International Series on Public Policy

Series Editors
B. Guy Peters
Department of Political Science
University of Pittsburgh
Pittsburgh, PA, USA

Philippe Zittoun
Research Professor of Political Science
LET-ENTPE, University of Lyon
Lyon, France

The International Series on Public Policy - the official series of International Public Policy Association, which organizes the International Conference on Public Policy - identifies major contributions to the field of public policy, dealing with analytical and substantive policy and governance issues across a variety of academic disciplines.

A comparative and interdisciplinary venture, it examines questions of policy process and analysis, policymaking and implementation, policy instruments, policy change & reforms, politics and policy, encompassing a range of approaches, theoretical, methodological, and/or empirical.

Relevant across the various fields of political science, sociology, anthropology, geography, history, and economics, this cutting edge series welcomes contributions from academics from across disciplines and career stages, and constitutes a unique resource for public policy scholars and those teaching public policy worldwide.

All books in the series are subject to Palgrave's rigorous peer review process: https://www.palgrave.com/gb/demystifying-peer-review/792492

More information about this series at
http://www.palgrave.com/gp/series/15096

John Connolly • Arno van der Zwet
Editors

Public Value Management, Governance and Reform in Britain

palgrave
macmillan

Editors
John Connolly
University of the West of Scotland
Paisley, UK

Arno van der Zwet
University of the West of Scotland
Paisley, UK

ISSN 2524-7301   ISSN 2524-731X (electronic)
International Series on Public Policy
ISBN 978-3-030-55585-6   ISBN 978-3-030-55586-3 (eBook)
https://doi.org/10.1007/978-3-030-55586-3

© The Editor(s) (if applicable) and The Author(s), under exclusive licence to Springer Nature Switzerland AG 2021
This work is subject to copyright. All rights are solely and exclusively licensed by the Publisher, whether the whole or part of the material is concerned, specifically the rights of translation, reprinting, reuse of illustrations, recitation, broadcasting, reproduction on microfilms or in any other physical way, and transmission or information storage and retrieval, electronic adaptation, computer software, or by similar or dissimilar methodology now known or hereafter developed.
The use of general descriptive names, registered names, trademarks, service marks, etc. in this publication does not imply, even in the absence of a specific statement, that such names are exempt from the relevant protective laws and regulations and therefore free for general use.
The publisher, the authors and the editors are safe to assume that the advice and information in this book are believed to be true and accurate at the date of publication. Neither the publisher nor the authors or the editors give a warranty, expressed or implied, with respect to the material contained herein or for any errors or omissions that may have been made. The publisher remains neutral with regard to jurisdictional claims in published maps and institutional affiliations.

This Palgrave Macmillan imprint is published by the registered company Springer Nature Switzerland AG.
The registered company address is: Gewerbestrasse 11, 6330 Cham, Switzerland

We dedicate this book to our friend and colleague Professor Duncan McTavish. Duncan planned on contributing to this book before his untimely death in November 2018. We hope that he would be pleased with how this book has come together. Many of the contributors to this book have been fortunate enough to have been mentored, encouraged and supported by Duncan over the years, for which we owe a great deal of gratitude.

Foreword

In the post-war era, two simple equations lay behind much of public policy. The first, which shaped the private sector of the economy, was *Value equals Price*. As Mariana Mazzucato has explained, a century and a half of controversy about the nature of value, running back through Marx and Ricardo to Adam Smith, was neatly brought to an end in the immediate post-war era. Products were valued by their price. Businesses came to be judged by the shareholder value they created. At macro-economic level, the economic success of countries was based on GDP growth which was also based on this simple equation. Everyone knew the equation was deeply flawed and, at best, a gross simplification, but as economies grew, businesses thrived and business schools devoted themselves to mathematical models (which also assumed the simple equation), pretty much everyone was happy with this self-deceit.

Meanwhile, policy for the public sector—funding for education, health and policing, for example—was based on the second equally simple equation, *Inputs equal Outputs*. Around the world, countries built schools, hospitals and thousands of miles of road or railway and claimed, on the basis of this equation, to be making a big difference. They employed more and more teachers, more and more nurses, more and more police officers and argued that thus they were improving education and health and reducing crime. Economists calculated the impact of education on the economy by measuring years of schooling rather than outputs or outcomes—in response, countries pushed up the school-leaving age, regardless of what students learnt or even whether the teachers actually showed up at school.

Again, everyone knew this equation was deeply flawed and, at best, a gross simplification, but economists could not think of anything better. Governments were generally happy too because it was easier to deliver a promise, for example, for a maximum class size or a given quantity of police officers than it was to improve literacy or cut crime. Public sector workforces supported the equation too, happy to agree that more meant better (and fewer meant worse) because it meant no accountability for outcomes.

The consequences of these two equations over 70 years or so were not all bad. Globally speaking, we became many times more wealthy, poverty was much reduced, health improved, life expectancy rose, more children and young people achieved higher standards, university education expanded dramatically, crime rose and then fell...but by the first decade of this century, the profound flaws in the two equations were becoming apparent.

In the private sector, *Value equals Price* led businesses to promote profit by, among other things, externalising costs—if waste could be poured down the river at no cost to the business, so be it. Market pressures, with businesses chasing quarterly evidence of profit and shareholder value, became increasingly short-term and global. The equation's biggest flaw was that it had no ethical context. Of course, many people in business were ethical in the way they conducted themselves, but by no means all. We had a series of scandalous cases such as Enron and WorldCom. Worse, economic growth occurred without any thought given to its sustainability. Climate change was one consequence, pollution of the oceans and loss of biodiversity were others, equally profound.

In the public sector, by the end of the twentieth century, similar flaws in the simplistic equation were becoming apparent too. Taxpayers were increasingly sceptical about what they got for their money. Some just wanted to pay less tax; others were willing to pay but only on condition they saw results. Not just more police, but less crime. Not just more transport, but more convenient, punctual rail services and less congestion. Not just more hospitals and doctors, but shorter waiting times and better health outcomes.

As a result, some governments set public targets so taxpayers could see what they were getting for their money. Public sector workforces were generally sceptical of this development; they feared being held accountable for results. I even heard the leader of one of America's major teacher unions argue against accountability for results on the grounds that 'teachers don't make that much difference'. In other words, she was willing to undermine public belief in the importance of teachers (and incredibly her members' sense of self-worth) in order to resist accountability and maintain *Inputs equal Outputs*.

Inputs equal Outputs had no ethical context either, though the professional ethics of the vast majority of doctors, nurses, teachers and public servants mitigated the consequences. Even so, with notable exceptions, performance around the world of public services, especially for families on low incomes, often fell short. Mediocrity ruled. Outcomes varied hugely by postcode.

And while targets helped where they were well designed, many governments did not have the courage to build a system around them. And in any case, targets were by no means a complete answer. They rarely took account of the long term or of the degree to which public expenditure was understood and supported by citizens, users and taxpayers.

In Britain, one advance was made when Gordon Brown asked Tony Atkinson of Oxford University to find a better way of measuring public sector productivity than *Inputs equal Outputs*. His report led to improvements in the way the Office for National Statistics accounted for public sector productivity, but the effect was largely retrospective and his report had little impact on policy-making or on the way in which public money was allocated in spending reviews.

Then in 2007–2008 came the global financial crisis. *Value equals Price*, you might have thought, would be blown out of the water by the crisis as the equation's lack of ethical basis and dire economic consequences were made plain. But no. To avoid total economic meltdown, public sector bailouts were required as the banks were considered 'too big to fail'. The financial services sector that had spent thirty years lobbying for ever less regulation discovered it could not manage without it. It even had the arrogance to claim that the fault for the crisis lay not with its own ethical failings but with the regulators for allowing them to do what they had done.

Economic growth rates stalled, public debt rose, government expenditure came under pressure. Austerity ruled. The answer in the public sector was not to change the simple equation—it was to squeeze the inputs side of it and hope for the best. At a level of generality, governments were forced to make a productivity argument—that less input should not necessarily lead to less output—but the imperative was to cut inputs and therefore control and ultimately reduce burgeoning debt, which would otherwise have been passed on to future generations.

When we finally emerged from austerity, while the two flawed equations remained largely in place, their long-term consequences were becoming apparent. A growing number of voices advocated alternatives.

In relation to *Value equals Price*, Mariana Mazzucato's book *The Value of Everything* raised fundamental questions about the equation's validity at both micro- and macro-economic levels. Meanwhile, the growing sense of a climate emergency, coinciding with the major financial and economic challenges of 2008–2018, put the issue of finding an alternative firmly on the agenda. How could we continue to measure GDP in the way we do given its ethical and environmental blindness? GDP survives still because there is no consensus on what the alternative might be, but it is increasingly being questioned.

While *Inputs equal Outputs* also remains influential, as illustrated by much of the political debate, it too has come under challenge, not before time. Ongoing international benchmarking, perhaps best exemplified by the OECD-PISA comparisons of education systems, has revealed that the correlation between inputs and outcomes is weak. It matters, not just how much you spend but how exactly you spend it!

Meanwhile, the UK Treasury, with the active support of successive chancellors and chief secretaries, has actively pursued alternative ways of thinking about public value. The starting point was the commissioning of a report from me on the subject, which was published with the budget in November 2017. Since then, the Treasury has pursued an innovative approach which, in spite of political uncertainty in Britain in the years 2016–2019, has begun to shape the dialogue between the Treasury and major spending departments.

My report made the case for a rounded perspective on public value, to replace the bankrupt concept *of Inputs equal Outputs*. Hence the Public Value Framework with four pillars.

Public Value Assessment Framework: Relationship Between Funding, Pillars and Outcomes

The first pillar requires that a given sum of public money delivers specified goals. The second pillar requires the fair, transparent and efficient allocation of the resources. The third pillar is an innovation—it suggests that for many areas of public expenditure we will get much better outcomes if the service user is not just a recipient but an engaged partner; think of tackling obesity, addressing mental health or enabling student learning. It also suggests that taxpayers/citizens need to see the rationale for each budget. If they support, or at least understand that rationale, the budget will have greater legitimacy.

The fourth pillar is another innovation. Public value is long term as well as short and medium term. This means that public service managers at every level need to think consistently about how they can ensure they leave the service for which they are responsible better than they found it. This is stewardship. It applies at the front line—a hospital manager, for example—and at national level—the permanent secretary of a government department.

Since my report was published, the application of this Framework has been piloted by the Treasury in collaboration with several government departments. The Framework was refined and improved as a result. Since then, Historic England has adopted and refined it further as a means of evaluating proposals. The Food and Farming Commission has strengthened it in relation to the natural environment and proposed its use in that domain. Recently, the Dutch government has decided to pilot its use too.

It would be foolish to suggest that this approach to public value answers all the questions, but it is a step forward and these early applications of it suggest it is practical and useful. The recently retired head of the National Audit Office, Sir Amyas Morse, has welcomed it as a significant advance.

My hope is that it will become central to the way the Treasury interacts with government departments and results in a common language in which to discuss public value. The result of that would be a richer, deeper dialogue about what public value is and how it is delivered. I also hope that others will build on it—which is why I welcome this book—and ensure ever deeper understanding of public value. With this in mind, John Connolly and Arno van der Zwet (and the contributors to their book) make a welcome contribution to public value thinking by examining the possibilities and challenges of delivering public value in Britain. There are lessons from this study that other state contexts beyond Britain should reflect on. In short, a focus on public value by governments should result in better services, more efficient use of public money, better outcomes for individual citizens and families and thus more people leading more fulfilled lives.

That surely is worth working for. And, if we succeed, while others dismantle *Value equals Price*, we could dance on the grave of *Inputs equal Outputs*.

2019   Sir Michael Barber

Sir Michael Barber is founder and chairman of Delivery Associates, an advisory firm which helps the government and other organisations to deliver improved outcomes for citizens. Sir Michael was Head of the Prime Minister's Delivery Unit from 2001–05, and Chief Adviser to the Secretary of State for Education on School Standards from 1997–2001. Before joining the government, he was a professor at the Institute of Education, University of London. He is the author of several books on deliverology, most recently *How to Run a Government: So that Citizens Benefit and Taxpayers Don't go Crazy* (2016). Other titles by him are: *Deliverology in Practice* (2015), *Deliverology 101* (2011) and *Instruction to Deliver* (2008). He is also a co-author of *Oceans of Innovation* (2012) and *An Avalanche is Coming* (2013).

Acknowledgements

Acknowledgements for John Connolly

First of all I would like to thank my co-editor, Arno, for his work on this book project. I fear that without his commitment, hard work and patience, this book would never have happened! In the acknowledgements for my previous book—*The Politics and Crisis Management of Animal Health Security* (Routledge Publishers)—I gave priority in the acknowledgements section to my wife (Jennifer) and to my two cheeky children (Robyn and Joshua). Back then, the kids didn't know all that much about my job but I guess they might have a *slightly* better idea these days—they are, after all, at the grand old ages of 9 and 7. I must admit, though, they remain fairly unimpressed! I'm quite pleased about that, I think, because they ensure that my feet are rarely far off of the ground. My extended family, and my non-academic friends, also have a better idea of what I do after I had the opportunity to share some of my work with them at my inaugural lecture at the University of the West of Scotland in August 2019. It was a night to remember and cherish. One of the greatest pleasures, for me personally, was that my father in-law, Jim, told me after the lecture that he was very proud of me—that meant a great deal. Jim has always been very kind and supportive to me over the years—so much so that I also think of him as my in-house handyman who is on-call most days to deal with crises as they arise. He doesn't get paid all that much for that job so I hope that my personal dedication of this book to him will suffice. Just don't ask me to do any wallpapering any time soon!

Acknowledgements for Arno van der Zwet

There are many colleagues and students that have directly or indirectly made a contribution that made this book possible and to whom I am immensely grateful. In particular, I am indebted to my fellow editor for giving me the opportunity to contribute to this book. This started off as John's book project, but I was happy to come on board when I moved to the University of the West of Scotland three years ago. However, no letters would have filled these pages, or at least those that I was responsible for, without the support of my wife Jennifer and three gorgeous children (Aletta, Thijs and Cas). The latter have no idea what daddy does (the former has some idea!) and 'don't like the stories he writes'. I would also like to thank my parents (all four of them) and parents-in-law for their encouragement and support at various stages of my academic career. When reflecting on achievements, we tend to think of those that are no longer with us. My stepdad, Gaston Schellekens, and father-in-law, Bill Lindsay, are two men that I have lost in recent years. They epitomised hard work, creativity and love, and despite having passed away far too young, I feel their support every day.

We would both like to thank colleagues at Palgrave for their support and patience over the past few years as well as all of the contributors to the book for their hard work and commitment. It is much appreciated!

About the Book

This book examines governance reform in Britain, with a particular focus on the period since 2010. The New Labour period (1997–2010) saw a fairly strong emphasis on governance reform. The decade or so since has seen major societal, economic and technological changes. We examine, through different analytical lenses, the extent to which the post-2010 period (under the Conservative government, with initial support being offered by the Liberal Democrats when they were part of the post-2010 coalition government) saw a departure from Labour-led reforms or whether the reforms were of a path-dependent nature.

Students of public administration will know that public sector reform is continuous and never ending, as is the political, social, cultural and technological context in which bureaucracies operate. Governance systems have to continually find new ways to address new and old challenges. Reform is invariably incremental and often reactive. However, there are occasions when the government of the day sets out a comprehensive reform agenda for the public sector that shifts the way in which the government's bureaucracy operates and changes many of the assumptions underpinning governance and the policy process. We approach this subject by using the concept of 'public value management'. Public value not only offers analyses that focus on governance from a *micro* or *meso* level (i.e. the leadership and operationalisation of policy implementation), but it also offers an opportunity to reflect on matters of statecraft and complexity at a systems-wide level in governance settings.

The book concludes that there has not been a major shift towards a new 'public value' paradigm in Britain and that key elements of the NPM paradigm remain prevalent. What the various contributions to this volume show is that there is an opportunity for more paradigmatic changes to UK governance but that post-2010, despite some examples of progress, has not seen the emergence of new governance agenda which concerns evaluating *how government works* on the basis of sustaining public value approaches. Austerity, Brexit and COVID-19 have distracted political leaders and limited the progress towards a new approach to governance reform.

The book calls for greater attention to be given to public value in the future to ensure that a value-based approach to 'reinventing government' is prioritised and sustained as part of modern British governance.

Contents

1 Introduction 1
John Connolly and Arno van der Zwet

2 Public Value in Britain: A 'Post-New Public Management' Environment? 15
John Connolly and Arno van der Zwet

3 Public Sector Reform in the UK: Key Developments, Debates and Political Responses in Challenging Times 45
Robert Pyper

4 Modes of State Governance, Populist Pressures and Public Sector Reform 87
Matthew Flinders and Christopher Huggins

5 Evidence-based Policy and Public Value Management: Mutually Supporting Paradigms? 115
Kathryn Oliver and Alec Fraser

6	Public Service Innovation: Challenges and Possibilities for Innovation Adoption Adina Dudau, John Finch, James Grant Hemple, and Georgios Kominis	149
7	Public Value Leadership in the Context of Outcomes, Impact and Reform Janice McMillan	173
8	Accountability and Networks: Mind the Gap Andrew Massey	201
9	Public Value Management in Brexit Britain Janice Morphet	227
10	Public Value Management: A Paradigm Shift? Arno van der Zwet and John Connolly	259
Index		287

Notes on Contributors

John Connolly is Professor of Public Policy at the University of the West of Scotland. He is a former public servant having previously worked in senior policy and evaluation positions in Scotland before joining the University of the West of Scotland in 2013. His main research interests include public sector reform, the politics of crisis management, evaluation, health security and social inequalities. He has led and contributed to a number of funded research projects (funders include the Scottish Government, National Health Service in Scotland, the Economic and Social Research Council and the British Council). He is the editor of the flagship journal of the Academy of Social Sciences—*Contemporary Social Science*—and is a senior fellow of the UK Higher Education Academy.

Adina Dudau is a senior lecturer at the University of Glasgow's Adam Smith Business School. Her research includes public sector management, accountability and innovation. Adina is a CIPD associate member and works with public sector and voluntary and community sector organisations for research, teaching and consultancy. Her researches have been published in *Public Management Review, Public Money and Management, Public Policy and Administration, European Management Review, Management Accounting Research* and *Academy of Management Learning and Education*.

John Finch is Professor of Marketing and Head of University of Glasgow's Adam Smith Business School. His research is in business-to-business marketing and market studies. John is a member of the Chartered

Institute of Marketing and has undertaken consulting work with a number of organisations (from large transnational corporations to SMEs) and his works have been published, among others, in *Research Policy*, *Marketing Theory*, *Industrial Marketing Management*, *Journal of Business Research* and *Cambridge Journal of Economics*.

Matthew Flinders is Professor of Politics and Founding Director of the Sir Bernard Crick Centre at the University of Sheffield. He is also president of the Political Studies Association of the United Kingdom and is a member of the Economic and Social Research Council. His research interests span political psychology, democratic governance and public management.

Alec Fraser is Lecturer in Government & Business at King's College London. His research centres on the use of evidence in policy-making and practice across the public sector with a particular focus on health and social care. He previously spent five years at the Policy Innovation Research Unit at the London School of Hygiene and Tropical Medicine. Prior to entering academia, he worked in NHS administration and management.

James Grant Hemple is Adjunct Lecturer in Management at the Adam Smith Business School, University of Glasgow. His main area of research is business-to-business marketing with a broader interest in market studies, business models and innovation. Grant holds a PhD in management from the University of Glasgow. His work has been presented at various conferences including the British Academy of Management (BAM), Industrial Marketing and Purchasing (IMP) and The International Society for Professional Innovation Management Conference (ISPIM Innovation Conference). Grant's academic interests complement his practical experience as a project manager, where he focuses on research and development within the public sector. Grant has also undertaken roles specialising in knowledge management and digital marketing.

Christopher Huggins is Senior Lecturer in Politics and Associate Dean for Learning, Teaching and Student Experience at the University of Suffolk. He completed his PhD at the University of Portsmouth and has held positions at Keele University, the University of Aberdeen and the University of the West of Scotland. His research interests centre on subnational and territorial politics and the impact of Brexit on devolution in the UK. He is also editor of the *Journal of Contemporary European Research*.

Georgios Kominis is Lecturer in Management Control at the University of Glasgow's Adam Smith Business School and undertakes research in public sector accounting, accountability and management control. He reviews for, and his works are published in, *Management Accounting Research*, *Public Management Review*, *European Management Journal* and *Financial Accountability and Management*.

Andrew Massey is Professor of Government and Academic Director of the International School for Government at King's College London. He is the author of more than 100 published books, papers and chapters. He has worked in a range of areas including British, European and US policy and politics. His main areas of research include comparative public policy, public administration and issues around the reform and modernisation of government and governance at all levels in the UK, USA, EU and globally. He is editor-in-chief of the journal *International Review of Administrative Sciences* and editor for the journal *Public Money and Management*.

Janice McMillan is Associate Professor in Public Management and Human Resource Development at Edinburgh Napier University. Her research interests include public management, human resource development and leadership, and she has written widely in these areas. With John Fenwick, she is co-editor of *Public Management in the Postmodern Era: Challenges and Prospects* (2010) and co-author of *Decentralizing the Civil Service: From unitary state to differentiated polity in the United Kingdom* (2003) (with Rod Rhodes, Paul Carmichael and Andrew Massey). She was chair of the Political Studies Association Public Administration Specialist Group 1995–2005 and vice-chair of the Public Administration Committee of the Joint University Council 2013–2016.

Janice Morphet is a visiting professor at the University College London. Janice has been engaged in planning and local government for over 50 years. She was chief executive of a unitary authority, head of a large university school of planning and landscape, senior adviser on local government to central government and a consultant. She has written widely on local government, planning, management, infrastructure and the EU, including Brexit.

Kathryn Oliver is a social scientist with interests in the use of evidence in policy-making, especially public health policy. She is particularly interested in the structure and function of networks in policy and practice and how these influence research impact and science policy more generally. Kathryn co-leads the *Transforming Evidence* initiative which is a cross-disciplinary network aiming to bring together knowledge about the making and use of evidence from across sectors and disciplines.

Robert Pyper is Emeritus Professor of Government and Public Policy at the University of the West of Scotland. His books, book chapters and academic journal articles span the fields of government, public policy and public management and include national and international analyses of civil service policy and management, public services reform and modernisation, devolved polities, official and political accountability, governance and parliamentary select committees.

Arno van der Zwet joined the University of the West of Scotland in 2017 as Lecturer in Politics and Public Policy. He has previously worked as a research fellow at the European Policies Research Centre at the University of Strathclyde, where he remains as a senior research associate. His research interests include territorial politics, regional policy, governance and identity studies. He has been a principal investigator for Economic and Social Research Council funded research as well as for projects funded by European institutions, such as the European Commission, European Parliament and ESPON. He is an expert panel member of regional and urban studies for the European Commission Joint Research Centre.

List of Figures

Fig. 4.1	Types of Multilevel Governance Transport-Related Carbon Emissions in Four Cities. Bache et al. (2015)	93
Fig. 4.2	Procurement as a percentage of government expenditure, 2004/05 to 2017/18. Davies et al. (2018, p. 6)	100
Fig. 6.1	The process of institutional hybridity in relation to governance modes	153
Fig. 6.2	Public and private value across modes of governance	155
Fig. 6.3	Service continuum (adapted from Laing 2003)	157
Fig. 6.4	*Public Utility Firm*'s regulatory framework	162

List of Tables

Table 1.1	Thematic shifts in emphasis between NPM and PVM	8
Table 2.1	Public Value Framework	23
Table 4.1	Types of Multilevel Governance	91
Table 5.1	How evidence interacts with paradigms of management	121
Table 5.2	Four PVM propositions and their implications for evidence use:	130
Table 6.1	Illustration of public value pursuit in *Public Utility Firm*	161

List of Boxes

Box 4.1	Hansard Society Audit of Political Engagement (2019)	107
Box 5.1	The search for public value: the example of higher education	131
Box 5.2	Recognising the legitimacy of stakeholders: the example of public and patient involvement	132
Box 5.3	Collaborative commissioning	134
Box 5.4	Adaptable learning	137

Introduction

John Connolly and Arno van der Zwet

> *I say this to governments around the world 'you should always treat the bureaucracy with respect, you should recognise what it can do but if you become a prisoner of it then you will achieve nothing, you will just go around in circles'. It is a longer debate to have and it is a very important debate to have because reinventing government has fallen off the political agenda in recent times and it really shouldn't because today, especially with changes in technology, this whole concept of how government itself works is in my view fundamentally important. But, as I say, I love the integrity of the civil service and in a crisis it was brilliant but when it comes to trying to making change, and I'm being very honest here, I found it inadequate.*
>
> —Former British Prime Minister Tony Blair: *10th August 2017; BBC Radio 4*

The above is an extract from an interview for the *Reflections* radio programme presented by Peter Hennessey (historian and expert in the history of British government) with the former British Prime Minister Tony Blair

---

J. Connolly (✉) • A. van der Zwet
University of the West of Scotland, Glasgow, UK
e-mail: john.connolly@uws.ac.uk; arno.van-der-Zwet@uws.ac.uk

© The Author(s) 2021
J. Connolly, A. van der Zwet (eds.), *Public Value Management, Governance and Reform in Britain*, International Series on Public Policy, https://doi.org/10.1007/978-3-030-55586-3_1

(1997–2007), who was reflecting on his time in office. Blair went on to note that he found the bureaucracy to have clear limitations when it came to implementing reform agendas for areas such as health, education, asylum and immigration policy and that the bureaucracy or civil service was 'unresponsive'. A more positive sentiment entered the interview later when Blair said that:

> What I do accept, and I think we did this in my last six or seven years, is that you can get to a much more balanced perspective where you liberate those within the bureaucracy who actually do want to make change and who are enthusiastic.

Tony Blair's sentiments about changing the machinery of government warrants a renewed focus, particularly due to the twin policy challenges of Brexit and the COVID-19 pandemic. In fact, the final manuscript for this book was submitted during a period of lockdown as part of the pandemic crisis management control measures. The added value of this project will be to offer contemporary debates, reflections and perspectives which will feed into future academic research about how, and to what extent, the contours of governance reform in Britain will, or need to, change in the context of Brexit and in the aftermath of the COVID-19 pandemic.

Aims of the Book

Our primary aim is to examine governance reform in Britain, with a particular focus on the period since 2010. However, the authors of this book also discuss pre-2010 governance developments when it is relevant to their argument or thematic area. In substantive terms, we examine the extent to which the post-2010 reforms, taken forward by the Conservative and Liberal Democrat coalition government (Con-Lib, for short), and the developments since the re-election of the Conservative government in 2015 and 2017, have served to represent a departure from the governance reforms implemented by the post-1997 Labour government. Our dominant aim is to engage with debates about whether there has been a paradigm shift from an era of new public management to that which can be described as 'public value management'. This academic endeavour requires an interrogation of the extent to which such conceptual development is evident in the context of public sector reform in Britain and whether there is evidence of reform agendas, leadership cultures and political narratives that emphasise 'public value'.

BRITISH GOVERNANCE: POST-NEW PUBLIC MANAGEMENT?

The public administration and management field has seen considerable conceptual development over the past thirty years. The traditional model of public administration (emphasising bureaucracy, hierarchy, lines of accountability and control) shifted as part of the new public management (NPM) agenda associated with Thatcherism post-1979 (Hood 1991). Economic policy reform towards monetarism, the rise of the New Right ideology and neo-liberalism led to a paradigm shift (Hall 1993), which meant that public administration academics became increasingly concerned with market mechanisms, efficiency, consumerism, outputs, regulation, competition, performance management and performance measurement. Although these terms still have considerable scholarly currency, NPM developments in the 1990s foregrounded the emphasis on perspectives such as 'governance' and 'modernisation', which aligned with a post-1997 Blairite agenda. This agenda had its roots in Thatcherism and continued under 'Majorism' post-1990 (Rhodes 1997; Cabinet Office 1999; Massey and Pyper 2005). The rise of 'governance' perspectives from the mid-1990s onwards reflected the triple developments of devolution in the UK (Marsh et al. 2003), increasing globalisation (Hay and Marsh 2000), and European integration (George 1998). As Judge (2014: 112) notes:

> In the UK, devolution upwards to the European Union and other international organisations and devolution down to Scotland, Northern Ireland, and Wales has transformed a unitary (or at least a union) state into a multi-level polity...characterised by non-standardised administrative structures, a complex institutional nexus and variegated decentralised policy processes.

One of the most enduring characterisations of the British state emerges from the view that the political system has become 'hollowed-out' and that the core and wider executive (although a prevailing actor) is just but one actor amongst several which cross-cut the public, private and third sectors (Bevir and Rhodes 2003). The characterisation of the 'hollowed-out' state promotes the idea of states remaining as 'gatekeepers' in that they are able to steer and terminate policy at a strategic level. Current debates gravitate around whether British governance is less about the state being a facilitator (amongst many facilitators) but more about the manner and style of statecraft whereby the state remains an architect of governance (Bevir 2010). In this respect, notions of 'metagovernance' and 'rescaling' become conceptual reference points for understanding the capacities and approaches relating to state actions.

If public administration is about 'how things work, how governments make decisions, apply, or enforce these decisions' (Massey and Pyper 2005: 4), then a focus on public value is about understanding the quality of governance reforms at multiple levels, including the extent to which these match public expectations. Nonetheless, there are debates in the academic literature about whether we have witnessed an end to NPM (Dunleavy et al. 2006; De Vries 2010; Reiter and Klenk 2019). These debates gravitate around what could be *the* successor to NPM. One notable candidate has been *New Public Governance* (NPG) (Osborne 2009). The arrival of NPG largely comes down to the argument that NPM thinking does not sufficiently address the external dynamics which shape public governance. There are also concerns about NPM's focus on intra-organisational forms, performance measurement, and its lack of account for understanding complex relationships. There are further important interpretations of public sector governance such as *New Public Service* (NPS), which emphasises the importance of the democratic and collaborative dimensions of modern governance (Denhardt and Denhardt 2007). NPS is also informed by Mark Moore's idea regarding creating *Public Value*, which calls for public managers to open up policy processes and rebalance power relationships to give citizens a greater role in shaping policy decision-making (Moore 1995). Creating public value is, therefore, about the implementation of governance strategies, which are valued by the public. It is perhaps understandable, therefore, why Dunleavy et al. (2006) questioned whether 'New Public Management is Dead'. In recent times, public value has become the centre of academic attention around the extent to which it is a distinctly new paradigm, superseding new public management (NPM). Yet, Stoker (2006, p.43), in his assessment of the move from public management to public value management, notes that '[c]laims that a new paradigm is emerging in any sphere of social and political study are rightly treated with scepticism'. This, in part, is because no conceptual approach in public administration scholarship is ever entirely new, and there are always connections to the past. We have sympathy with this perspective but recognise that *debates* about 'whether

NPM is dead' are not actually dead given that NPM-informed thought regarding managerialism in the public sector remains very relevant today. The COVID-19 pandemic, for example, has led to questions about how public services, and their leaders and managers, can negotiate the coming years of economic recovery and what this means for the management and organisation of services. How can we better understand the next steps in British governance if we do not understand the governance terrains from which we have emerged? In order to take such steps forward, there needs to be recognition that a 'one size concept fits all' approach has major pitfalls for understanding the complexities around public sector reform in Britain. Some of the NPM battles may have been won within the academic community, but the war is certainly not over. A successor—if there is going to be one—has not yet emerged victoriously to stake its claim as a new all-encompassing paradigm.

Crises can serve to expose the degree of progress towards effective governing approaches. Future research will tell us much more about changes in British governance as a result of Brexit and the COVID-19 crisis. What can be argued with a degree of confidence is that the challenges of the pandemic have served to expose the performance of governance leadership and processes. There has been evidence of a lacklustre approach to introducing the national lockdown (when there was evidence of the inevitability of the global pandemic), problems with the supply of personal protective equipment (PPE), a lack of support for care homes, capacity issues surrounding test and trace systems, a lack of lessons learned from the large-scale pandemic simulation 'Exercise Cygnus' in 2016, problems with the implementation of science and advisory structures, and moral questions surrounding the conduct of powerful government figures when it comes to contravening national lockdown measures (such as the behaviour of a senior special adviser to the Prime Minister, Dominic Cummings) (Altmann 2020; Blackburn 2020; Ford 2020; Foster and Neville 2020; Haddon 2020; Nickson et al. 2020; Nuki 2020). These are just some of the problems. It could also be argued that all of these issues have, in different ways, contributed to questions about the need for public value-based leadership and this includes evaluating state capacity levels. Brexit is also relevant to the handling of the pandemic given that the politics of disengagement from EU vaccine procurement initiatives can be explained by a careless separatist governance mentality at the expense of measured governance when it comes to de-coupling from the EU. The matter of state capacities, as we disentangle from the EU (or 'de-Europeanise'), will continue to be a topic of interest for those working across multiple policy sectors that were previously Europeanised (see Connolly et al. 2020) but governing through this process in a period of post-COVID recovery has to be an ongoing concern for those studying public value. It is the case, however, that there are never guarantees that crises will lead to sweeping governance changes (Connolly 2016), but this book helps to formulate and draw together important debates and perspectives for assessing future changes in the leadership and organisation of the public sector in the context of contemporary governance. As part of this journey, we recognise that new ideas located under the overarching concept of public administration have some common features around disaggregated government, and the growing importance of governing through complex multi-level networks in which the creation and delivery of policy are dependent upon effective public sector leadership and collaborative working.

With this in mind, the dominant conceptual reference point for this book is public value management and leadership within a network governance environment (Moore 1995; Alford and Hughes 2008; Stoker 2006; Williams and Shearer 2011; Hartley et al. 2015; Bryson et al. 2017; Andrews 2019). Rhodes and Wanna (2007: 408) are critical about the term 'value' because of its inherent ambiguity in that 'it can mean all things to all people'. However, 'value' is in good company given we are not short of terms in public administration studies that have an element of ambiguity about them. In fact, the closest relative to public value is 'policy success' in that, just like public value, the long-standing issue associated with understanding success and failure in public governance studies has been the general absence of fixed criterion for making judgements about success and failure—warranting the accusation that making such judgements is 'in the eye of the beholder'. McConnell (2010: 17) reflects thoughtfully on this issue by suggesting that '[o]verall, differing perspectives on how easily (or otherwise) public value can be measured indicate that any analysis of policy success needs to deal with broadly similar issues'.

Students, researchers and practitioners have been dealing with even more terms that represent a new phase in the literature within British public management and administration. Examples include empowerment, contribution, co-production, improvement, result-orientation, engagement, impact, capacity, deliberation, learning, and evidence-based policy-making and practice (to name some). Yet although these terms provide an indication of how the discipline has developed, it would be incorrect to assume that there are clear lines of conceptual demarcation between any of them. Further key concepts which emerge throughout the book include multi-level governance (Bache et al. 2016), metagovernance (Sørensen and Torfing 2009), Europeanisation (Bache and Jordan 2006), complexity (Kickert et al. 1997), networks (Rhodes 1997; Bevir and Richards 2009), evidence-based policy-making (Oliver et al. 2014), partnerships (Osborne 2000), accountability (McGarvey 2001), policy innovation (Osborne and Brown 2013), policy success and failure (Marsh and McConnell 2010; McConnell 2016) and public value leadership (Hartley et al. 2015). The evaluative endeavour of the book is to address whether we have witnessed a paradigmatic shift from NPM to public value management (PVM) in the context of British governance. Public value is inextricably linked with how public services are organised (public management), hence the use of the phrase 'public value management'—in short, 'management matters' in governance reform (Connolly and Pyper 2020). In order to foreground the rest of the book, Table 1.1 highlights the thematic shifts in emphasis between NPM and PVM.

Post-NPM debates are not the same as those in relation to 'traditional public administration' versus NPM debates given that the dominant economic model has largely been maintained within both NPM and PVM. It is the modern policy narratives and ways of governing which have changed towards emphasising complexity and network approaches to governance. Indeed, the 2008 global financial crisis or the 'credit crunch' did not lead to a retreat back towards Keynesianism, and some would argue that the outcome was a strengthening of neo-liberalism as a result of austerity politics and the cuts to public expenditure during the post-2010 Conservative and Liberal Democrat coalition government's time in office. The other dimension is that terms such as reform, modernisation, continuous improvement and empowerment run the risk of representing no more than political strategies in phraseology for masking policy and programme failures, the warped presentation of successes and the purposeful act of blurring lines of accountability. Indeed, political language and labels are important tools for conducting the art of culpability avoidance or gaming (Hood 2002; Edelman 2013; Bache et al. 2015). It is important to recognise that when there is increasing complexity in governance landscapes, there are enhanced opportunities for performance failures, transaction costs, ambiguities in policy and organisational relationships and fuzzy lines

Table 1.1 Thematic shifts in emphasis between NPM and PVM

	New Public Management	Public Value Management
Key objectives of the system	Managing inputs and outputs in a way that ensures economy and responsiveness to consumers.	The overarching goal is achieving public value, which in turn involves more of a focus on effectiveness in tackling the (often complex) problems that the public care about.
Definition of public interest	Aggregation of individual preferences, captured in practice by senior politicians or managers supported by evidence about customer choice.	Individual and public preferences produced through a complex process of interaction involving deliberative reflection over inputs and opportunity costs.
Preferred system for service delivery	Private sector or tightly defined arm's-length public agency.	Menu of alternatives selected pragmatically and a reflexive approach to intervention mechanisms to achieve outputs.
Approach to public service ethos	Public sector ethos is less favoured compared to customer service.	No single sector has a monopoly on public service ethos. Maintaining relationships through shared values is seen as essential.
Dominant model of accountability	Separation of politics and management; politics to give direction, but not hands-on control; managers to manage, additional loop of consumer assessment built into the system.	Elected leaders, managers and key stakeholders involved in search for solutions to community problems and effective delivery mechanisms. The system, in turn, is subject to challenge through elections, referendums, deliberative forums, scrutiny functions and shifts in public opinion.
Role of managers	To help define and meet agreed performance targets.	To play an active role in steering networks of deliberation and delivery, and maintain the overall capacity of the system.

Source: Adapted from Stoker (2003)

of accountability. As Judge (2014: 180) notes, multi-layered perspectives represent what can be described as an 'interactive vortex'—hardly a metaphor that instils a sense of clarity, order and delineation. Nonetheless, policy actors at multiple levels of governance increasingly need to manage complexity and are often responsible for the delivery of programmes and services, for evidencing their impact and demonstrating public value in complex environments which, taken together, have implications for the architectonics of the state.

STRUCTURE OF THE BOOK

Chapter 2 (by John Connolly and Arno van der Zwet) contextualises the subsequent chapters of the book by introducing key themes and perspectives. It sets the foundations for the book by identifying how and why the academic literature has questioned whether we are now witnessing an end to new public management with key reference to the British context. The chapter discusses key concepts and introduces the themes which feature throughout the book. Chapter 3 (by Robert Pyper) considers the developments in public sector reform since the election of the Conservative-Liberal Democrat government in 2010. The chapter assesses evidence of alignment and divergence in public sector reform agendas and processes across the UK. Chapter 4 (by Matthew Flinders and Christopher Huggins) addresses modes of governance with a focus on populist pressures. The authors conclude with the argument that a public value approach has the potential to act as a 'glue' for binding the infrastructure of the modern state but also as the essence of democratic governance. Chapter 5 (by Kathryn Oliver and Alec Fraser) considers the role(s) of evidence as part of public service reform processes. Chapter 6 (by Adina Dudau, John Finch, James Grant Hemple and Georgios Kominis) focuses on 'innovation' in the context of British governance and public sector reform. This chapter draws on examples of innovative processes in public sector reform and identify the conditions in which public sector innovations have taken place. This discussion links with governance perspectives by considering the modes of governance that are most suitable for enabling innovation and the ways in which innovation can be evaluated. Chapter 7 (by Janice MacMillan) highlights the challenges of demonstrating the impact and successes of public sector reform. It particularly considers the importance of public leadership in relation to public value. The chapter highlights how public sector reform projects can achieve public value outcomes through participative approaches to policy planning and evaluation. Chapter 8 (by Andrew Massey) focuses on the accountability dimensions of contemporary reform agendas. This analysis also addresses issues such as blame-gaming and culpability avoidance and how network-based approaches to reform pose difficulties for lines of accountability. The author highlights that greater clarity, transparency and accountability can only be effective in modern governance contexts if there are political commitments to monitor and audit complex lines of accountability, authorisation and control. Chapter 9 (by Janice Morphet) reflects on how Brexit could impact on a public value management policy framework in the UK and that this is an area which requires research in the longer-term. Finally, Chapter 10 (by van der Zwet and Connolly) reflect on the debates regarding whether we are living in a time of post-NPM. The chapter examines to what extent we have seen new processes of policy-making, new practices in relation to programming and monitoring policy outcomes, and new political narratives that support public value management. In the final part of the chapter, we discuss the main themes identified in the other chapters of the book and consider the prospects for public sector reform in light of Brexit and the COVID-19 pandemic.

References

Alford, J., & Hughes, O. (2008). Public Value Pragmatism as the Next Phase of Public Management. *The American Review of Public Administration, 38*(2), 130–148.

Altmann, R. (2020). The Lesson of the Covid-19 Care Homes Tragedy: Renationalising is no Longer Taboo. https://www.theguardian.com/commentisfree/2020/jul/06/covid-19-care-homes-tragedy-renationalise-crisis

Andrews, L. (2019). Public Administration, Public Leadership and the Construction of Public Value in the Age of the Algorithm and 'Big Data'. *Public Administration, 97*(2), 296–310.

Bache, I., & Jordan, A. (2006). The Europeanization of British Politics. In *The Europeanization of British Politics* (pp. 265–279). London: Palgrave Macmillan.

Bache, I., Bartle, I., Flinders, M., & Marsden, G. (2015). Blame Games and Climate Change: Accountability, Multi-Level Governance and Carbon Management. *The British Journal of Politics and International Relations, 17*(1), 64–88.

Bache, I., Bartle, I., & Flinders, M. (2016). Multi-Level Governance. In *Handbook on Theories of Governance*. Edward Elgar Publishing.

Bevir, M. (2010). *Democratic Governance*. Princeton University Press.

Bevir, M., & Rhodes, R. (2003). *Interpreting British Governance*. Routledge.

Bevir, M., & Richards, D. (2009). Decentring Policy Networks: Lessons and Prospects. *Public Administration, 87*(1), 132–141.

Blackburn, P (2020). A Hidden Threat: Test-and-Trace Failure Edges Closer. https://www.bma.org.uk/news-and-opinion/a-hidden-threat-test-and-trace-failure-edges-closer

Bryson, J., Sancino, A., Benington, J., & Sørensen, E. (2017). Towards a Multi-Actor Theory of Public Value Co-Creation. *Public Management Review, 19*(5), 640–654.

Cabinet Office. (1999). *Modernising Government*. London: The Stationery Office.

Connolly, J. (2016). *The Politics and Crisis Management of Animal Health Security*. Routledge.

Connolly, J., & Pyper, R. (2020). The Leadership and Management of Public Services Reform in Scotland. In M. Keating (Ed.), *The Oxford Handbook of Scottish Politics*. Oxford University Press.

Connolly, J., Zwet, A. V. D., Huggins, C., & McAngus, C. (2020). The Governance Capacities of Brexit from a Scottish Perspective: The Case of Fisheries Policy. *Public Policy and Administration*, 0952076720936328.

De Vries, J. (2010). Is New Public Management Really Dead? *OECD Journal on Budgeting*, 10(1), 1–5.

Denhardt, J. V., & Denhardt, R. B. (2007). *The New Public Service: Serving, Not Steering*. ME Sharpe.

Dunleavy, P., Margetts, H., Bastow, S., & Tinkler, J. (2006). New Public Management is Dead—Long Live Digital-Era Governance. *Journal of Public Administration Research and Theory*, 16(3), 467–494.

Edelman, M. (2013). *Political Language: Words that Succeed and Policies that Fail*. Elsevier.

Flear, M. (2020). EU Joint Procurement - UK's Delayed Participation Undermines Delayed the NHS and Risks Lives. https://ukandeu.ac.uk/eu-joint-procurement-uks-delayed-participation-undermines-the-nhs-and-risks-lives/

Ford, J. (2020). The Battle at the Heart of British Science over Coronavirus. https://www.ft.com/content/1e390ac6-7e2c-11ea-8fdb-7ec06edeef84

Foster, P & Neville, S. (2020). How Poor Planning Left the UK without enough PPE. https://www.ft.com/content/9680c20f-7b71-4f65-9bec-0e9554a8e0a7

George, S. (1998). *An Awkward Partner: Britain in the European Community*. Oxford: Oxford University Press.

Haddon, C. (2020). The government's handling of the Dominic Cummings row has led to a loss of public trust. https://www.instituteforgovernment.org.uk/blog/government-handling-dominic-cummings-loss-public-trust

Hall, P. A. (1993). Policy Paradigms, Social Learning, and the State: The Case of Economic Policymaking in Britain. *Comparative Politics*, 25, 275–296.

Hartley, J., Alford, J., Hughes, O., & Yates, S. (2015). Public Value and Political Astuteness in the Work of Public Managers: The Art of the Possible. *Public Administration*, 93(1), 195–211.

Hay, C., & Marsh, D. (2000). *Demystifying Globalization*. New York: St.

Hood, C. (1991). A Public Management for All Seasons? *Public Administration*, 69(1), 3–19.

Hood, C. (2002). The Risk Game and the Blame Game. *Government and Opposition*, 37(1), 15–37.

Judge, D. (2014). *Democratic Incongruities*. Palgrave Macmillan.

Kickert, W. J., Klijn, E. H., & Koppenjan, J. F. (Eds.). (1997). *Managing Complex Networks: Strategies for the Public Sector*. Sage.

Oliver, K., Lorenc, T., & Innvær, S. (2014). New Directions in Evidence-Based Policy Research: A Critical Analysis of the Literature. *Health Research Policy and Systems, 12*(1), 34.

Marsh, D., & McConnell, A. (2010). Towards a Framework for Establishing Policy Success. *Public Administration, 88*(2), 564–583.

Marsh, D., Richards, D., & Smith, M. (2003). Unequal Plurality: Towards an Asymmetric Power Model of British Politics. *Government and Opposition, 38*(3), 306–332.

Massey, A., & Pyper, R. (2005). *Public Management and Modernisation in Britain*. Palgrave.

McConnell, A. (2010). *Understanding Policy Success: Rethinking Public Policy*. Macmillan International Higher Education.

McConnell, A. (2016). A Public Policy Approach to Understanding the Nature and Causes of Foreign Policy Failure. *Journal of European Public Policy, 23*(5), 667–684.

McGarvey, N. (2001). Accountability in Public Administration: A Multi-Perspective Framework of Analysis. *Public Policy and Administration, 16*(2), 17–29.

Moore, M. H. (1995). *Creating Public Value: Strategic Management in Government*. Harvard University Press.

Nickson, S., Thomas, A., & Mullens-Burgess, E. (2020). Decision Making in a Crisis: First Responses to the Coronavirus Pandemic, Institute for Government. https://www.instituteforgovernment.org.uk/sites/default/files/publications/decision-making-crisis.pdf

Nuki, P (2020). Exercise Cygnus Uncovered: The Pandemic Warnings Buried by the Government. https://www.telegraph.co.uk/news/2020/03/28/exercise-cygnus-uncovered-pandemic-warnings-buried-government/

Osborne, S. (2000). *Public-Private Partnerships for Public Services: An International Perspective*. Routledge.

Osborne, S. (2009). *The New Public Governance? Emerging Perspectives on the Theory and Practice of Public Governance*. Routledge.

Osborne, S. P., & Brown, L. (Eds.). (2013). *Handbook of Innovation in Public Services*. Edward Elgar Publishing.

Reiter, R., & Klenk, T. (2019). The Manifold Meanings of 'Post-New Public Management'—A Systematic Literature Review. *International Review of Administrative Sciences, 85*(1), 11–27.

Rhodes, R. A. (1997). *Understanding Governance: Policy Networks, Governance, Reflexivity and Accountability*. Open University Press.

Rhodes, R. A., & Wanna, J. (2007). The Limits to Public Value, Or Rescuing Responsible Government from the Platonic Guardians. *Australian Journal of Public Administration, 66*(4), 406–421.

Sørensen, E., & Torfing, J. (2009). Making Governance Networks Effective and Democratic Through Metagovernance. *Public Administration, 87*(2), 234–258.

Stoker, G. (2003). *Public Value Management (PVM): A New Resolution of the Democracy/Efficiency Trade Off*. Institute for Political and Economic Governance (IPEG), University of Manchester.

Stoker, G. (2006). Public Value Management: A New Narrative for Networked Governance? *The American Review of Public Administration, 36*(1), 41–57.

Williams, I., & Shearer, H. (2011). Appraising Public Value: Past, Present and Futures. *Public Administration, 89*(4), 1367–1384.

CHAPTER 2

Public Value in Britain: A 'Post-New Public Management' Environment?

John Connolly and Arno van der Zwet

INTRODUCTION

As the introduction to this book highlighted, the study of public administration has seen a conceptual shift from new public management (NPM) to more of a focus on public value, including the leadership and management strategies to achieve and demonstrate value (sometimes referred to as 'public value management'). The public value lens has yet to be applied to governance reform within the British context to any significant extent. This book seeks to make in-roads in this respect (see Coats and Passmore 2008). It is important to note, however, that public value is not just about how government programmes are implemented or only a *meso-* or *micro-*level concern for implementing initiatives, policies and interventions (as important as that is). Rather, public value is also about governance approaches to manoeuvring within policy systems, or the 'craft' of, government. It is about the leadership strategies and approaches for building

J. Connolly (✉) • A. van der Zwet
University of the West of Scotland, Glasgow, UK
e-mail: john.connolly@uws.ac.uk; arno.van-der-Zwet@uws.ac.uk

© The Author(s) 2021
J. Connolly, A. van der Zwet (eds.), *Public Value Management, Governance and Reform in Britain*, International Series on Public Policy, https://doi.org/10.1007/978-3-030-55586-3_2

capacity for multiple actors to be able to generate value (Morse 2010; Liddle 2018; Hartley et al. 2019; also see McMillan's chapter in the current volume). Public value recalibrates traditional public administration perspectives regarding lines of accountability, which is that public managers are accountable to their political masters, to the idea that the accountability of public managers is more aligned to the private sector imperative of customer-focused 'shareholder value' (Pyper 2015, p. 30). Stoker (2006) notes that, in the context of modern governance, an essential aspect of public value 'involves networks of deliberation and delivery'. Public value, therefore, could be regarded as an approach that promotes the widening of the stakeholder net, emphasising collaboration. In this vein, there is a notion of governance complexities and multidirectional accountabilities invoked by public value interpretations.

The subsequent chapter in this volume, by Robert Pyper, considers public sector reform in the context of the developments in British public administration. To frontload further debates within the book, the present chapter addresses key themes and issues relating to public value, governance and reform. It starts by considering NPM in the context of British governance and then focuses on major themes associated with public value, including complexity, networks, outcomes, evaluation, co-production and trust. The chapter ends by discussing key issues with regards to measuring and establishing public value. Overall, the chapter calls for analyses of governance reform to avoid over-claiming that NPM is over and that cumulative changes over time expand our understanding of NPM ideas, rather than replace them.

The British Governance Context

The impact of NPM on the British civil service in the 1980s through to the 1990s has been very well documented, particularly in terms of the impact of agencification (or 'quangoization'), a consumerist approach to public service provision, outsourcing previously state-provided services, competitive tendering, corporate management approaches in the public sector, and the rise of public sector performance measurement and management systems (e.g. Politt 1989; Dunleavy and Hood 1994; Rhodes 2000; Politt and Dan 2013). The rise of monetarism and the New Right ideology introduced private sector and market-based mechanisms into the operation of the public sector as opposed to more Weberian bureaucratic approaches, for example, tighter command and control within hierarchical structures. These developments are linked with governance debates about how and whether the British state was being 'hollowed out', decentralised and essentially becoming a 'differentiated polity' (Rhodes 1997; Bevir and Rhodes 2003) as a result of the territorial patterns of devolution for Scotland, Wales and Northern Ireland post-1999. The added dimension, of course, is the (pre-Brexit) policy context of the widening and deepening of European integration (given Britain's membership of the European Union)—described, for short, as 'Europeanisation' or 'multi-level governance' (Bulmer and Burch 2005). The 'hollowed out' state thesis has, however, been questioned by Marsh et al. (2003) who argue that this argument is overstretched and that the core UK executive remains the most powerful actor in the policy process. It is claimed that the British political traditions of the dominance of the 'Westminster model' (i.e. the concentration of power to key political institutions) have remained dominant within the UK political system (see Judge 1993, 2005).

It is possible to point to two major examples in contemporary British politics that support such an argument. First, the decision to leave the European Union (known widely as 'Brexit') as a result of the referendum result on 23 June 2016 (result: 51.9% to leave; 48.1% to remain) has dominated British politics in recent years. The political machinations since the referendum have highlighted the acute uncertainties about what a 'post-Brexit Britain' will mean and look like for the economy, immigration, agriculture, fisheries and citizenship status (to name but some). The narrative of 'taking back control' of the UK's sovereignty (language used persistently by 'leave' [the EU] campaigners) was a direct plea to reassert the role of British political institutions and thus serves to challenge the supranational governance contribution to the 'hollowing out of the state' argument (see Rhodes 1997; Jessop 2004).

A further example is the election of the Scottish National Party (SNP) as the party of government in Scotland in 2007 following two successive Labour and Liberal Democrat coalition administrations (1999–2002 and 2003–2007) in post-devolution Scotland in 1999. Given that the political *raison d'être* for the SNP is independence for Scotland, the Scottish government embarked on an incremental campaign to have an independence referendum (known as 'indy ref'). The independence referendum of 18 September 2014 produced a 'no' vote (55.3% compared to 44.7% who voted yes to independence). The Brexit vote gave more momentum to the SNP's aims given that a breakdown of the Brexit referendum results showed that 62% of Scottish voters sought to stay in the EU (resulting in the SNP claiming that Scotland was being dragged out of the EU against its will). There is, however, a lack of evidence of any 'Brexit bounce' in Scottish public opinion in support of another independence referendum in Scotland (Montagu 2019, pp. 45–46). The twin developments of Brexit and the result of the 2017 General Election has reaffirmed the dominance of the state at the UK level and has served to reinforce Marsh et al.'s (2003) argument that the Westminster model is dominant in British politics. The overall point here is that the constitutional and political context *matters* to how we understand the patterns of British governance. This also matters in terms of the forms and architectures of how governance systems are led, organised and operationalised (see Flinders and Huggins in the present volume). Moreover, debates about developments in public sector reform that address notions of public value should identify the sub-concepts or themes that might be considered as different from NPM and how these matter for how we understand British governance.

Public Value: An Emphasis on Evaluation and Complexity

Public value emphasises complexity to a far greater extent than NPM, and this warrants the need for adaptive leadership and the ability to navigate multiple accountabilities (Benington and Turbitt 2007). Talbot (2009, p.169) reflects on the fact that 'public value seems to have the advantage of looking simultaneously forward and backward'. For example, in the UK, performance management targets and the '3Es' (economy, efficiency and effectiveness), which are associated with NPM from the late Thatcher era (with continued focus under John Major's government up until 1997), remain relevant for public value perspectives. At the same time, public value perspectives exhibit more ambition about having in place responsive and resilient, or in Stoker's (2005) terms, 'agile' public services. Public value places less emphasis on the 'consumerist' and the private sector orientations of understandings of NPM, and, instead, public value elevates the importance of the citizen as a partner in the development and implementation of services. In this respect, co-production and participatory governance helps us to focus on the design of public sector programmes based on the logic that if the end-user is involved in design process then it will reduce the risk of policy or programmatic failures (Bovaird 2007; McConnell 2015).

A major consideration for adopting a co-productive approach to public services is that the approach can offset long-standing and ever-present post-implementation evaluation findings—that programmes, policies and interventions were not fit for purpose in the first place (Mayne 2013). The issue of evaluation, therefore, is important because public value takes conceptual thinking about the design of services in the public sector away from outputs (i.e. the direct result of policy activities). For instance, in August 2017, the Office for National Statistics reported that employment in the UK was 32.1 million (77.1% of the population), and this was the highest (pre-pandemic) since modern records began in 1971 (ONS 2017). At an output level, this might be a policy success, but what this does not tell us about the value or outcomes of such changes in the rate of employment, for example, what type of employment? Are people happier in their jobs? What about the 'working poor' and the rise of inequalities as a result of austerity? What about job security? These are public value-based questions.

Public Value and Accountability

Accountability structures need to be shaped in order to support the creation of public value (Kelly et al. 2002; see also Massey's chapter in this volume). The democratic nuance of public value, according to Stoker (2006), is to give more relative weightage to democratic participation compared to NPM perspectives, with the latter giving more relative weightage to efficiency. The politics-administration dichotomy (i.e. Woodrow Wilson's separation of the two spheres) and clearer lines of accountability (in a Weberian sense) are subject to challenge in contemporary public administration or, as Svara (2001) considers, can be described as 'mythological'. The traditional tension between politicians and public managers comes from the fact that politicians seek to maintain electoral victory whereas a public manager's intention, in principle at least, is to maintain professional integrity and to deliver services to the public efficiently and effectively. However, the 'fading legacy of Woodrow Wilson' (Martin 1988) emerges from the advancement of bureaucratic/administrative leadership which can ultimately shape policy agendas and increase accountability of the bureaucracy towards democratic channels e.g. senior officials giving evidence to politicians via parliamentary committees, which is, in turn, televised and covered by the media. Overt and influential bureaucratic leadership is not something that is visible at all times and across all policy sectors. As Peters and Pierre (2001) note, there is a continuum ranging from a clear separation between politicians and officials to an intense interactive set of relations whereby the 'bureaucratic government' is powerful in shaping policy preferences. This is particularly the case when officials have technocratic expertise, which politicians rarely have, and having knowledge puts officials in powerful positions (Peters and Pierre 2008).

In a modern era of digital governance and evidence-based policymaking, the need to legislate on matters of scientific or technical public policy (e.g. pandemics, climate change, poverty, inequalities, migration) means that there are opportunities for technocratic actors to have authoritative positions within policy domains (Zito 2015). The uncertainties that come from the forces of globalisation, which is often the driver for modern wicked problems, *require* a network-based approach to public sector governance, and this, moreover, necessitates public managers to do less managing, and more leading, as they negotiate power struggles with politicians. That is not to say that officials themselves do not enter into conflict with each other given that inter- and intra-bureaucratic conflict is a feature of governmental life, especially in times of uncertainty and crisis (Connolly 2016a, pp. 19–20). Yet, if we reflect further on Kelly et al.'s (2002) view that accountability structures are shaped to structure the creation of public value, then this invokes a sense of institutional entrepreneurialism with regards to enhancing citizen engagement and co-productive practices in the making of public policy. The politics of this, however, is that this aids and abets a form of statecraft which produces an empowerment-heavy approach to governance (akin to the 'enabling state'). According to Rhodes and Wanna (2007), this risks blame-shifting. The darker side of public value is considered by Bryson et al. (2014, p. 451). They suggest that public value could be seen as a rhetorical strategy to advance the interests of bureaucrats. In other words, a public value focus on the bureaucracy risks the accumulation of bureaucratic power for non-elected, rather than elected, leaders.

The Importance of Leaders Within Policy Systems

Williams and Shearer (2011, p. 14) single out the work of Alford and Hughes (2008) and Gains and Stoker (2009) and discuss the distribution of responsibility for value-creation. Key agents for promoting and enabling public value within decentralised environments are those who operate at *meso*-levels within policy systems, rather than at the top. These actors can be described as 'catalytic' leaders (Luke 1997), given that they are change agents who, or at least attempt to, galvanise silos and lead across boundaries. Williams (2012, p.103) maintains that such individuals are responsible for multilateral brokerage, coordination and integration who 'manage within interorganizational theatres'. This reflects the complexities of modern governance whereby a multitude of factors and circumstantial drivers shape organisational imperatives and behaviours within the public sector, necessitating public policy and administration analysts to respect the contextual influences that have implications for the marshalling and execution of public value processes in network-based environments.

'Contextualization' (Politt 2002), therefore, is an important idea that has been recognised by scholars in that different state contexts will bring their own nuances for approaching public sector reform (see Pyper 2015, pp. 24–28). This is in no small part due to the need to adapt as a result of the particular external challenges of globalisation, COVID 19, austerity, crises (e.g. the legacy of the 2008 global financial crisis) and the implications of changes in global governance (Brexit, for example) coupled with internal dynamics of the structures and sub-structures of the political system. A further public value interpretation of role of the modern public manager is the need to understand the outcomes, or 'value-added', of public sector reform and initiatives. It is often those leaders embedded within policy systems that have partnership bridging functions that are crucial for achieving public value. With this in mind, Williams and Shearer (2011, p.14) suggest that there needs to be more 'research into, and evaluation of, the applicability of public value to the local strategic management level'. The value of *meso*-level leaders themselves merits further research given that there are clearly barriers for such actors to *lead for public value*. The pursuit of public value requires the system itself to have a culture of innovation and political masters who are supportive of risk-taking and an uncluttered stakeholder landscape (where such leaders know what they have direct control over and what they can indirectly influence) but this is by no means guaranteed within the realities of complex public service environments (Rhodes and Wanna 2007; Connolly and Pyper 2020).

Public value also requires ethical leadership. There are negative consequences for the effectiveness of governance if this is absent. As a case in point, in January 2019 the Committee on Standards in Public Life (an independent advisory non-departmental public body that advises the prime minister on ethical standards across the whole of public life) published a report based on evaluations of corporate failure within local government. There were investigations into Tower Hamlets (failures in financial, prudence and management), Doncaster (culture of bullying—individual councillor behaviours at Doncaster were 'venomous, vicious, and vindictive') and Northamptonshire (breakdown in the scrutiny processes and the structures of accountability and objectivity). This led the report to conclude that identified failures in ethical and leadership cultures were the source of problems (Committee on the Standards in Public Life 2019). The point here is that if ethical matters are not attended to with due care in public governance, then this has negative consequences for the accrual of public value (of which trust is vitally important). Furthermore, and as noted earlier in this section of the chapter, leadership cultures that promote trust-building are fundamental to achieving value. A shift towards outcomes, at its best, is a way to lead agendas and engage with stakeholders in order to pursue shared goals.

PUBLIC VALUE: A SHIFT TO OUTCOMES

One of the most significant drivers to promote public value emerged in 2017 via Sir Michael Barber's report: *Delivering better outcomes for citizens: Practical steps for unlocking public value*. The Barber report was commissioned by the UK Treasury to understand how the Treasury (and wider government departments) can organise themselves to deliver public value (also see the Foreword in this volume). The report introduces a 'Public Value Framework' (PVF) which promotes Mark Moore's work to encourage public managers to manage resources to produce better outcomes (Barber 2017, p. 24). The PVF, according to the report, promotes two main agendas. First, the goal was for the PVF to 'form the basis for the ongoing dialogue across the public sector on public value, thereby creating a common language on how to improve it' (Barber 2017, p. 25). This is based on the idea of disseminating best practice, sharing learning and producing 'new dialogues' across government departments. Second, the intention of the PVF was for it to stimulate 'the agenda for periodic Public Value Reviews through which the Treasury, in collaboration with departments would examine in-depth major areas of public expenditure' (Barber 2017, pp. 25–26) (see also Pyper's chapter in this volume for more details on the establishment of the Barber review). What this

Table 2.1 Public Value Framework

Four Pillars	16 areas to consider
Pursuing Goals	• Understanding goals and indicators
	• Degree of ambition
	• Progress towards indicators and goals
Managing Inputs	• Processes to manage resources
	• Quality of data and forecasts
	• Benchmarking and cost control
	• Cost shifting
Engaging Users and Citizens	• Public and taxpayer legitimacy
	• User/client experience and participation
	• Key stakeholder engagement
Developing Systems Capacity	• Capacity to innovate and learn from innovation
	• Capacity to plan and deliver
	• Capacity to engage with the delivery chain
	• Capacity to work across organisational boundaries
	• Capacity of the workforce
	• Capacity to review performance data and evaluate impact

Source: Barber (2017)

highlights, therefore, is a call for more of an evaluative culture focused on the achievement of outcomes and continuous improvement, which are grouped in the report around 'Four Pillars', as noted in Table 2.1:

Two years after the publication of the Barber review, a 2019 report by the House of Commons Public Accounts Committee (PAC), which reflected on the goals of the Barber report, investigated the work of the Treasury in the context of improved government planning and spending. This was essentially a progress report about the UK government's approach to adopting public value-based thinking. The PAC report found that:

> we remain concerned that planning and spending are treated as disparate. We found compelling evidence that departments are not incentivised to plan for the longer-term, and they are repeatedly over-optimistic when planning for what they can deliver, by when and for how much. Unless action is taken to correct these issues, the government's long-standing problems of short-term thinking, sticking plaster funding and cost-shunting will persist, resulting in poorer quality, less sustainable and joined-up services. Ultimately, this means that the needs of the public, who rely on and fund these vital services, can fall through the cracks. (Public Accounts Committee Report 2019, p. 3)

For public value to be successful, there needs to be a long-term perspective on the changes that need to be made (avoiding short-termism), implementation of programmes need to be evidence-based (i.e. realistic and not overoptimistic), and the breaking down of silo working (to enable joined-up collaborative governance approaches)—with all of this being on the basis that planning and evaluation need to be dovetailed rather than being separate functions (see also Connolly 2016b). A key lesson from both reports (the Barber review and the PAC) is the importance of understanding what the public value literature tells us about 'how to do' public value and what public managers need to think about when managing programmes and departments.

The idea of policy 'outcomes' is becoming ever more a part of the lexicon of public management and administration as a consequence of questions such as 'what is the difference this policy and programme has made?', 'what is the change?' and 'how do we know?'. Although performance measurement has been a key tenet of NPM, this provides an output-focused account of what is being delivered rather than the outcome(s) accrued from such activities. Theories of change modelling and outcome frameworks help decision-makers and service managers to inform planning and to evaluate the value or contribution that programmes are making within complex contexts (Craig 2013; Connolly et al. 2018). There is also the argument that visions of outcomes for public services are out of sync with what is achievable at *meso-* or *micro-*levels - it is the latter levels which do the heavy lifting. Another way to consider this is that modern governance calls into question whether or not the change agents are those who occupy elite-level positions in the central offices of government or whether they are situated within partnership contexts at lower levels within the policy system.

Regrettably, the public value and evaluation literatures do not talk to each other to a sufficient extent. The ways in which the public management literature considers outcomes-focused approaches include, but are not limited to, results-based management (Mayne 2007; Try and Radnor 2007), theory-based evaluation (Weiss 1997; Douthwaite et al. 2017), programme evaluation (Calder 2013; Newcomer et al. 2015) and contribution analysis (Bannister and O'Sullivan 2013; Befani and Mayne 2014; Connolly 2016b). These are all branches of the same tree for understanding value. Outcomes-focused approaches are not particularly new. Logic modelling, as an approach for mapping outcomes, has been a feature of strategic and programme planning within the public sector for many decades (at least since the 1970s). Knowlton and Phillips (2012, p.6) note that the US Agency for International Development's 1971 logical framework approach and Claude Bennett's 1976 hierarchy of programme effectiveness were amongst the earliest uses of such a tool which visually represented programmes of work. The academic world then saw the advancement and promotion of logic models in the seminal academic writings (by Carol Weiss (1995), for example). The change towards more attention being given to impact and outcomes means that tools, such as logic models, are commonly used as part of the armoury of contemporary public managers.

In Britain, the value for money (VFM) and best value (Boyne 2000; Audit Scotland 2020) agendas promoted the idea that service-level reforms should be more sustained, not just short-term reform, and that levels of sustainability should be monitored and evaluated. This was a step change towards an outcomes-focused approach to reform in the public sector, emphasising:

- Evaluative organisational cultures (Benington 2011; Mayne 2017);
- Evidence utilisation (Patton 2008; Oliver et al. 2014)
- Knowledge brokerage (Ward et al. 2009; Reid et al. 2017)
- Collaborative and partnership working (Huxham and Vangen 2013; O'Leary 2015[1]).
- Organisational learning and improvement (Rashman et al. 2009; Hartley et al. 2013)
- Dovetailing between planning and evaluation (Connolly 2016b; Vedung 2017)
- Participatory approaches to planning and evaluation (Abelson et al. 2013; Lovan et al. 2017)
- Public leadership and advocacy (Wallis and Gregory 2009; Morse 2010; Ospina 2017)
- Monitoring and impact evaluation (Bozeman and Sarewitz 2011; Vedung 2017)
- Public sector as a complex system[2] (Agranoff 2007; Geyer and Cairney 2015)

[1] O'Leary (2015, pp. 87–88) highlights that studies of collaboration and partnerships suffer from a lack of definitional commonality to describe collaborative public management, with studies using various units of analyses with regards to who is the lead agent of collaboration and whether collaborations happen by chance, are formal or informal.
[2] This is based on public managers needing a rounded view of the policy sector and context by undertaking a stakeholder analysis and multi-level evaluations at *macro-* (national), *meso-* (agency or partnership level) and *micro-*levels (ultimate point of implementation).

Policy narratives, supported by the post-1997 Labour government, signified a shift towards the language of outcomes. Kelly et al. (2002) note that this was directly linked to the pursuit of public value on the basis of having a 'whole of government' approach to public administration, underpinned by modernisation processes. Also referred to as 'joined-up government', there is a strong sense of utopianism when advocating joined-up approaches. This is not unlike Hogwood and Gunn's argument regarding the unreachable objective of achieving perfect implementation (Hogwood and Gunn 1984). Yet, policy-makers know that there are systemic problems when it comes to *not* joining-up. Bureau-political conflict (Rosenthal et al. 1991), a lack of clarity of ownership over tackling problems that transcend policy sectors (Wilkins 2002), minimal stimuli to foster innovation—both in an intra- and interorganisational sense (Clarke and Stewart 1997)—are likely to be left wanting. The outcome of 'too much' joined-up government, or being instructed to do so by those in political authority, might lead to resentment due to forced collaboration. This would dampen the possibilities for creativity which can be borne out of a moderately conflictual and competitive environment. That being said, Ling (2002) notes that aspects of joined-up government entail shifts in governing arrangements which include new accountabilities and incentives (e.g. shared outcome targets), new ways of working across organisational boundaries (including shared leadership and budgeting processes), new ways of delivering services (e.g. joint delivery across sectors and greater scope for consultation with the end-user) and new types of organisation (e.g. information-sharing, shared cultures and capacity building).

Co-producing Public Value: Features Politics and Trust

Adopting an outcomes approach to public sector reform interlinks with notions of democratic engagement in policy design processes and the need for policy-makers to reach those who are ultimately affected by decisions (see also McMillan's chapter in this volume which addresses co-production in the context of public value leadership). According to the New Economics Foundation (2008, pp. 12–13), co-production can be described as follows:

- Providing opportunities for personal growth and development to people, so that they are treated as assets, not burdens, on an overstretched system.

- Investing in strategies that develop the emotional intelligence and capacity of local communities.
- Using peer support networks instead of just professionals as the best means of transferring knowledge and capabilities.
- Reducing or blurring the distinction between producers and consumers of services by reconfiguring the ways in which services are developed and delivered.
- Allowing public service agencies to become catalysts and facilitators rather than simply providers.
- Devolving real responsibility, leadership and authority to 'users', and encouraging self-organisation rather than direction from above.
- Offering participants a range of incentives which help to embed the key elements of reciprocity and mutuality.

These are challenging principles for policy-makers and bureaucratic actors to live by, and there is the danger that the language of co-production is used as a symbolic mechanism to convey the impression that users are fundamental for policy creation. Flinders et al. (2016) discuss the 'hidden politics' of co-production. They argue that it can be highly consuming in terms of time and emotion, ethically complex, suffers from inconsistencies, and is vulnerable to changes in wider political circumstances. Co-production, as noble in intention as it might be, will be subject to false starts by the fundamental prevalence of acute inequalities i.e. not all citizens will feel like they are candidates for co-production (Mackenzie et al. 2013). That is not to say that co-production cannot be an 'intrinsic good' or that it does not have the potential to support well-being (Needham and Carr 2009), nor that it cannot be used as a preventative approach for diagnosing societal problems before they require policy interventions (Needham and Carr 2009; Slay and Stephens 2013).

In the spirit of deliberative democracy, there are mutual benefits for citizens being part of decision-making processes. Decision-makers can understand what 'value' means to the user of services and enable them to access the experiential learning of citizens. At the same time, there is the potential for co-production to foster more cohesive communities, which serves, *inter alia*, to create social capital (Griffiths and Foley 2009). That being said, there is no getting away from the fact that co-production is an example of another 'woolly-word' in public policy (Osborne et al. 2016, p. 640) and there is scarce evidence of the value (be in terms of cost implications or efficiencies accrued) of being co-productive as a service designer

(Voorberg et al. 2014). The politics of co-production is also about the intended and unintended manoeuvring of the use of the term. Bovaird et al. (2017, p. 363) argue that much of the rhetoric and practice about co-production privilege the citizen's voice in policy and service development 'rather than getting them to do things for themselves and for each other'. In other words, as the New Economics Foundation notes, there are those in policy circles who use co-production as a term to mean no more than consultation (New Economics Foundation 2008, p. 15). Such perspectives are also not helped by the inability to demonstrate the value of co-production beyond specific and often localised sectors, which are contexts that are naturally riper for co-productive practice. As Osborne et al. states (2016, p. 643):

> Services such as residential care and education are clearly instances where co-production and value co-creation are high, with almost constant, direct face-to-face contact between the service user and the service provider. By contrast, they are rather lower for electronic financial services, such as tax returns, because production and consumption occur through the medium of an electronic interface that does not have the interpersonal immediacy of face-to-face contact–in this case, the co-production of a financial service is essentially passive (the inputting of financial data for their tax return by a citizen or choosing from a list of preset options, for example), mediated through a virtual interface.

This points to the fact that the evaluative qualities of co-production, if we accept that co-productive practice is a cornerstone of public value, are of little value. If the modern public sector is occupied within complex governance landscapes, which might be 'morass-like' (Pugh and Connolly 2016), then perhaps the question should be less about the scalability of co-production but more about having a culture that allows for co-production to be sustained. The cultural dimension is important here, however, in that the culture requires public sector leaders and managers to allow for those engineering co-production to 'intelligently fail' and to be experimental, which is obviously not without its risks in the context of public sector accountability with the ever-present risk of blame games and electioneering. This is especially the case if intelligent failure/experimentation leads to maladministration, which can, moreover, lead to the tightening of bureaucratisation. As Bovaird and Loeffler (2012, original emphasis) suggest, on the topic of resource capacities, 'co-production may be 'value for money', but it usually cannot produce value *without* money'.

Farazmand (2009: 1016) also notes that 'nothing gets done without administrative capacity' and that capacity is the 'core of government'. In public administration terms, capacities are the institutional energy which, if managed properly, play a necessary part avoiding policy failure (Howlett 2012; Wu et al. 2015; Dunlop 2017). In this respect, studies of public value need to do more to focus on the capacities to enable meaningful co-production in the first place.

Reciprocity and trust have been cited as key to producing public value (Kelly et al. 2002; Talbot 2008). If public value includes the presence of competitiveness (e.g. choice and relative quality), collaboration (e.g. co-production and partnership working), control (e.g. resilience, standard-setting, efficacies) and creativity (e.g. transparency accountability and innovation), then, according to Talbot (2008, p. 19), all of these ambitions of public value will be undermined in the absence of trust and legitimacy. The chapters of this book address these issues in different ways, but there is a lack of equivocal evidence to suggest that co-production leads to increased trust between citizens and public services (Bovaird and Loeffler 2012; Fledderus et al. 2014). Trust can be measured, according to Talbot (2008, p. 19), by stakeholder, user and public surveys, analyses of audits and inspections and levels of complaints. Yet measuring public value is by no means straightforward. This is where the chapter will now turn.

Making Judgements About the Presence of Public Value

As noted in the introduction of this book, establishing public value is a close friend (or, in McConnell's (2010, p. 15) terms, a 'surrogate') for understanding policy success in public policy and administration. Researchers have been wrestling for some time with how to evaluate success (and failure), including how to plausibly make claims about the value that has been accrued as a result of the implementation of a set of programmes and initiatives within complex political environments. McConnell (2010, pp. 16–17) notes how public value and debates about establishing success has similar challenges and complexities to consider in that they are both slippery and ambiguous, neither is devoid of internal conflicts (e.g. part of a system or process might be of value, whereas others might be less so) and the importance of cultural and policy context dependence (e.g. value accrued in one geopolitical environment might not be suitable for translation into others).

Furthermore, similarities emerge when it comes to cutting through contested perspectives about 'what' and 'how' to measure value. This is no easy task if we consider that, as Stoker (2006, p.42) noted, 'the judgment of what is public value is collectively built through deliberation involving elected and appointed government officials and key stakeholders'. Reaching collective agreements, and having in place the right deliberative forums that address the self-interests of actors, and the inevitable power dynamics and imbalances, is not quite utopian but, in practice, very difficult if, for instance, 'other stakeholders' also include citizens. The public manager's role, according to Bryson et al. (2004, p. 447), is to play an 'active role in helping create and guide networks of deliberation and delivery and help to maintain and enhance the overall effectiveness, accountability, and capacity of the system'. This also includes evaluating the impact of change processes that are aimed at creating public value. Bryson et al. (2004, p. 450) cite Meynhardt (2009, p. 212) who argues that this happens at two levels. First, evaluation is about 'how the basic needs of individuals, groups, and society as a whole are influenced in relationships involving the public' and 'public value is also about value from the public' when it is 'drawn from the experience of the public'. This points to the need for the co-production of public value evaluations.

If NPM management focused more on the strategies for implementing performance improvement regimes, then the process of managing public value is about organising policy and organisational strategies so that there are capacities to enable the monitoring and evaluation of implementation processes in the long term. Blaug et al. (2006, p. 5) go as far to say that there can be measurement strategies in the public sector, and across policy systems, which can end up 'destroying' public value, and the risks of this are associated with standardisation practices of reducing performance down to input- and output-based measures (such as hospital waiting times and exam results). Even if we consider non-political systems-based contexts, such as research on the performance value of engineering systems (which might be generally associated within monitoring-based measures), there is recognition of the need to understand alterative contextual and often qualitative measures for assessing the resilience levels of engineering systems (see Cimellaro et al. 2016). However, no matter the sector (public or private), measuring public value requires leadership and the bureaucratic capacities in order to allow public value to be realisable and evaluable. The PAC report's major criticisms of the Treasury's (and Whitehall's) progress towards delivering a sustainable approach to public value addressed the issue of capacity directly, which has not been helped by high turnover rates and the need to recruit more talent from outside Whitehall. It notes that:

> Given the instrumental role they play [civil servants] in advising ministers, stewarding submissions for new spending and challenging the realism of departments' plans, Treasury spending teams need to be highly-skilled and effective, as well as having very specific expertise to particular departments. The Treasury is, by its own admission, a 'young department' with high staff turnover … As a result, we see poor forecasting, planning and understanding of the long term. The Cabinet Office reports that it is helping departments to plan better, for example by getting departments to self-assess their planning maturity. To better inform ministerial decisions the Cabinet Office and the Treasury say that they are building functional capability and experience back into the civil service, but it will take time. It is vital that the right skills and experience are in place to achieve a culture of challenging objectives, plans and progress. (PAC Report 2019, p. 5)

These issues also need to be considered in light of the governance lessons to be learned from the COVID-19 pandemic i.e. focusing on matters of statecraft and governance capacities will be key for establishing public value. The often cited landmark on how to approach public administration within government came as a result of the 1999 *Modernising Government* White Paper which focused on addressing aspects of quality in public services with an emphasis on joined-up government (Cabinet Office 1999). Bryson et al. (2014, p. 452), in discussing the New Labour government's approach to public value under Tony Blair, argued that, at that time, public value was used more in a way of thinking about performance, outcomes, legitimacy and trust. Blair himself, on reflecting on his time in office, particularly the last six years of his premiership (2001–2007), highlighted how the government sought to adopt 'a balanced perspective' by making use of external advisers as well as drawing on the expertise within the civil service whilst recognising the distinct limitations of the bureaucracy:

> I say this to governments around the world, you should always treat the bureaucracy with respect, you should recognise what it can do but if you become a prisoner of it then, believe me, you will achieve nothing, you will just go around in circles. (BBC Radio 4; Reflections with Peter Hennessey, Tony Blair: 10th August 2017)

Tony Blair was quoted in the introductory chapter to this book from the same interview, and he went on to say that the 'reinventing government' agenda has went off the radar. The post-2008 global financial crisis austerity agenda, coupled with Brexit (see Morphet's chapter in this volume), has been a major *macro*-political distraction away from the art of governing and learning. Perhaps the lack of priority afforded by the UK government to such matters explains the findings of the 2019 PAC report. In essence, governance capacities are the lifeblood for enabling monitoring, evaluation and innovation to happen in the first place, let alone for it to be sustained. In contemporary Britain, the post-2010 welfare reform agenda challenges not just health and social inequalities and the fabric of communities but it has implications for what can be considered to be, in common parlance, as the organisational 'nice to dos'—these include training and evaluation budgets. There are risks in times of austerity that the impact side of evaluation (in terms of assessing outcomes) becomes deprioritised over performance measurement and monitoring, which is more in the domain of *process* rather than *impact* evaluation. In such a context, the logic follows that less can be said about the value-added of service delivery in such a context. That being said, public managers and leaders are encouraged by Blaug et al. (2006, p. 52), who draw on the work of the Australian Government Productivity Commission (2005), to consider the following aspects for evaluating public value:

- *Effectiveness* indicators to reflect how well the outputs of a service achieve the stated objectives of that service.
- *Efficiency* indicators to reflect how well services use their resources to produce outputs and achieve outcomes.
- *Output* indicators of service delivery. Output indicators can be grouped according to the desired characteristics of a service—for example, accessibility, appropriateness or quality—which may differ across services.
- *Outcome* indicators to provide information on the impact of a service on the status of an individual or a group, and on the success of the service area in achieving its objectives.
- *Quality* indicators to reflect the extent to which a service is suited to its purpose and conforms to specifications. Information about quality is particularly important for performance assessment when there is a strong emphasis on increasing efficiency.

- *Access* indicators to reflect how easily a community can obtain a delivered service, for example, access to school education. Access has two main dimensions: timeliness and affordability. Timeliness indicators include waiting times (e.g. in hospitals). Affordability indicators relate to the proportion of income spent on particular services (e.g. out-of-pocket expenses towards the provision of childcare).
- *Appropriateness* indicators to measure how well services meet the needs of citizens. This allows for services to develop measurable standards of service need against which current levels of service can be assessed and levels of over- or under-servicing identified.
- *Equity* indicators are needed. These have horizontal and vertical dimensions. In the context of performance measurement for service delivery, horizontal equity is exhibited when everyone is allowed to access the service. Service delivery exhibits vertical equity when it accounts for the special needs of certain groups in the community and adjusts aspects of service delivery to suit these needs. This approach may be needed where geographic, cultural or other reasons might mean that some members of the community have difficulty accessing the service.

These are helpful ways of developing evaluative thinking for public sector governance, but assessing the contribution of a service or programme, in terms of understanding the value that they offer society, can be resource intensive. In austere times, public managers tend to remain in a 'performance measurement' mode of thinking. Performance measurement data, alongside softer data (often of a qualitative nature), *can* be used to tell a trustworthy story of impact. In fact, governance is often about storytelling as a way of constructing realities to help navigate through having too much or inconclusive information, which warrants the need for interpretations to generate policy narratives (Shanahan et al. 2011; Jones et al. 2014; Oppermann and Spencer 2016). Bevir (2011) makes the case that storytelling in public administration should be defended, and Stark and Head (2018) maintain that storytelling is a way of dealing with institutional amnesia or memory loss. Jones and Crow (2017) also make the case that scientific research needs to take storytelling literally in that communicating policy solutions requires a narrative-based structure whereby there is a 'plot' with a moral to the story which unearths a plausible 'solution' to a problem that is frontloaded by 'scene-setting' and 'character development'.

What this indicates is that there might be 'hard data' collected routinely about the impact of a service or programme, but the use of data to make sense of value might be lost when those who need to know the value of a policy, programme, intervention and service do not recognise the ways in which the information is collected or packaged. Stevens (2011) reported on an observational study of British civil servants and concluded that although officials showed a commitment to using evidence, the complexity of evidence, and its volume, necessitated the formulation of persuasive policy stories. To be fair to policy-makers, academics are not always equipped with the experience or skills to support policy-makers in answering the questions that they want to know, despite the increasing importance of the impact agenda in academia. That being said, there is now more research on how academic research can influence policy in recognition of the fact that there is far from a loving marriage between research evidence and policy-making (see Oliver and Cairney 2019). Yet, it is important for policy-makers to value evidence, not least because it helps to legitimise policy decision-making (see the chapter by Kathryn Oliver and Alec Fraser in the current volume). If that is all that evidence does, however, then that underplays its role in the context of public value. There is more of a policy audience available now than ever in the British context when it comes to sharing evidence with policy-makers (Cairney et al. 2016). The increased role of parliamentary select committees in recent decades, which hear evidence and conduct their own investigations, is an example in this context. Parliamentary committees are now regarded as alternative career path for parliamentarians who can create a name for themselves, normally as committee chairs. In the Westminster Parliament, for example, the chairs of select committees are elected by fellow MPs, rather than party whips, which enhances their credibility and independence. The profile of committees has also been raised by taking evidence from public figures. For example, in 2016, Business, Innovation and Skills (BIS) Committee and Work & Pensions Committee heard evidence from Arcadia Group's Chairman, Philip Green, as part of their inquiries relating to the British Home Store's (BHS) pension fund deficit, which included heated exchanges between MPs and Philip Green. Committees have also been a route for those in the public eye to share their experiences. Comedian Russell Brand shared his experiential learning as part of a drugs policy inquiry with the Home Affairs Select Committee in 2012 (BBC 2012), and even the late (and great!) Lemmy Kilmister from *Motörhead* gave a talk at the Welsh Assembly, calling for the decriminalisation of heroin (BBC 2005). These might be examples of exceptional high-profile ways in which select committees engage with matters relevant to public policy, but what often flies under the radar is the everyday workings of committees in taking evidence from academics and representatives from civil society as part of a range of investigations. This is not to say that select committees are always effective, nor are those that are called to give evidence always representative of wider society (Geddes 2017), but opportunities for evidence to be heard has seen a positive shift forward in recent decades.

This talks to a broader point that the widespread dissemination of evidence is now commonplace and is an important function of democratic processes. McConnell (2010, p. 181) highlights that governments are less likely to fear critical evaluations of performance over those evaluations that might be accused of being interfered with or blocked by government (or being seen as a 'whitewash'). Indeed, the word *politics* in the phrase 'politics of evaluation' is more often than not due to the risks of evaluations being subject to control by powerful actors, for example, funders controlling the terms and remit of evaluations and with regards to how and when they are disseminated (Weiss 1993; Datta 2011). An even broader point, but an important one, is that for evaluations of public value to have a realistic opportunity of being able to research and report on value-based questions, there is a need for investment in the governance capacities to institutionally embed evaluation to allow leaders and managers within public services to have the space to organise their work to underpin programmes with evaluation. Embedding meaningful evaluation, culturally and operationally, is crucial in efforts to achieve public value.

Conclusions

A public value perspective on the public sector makes up for the shortcomings of new public management. Kelly (2002, pp. 9–10) identifies that 'the practice of the new public management often emphasised narrow concepts of cost-efficiency over other considerations (i.e. the focus was on technical rather than allocative efficiency)'. Massey (2007, p. 20) captures the essence of the need to avoid a narrow perspective on public administration by arguing that 'in the modern, post-NPM world of public administration, there is no Stalinist one-size-fits-all, context is everything'. This means that a grand theory of public value and how it is to be applied is not something that is particularly realistic or useful. Pyper (2015, p. 31) notes that 'public value itself certainly adds to our understanding of the complexities and challenges of modern public administration. It is not a successor paradigm in its own right'. What public value *does* provide is a way to recalibrate conceptual positions towards one that accounts for how institutional and policy relationships are shaped by social, political, economic and technological contexts.

This chapter has highlighted key conceptual themes that will be of importance for the remainder of the book but it has done so by calling for students of public value to dovetail this area of research with that of evaluation research and ideas. Furthermore, the more one delves into the public value literature, the less important a single definition (or even a set of definitions) seems to become in that the 'value of public value' is to understand *what it is associated with* (e.g. networks, innovation, leadership, advocacy, evidence, collaboration, learning, improvement, evaluation, participation, impact and complexity). If claims were made that there was even a fairly strong degree of conceptual clarity associated with public value, then authors would be accused of being unrealistic and not taking into account the complexities of public governance. It is plausible to suggest a combination of being cautious to avoid overinflating what is 'new' in public administration, given that institutional change is inherently conservative, yet there are dangers of being overly conservative about the propensity for public administration to not change and innovate. As Streeck and Thelen (2005, p. 8) noted, in their study of institutional changed, that 'we must avoid being caught in a conceptual schema that provides only for either incremental change … or disruptive change'. With this in mind, one way to conceive of public value is that it is the result of cumulative change from a phase of NPM, rather than it emerging as a paradigmatic replacement in its own right. Such debates are explored in some detail throughout the book by pursuing a number of themes related to leading and managing public value processes. The next chapter, by Robert Pyper, considers such debates in the context of contemporary public sector reform.

References

Abelson, J., Blacksher, E. A., Li, K. K., Boesveld, S. E., & Goold, S. D. (2013). Public Deliberation in Health Policy and Bioethics: Mapping an Emerging, Interdisciplinary Field. *Journal of Public Deliberation, 9*(1), 5.

Agranoff, R. (2007). *Managing within Networks: Adding Value to Public Organizations*. Georgetown University Press.

Alford, J., & Hughes, O. (2008). Public Value Pragmatism as the Next Phase of Public Management. *The American Review of Public Administration, 38*(2), 130–148.

Audit Scotland. (2020). *Best Value*. Retrieved from https://www.audit-scotland.gov.uk/our-work/best-value.

Australian Government Productivity Commission, Report on Government Services. (2005). *Report of the Steering Committee for the Review of Government Service Provision*. Canberra.

Bannister, J., & O'Sullivan, A. (2013). Knowledge Mobilisation and the Civic Academy: The Nature of Evidence, the Roles of Narrative and the Potential of Contribution Analysis. *Contemporary Social Science, 8*(3), 249–262.

Barber, M. (2017). *Delivering Better Outcomes for Citizens: Practical Steps for Unlocking Public Value*. Commissioned by HM Treasury. Retrieved from https://www.gov.uk/government/news/sir-michael-barber-report-into-improving-value-in-public-spending-published.

BBC. (2005). Motorhead's Lemmy Rocked the Welsh Assembly. Retrieved from https://www.bbc.co.uk/news/av/uk-wales-35193418/archive-motorhead-s-lemmy-rocked-the-welsh-assembly.

BBC. (2012). Russell Brand Calls for More Compassion for Drug Users. Retrieved from https://www.bbc.co.uk/news/uk-politics-17823272.

Befani, B., & Mayne, J. (2014). Process Tracing and Contribution Analysis: A Combined Approach to Generative Causal Inference for Impact Evaluation. *IDS Bulletin, 45*(6), 17–36.

Benington, J. (2011). From Private Choice to Public Value? In J. Benington & M. H. Moore (Eds.), *Public Value: Theory and Practice* (pp. 31–51). New York: Palgrave Macmillan.

Benington, J., & Turbitt, I. (2007). Policing the Drumcree Demonstrations in Northern Ireland: Testing Leadership Theory in Practice. *Leadership, 3*(4), 371–395.

Bevir, M. (2011). Public Administration as Storytelling. *Public Administration, 89*(1), 183–195.

Bevir, M., & Rhodes, R. (2003). *Interpreting British Governance*. Routledge.

Blaug, R., Horner, L., & Lekhi, R. (2006). *Public Value, Citizen Expectations and User Commitment. A Literature Review*. London: The Work Foundation.

Bovaird, T. (2007). Beyond Engagement and Participation: User and Community Coproduction of Public Services. *Public Administration Review, 67*(5), 846–860.

Bovaird, T., & Loeffler, E. (2012). From Engagement to Co-Production: The Contribution of Users and Communities to Outcomes and Public Value. *Voluntas: International Journal of Voluntary and Nonprofit Organizations, 23*(4), 1119–1138.

Bovaird, T., Flemig, S., Loeffler, E., & Osborne, S. P. (2017). Debate: Co-Production of Public Services and Outcomes. *Public Money & Management, 37*(5), 363–364.

Boyne, G. (2000). Developments: External Regulation and Best Value in Local Government. *Public Money and Management, 20*(3), 7–12.

Bozeman, B., & Sarewitz, D. (2011). Public Value Mapping and Science Policy Evaluation. *Minerva, 49*(1), 1–23.

Bryson, J. M., Crosby, B. C., & Bloomberg, L. (2014). Public Value Governance: Moving beyond Traditional Public Administration and the New Public Management. *Public Administration Review, 74*(4), 445–456.

Bulmer, S., & Burch, M. (2005). The Europeanization of UK Government: From Quiet Revolution to Explicit Step-Change? *Public Administration, 83*(4), 861–890.

Cabinet Office. (1999). *Modernising Government, Cm 4310*. London: The Stationery Office.

Cairney, P., Oliver, K., & Wellstead, A. (2016). To Bridge the Divide between Evidence and Policy: Reduce Ambiguity as much as Uncertainty. *Public Administration Review, 76*(3), 399–402.

Calder, J. (2013). *Programme Evaluation and Quality: A Comprehensive Guide to Setting Up an Evaluation System*. Routledge.

Cimellaro, G. P., Renschler, C., Reinhorn, A. M., & Arendt, L. (2016). PEOPLES: A Framework for Evaluating Resilience. *Journal of Structural Engineering, 142*(10), 04016063.

Clarke, M., & Stewart, J. (1997). *Partnership and the Management of Co-Operation*. Birmingham: School of Public Policy, University of Birmingham.

Coats, D., & Passmore, E. (2008). *Public Value: The Next Steps in Public Service Reform*. London: Work Foundation.

Committee on Standards in Public Life. (2019). *Review of Local Government Ethical Standards*. London: CSPL. Retrieved from https://www.gov.uk/government/collections/local-government-ethical-standards.

Connolly, J. (2016a). *The Politics and Crisis Management of Animal Health Security*. Routledge.

Connolly, J. (2016b). Contribution Analysis as an Approach to Enable Public Managers to Demonstrate Public Value: The Scottish Context. *International Journal of Public Sector Management, 29*(7), 690–707.

Connolly, J., & Pyper, R. (2020). The Leadership and Management of Public Services Reform Under the SNP in Scotland: Multi-Level Challenges within a Network Governance Context. In M. Keating & C. McAngus (Eds.), *Handbook of Scottish Politics*. Oxford University Press.

Connolly, J., Reid, G., Knoll, M., Halliday, W., & Windsor, S. (2018). The Sustainability of Knowledge Brokerage of the Mental Health Improvement Outcomes Framework in Scotland: A Follow-Up Analysis. *Evidence & Policy: A*

Journal of Research, Debate and Practice. Retrieved from https://www.ingentaconnect.com/content/tpp/ep/pre-prints/content-ppevidpol1600055r3.

Craig, N. (2013). Seeing the Wood and the Trees: Using Outcomes Frameworks to Inform Planning, Monitoring and Evaluation in Public Health. *Journal of Public Health, 35*(3), 467–474.

Datta, L. E. (2011). Politics and Evaluation: More than Methodology. *American Journal of Evaluation, 32*(2), 273–294.

Douthwaite, B., Mayne, J., McDougall, C., & Paz-Ybarnegaray, R. (2017). Evaluating Complex Interventions: A Theory-Driven Realist-Informed Approach. *Evaluation, 23*(3), 294–311.

Dunleavy, P., & Hood, C. (1994). From Old Public Administration to New Public Management. *Public Money & Management, 14*(3), 9–16.

Dunlop, C. A. (2017). Policy Learning and Policy Failure: Definitions, Dimensions and Intersections. *Policy & Politics, 45*(1), 3–18.

Farazmand, A. (2009). Building Administrative Capacity for the Age of Rapid Globalization: A Modest Prescription for the Twenty-First Century. *Public Administration Review, 69*(6), 1007–1020.

Fledderus, J., Brandsen, T., & Honingh, M. (2014). Restoring Trust through the Co-Production of Public Services: A Theoretical Elaboration. *Public Management Review, 16*(3), 424–443.

Flinders, M., Wood, M., & Cunningham, M. (2016). The Politics of Co-Production: Risks, Limits and Pollution. Evidence & Policy: A Journal of Research. *Debate and Practice, 12*(2), 261–279.

Gains, F., & Stoker, G. (2009). Delivering 'Public Value': Implications for Accountability and Legitimacy. *Parliamentary Affairs, 62*(3), 438–455.

Geddes, M. (2017). Committee Hearings of the UK Parliament: Who Gives Evidence and Does this Matter? *Parliamentary Affairs, 71*(2), 283–304.

Geyer, R., & Cairney, P. (Eds.). (2015). *Handbook on Complexity and Public Policy.* Edward Elgar Publishing.

Griffiths, S., & Foley, B. (2009). *Collective Co-Production: Working Together to Improve Public Services.* Local Authorities & Research Councils' Initiative (2010) Co-Production: A Series of Commissioned Reports, Research Councils, Swindon, UK.

Hartley, J., Sørensen, E., & Torfing, J. (2013). Collaborative Innovation: A Viable Alternative to Market Competition and Organizational Entrepreneurship. *Public Administration Review, 73*(6), 821–830.

Hartley, J., Sancino, A., Bennister, M., & Resodihardjo, S. L. (2019). Leadership for Public Value: Political Astuteness as a Conceptual Link. *Public Administration.* Retrieved from https://onlinelibrary.wiley.com/doi/pdf/10.1111/padm.12597?casa_token=460ecuXk9IcAAAAA:QYh1jqiqao2NLf8AlsbkwGvTu3CyV-ng33mj9fhGanGB8yxQxGsNCgkM1Pq66jbI4B-JUu6b2mTBlA.

Hogwood, B. W., & Gunn, L. A. (1984). *Policy Analysis for the Real World*. Oxford: Oxford University Press.
Howlett, M. (2012). The Lessons of Failure: Learning and Blame Avoidance in Public Policy-Making. *International Political Science Review, 33*(5), 539–555.
Huxham, C., & Vangen, S. (2013). *Managing to Collaborate: The Theory and Practice of Collaborative Advantage*. Routledge.
Jessop, B. (2004). Hollowing Out the 'Nation-State' and Multilevel Governance. In P. Kennett (Ed.), *A Handbook of Comparative Social Policy*. Cheltenham, UK: Edward Elgar Publishing.
Jones, M. D., & Crow, D. A. (2017). How Can We Use the 'Science of Stories' to Produce Persuasive Scientific Stories? *Palgrave Communications, 3*(1), 53.
Jones, M. D., McBeth, M. K., & Shanahan, E. A. (2014). *The Science of Stories*. New York: Palgrave Macmillan.
Judge, D. (1993). *The Parliamentary State*. Sage.
Judge, D. (2005). *Political Institutions in the United Kingdom*. Oxford: Oxford University Press.
Kelly, G., & Muers, S. (2002). *Creating Public Value—An Analytical Framework for Public Service Reform*. London: Cabinet Office Strategy Unit. Retrieved from http://www.strategy.gov.uk.
Kelly, G., Mulgan, G., & Muers, S. (2002). *Creating Public Value—An Analytical Framework for Public Service Reform*. London: Cabinet Office Strategy Unit. Retrieved from http://www.strategy.gov.uk.
Knowlton, L. W., & Phillips, C. C. (2012). *The Logic Model Guidebook: Better Strategies for Great Results*. Sage.
Liddle, J. (2018). Public Value Management and New Public Governance: Key Traits, Issues and Developments. In *The Palgrave Handbook of Public Administration and Management in Europe* (pp. 967–990). London: Palgrave Macmillan.
Ling, T. (2002). Delivering Joined-Up Government in the UK: Dimensions, Issues and Problems. *Public Administration, 80*(4), 615–642.
Lovan, W. R., Murray, M., & Shaffer, R. (2017). *Participatory Governance: Planning, Conflict Mediation and Public Decision-Making in Civil Society*. Routledge.
Luke, J. S. (1997). *Catalytic Leadership*. San Francisco: Jossey-Bass.
Mackenzie, M., Conway, E., Hastings, A., Munro, M., & O'Donnell, C. (2013). Is 'Candidacy' a Useful Concept for Understanding Journeys through Public Services? A Critical Interpretive Literature Synthesis. *Social Policy and Administration, 47*(7), 806–825.
Marsh, D., Richards, D., & Smith, M. (2003). Unequal Plurality: Towards an Asymmetric Power Model of British Politics. *Government and Opposition, 38*(3), 306–332.

Martin, D. W. (1988). The Fading Legacy of Woodrow Wilson. *Public Administration Review*, 631–636.
Massey, A. (2007). *Context is everything*. Public, July, 20.
Mayne, J. (2007). Challenges and Lessons in Implementing Results-Based Management. *Evaluation, 13*(1), 87–109.
Mayne, J. (2013). *Enhancing Evaluation Use*. SAGE.
Mayne, J. (2017). Independence in Evaluation and the Role of Culture. In J. Barbier & P. Hawkins (Eds.), *Evaluation Cultures Sense-Making in Complex Times* (pp. 111–144). Routledge.
McConnell, A. (2010). *Understanding Policy Success: Rethinking Public Policy*. Macmillan International Higher Education.
McConnell, A. (2015). What is Policy Failure? A Primer to Help Navigate the Maze. *Public Policy and Administration, 30*(3-4), 221–242.
Meynhardt, T. (2009). Public Value Inside: What is Public Value Creation? *Intl Journal of Public Administration, 32*(3–4), 192–219.
Montagu, I. (2019). Scotland. In *Brexit and Public Opinion*. UK in a Changing Europe. Retrieved from https://ukandeu.ac.uk/wp-content/uploads/2019/01/Public-Opinion-2019-report.pdf.
Morse, R. S. (2010). Integrative Public Leadership: Catalyzing Collaboration to Create Public Value. *The Leadership Quarterly, 21*(2), 231–245.
Needham, C., & Carr, S. (2009). *Co-Production: An Emerging Evidence Base for Adult Social Care Transformation*. Social Care Institute for Excellence.
New Economics Foundation. (2008). Co-Production: A Manifesto for Growing the Core Economy. Retrieved from https://neweconomics.org/uploads/files/5abec531b2a775dc8d_qjm6bqzpt.pdf.
Newcomer, K. E., Hatry, H. P., & Wholey, J. S. (Eds.). (2015). *Handbook of Practical Program Evaluation*. San Francisco, CA: Jossey-Bass & Pfeiffer Imprints, Wiley.
O'Leary, R. (2015). From Silos to Networks. In M. Guy & M. Rubin (Eds.), *Public Administration Evolving: From Foundations to the Future* (pp. 84–101). Routledge.
Office for National Statistics. (2017). UK Labour Market: May 2017. Retrieved from https://www.ons.gov.uk/employmentandlabourmarket/peopleinwork/employmentandemployeetypes/bulletins/uklabourmarket/may2017.
Oliver, K., & Cairney, P. (2019). The Dos and Don'ts of Influencing Policy: A Systematic Review of Advice to Academics. *Palgrave Communications, 5*(1), 21.
Oliver, K., Innvar, S., Lorenc, T., Woodman, J., & Thomas, J. (2014). A Systematic Review of Barriers to and Facilitators of the Use of Evidence by Policymakers. *BMC Health Services Research, 14*(1), 2.
Oppermann, K., & Spencer, A. (2016). Telling Stories of Failure: Narrative Constructions of Foreign Policy Fiascos. *Journal of European Public Policy, 23*(5), 685–701.

Osborne, S. P., Radnor, Z., & Strokosch, K. (2016). Co-Production and the Co-Creation of Value in Public Services: A Suitable Case for Treatment? *Public Management Review, 18*(5), 639–653.

Ospina, S. M. (2017). Collective Leadership and Context in Public Administration: Bridging Public Leadership Research and Leadership Studies. *Public Administration Review, 77*(2), 275–287.

Patton, M. Q. (2008). *Utilization-Focused Evaluation*. Sage Publications.

Peters, B. G., & Pierre, J. (2001). Developments in Intergovernmental Relations: Towards Multi-Level Governance. *Policy & Politics, 29*(2), 131–135.

Peters, B. G., & Pierre, J. (Eds.). (2008). *Politicians, Bureaucrats and Administrative Reform*. Routledge.

Politt, C. (1989). Performance Indicators in the Longer Term. *Public Money & Management, 9*(3), 51–55.

Politt, C. (2002). Clarifying Convergence. Striking Similarities and Durable Differences in Public Management Reforms. *Public Management Review, 4*(1), 471–492.

Politt, C., & Dan, S. (2013). Searching for Impacts in Performance-Oriented Management Reform: A Review of the European Literature. *Public Performance & Management Review, 37*(1), 7–32.

Public Accounts Committee. (2019). *House of Commons Committee of Public Accounts: Improving Government Planning and Spending*. Seventy-Eighth Report of Session 2017–19, January 30.

Pugh, M., & Connolly, J. (2016). A Review of Contemporary Linked Challenges for Scottish Local Government. *Scottish Affairs, 25*(3), 317–336.

Pyper, R. (2015). Public Administration, Public Management and Governance. In A. Massey & K. Johnston (Eds.), *The International Handbook of Public Administration and Governance (pp. 13–34)*. Edward Elgar Publishing Limited.

Rashman, L., Withers, E., & Hartley, J. (2009). Organizational Learning and Knowledge in Public Service Organizations: A Systematic Review of the Literature. *International Journal of Management Reviews, 11*(4), 463–494.

Reid, G., Connolly, J., Halliday, W., Love, A. M., Higgins, M., & MacGregor, A. (2017). Minding the Gap: The Barriers and Facilitators of Getting Evidence into Policy when Using a Knowledge-Brokering Approach. *Evidence & Policy: A Journal of Research, Debate and Practice, 13*(1), 29–38.

Rhodes, R. A. (1997). *Understanding Governance: Policy Networks, Governance, Reflexivity and Accountability*. Open University Press.

Rhodes, R. A. (2000). The Governance Narrative: Key Findings and Lessons from the ERC's Whitehall Programme. *Public Administration, 78*(2), 345–363.

Rhodes, R. A., & Wanna, J. (2007). The Limits to Public Value, Or Rescuing Responsible Government from the Platonic Guardians. *Australian Journal of Public Administration, 66*(4), 406–421.

Rosenthal, U., Hart, P. T., & Kouzmin, A. (1991). The Bureau-Politics of Crisis Management. *Public Administration, 69*(2), 211–233.

Shanahan, E. A., Jones, M. D., & McBeth, M. K. (2011). Policy Narratives and Policy Processes. *Policy Studies Journal, 39*(3), 535–561.

Slay, J., & Stephens, L. (2013). *Co-Production in Mental Health: A Literature Review*. London: New Economics Foundation.

Stark, A., & Head, B. (2018). Institutional Amnesia and Public Policy. *Journal of European Public Policy*, 1–19.

Stevens, A. (2011). Telling Policy Stories: An Ethnographic Study of the Use of Evidence in Policy-Making in the UK. *Journal of Social Policy, 40*(2), 237–255.

Stoker, G. (2005). Public Value Management—A New Narrative for Networked Governance? *The American Review of Public Administration, 36*(1), 41–57.

Stoker, G. (2006). Public Value Management: A New Narrative for Networked Governance? *The American Review of Public Administration, 36*(1), 41–57.

Streeck, W., & Thelen, K. (2005). Introduction: Institutional Change in Advanced Political Economies. In W. Streeck & K. Thelen (Eds.), *Beyond Continuity: Institutional Change in Advanced Political Economies*. Oxford: Oxford University Press.

Svara, J. H. (2001). The Myth of the Dichotomy: Complementarity of Politics and Administration in the Past and Future of Public Administration. *Public Administration Review, 61*(2), 176–183.

Talbot, C. (2008). *Measuring Public Value*. London: The Work Foundation.

Talbot, C. (2009). Public Value– The Next 'Big Thing' in Public Management? *International Journal of Public Administration, 32*(3–4), 167–170.

Try, D., & Radnor, Z. (2007). Developing an Understanding of Results-Based Management through Public Value Theory. *International Journal of Public Sector Management, 20*(7), 655–673.

Vedung, E. (2017). *Public Policy and Program Evaluation*. Routledge.

Voorberg, W. H., Bekkers, V. J. J. M., & Tummers, L. G. (2014). A Systematic Review of Co-Creation and Co-Production: Embarking on the social innovation journey. *Public Management Review, 17*(9), 1333–1357

Wallis, J., & Gregory, R. (2009). Leadership, Accountability and Public Value: Resolving a Problem in "New Governance"? *Intl Journal of Public Administration, 32*(3-4), 250–273.

Ward, V., House, A., & Hamer, S. (2009). Knowledge Brokering: The Missing Link in the Evidence to Action Chain? *Evidence & Policy: A Journal of Research, Debate and Practice, 5*(3), 267–279.

Weiss, C. H. (1993). Where Politics and Evaluation Research Meet. *Evaluation Practice, 14*(1), 93–106.

Weiss, C. H. (1995). Nothing as Practical as Good Theory: Exploring Theory-Based Evaluation for Comprehensive Community Initiatives for Children and

Families. *New Approaches to Evaluating Community Initiatives: Concepts, Methods, and Contexts, 1*, 65–92.

Weiss, C. H. (1997). How Can Theory-Based Evaluation Make Greater Headway? *Evaluation Review, 21*(4), 501–524.

Wilkins, P. (2002). Accountability and Joined-Up Government. *Australian Journal of Public Administration, 61*(1), 114–119.

Williams, P. (2012). The Role of Leadership in Learning and Knowledge for Integration. *Journal of Integrated Care, 20*(3), 164–174.

Williams, I., & Shearer, H. (2011). Appraising Public Value: Past, Present and Futures. *Public Administration, 89*(4), 1367–1384.

Wu, X., Ramesh, M., & Howlett, M. (2015). Policy Capacity: A Conceptual Framework for Understanding Policy Competences and Capabilities. *Policy and Society, 34*(3-4), 165–171.

Zito, A. R. (2015). Expertise and Power: Agencies Operating in Complex Environments. *Politics and Governance, 3*(1), 73–89.

CHAPTER 3

Public Sector Reform in the UK: Key Developments, Debates and Political Responses in Challenging Times

Robert Pyper

This chapter grounds the concepts and themes established in Chap. 2 of this volume within public sector reform developments in Britain, with a specific focus on the period since 2010. We begin by examining the meaning of, and driving motivations for, public sector reform, and consider the extent to which, in the UK context, public value management provides us with a binding analytical narrative through which we might better understand policy and practice around public sector reform. The key factors conditioning and contextualising the changed environment in the public sector are set out before we discuss central and devolved governmental approaches to public sector reform across the UK in the turbulent period since 2010. The chapter concludes with an assessment of the evidence of alignment and divergence in public sector reform agendas and processes across the UK over this period.

R. Pyper (✉)
University of the West of Scotland, Paisley, UK
e-mail: Robert.Pyper@uws.ac.uk

© The Author(s) 2021
J. Connolly, A. van der Zwet (eds.), *Public Value Management, Governance and Reform in Britain*, International Series on Public Policy, https://doi.org/10.1007/978-3-030-55586-3_3

Meanings, Drivers and Motivations

Although ostensibly straightforward, 'public sector reform' can be an elusive concept, and, in practice, what we have across the UK are several, often distinct, reform processes. These can assume different shades of meaning and emphasis depending upon the conceptual or theoretical perspectives through which they are viewed. 'Change management', 'modernisation', 'innovation', 'service improvement', 'efficiency drives' and other phrases can be used to encapsulate specific features of reform agendas, which can in turn be viewed through the prism of paradigm shifts which chart the journey from 'public administration' to 'new public management', to 'governance', 'new public governance' and beyond, to 'public value management' (see, e.g. Alford and Hughes 2008; Bevir 2013; Christensen and Laegreid 2011a, b, c; Hartley et al. 2015; Hood 1991; Moore 1995; Newman 2005; O'Flynn 2007; Osborne 2011; Rhodes 1997; Rhodes et al. 2003; Rhodes and Wanna 2007). 'Reform' might apply in the context of the policies or statutes which govern the substance, nature and form of specific services, or to organisational structures and processes through which services are formulated and delivered.

Within this, we have the increasingly complex definitional questions surrounding 'public services'. For example, is a flow of public money into a service sufficient to justify the continuing use of the concept, even if the delivery mechanism and some key lines of accountability have been located in the private or not-for-profit sectors? Such matters merit detailed attention in their own right, but are worth raising here as useful correctives to the temptation to assume a universally accepted understanding of 'public sector reform'.

The key drivers and motivations for public service reform are the desire to improve service management, strengthen ministerial control, enhance service delivery, achieve efficiency gains, cut staff numbers, reduce costs, fulfil ideological objectives and/or apply the lessons contained in voguish managerial prescriptions. As noted by Hood (1991, pp. 4–5), there are increased emphases here on the disciplined use of resources, greater managerial autonomy and 'flexibilities', competition via tendering and contractualisation, disaggregation through structural change and privatisation and the application of performance standards and measurement. Additionally, the drive to integrate services in spheres such as health and social care became a key feature of subsequent modernisation agendas.

In the UK, the period since the mid-1970s has seen public service reform agendas driven by a confluence of ideas, stemming from three schools of thought (Chicago: Friedmanite; Austria: Hayekian; Virginia: public choice theorists including Niskanen), and formulated into the 're-invention' of government around the practices of the new public management. By the 1990s and 2000s, these were moulded into a specifically British reform context (described as 'modernisation', and encapsulating within it new concepts of 'governance') incorporating elements of European policy-making and governance, as well as features of bureaucratic statism seen most obviously in the regimes of 'performance targets' (for a detailed discussion of these reform trajectories, see Massey and Pyper 2005, pp. 27–39). The 2010–2015 Conservative-Liberal Democrat coalition attempted to stake out new reform territory which would open public services to an increasingly varied range of providers and lead to a new configuration of relationships between the state and the networks of civil society and the free market, as an explicit reaction to the perceived bureaucratic centralism of New Labour (see HM Government 2011). However, analysis of this approach suggested that the 'bottom-up narrative cannot disguise the fact that the Coalition partners were not averse to top-down hierarchical governance when politically expedient …', and there is evidence of reform synergies and continuities across the New Labour and coalition periods framed around 'a curious hybrid of bureaucratic control and market competition' (Painter 2013, pp. 7, 15). The economic, financial and political context of austerity meant that the coalition, and its successor Conservative administrations from 2015 onwards, pursued public sector reform while giving increased weight to some of the reform drivers we listed above: specifically, efficiency gains, integration of service provision, cutting staff numbers and reducing costs.

Analysts have emphasised the key roles played by elites in public sector reform processes. The composition of the elites (broadly defined as political executives and senior officials) may alter; they are often influenced by external factors ('ideas' and 'pressures', including, in recent times, globalisation and the international financial crises) and their plans are subject to unintended consequences and distortions during implementation within the structures and sub-structures of the political system (see also Pyper 2015; Dunleavy 2019). However, reform 'tends to begin in the upper, rather than the lower reaches of governance …' (Pollitt and Bouckaert 2011, p. 33). Citing the work of Goodin (1996) on the theory of institutional design, Pollitt and Bouckaert argue that:

> it is the exception rather than the rule for reform schemes to be comprehensive, even in intent. Reformers try to improve this or that institution or programme, or sometimes a whole sector (health, education), but they seldom attempt to remodel the entire sweep of public sector institutions in one go. (Pollitt and Bouckaert 2011, p. 34)

This is debatable, however, as it might be argued that, for example, the Blair administration's *Modernising Government* programme represented an attempt (albeit flawed) to produce a sector-wide blueprint for reform (Prime Minister 1999), and the 2010–2015 UK coalition government's Open Public Services White Paper (HM Government 2011) was a similar (and arguably similarly flawed; see Painter 2013) attempt to provide an overarching statement of intent. Even where there is no comprehensive plan per se, there is usually at the minimum a broad guiding outlook or philosophy. Nonetheless, as Pollitt and Bouckaert rightly point out,

> it is easy to exaggerate the degree of intentionality in many reforms …although … intentional acts of institutional redesign have been crucial …this should not be read as an elevation of organizational elites into God-like designers who are routinely able to realize bold and broad schemes of improvement. (Pollitt and Bouckaert 2011, p. 34)

Public Value: A Reform Narrative?

Here, the question arises regarding the extent to which, in the UK context, public value management provides us with an intentional binding analytical narrative through which we might better understand policy and practice around public sector reform. Talbot (2011) argues that:

> Public value essentially tries to weld together ideas about efficiency and effectiveness in the provision of public services with notions of democratic legitimacy and trust – in some ways it could be seen as a synthesis of older public administration and public interest ideas with aspects of NPM. (Talbot 2011, p. 27)

As we saw during the discussion of public value management in Chap. 2, the concept is closely associated with, *inter alia*, co-production, co-creation, citizen participation in service design and delivery, autonomy, accountability, emphasis on outcomes, devolution of authority, evaluative and learning-based organisational cultures, continuous innovation, improvement, network management and collaboration and partnership working (Alford and Hughes 2008; Bryson et al. 2014; Bryson et al. 2017; Hartley et al. 2015; Moore 1995; O'Flynn 2007; Stoker 2006; Williams and Shearer 2011). There is, therefore, an intrinsic connection between the normative understanding of public value and the modernisation and reform foci within public management—hence the perceived utility of the concept of public value management, with its concern for cross-sectorial approaches to leadership and management, and the core significance of valued management in the delivery of modern public governance reform agendas (Wright and Pandey 2009, p. 86). All of these have featured in the varied reform and modernisation programmes which have swept across the public services landscape in the UK since 2010. Notwithstanding this, the lacunae and weaknesses within public value theory, including its working assumption that the public interest aligns with the interests of public managers, have led to reformulations, exemplified by Talbot's proposed incorporation of 'self-interest, public interest and procedural interest' as a framework for enhancing the utility of the concept (Talbot 2011).

Where should we properly locate public value in the context of the successive and overlapping drivers of reform and 'modernisation'? Pyper (2015) argued that the overarching umbrella of public administration remains a useful organising principle through which we can make sense of successive waves of reform variously described as managerialism, new public management, 'modernisation' per se and governance, through to the new public governance and public value. Newman (2011) sought to bring a degree of coherence to a line of succession from public administration through NPM to governance, giving emphasis to the concepts of empowerment and participation, which she had earlier outlined in the context of a 'remaking of the public sphere' (Newman 2005). Although Newman's work was not concerned directly with public value, there is an inherent link here to the concept's founding ideas (see Moore 1995; Coats and Passmore 2008; Bennington and Moore 2011). These integrated within public administration and management the strategic imperative to enhance value in a fashion similar to that found in the private sector, where the addition of 'shareholder value' is an intrinsic objective. At its core,

> Public value argues that public services are distinctive because they are characterised by claims of rights by citizens to services that have been authorised and funded through some democratic process … It is designed to get public managers thinking about what is most valuable in the service that they run and to consider how effective management can make the service the best

that it can be ... engaging with citizens is not an exercise in giving the public what they want or slavishly following the dictates of public opinion polls. Public value offers a framework for how the information gathered using these processes should be used to improve the quality of the decisions that managers take. It calls for a continuing dialogue or conversation between public managers and citizens. (Coats and Passmore 2008, p. 4)

In all of this, there is a clear requirement for the embrace of cultural change within public sector organisations, and for strategic leadership, and there are consequential, vitally important, questions around the nature of leadership, organisational learning and changes to organisational culture (see also McMillan's chapter on public value leadership in this volume). The dissemination and inculcation of concepts such as public value rely, to a considerable extent, upon the effectiveness of leadership in securing cultural change. In the UK context, this leads to a focus on the importance of public sector reform leadership in Whitehall as a vanguard for change agendas, but also the synergetic relationships between modernisation and reform agendas at the centre and across the wider public sector, with, depending on timing and circumstances, initiatives being led by the centre or by the localities.

In the UK, the explicit and universal adoption of public value management as a reform framework and policy driver was initially difficult to discern. A relatively early attempt by the Strategy Unit in the Cabinet Office (see Kelly et al. 2002) to spark intra-governmental support for the core public value ideas had some limited success and ministerial support, but 'HM Treasury largely absented itself from the discussions ...and they ... apparently remained sceptical' (Talbot 2011). It was not until 2017 that this Treasury scepticism began to shift, at least to some extent, when a major review of Whitehall efficiency was sanctioned, with an application of public value at its core.

The person who headed the review, Sir Michael Barber (who provided the *Foreword* to this book), personifies this incremental shift and the increasing emphasis on public value within the paradigms set out above. A senior policy adviser (on school standards) to the Secretary of State for Education and Employment between 1997 and 2001, Barber moved to work at the heart of the Blair government's modernisation agenda, as head of the Prime Minister's Delivery Unit between 2001 and 2005. In this role, he led the drive to deploy fresh methods to refine targets and create a renewed focus on the delivery of qualitative improvements to public services in key policy spheres including health, education and justice. Barber's account of his time as head of the Delivery Unit became one of the defining texts of Blairite modernisation (Barber 2007). After leaving government, Barber became a partner at McKinsey and Company, founded the US Education Delivery Institute, served as a Chief Education Adviser at Pearson and set up Delivery Associates, a public sector advisory group. In 2016, in seeking to answer the question of 'how to run a government', he deployed the ideas and concepts of Mark Moore in arguing that governments should organise regular 'productivity reviews' using Moore's four key criteria for maximising public value (Barber 2016).

As the Treasury's initial scepticism about the applicability of the public value concept waned, in early 2017, Barber was commissioned to lead a review of civil service efficiency. Previous, high-profile exercises of this type (see, e.g. Gershon 2004 and Green 2010) had produced extensive lists of recommendations, but significant gaps between the claimed potential savings and the results achieved. In launching Barber's review, the Treasury made it clear that he was being asked to focus on broader, long-term approaches and strategies rather than the detail of specific savings which were required from government departments as part of the ongoing efficiency targets associated with the 'austerity' programme (Foster 2017; HM Treasury 2017). Notwithstanding this, it was perhaps significant that the Treasury was the lead department in the commissioning of Barber (although the work was approved and supported by the Cabinet Office) and there was a clear emphasis on the financial dimensions of the work in the accompanying statements made by the ministers, David Gauke, Chief Secretary to the Treasury, and Ben Gummer, Minister for the Cabinet Office (HM Treasury 2017). Neither minister mentioned the concept of public value in their statements. However, the general announcement from the Treasury made clear that 'the project team will … consult widely across government and with international experts to look at what incentives deliver excellent public value', and, importantly, Barber himself saw the task of his review as helping to position 'the UK as a global leader in maximising the public value of every tax pound' (HM Treasury 2017).

Working with a team, Barber drew upon public value theory and practice and consulted widely across Whitehall and, particularly, with the relevant sections of the Cabinet Office and departmental Permanent Secretaries (Barber 2017, particularly Appendix C of the review). The report was published in November 2017 (Barber 2017) and was promptly welcomed at a Treasury roundtable event addressed by Sir Jeremy Heywood, Cabinet Secretary and Head of the Civil Service, and Elizabeth Truss, Chief Secretary to the Treasury (Civil Service Blog 2017; Johnstone 2017). The report contained seven chapters which examined the importance of public sector productivity, previous and existing efficiency initiatives and their outcomes, lessons from the academic community, the content and deployment of a Public Value Framework and the recommended next steps for government. At the heart of the report was Barber's conceptualisation of a 'Public Value Framework' which would facilitate tracking progression from the total funding provided for a policy or programme, and the effective utilisation of this funding via 'Four Pillars of the Public Value Assessment Framework' to deliver outcomes and maximise value for the taxpayer (Barber 2017: 6). The 'Four Pillars' concerned 'Pursuing Goals', 'Managing Inputs', 'Engaging Users and Citizens' and 'Developing System capacity', and within these, there were 16 'areas to consider' (Barber 2017: see Appendix A of the review) with criteria to allow for judgements to be made against a coloured 'traffic-light' system (green, amber/green, amber/red and red). Key elements of the cultural change deemed necessary by Barber related to the working relationships and extant organisational perceptions across Whitehall. In particular, he argued that the traditional mutual suspicion between the Treasury on the one hand, and spending departments on the other, would have to be overcome.

> Occasionally relationships between the Treasury and departments have become challenging. The Treasury has been seen as not just interested in controlling expenditure … but taking a negative standpoint in case a new idea might lead to new costs. It can also be seen as stifling departmental performance through restrictive budgeting rules and layers of process, and then conducting the occasional shake down when the coffers run low. Meanwhile departments can be seen from the Treasury perspective as the covetous children, unconcerned by the family's financial situation and keen to spend every penny they have however they choose. (Barber 2017, p. 37)

Barber believed that there was evidence, across Whitehall, of a willingness to embrace the cultural change needed to deliver successful implementation of his public value framework. The requirement Barber identified for effective strategic leadership, coupled with cultural change, applied in all elements of the public sector where public value was being deployed as a driver for modernisation and reform. The importance of the Whitehall dimension lay in its status as a national-level exemplar and as a strategic force for, and coordinator of, public sector reform programmes. Despite the report's positive reception, and the government's commitment to the pilot schemes, in the autumn of 2018, the National Audit Office noted that the Treasury had 'not yet decided how best to implement the findings' of the Barber review, and stressed the need for progress:

> We welcome the move towards better understanding and measuring of public value and expect HM Treasury to take this work forward at pace. (National Audit Office 2018c, p. 7)

As will be argued in the substantive analysis provided in Chap. 10 of this volume, helpful although its insights are in many respects, public value management ultimately does not represent a paradigmatic shift per se but represents an evolutionary development within the broad NPM/governance sphere, with elements of its prescriptions being adopted and given varied degrees of emphasis as deemed appropriate and as influenced by political and managerial drivers of change.

CONDITIONING AND CONTEXTUALISATION

When assessing central and devolved governmental approaches to public sector reform across the UK in the period since 2010, we might view the key developments through analytical prisms which would allow us to consider reform by chronological periods (tenures of governments), by geographical entity (national and subnational), by public service category (e.g. health and education) or by theme (rationalising structures and process, enhancing quality of service delivery, achieving efficiencies and so on). However, the weakness of each of these approaches, taken in isolation, is that we could ignore or minimise the impact of some fundamental externalities. This has been a period of significant turbulence and increasing complexity in the UK governance. Public sector reform in these times has been conditioned and contextualised by a range of factors, most importantly, variations in party-political control, management of the consequences flowing from the 2008 banking and financial crisis and the effects of constitutional churn, turbulence and upheaval around, respectively, the issues of Scottish independence and discontinuity on the governance arrangements for Northern Ireland and the aftermath of the 2016 referendum on the UK's EU membership. In an attempt to square the circle and cover our topic as holistically as possible, some reflections on each of these four key externalities will be offered before we turn to a broad geographical approach, built around government chronologies, but with the externalities, conditioning factors and contexts played into the analysis appropriately. We will also offer some reflections on the extent to which the disaggregated political and constitutional structure of the UK, encompassing asymmetric devolution, has impacted on the idea of a coordinated central driver in public sector reform. First, let us turn to the four conditioning and contextualising factors.

Party-Political Variables and Turbulence

The political context within which public sector reform has taken place in the period under consideration here has seen significant variations in party-political control, with UK central government led in turn by a Conservative-Liberal Democrat coalition between 2010 and 2015, a Conservative small majority between 2015 and 2017, a Conservative minority dependent on support from the Democratic Unionist Party from 2017 to 2019, and a new majority Conservative Government from December 2019. In this period, the devolved governments have been led by Nationalists (in Scotland), the Labour Party (in Wales, governing in turn in coalition with Plaid Cymru, alone, and in coalition with the Liberal Democrats) and the Democratic Unionists and Sinn Fein (in Northern Ireland, until 2017, when there was a failure to agree on a new administration). Within this political context, public sector reform agendas have to be viewed through numerous prisms, including the path-dependency issues around the substantial legacy of New Labour's public service modernisation programme in the period leading up to 2010, and the pre-2010 experiences of the respective devolved administrations. We discuss these issues in the appropriate sections below.

Fall-Out from 2008: 'Austerity'

The second conditioning factor stemmed from the global financial crisis of 2008, which had its origins in the collapse of the subprime mortgage market in the United States the previous year, and triggered severe pressure on a wide range of financial institutions, including the Lehman Brothers investment bank, which went into bankruptcy in September 2008. In the

UK, the Labour government announced a £500 billion rescue package for the banking sector in October 2008, and took an 81% shareholding in the huge, but ailing, Royal Bank of Scotland, effectively taking it into public ownership in order to save the bank from imminent collapse (see Darling 2011, see chapters 3, 4, 5, 6, and 7). Managing the extended and extensive fall-out from the 2008 banking and financial crisis created an acute strategic management challenge for the UK government in the following years (see Beech and Lee 2015; Broadbent et al. 2011; Hood and Dixon, 2013, 2015; Kickert 2012; Laws 2016; McCann 2013; Seldon and Snowdon 2015). The impact on public finances was severe. Although the National Health Service and education budgets were ring-fenced to protect them from the most serious effects of budget cuts, the post-2010 Coalition and Conservative governments launched a dual attack on the current budget deficit and the scale of national debt in relation to GDP, and this led to rolling programmes of public expenditure cuts coupled with tax increases. The spending reductions took £41billion out of departmental budgets between 2010 and 2013, with further cuts of £4 billion over the next four years (Emmerson 2017). This embrace of 'austerity', which signified reduced resourcing for public services in real terms, played into public sector reform debates in two ways. For politicians who favoured an anti-statist or reduced state approach to governance, the crisis represented something of an opportunity to pursue policy approaches to these ends. For others, the sheer scale of the resourcing cuts necessitated genuinely refocussed approaches to public sector reform.

Constitutional Churn 1: Consequences of the Scottish Independence Question and Governance Turmoil in Northern Ireland

The third conditioning factor flowed from the significant constitutional turbulence which affected two of the loci within the UK's asymmetric devolution arrangements in the period after 2010, with consequential impacts (reshaping or, arguably, marginalisation) upon approaches to public sector reform. In Scotland, the question of independence became a recurring issue due to the strong electoral performance of the SNP in successive elections, while in Northern Ireland, there was an apparently inherent level of discontinuity in the governance arrangements stemming from political upheavals. In relative terms, constitutional issues produced significantly less churn in Wales, where the focus was on the implementation of the recommendations of the Silk Commission (Commission on

Devolution in Wales 2012, 2014) via the Wales Acts of 2014 and 2017 (which dealt, respectively, with the extension of fiscal powers and legislative powers).

The 2011 elections to the Scottish Parliament saw the emergence of a majority SNP government committed to holding a referendum on independence, and after intermittent discussions between the nationalists and the UK coalition government, in January 2012, a referendum was offered by the UK government on a straight 'yes' or 'no' question to independence (see Seldon and Snowdon 2015, specifically chapter 11). This ignited an extended campaign, in advance of the official campaign launch some time later, and the referendum was held in September 2014 (see Arnott 2015; Jeffery 2016; Seldon and Snowdon 2015, specifically chapter 33). The winning margin for the 'No' campaign was clear (55.3% to 44.7%). The SNP launched a campaign for a second referendum on Scottish independence after the Brexit referendum, with resultant tensions between the nationalist/separatist government in Edinburgh and the unionist government in London. As noted below, a public sector reform agenda was pursued by Scottish governments in the period under consideration here, but this was in the broader context of an overriding constitutional imperative, with an almost continuous period of campaigning from 2011 onwards. The Scottish First Minister, Nicola Sturgeon, acknowledged that the constitutional focus 'ultimately transcends the issues of Brexit, of oil, of national wealth and balance sheets and of passing political fads and trends' (Sturgeon 2016).

One consequence of the 2014 independence referendum was the UK government's delivery of its commitment to enhance devolution. Following the 'No' vote, an All-Party Commission led by Lord Smith of Kelvin took evidence and, in November 2014, published a report (see Smith 2014; Scottish Parliament 2015), which formed the basis for the 2016 Scotland Act. The latter, *inter alia*, conferred constitutional permanence on the Scottish Parliament and Scottish Government, strengthened Edinburgh's control over social security benefits as well as devolved power over income tax rates and bands. At the same time, steps were taken to address the so-called West Lothian Question and the anomalous situation whereby Westminster MPs from Scottish constituencies could vote on legislation affecting only or mainly England, while, post-devolution, MPs from English constituencies had no similar rights to vote on purely Scottish issues. In 2015, the Conservative government took steps to implement the key recommendations of the McKay Commission (2013) regarding

'English Votes for English Laws' (EVEL). This resulted in new processes, within which the Speaker of the House of Commons makes rulings on the elements of bills which refer to England only, or to England and Wales, and these elements are then scrutinised via either an England-only standing committee (in the case of matters relating to England and Wales) or in a Legislative Grand Committee (see Kelly 2017). Although they functioned relatively well in some respects, the new processes were subject to criticism on grounds of, *inter alia*, complexity, lack of clarity in the new Standing Orders and placing the Speaker in an unnecessarily controversial position (see Gover and Kenny 2016; Public Administration and Constitutional Affairs Committee 2016a).

In Northern Ireland, the period after 2011 was characterised by relative stability during the period of the UK Coalition government (see Gormley-Heenan and Aughey 2015), followed by a time punctuated by periodic political upheaval and, eventually, suspension of the Executive. After the Northern Ireland Assembly elections of May 2011, a multiparty Executive was formed, led by the Democratic Unionist Party's (DUP) Peter Robinson as First Minister, and Sinn Fein's Martin McGuinness as Deputy First Minister. The United Ulster Unionists (UUP) withdrew from the Executive in August 2015 following a murder allegedly carried out by members of the Provisional IRA (Irish Republican Army) with links to Sinn Fein. The following month, Peter Robinson stepped down as First Minister, having failed to have the Assembly adjourned (McDonald and Watt 2015). After briefly resuming his duties, Robinson finally resigned as leader of the DUP and First Minister in January 2016 (McDonald 2015), being replaced by Arlene Foster, also of the DUP. Elections in May 2016 led to a new three-party Executive (DUP, Sinn Fein and Independent Unionist) being formed (Russell 2016). This government fell in January 2017 following the resignation of the Deputy First Minister, McGuinness, in protest at the refusal of the First Minister (Foster) to step aside from her role pending an investigation into the failure, with significant loss of public money, of the Renewable Heat Incentive scheme, for which Foster had previously held responsibility (Breen 2018; McDonald 2017). McGuinness' resignation forced an election after which the DUP retained its position as the largest party (Russell 2017), but Sinn Fein refused to agree a power-sharing agreement for a new Executive with Foster as First Minister. Negotiations were held, several deadlines passed without agreement on the formation of a new Executive and the stalemate continued throughout 2017, 2018 and into 2019, leaving Northern Ireland without an Executive and with administrative matters being managed by officials (Kelly 2018; McDowell 2017). Cross-party negotiations on the formation of a new Executive re-opened in the spring of 2019, resulting in a new administration in January 2020.

The net effect of this political and constitutional turbulence in Northern Ireland has been a degree of strategic planning blight and relative lack of focus on matters relating to public sector reform, as the more fundamental issues of political control and governance have been in flux.

Constitutional Churn 2: Brexit

The fourth conditioning factor emerged from the upheaval which followed the 2016 referendum on the UK's membership of the European Union. The Conservative party fought the 2015 UK general election on a pledge to hold a referendum on the country's membership of the EU. As leader of the new majority Conservative government, David Cameron fulfilled this commitment by calling the referendum for June 2016 (Cowley and Kavanagh 2016; Seldon and Snowdon 2016; Shipman 2017). The outcome was a vote to 'Leave' rather than 'Remain' by a margin of 51.9% to 48.1%.

For the UK, there were short- and medium-term political consequences. An immediate outcome was the resignation of the Prime Minister David Cameron, and his replacement by Theresa May, following a leadership election within the Conservative Party. Within nine months, May had called a General Election in an attempt to secure an increased Commons majority and strengthen her position for the forthcoming negotiations with the EU on the UK's withdrawal. However, the outcome of the 2017 General Election left the Conservative Party short of an overall majority and dependent upon the Democratic Unionist Party for support in a 'confidence and supply' arrangement (Shipman 2018). The 2016 referendum therefore led to a change in the premiership (with associated changes in the ministerial ranks at cabinet and sub-cabinet levels, leading to political turbulence across Whitehall departments) and the emergence of a minority government. The turbulence and uncertainty continued as Theresa May's position as prime minister and the stability of her government were repeatedly questioned while the UK entered formal negotiations to leave the EU by the end of March 2019 after invoking Article 50 of the Treaty on European Union (which triggers a withdrawal process) in the spring of 2017. At each stage of the negotiation process with the EU, May's government faced significant opposition from both pro- and anti-Leave (Brexiteers and Remainers) factions within the Conservative Party, and in Parliament, together with periodic ministerial resignations (Shipman 2018). Failure to secure parliamentary approval for the government's Withdrawal Agreement led to an extension of UK membership of the EU until the end of October 2019. Theresa May's position deteriorated further in this context. In May 2019, she announced her resignation. Boris Johnson became leader of the Conservative Party and thus prime minister in August 2019. Following much political posturing and promises around leaving the EU at the end of October 2019, the Westminster Parliament legislated to compel the prime minister to request an extension to Britain's withdrawal from the EU, much to the prime minister's disagreement, until the end of January 2020. The UK government won a vote in Parliament to hold an election on 12 December as a strategy, although not one without risk, to try to secure an overall majority in order to finalise Brexit. The risk paid off and the Conservatives under Johnson's leadership were returned as the governing party in the UK, with a majority of 80 seats secured in the Westminster Parliament. The Westminster Parliament subsequently ratified The EU withdrawal legislation, and the UK left the EU at 11 p.m. on 31 January 2020. This initiated what is known is a transition period that is set to end on 31 December 2020. It is unclear how all these political events will unfold and what their short-, medium- and long-term implications will be for public value given the governance distractions caused by Brexit politics. The UK's departure from the European Union has had, and will have, consequences for every area of Europeanised public policies, the future state of the public finances (due in part to uncertainty about the impact of Brexit on commercial and industrial activity and the consequential tax revenues available) and the relations between the component parts of the UK state. The latter were especially acute in Northern Ireland, which became one of the key foci in the negotiations with the EU. This was due to the implications of the land border between a future non-EU member and a member state within the island of Ireland, and in Scotland, where the SNP government seized on the Brexit issue as a potential trigger for a second independence referendum. A date has yet to be set for the latter, with the UK government refusing to grant permission for a second, disruptive referendum only a relatively short time after the first.

In Whitehall, at a time when the overall size of the civil service was at its lowest since the Second World War, over 600 officials were transferred from the Cabinet Office's Europe Unit, the Foreign and Commonwealth Office's Europe Directorate, the UK's Permanent Representation to the EU and other parts of the system of government, into a new Department for Exiting the European Union, under a ministerial team headed by a cabinet minister (Owen and Munron 2016). Additionally, all other government departments faced the challenge of planning for the impact of Brexit on their own policies, commitments and activities, based on the shifting possibilities around the specific form of the UK's withdrawal (Menon et al. 2017). The disruptive effect has been summarised as including

> delayed decisions and an inability to make trade-offs …inordinate secrecy and a lack of transparency …inconsistent assumptions and the difficulty of aligning plans…ineffective external engagement and a lack of detail…struggling to get the right people and keep them. (Owen et al. 2018, pp. 4–5)

The net effect of the extensive political and administrative disruption and uncertainty in the wake of the 2016 referendum was a fundamental re-prioritisation within the UK's polity. The ongoing delivery of public services now took place in a context within which future planning and reform agendas had become circumscribed by the *realpolitik* of Brexit.

PATH DEPENDENCIES AND DYSFUNCTIONALITIES

Taking account of these conditioning and contextualisation factors, we can now advance our understanding of the broad public sector reform agenda post 2010. We will reference some core elements of continuity stemming from the path dependencies of earlier reform programmes and initiatives, and provide evidence of vulnerabilities resulting in part from the conditioning factors and in part from inherent problems associated with, for example, the incorporation of third-sector providers into the public service arena, and the limitations of contractualisation.

Whitehall Reform Themes

In broad terms, the major UK civil service reform themes and agendas over the period since 2010 exhibit fundamental continuity with the reforms of the post-1997 Blair/Brown Labour governments, and those of their immediate Conservative predecessors of the 1990s and late 1980s. These manifested themselves in successive waves of managerial and structural reforms, encapsulated in a 'modernisation' agenda, which manipulated service delivery structures to create a mix based on agencification plus more traditional departmental structures, stressed the customer-focus and consumerist agenda as a driver for service improvement and delivery, rolling reviews of public sector efficiency and capability, and the introduction of human resources reforms designed to address the challenges around diversity and professional skills development (for a summary of the roots of all of this, see Burnham and Pyper 2008, pp. 139–154, Barber 2007).

The rhetoric of the incoming government of 2010 suggested an innovative approach to civil service reform. There was a focus on the scope for greater savings in departmental budgets, the need to shift the balance in service delivery to the components of 'the Big Society' (charities, NGOs, communities) and a requirement for officials to become involved in 'social action' which was to be addressed by transforming 'the civil service into a "civic service" by facilitating 'social action' by officials. Departmental targets were to be replaced with business plans, senior managers would be accountable to departmental boards, there was to be greater openness on civil service pay and new systems of rewards were to be introduced (as well as removal of 'least effective' officials) (Conservative Party 2010). Arguably, certain of these themes can be linked to dimensions of public value management's emphasis on citizen participation, devolution of authority and partnership working, although these were not explicitly recognised or embraced.

None of this was particularly revolutionary, however, and in practice, a gradualist modernisation approach continued from the Blair/Brown era through the civil and public service reform approaches of the 2010–2015 Coalition and into the Conservative governments that followed (Pyper 2013). In the post-2010 period, the most significant attempt to encapsulate a civil service reform agenda in a single document, akin to the strategies embraced by governments of the past, running back to the Fulton Report of 1968, via the Next Steps Report of 1988 and the Modernising Government White Paper of 1999, was the Civil Service Reform Plan of 2012 (HM Government 2012). This document set the agenda for Whitehall reform for the period of the Coalition government and its Conservative successors. It attempted to collate and develop the thinking carried out on civil service matters by the Conservatives pre-2010, align this with the austerity policies put in place over the two years since the election and set a course for future reform. This course was duly followed. David Cameron positioned the initiative within the evolutionary development of the civil service since Northcote-Trevelyan (HM Government 2012, p. 2). The document examined the strengths of the civil service (including its range of skills and experience, flexibility and agility, particularly in crises, and core values), the change imperative (this was explicitly linked to the economic recession) and a reform agenda framed around issues relating to the size and shape of the civil service (by 2015, it was to be 23% smaller than in 2010, with around 380,000 staff), improved policy-making capability, the challenges in implementing policy and securing accountability, strengthening skills and improving performance and ensuring that appropriate staff recognition and rewards systems were put in place. One critic argued that the Plan 'ignored history almost completely', was largely 'old wine in very old, but relabelled bottles', but nonetheless had some positive points (Talbot 2012), although the independent Institute for Government was marginally more positive about the Plan's scope and purpose (see Riddell 2012; Thomas 2012). Implementation of the Civil Service Reform Plan became closely associated with reductions in the size of government departments as a fundamental element of the austerity agenda. Although the Plan's lowest target figure was not met, six successive years of cuts from 2010 onwards took out one-fifth of the staff and produced the smallest civil service in the post-war period (384,260 fte in June 2016). Numbers began to rise again under the May government (to 400,170 by June 2018) as Whitehall prepared for Brexit (all figures here are from Institute for Government 2018).

This agenda, and the aforementioned partial embrace of public value via the Barber Report, provided, at best, very limited evidence of a 'joined-up' approach linking civil service issues and themes to a broader public service reform strategy, and by 2017, the need to address the deficits in coordination through the creation of a Department for Public Sector Reform was being proposed (Regan 2017). However, there was no sign of such an ambitious approach being taken, and in a speech on 'Civil Service Transformation', the organisation's Chief Executive offered only a set of generalities on 'how' and 'where' officials work, and the need for expertise to be enhanced (Manzoni 2018).

Limits to a 'Big Society'

Similar to the search undertaken by the New Labour administrations for a binding policy narrative badged as the 'Third Way' (and its various offshoots), the Conservatives under David Cameron's leadership embraced the concept of the 'Big Society' and took this into their Coalition with the Liberal Democrats as a policy driver (Fenwick and Gibbon 2017; Woodhouse 2015). An amalgam of ideas around empowering communities, encouraging volunteerism, enhancing localism and supporting mutuals and charities, with implicit rather than explicit linkages across to the driving themes of public value management, this sought to fill the vacuum being created by the scaling down of government associated with austerity, by offering a vision of effective social action beyond the confines of formal government structures, at all levels (see Fenwick and Gibbon 2016). In Whitehall, an apparatus was established to coordinate (the Big Society Network) and pump-prime (Big Society Capital) the initiative. The Big Society peaked as a formal policy driver in 2010–2013, after which it became less prominent, due partly to controversies surrounding some of its elements, including reductions in grants to charities and the increasing success of the private, rather than the third, sector in securing government contracts (Butler 2015). Notwithstanding this, the initiative's spirit had roots in a significant trend which had emerged from the New Public Management and modernisation agendas of the recent past, and this continued to run through the work of the governments beyond 2013. This involved enabling voluntary organisations, charities and social enterprises to deliver public services (for more on the movement towards the delivery of core social services by the voluntary sector, see Austin 2003, and Fenwick and Gibbon 2016). There is a clear association here with some elements of the public value management agenda, including co-creation, citizen participation in service design and delivery, devolution of authority and collaboration and partnership working. The risks associated with this policy trend were exemplified in a series of major failings, one of the most graphic being Kids Co. The collapse of this charity raised serious questions about governance and the risks of devolving policy and financial resources from central and /or local government via loose subcontracting arrangements, to third-sector/voluntary bodies.

Keeping Kids Company, generally known as Kids Company, or Kids Co, was founded in 1996 by Camila Batmanghelidjh, as a charity aiming to providing practical, emotional and educational support to vulnerable children, young people and adults through 12 centres and partnerships with 40 schools in London, Bristol and Liverpool. Kids Co claimed to support 36,000 individuals, although this figure was disputed by MPs who subsequently investigated the matter (Public Administration and Constitutional Affairs Committee 2016b, paras 26–36), and was funded through a combination of private donations and £42 million of public funds allocated by the UK central government, plus an additional £4 million from local authorities and lottery grants, between 1996 and 2015. Operating on a demand-led model, with many of its clients self-referring, Kids Co embraced the principle that no child should be turned away. Ineffective financial management produced operating crises and, eventually, a major breakdown in 2015, when the charity sought emergency funding of £3 million from the government. Overriding the formal objection of the Permanent Secretary to the Cabinet Office, two government ministers approved payment of this money, with conditions relating to the restructuring of Kids Co, and the cash was transferred on 30 July 2015, one day before a police investigation began into allegations of sexual abuse within the charity. The government sought to recover its emergency support due to concerns about a possible breach of grant conditions (some of the money was being used to pay salaries). Matching support funds from a private source failed to materialise, and Kids Company collapsed on 5 August. There followed investigations by the Metropolitan Police, the Charity Commission and by two House of Commons select committees (Public Accounts Committee 2015; Public Administration and Constitutional Affairs Committee 2016b).

The collapse of Kids Co raised serious concerns about criminality, financial mismanagement, weak regulation and accountability, audit failures, and insider access for a high-profile charity and its charismatic leader. Beyond this, the case exposed weaknesses in a vision of public service delivery which delegated responsibilities and resources for the care and support of vulnerable people to poorly managed and weakly regulated non-state bodies.

Localism on the Brink

A key feature of the Big Society agenda, enshrined in the Localism Act of 2011, was the drive to devolve decision-making powers from the centre to communities in England, via a series of reforms which would allow for elected mayors, facilitate local referenda and enhance the powers of local authorities. This was accompanied by the abolition of the former Regional Development Agencies and the emergence of new Local Enterprise Partnerships between local authorities and businesses, decentralisation of receipts from business rates, the announcement of Chancellor of the Exchequer George Osborne's new 'Growth and City Deals' (agreements between Whitehall and English local authorities) and new Enterprise Zones, including the 'Northern Powerhouse' economic regeneration initiative (see Smith and Wistrich 2016). Again, it is possible to discern implicit thematic linkages to the devolution of authority dimensions of public value management.

However, it gradually became clear that local government would be the element of the public sector most dramatically affected by the austerity regime. During the early phase of austerity, councils generally managed to spend within their income, but from 2015 to 2016, current expenditure was increasingly being funded from cash reserves as demands for services (particularly adult social care) increased inexorably. The National Audit Office found that, for the period 2010–2018, there had been a real-term reduction of 49.1% in central government funding for English local authorities and of 28.6% in councils' spending power (defined as government grant support plus council tax receipts), and, consequently, up to 15 local authorities were in danger of financial collapse (National Audit Office 2018a, p. 4). The reality of this situation was brought home most forcibly in 2018 when a long-running financial crisis at Conservative-led Northamptonshire County Council came to a head in the form of a £70 million budget shortfall. Following the resignation of the Council leader, it moved to formulate an emergency plan under which it would introduce major cuts to jobs and services, reducing the latter to a bare minimum 'core offer', which would allow the council to meet only its strict legal commitments, and propose a restructuring of the Northamptonshire council map with the creation of a new single-tier structure (Butler 2018). This type of restructuring was being considered across many English local authorities, raising concerns about the impact on communities and localism (Copus 2018).

By 2018, it was becoming clear that local government was the sphere where public sector reform was being driven not by reflection and strategy, let alone public value management, but by crisis management.

Contractualisation Traps

Beginning in the 1980s, and running through the public sector reform programmes of successive governments over the period since then, the process of contracting-out delivery and provision of government functions and services and infrastructure projects has been a recurring theme in the New Public Management, modernisation and governance agendas. In softer focus, the collaboration and partnership working elements of public value management might be said to feature here. In part ideological, in part based on a hard pragmatism around the limitations of short-term public finance, contractualisation took many shapes and forms, and was badged under various initiatives as, *inter alia*, the private finance initiative (PFI) and public-private partnerships (PPP). Although this strain of public sector reform remained a popular option for the governments in the period under consideration here, recurring problems with contractualisation were apparent and can be exemplified with reference to two major cases.

The 2017 fire at the Grenfell Tower housing block in London, in which 71 people died, raised serious questions about the management of subcontracts for housing renovation projects, the complexity of the contractual relationships across these commercial networks and the weaknesses in the accountability systems, which apparently contributed to this disaster.

Following the fire, the Royal Borough of Kensington and Chelsea revoked the contract of the management organisation to which it had subcontracted control of its housing stock and resumed direct responsibility for the estate on which the Grenfell Tower is located (Godden 2017). A set of internal inquiries was established by the Borough Council and the London Fire Brigade, and a public inquiry was launched in June 2017. The cumulative findings of these inquiries would shape the long-term impact of Grenfell, but there was sufficient immediate evidence to suggest that there had been significant major failings in the contractualisation processes.

The local authority had subcontracted the management of its entire housing stock, including the Grenfell Tower block, to the Kensington and Chelsea Tenant Management Organisation (KCTMO). This organisation's board had representatives from the resident population of the local council properties, the Borough Council and three independent members (Kensington and Chelsea Tenant Management Organisation 2006). As part of a renovation project at the Grenfell Tower, new exterior cladding was fitted in 2015–2016. It was this cladding which contributed to the rapid spread of the fire. Rydon Ltd submitted a bid for the renovation work which was £2.5 million lower than an original contractor and was given the contract by the KCTMO (Gapper 2017). The work was then subcontracted to multiple firms, and, as part of these arrangements, a cheaper form of exterior cladding was used (Gapper 2017). In this scenario, it became increasingly difficult to discern the precise roles, responsibilities and accountabilities of the Borough Council, the KCTMO and the myriad of subcontractors.

These contractual arrangements were not unique to the Royal Borough of Kensington and Chelsea, and the Grenfell disaster raised important questions about the failure of the complex, extended accountability relationships spawned by such approaches. The relationships between the local authority, the Kensington and Chelsea Tenant Management Organisation (KCTMO), Rydon Ltd and the companies to which Rydon subcontracted the various elements of the work for the Grenfell Tower refurbishment project could be seen across many capital, construction and service delivery projects in the public sector. Following the disaster, concerns were raised by the Royal Institute of British Architects about the lack of a single point of responsibility for the refurbishment project and the need for new 'Principal Designer' and 'Principal Contractor' roles in this sphere of public sector contractualisation as a means towards securing greater clarity and accountability (Royal Institute of British Architects 2017, p. 19).

Another significant failing in the contractualisation regime was exposed by the collapse of the second-largest construction company in the UK, Carillion, which went into liquidation in January 2018. Carillion had 43,000 employees (19,000 of whom were UK-based), and, despite posting positive accounts and reports in 2017, went into liquidation a few months later, owing £2 billion to 30,000 suppliers and subcontractors and with pension liabilities of £2.6 billion (Business, Energy and Industrial Strategy and Work and Pensions Committees 2018, pp. 4–6). Carillion had 420 contracts across the UK public sector, involving hospitals, schools, prisons, transport and the armed forces, and the Cabinet Office was obliged to take the extraordinary step of allocating £150 million to the Official Receiver in order to ensure the continuity of public services after the company's collapse (National Audit Office 2018b, p. 4).

The cases above represent only a part of the accumulation of crises and failures across the extensive span of contractualisation and outsourcing, which also included, *inter alia*, the inability of the security firm G4S to deliver on its commitments for the 2012 London Olympics, and repeated failures by companies across the health, social care and probation services (Walker 2018). These failures led to arguments for a new phase of public sector reform, within which a fundamental review of this entire approach to the management and delivery of huge areas of public service activity would accumulate lesson-learning and lead to agreement on a new way forward (see, e.g. Public Administration and Constitutional Affairs Committee 2018; Walker and Tizard 2018). However, it would take a significant rebalancing of the contractualisation agenda, away from the financially and ideologically driven approach of the past, to align it with the co-production, co-creation, collaboration and partnership working imperatives of public value management—both in principle and in practice. One example of this approach might be seen in the City Deals initiative, launched in 2013, which modelled new government-city agreements based around support for local projects, economic development and job-creation (see O'Brien and Pike 2015).

Developments in Scotland

In Scotland, as in Wales and Northern Ireland, the public sector is balanced between a wide range of bodies and functions which are devolved, and others which remain reserved to the UK central government (see McTavish 2014). Beyond foreign policy, defence and national security, the latter most obviously includes the civil service, and most functions of the Department of Work and Pensions and the Treasury. Following the 2014 independence referendum and the recommendations of the Smith Commission, the Scotland Act of 2016 extended devolution in Scotland beyond the scope of the original 1998 Act, particularly in the realms of taxation and social welfare benefits. The Scottish Parliament was given extended powers over tax rates and bands, and new powers to create certain types of benefits as well as powers over discretionary payments within certain extant benefits reserved to the UK government (see Berry and Kidner 2016; Berthier 2016). During the first phases of the devolution settlement in Scotland, the focus was largely upon consolidating the new governance arrangements, and limited attention was paid to further public sector reform. There were some initiatives around interagency collaborations, joint service delivery, integrated public services, joined-up approaches and partnership working, but the working understanding was that the extant pattern of public service bodies would remain.

Still within the constitutional context of the unified British civil service, the large part of the civil service in Scotland, which worked to the Edinburgh government, moved from a traditional departmental structure to a set of Directorates framed around the cross-cutting policy portfolios of the cabinet secretaries (ministers) (see Parry 2016). With the exception of the very poorly managed move from a regionally based structure to a centralised, single Police Service of Scotland in 2013 (see below), there remained an abiding faith in the extant public sector structures and the power of espoused rhetoric about integration and collaboration, coupled with coordination with the private and not-for-profit sectors, to deliver results and enhance service delivery. Throughout the period under consideration here, there was no appetite for challenging the inherited organisational silos in the health service and local government, which inhibited progress towards a genuinely inclusive and integrated public services model.

In 2011, the Christie Commission analysed possible forward paths for the delivery of public services around service integration and a common public service ethos. Subsequently, a new agenda merged around the themes of 'prevention', 'partnership', 'workforce development' and 'performance' (Scottish Government 2011). 'Public service reform' became based upon the Scottish Government's core agendas relating to 'Efficiency and Transformational Government', 'Community Planning' and 'External Scrutiny'. Notwithstanding its title, The Public Services Reform (Scotland) Act of 2010 lacked a strategic focus, but followed through on some Christie recommendations by concentrating on some specific changes featuring outcome agreements, efficiency savings, more shared services in a few areas of provision and a focus on early intervention. In the following years, three drivers emerged to push the public services reform agenda in Scotland: the National Performance Framework (NPF), the Community Empowerment (Scotland) Act and the integration agenda for health and social care via the Public Bodies (Joint Working) (Scotland) Act.

The NPF, introduced in 2007 as an element of the spending review, was revised in 2011 (see Campbell 2012), in 2016 (Scottish Government 2016) and in 2018 (Scottish Government 2018). Styled as 'a single framework to which all public services in Scotland are aligned', it comprises a set of 'High Level Targets' (growth, productivity, participation, population, solidarity, cohesion, sustainability) and 'Strategic Objectives' ('Wealthier & Fairer; Smarter; Healthier; Safer & Stronger; Greener'), all of which are linked to 'National Outcomes' (originally 16, scaled down to 11 in 2018) and 'National Indicators' (originally 55, increased to 81 in 2018). Within the NPF, 'the reform journey is a partnership with local government and the third sector that helps ensure our public services are sustainable, meet the needs of citizens and improve the lives of Scotland's people' (Scottish Government 2018). Performance against these National Indicators in key public service areas including education and health was distinctly mixed (see Connolly and Pyper 2020).

Linked to the NPF, the 2015 Community Empowerment (Scotland) Act required ministers to 'consult on, develop and publish a set of national outcomes for Scotland' and gave 'local communities a right to challenge local public service delivery if it is not meeting their needs'. The Act further required services to be planned, delivered and monitored through partnerships (including the health service, local authorities, the police services, community groups and the third sector). In line with the wider trend across the UK, the Public Bodies (Joint Working) (Scotland) Act 2014 provided a legal framework for the integration of health and social care provision and produced new public bodies ('Integration Authorities') in an attempt to break down barriers to joint working between NHS Boards and local authorities, and deliver budget savings (see Burgess 2016). It has been argued that the prevailing effect of these three key policy instruments has been to consolidate the post-1999 approach which eschews grappling with the bigger, strategic issues around public service leadership and structures, in favour of centrally devised policy drivers which tend to intensify the effects of network governance, engender micro-management from Edinburgh and negate the spirit of public value management (Connolly and Pyper 2020).

Developments in Wales

In the period since 2010, the public sector reform agenda in Wales has followed a pattern similar to that seen in England and in Scotland, with rhetoric espousing the need for central steering, continuous improvement and more effective service deliver, but in practice a fairly dispersed approach being in evidence. A Public Service Leadership Group was chaired by the Minister for Local Government and Government Business, but the directorates' structure dispersed themes, as in Scotland. The PSL Group comprised 'senior leaders who represent public services and geographical areas across Wales'. Public sector reform issues were subsequently located within the portfolio of the Minister of Public Services. In 2013, a seven-person Commission on Public Service Governance and Delivery, chaired by Sir Paul Williams, was charged with oversight of progress and produced a report in January 2014 (Welsh Government 2014). This set out a series of recommendations relating to scale and complexity; governance, scrutiny and delivery; leadership, culture and values; and performance and performance management. The report stressed that structural changes were 'necessary and indeed urgent', and to be successful, these needed to be combined with wider changes to governance, scrutiny, accountability, leadership, culture, values and performance management. The Collaborative Footprint for Public Services in Wales provided a framework within which public services could develop consistent approaches to new collaborative working arrangements, clarity on how public services should collaborate, greater stability and reduced complexity. It identified six geographical 'collaborative areas' for managing the 'Footprint'. Additionally, there were Local Service Boards, 'where the leaders of local public and third sector organisations come together to take collective action to ensure public services are effective and citizen focussed'. In the Directorate structure, the Local Government and Communities Directorate was the location of the most obvious set of responsibilities for public service reform, but it is also worth noting that the remit of the Strategic Planning, Finance and Performance Directorate included responsibility for providing 'advice and guidance across the Welsh public sector' (for links to these groups, fora and policy statements, see www.wales.gov.uk/topics/improvingservices). The Programme for Government section of 'Public Services in Wales' reiterates the commitments to 'continuous improvement', 'funding supporting stronger and more effective service delivery' and 'effective collaboration between public services' (Welsh Government 2017).

The challenges around these familiar themes became increasingly acute as budgets were constrained and as Brexit loomed. In Wales, there is perhaps greater emphasis than elsewhere on the geographical dispersal of reform processes. On the whole, however, the impression is of an atomised, disaggregated approach to the management of public service reform. More focussed and strategic political and official leadership was identified as a vital perquisite for effective implementation of the public sector reform agenda in Wales:

> While Wales is good at analysis and ambition … implementation has been poor …Talk of the need for services to be 'joined-up' and 'responsive to need' has a long history; as does the call for local level innovation, and spreading of best practice. In that sense, the public sector reform agenda hasn't shifted hugely. But there has been a growing realisation that achieving reform is going to require new approaches. Which is why the …focus on leadership is to be welcomed. But it will require more than leadership … (it) will require systemic change across the Welsh public sector. (Bristow 2015)

Developments in Northern Ireland

As a consequence of the post-2002 Review of Public Administration in Northern Ireland (see Office of the First Minister and Deputy First Minister 2003; Knox and Carmichael 2005), which encompassed most public services, including health, local government, social welfare and school education (while excluding the Northern Ireland civil service and the executive agencies), there was a reasonably consistent and coordinated attempt to drive forward cohesive strategic coordination of public service reform from Belfast. Under a formal description of 'Civil Service Reform in Northern Ireland', the reform agenda actually encompassed the broader public services, and, in 2014, the Northern Ireland Executive commissioned a strategic review of public sector reform from the OECD (this was the first subnational governance review by the latter). The review (OECD 2016) focussed on improvements in the quality of public services, value for money and the scope for further reforms, and it produced 30 main recommendations across 9 reform themes, most of which were accepted by the Executive and formulated into a new outcome-based Programme for Government. Major emphasis was placed on improving the delivery of public services and governance through a common set of priorities, working across departmental boundaries, coordinating delivery, using public engagement as a reform enabler and using evidence-based decision-making by intervening early to address social problems (Northern Ireland Executive 2017). In a reform theme which was increasingly common across the UK, particular emphasis was placed on an integration programme for the delivery of health and social care (Thompson 2016). A specific local context here was the long-standing (effectively dating back to 1920) devolution of social security policy to Northern Ireland (see Gormley-Heenan and Aughey 2015, pp. 200–201). The overall reform programme was located within the Office of the First Minister and Deputy First Minister, with the Head of the Civil Service leading the change process across the NICS Departments in Programme for Government delivery plans, via the coordinating mechanism of the Public Sector Reform Division of the Department of Finance. Notwithstanding this strategic approach, the political stalemate in Belfast, budget cuts and the uncertainties surrounding the Brexit process were seen as significant barriers to the success of the public sector reform process in Northern Ireland by Deloitte (2018), and CIPFA called for a renewed commitment to reform and greater coordination of public services (Rensch 2017).

Conclusion: Divergence Over Alignment

Taking account of the collective impacts of the putative shift in the binding analytical narrative towards public value management, the effects of partisan differences and constitutional churn across the component polities of the state, together with the impacts of austerity and Brexit, we can now conclude by offering some observations on alignment and divergence in public sector reform agendas and processes across the UK.

Evidence from the post-2010 period provides confirmation that devolution in the UK, building upon some historical traditions of relative regional/subnational autonomy in some spheres of service provision and the asymmetrical character of the late 1990s constitutional innovations, leads to variations in the management of public service reform. Beyond that, even in the case of the still largely 'unified' elements of the public services, such as the civil service, the reform agendas are subject to potentially significant local variations due to the emerging distinctive cultures within these bodies in the devolved polities. Does 'public sector reform' have a single, agreed meaning in the UK context, let alone a binding analytical narrative around something like public value management? For this to be feasible, there would have to be evidence of common themes and purposes around which the reform agendas across diverse public service sectors and the geographical and political entities of the devolved polities can coalesce. Alternatively, it is possible that 'public sector reform' has a limited conceptual utility due to the gulf between the centre's rhetoric about reform as a holistic idea (as deployed repeatedly by successive UK governments, in one form or another) and the realities of a) different 'reform' priorities in distinct service sectors, and b) within service sectors, different 'reform' priorities in the distinct geographical entities of the UK. This recalls Rhodes' 'hollowing out' thesis and the impact of the differentiated polity:

> Put simply, government and policy in Britain have become messy. Indeed, British territorial governance is rapidly becoming a case of many exceptions and few rules. (Rhodes et al. 2003, p. 33)

The meaning and implications of public sector reform are therefore contested in the context of the messy realities of the cluttered, and often confused, UK polity. Reform in a differentiated polity with asymmetrical devolution cannot be simple and straightforward. The outcome is a curious mix of aligned and partially aligned reform agendas and practices, with a few common subthemes such as partnership working, community involvement and joint services and integration, which we might loosely link to public value management. The overall impression, however, is of a spectrum of divergence and the lack of an overall binding narrative.

Within the civil service, there is arguably the clearest example of a public sector reform programme with a fairly common currency across the component parts of the UK (including Northern Ireland, where, although the organisational structure and identity is distinct, the reform themes are very similar). The devolution settlements for Scotland and Wales made clear that the concept of the unified civil service was to remain, and there would be no distinct, devolved civil services in Edinburgh and Cardiff. Notwithstanding this, the evolving cultures and practices in the devolved administrations, as well as the differences in political leadership, have served to create a loosening of the ties to Whitehall in some respects, and a growing impression of distinctiveness, albeit still within the formal constitutional context of unity. Although the civil service in Scotland and Wales was therefore formally included in the reform agenda pursued by the post-2010 coalition government (see Pyper 2013), in the same way that it had been included in the waves of civil service reform which flowed from the decisions of the previous Labour governments (see Burnham and Pyper 2008), the reality was that the devolved polities explicitly or implicitly sought to distance themselves from the latest manifestation of civil service reform. Even in this most obvious instance of theoretical alignment, there appeared to be some reluctance on the part of both the Welsh and Scottish governments to be seen to be fully identified with the Whitehall civil service reform agenda. In contrast with the Cabinet Office website, there were no obvious links from the civil service sections of the Welsh and Scottish Government websites to the civil service reform programme. The Coalition government's 'Civil Service Reform Plan' apparently did not apply to the civil service in Scotland, where a separate reform agenda was taken forward via the business plans of the Scottish Government. However, the latter were not civil service reform plans per se, and did not engage with the core issues contained in the Whitehall document (see Housden 2014). This was the first example in modern history of a civil service reform agenda (see, e.g. Fulton, Next Steps, Modernising Government) having an application limited to Whitehall.

Contrary to its denomination, it becomes increasingly unfeasible to view the National Health Service as an organisation featuring an aligned,

UK-wide reform agenda. The NHS illustrates in microcosm the complexities which lie beneath the surface description of a core UK-wide 'public sector'. The organisational and structural realities of health service provision vary significantly across its component elements in England, Wales, Scotland and Northern Ireland (see Doheny 2015). Lest we overemphasise the specific impact of devolution on the differentiated polity, it is worth reminding ourselves that the NHS in Scotland has always had a separate basis in statute (the 1947 National Health Service (Scotland) Act), and its own structural and policy particularities. Once we move beyond the core principles of the NHS, including the provision of care which is free at the point of need, the working realities of the service have become increasingly varied across the component elements of the UK, with obvious contrasts in structures and philosophies seen in the array of Trusts (under the terms of the 2012 Health and Social Care Act, which applied only to England), Clinical Commissioning Groups in England (with the Health Boards in Scotland and Wales) and the organisational integration of health with social care in Northern Ireland. There are a myriad of policy strategies which emphasise the differences in approach in the specific polities (see, e.g. the Scottish Government's health 'Quality Strategy', '2020 Vision', 'Integration of Adult Health and Social Carer', 'Scottish Patient Safety Programme' and the Welsh Government's 'Together for Health' and '21st Century Healthcare' strategies, to name but a few). We can discern certain common features across some of the component entities of the UK, for example, the commissioner-provider split common to England and Northern Ireland; the use of quangos in England, Scotland and Wales; organisational integration of all health services in Scotland, Wales and Northern Ireland (see Gray and Birrell 2013 on all of this). Nonetheless, the overall impression is of geographically specific reform agendas, to the point where the drive to be different might even have resulted in lost opportunities for useful policy learning and transfer (see Moon 2013, for a critique of Rhodri Morgan's management of health policy in Wales from this perspective). Another example of significant divergence in reform agendas within a particular and fundamental service sphere can be seen in the realm of policing. Beyond Northern Ireland, where there was a tradition of a single territorial police service (the Royal Ulster Constabulary, and, from 2001, as part of the peace process reform agenda, the Police Service of Northern Ireland). The structure of policing in the UK was aligned with current or past local authority maps. The desirability of moving to single, national police bodies in

England, Wales and Scotland, as a means to secure greater strategic efficiency and effectiveness, was usually countered by concerns about compromising local priorities and accountabilities. However, a renewed focus on the need for greater strategic purpose, coupled with increasing concerns about budgets, led to significant change in Scotland. The Police and Fire Reform (Scotland) Act 2012 created a new Police Service of Scotland from April 2013. This merged the extant eight regional forces and the Scottish Crime and Drug Enforcement Agency and incorporated within its structure the Scottish Police Services Authority (which includes the Scottish Police College). The new organisation was effectively a national police service for Scotland, although it excluded the policing bodies reserved to Whitehall under the devolution settlement (Ministry of Defence Police, Civil Nuclear Constabulary and the British Transport Police). The chief constable heads an Executive team of assistant chief constables and deputy chief constables, and is accountable to the Scottish Police Authority. These new accountability relationships proved to be complex and problematic (see Dickie 2015; Thomson et al. 2015). Local policing commanders are based in each of Scotland's local authority areas, although the relationships between councils (which, under the 2012 Act, are empowered to 'shape and scrutinise local delivery of policing') and the local establishment of Police Scotland altered as the new organisation developed and the formal agreements with the local authorities were put in place.

The move to create a single Scottish police service can be contrasted with the retention of the regionally based police bodies in Wales, where a proposal in 2006 to create a single Welsh force through the merger of the four extant forces was dropped in the face of strong opposition. In England, the sheer scale of policing (the Metropolitan Police Service alone is almost twice the size of the new Police Service of Scotland), in addition to strongly held views about localism and accountability, mitigated against the creation of a single national force, although some observers saw the Scottish example as a potentially useful precedent (see, e.g. The Economist 2013). The reform agenda here, and in Wales, has been very different, and serves to emphasise the extent to which this area of public service reform encapsulates quite divergent themes and priorities. In part, the emphasis has been on attempts to enhance local accountability through the election of police and crime commissioners. The Police Reform and Social Responsibility Act 2011 allowed for the replacement of the local Police Authorities by new PCCs, who have responsibility for creating local 'police and crime plans' and managing the police budget, while being held to account by new Police and Crime Panels which give representation to each local authority in the area covered. Forty-three PCCs were put in place, via elections notable for low turnout, plus the Mayor of London as effective PCC for the Metropolitan Police and the City of London Corporation as the collective policing body for the City of London Police. Additional elements of the police service reform agenda for England and Wales flowed from the outcomes of the Winsor Report, which was published in two parts (Secretary of State for the Home Department 2011, 2012). This made a series of recommendations, accepted in principle by the government, concerning the deployment of police officers and staff, performance-related pay, pay scales and salaries, the recruitment and retirement processes for police officers and the mechanisms for agreeing on pay and conditions of service. The Winsor Report contains many of the keynotes of NPM, modernisation and governance, with emphasis on the need for chief constables to be given 'the modern management tools they require', and the creation of 'flexible and efficient' workforces with the skills required for the challenges of the next three decades.

On policing, therefore, we can summarise by saying that although many of the specific policy delivery and management challenges may be rather similar, there is a marked contrast in the emphasis placed on structural and organisational change in policing in Scotland, with the drive for local elected PCCs and a reform blueprint in the shape of the Winsor Report in England and Wales, while the specific circumstances of Northern Ireland dictate a different pattern there.

Overall, the challenge is to find a single public service where there is a complete alignment in reform terms across the UK. Four factors have driven the differentiation and dealignments:

- Embedded, traditional and historical variations in aspects of service provision and development, as seen in, for example, the NHS in Scotland.
- Devolution per se (the 'event'), which consolidated and expanded the range of decentralisation in service provision.
- The devolution process and experience since the 1990s, particularly the emergence of governing executives of different political persuasions in the component parts of the overall UK polity.
- The distractions caused by the contextual and conditioning factors discussed above, which, cumulatively, have served to create policy diversions and prioritised matters other than public sector reform.

The meaning and implications of public sector reform are contested in the context of the messy realities of the cluttered and often confused UK polity. Reform in a differentiated polity with asymmetrical devolution cannot be simple and straightforward. The outcome is a curious mix of aligned and partially aligned reform agendas and practices, with a few common subthemes such as partnership working, community involvement, performance strategies driven by outcome agreements, cross-agency working, joint services provision, and service-user focus and integration, each of which we might loosely link to public value management. The overall impression, however, is of a spectrum of divergence and the lack of an overall binding narrative. Instead, we find disaggregation and atomisation with no coordinated approach to public sector reform, even in the devolved polities where there is, ostensibly, clearer scope for more strategic and holistic arrangements. Policy learning and transfer have been relatively unexploited, partly because of the difference in political leaderships across the elements of the UK state (see Paun et al. 2016) and partly because of the reluctance by the centre to risk infringing upon the autonomies which flow from devolution. All of this needs to be seen in the context of the negative impacts of the contextual and conditioning factors discussed in this chapter.

REFERENCES

Alford, J., & Hughes, O. (2008). Public Value Pragmatism as the Next Phase of Public Management. *The American Review of Public Administration, 38*(2), 130–148.

Arnott, M. (2015). The Coalition's Impact on Scotland. In M. Beech & S. Lee (Eds.), *The Conservative-Liberal Coalition. Examining the Cameron-Clegg Government.* Houndmills: Palgrave Macmillan.

Austin, M. J. (2003). The Changing Relationship between Nonprofit Organizations and Public Social Service Agencies in the Era of Welfare Reform. *Nonprofit and Voluntary Sector Quarterly, 32*(1), 97–114.

Barber, M. (2007). *Instruction to Deliver. Fighting to Transform Britain's Public Services.* London: Methuen.

Barber, M. (2016). *How to Run a Government So That Citizens Benefit and Taxpayers Don't Go Crazy.* London: Penguin.

Barber, M. (2017). *Delivering Better Outcomes for Citizens: Practical Steps for Unlocking Public Value.* London: OGL.

Beech, M., & Lee, S. (Eds.). (2015). *The Conservative-Liberal Coalition. Examining the Cameron-Clegg Government.* Houndmills: Palgrave Macmillan.

Bennington, J., & Moore, M. H. (Eds.). (2011). *Public Value: Theory and Practice*. Houndmills: Palgrave Macmillan.

Berry, K., & Kidner, C. (2016). *Scotland Act 2016: Discretionary Payments and New Benefits*. Scottish Parliament Information Centre, Briefing 16/50, 3 June, Scottish Parliament, Edinburgh.

Berthier, A. (2016). *Tax Progressivity and the Scottish Rate of Income Tax*. Scottish Parliament Information Centre, Briefing 16/15, 10 February, Scottish Parliament, Edinburgh.

Bevir, M. (2013). Governance as Theory, Practice and Dilemma. In M. Bevir (Ed.), *The Sage Handbook of Governance*. London: Sage.

Breen, S. (2018). How RHI "Scandal" Sparked a Row that Brought Down the Assembly. *Belfast Telegraph*, 13 September.

Bristow, D. (2015). *Public Sector Reform in Wales: The Leadership Challenge*. Public Policy Institute for Wales. Retrieved from ppiw.org.uk/blog-public-sector-reform-in-wales-the-leadership-challenge/.

Broadbent, J., Massey, A., & Lavender, M. (2011). Editorial: Provision of Public Services in Troubled Times. *Public Money and Management, 31*(6), 379.

Bryson, J. M., Crosby, B. C., & Bloomberg, L. (2014). Public Value Governance: Moving beyond Traditional Public Administration and the New Public Management. *Public Administration Review, 74*(4), 445–456.

Bryson, J., Sancino, A., Benington, J., & Sørensen, E. (2017). Towards a Multi-Actor Theory of Public Value Co-Creation. *Public Management Review, 19*(5), 640–654.

Burgess, L. (2016). *Integration of Health and Social Care*. Scottish Parliament Information Centre Briefing 16/70, 24 August, Scottish Parliament, Edinburgh.

Burnham, J., & Pyper, R. (2008). *Britain's Modernised Civil Service*. Basingstoke: Palgrave Macmillan.

Business, Energy and Industrial Strategy and Work and Pensions Committees. (2018). *Carillion*, Second Joint Report 2017–19, HC769

Butler, P. (2015). Why the "Big Society" is Now Just a Hashtag for Coalition Hypocrisy. *The Guardian*, 20 January.

Butler, P. (2018). Northamptonshire Council Backing "Bare Minimum" Service Plan. *The Guardian*, 9 August.

Campbell, A. (2012). *The National Performance Framework and Scotland Performs*. Scottish Parliament Information Centre Briefing 12/12, 7 February, Scottish Parliament, Edinburgh.

Christensen, T., & Laegreid, P. (Eds.). (2011a). *The Ashgate Companion to New Public Management*. Farnham: Ashgate.

Christensen, T., & Laegreid, P. (2011b). Introduction. In T. Christensen & P. Laegreid (Eds.), *The Ashgate Companion to New Public Management*. Farnham: Ashgate.

Christensen, T., & Laegreid, P. (2011c). Beyond NPM? Some Developmental Features. In T. Christensen & P. Laegreid (Eds.), *The Ashgate Companion to New Public Management*. Farnham: Ashgate.

Civil Service Blog. (2017). *The Barber Public Value Review*. Retrieved from https://civilservice.blog.gov.uk/2017/11/29/the-barber-public-value-review.

Coats, D., & Passmore, E. (2008). *Public Value: The Next Steps in Public Service Reform*. London: The Work Foundation.

Commission on Devolution in Wales. (2012). *Empowerment and Responsibility: Financial Powers to Strengthen Wales*. Cardiff: Commission on Devolution in Wales.

Commission on Devolution in Wales. (2014). *Empowerment and Responsibility: Legislative Powers to Strengthen Wales*. Cardiff: Commission on Devolution in Wales.

Connolly, J., & Pyper, R. (2020). The Leadership and Management of Public Services Reform in Scotland. In M. Keating (Ed.), *The Oxford Handbook of Scottish Politics*. Oxford University Press.

Conservative Party. (2010). *Invitation to Join the Government of Britain. The Conservative Manifesto 2010*. London: Conservative Party.

Copus, C. (2018). Proposed Larger Councils Could Take the Local from Local Government. *The Guardian*, 3 May.

Cowley, P., & Kavanagh, D. (2016). *The British General Election of 2015*. Houndmills: Palgrave Macmillan.

Darling, A. (2011). *Back from the Brink. 1000 Days at Number 11*. London: Atlantic Books.

Deloitte. (2018). Northern Ireland. The State of the State. In *Citizens, Government and Business: The State of the State 2017–18*. London: Deloitte.

Dickie, M. (2015). Scottish Police Beset By Controversies. *Financial Times*, 7 August.

Doheny, S. (2015). *The Organisation of the NHS in the UK: Comparing Structures in the Four Countries*. National Assembly for Wales Research Service, Research Paper 15/020, May, National Assembly for Wales, Cardiff.

Dunleavy, P. (2019). "The Bureaucracy" as an Interest Group. In R. Congleton, B. Grotman, & S. Voigt (Eds.), *The Oxford Handbook of Public Choice*. Oxford: Oxford University Press.

Emmerson, C. (2017). *Two Parliaments of Pain: The UK Public Finances 2010 to 2017*. IFS Briefing Note BN199, Institute for Fiscal Studies, London.

Fenwick, J., & Gibbon, J. (2016). Localism and the Third Sector: New Relationships of Public Service? *Public Policy and Administration, 31*(3), 221–240.

Fenwick, J., & Gibbon, J. (2017). The Rise and Fall of the Big Society in the UK. *Public Money and Management, 37*(2), 126–130.

Foster, M. (2017). Key Blair Adviser Picked to Lead "Serious" Civil Service Efficiency Review. *Civil Service World*, 6 March. Retrieved from www.civilserviceworld.com/articles/news/key-blair-adviser-picked-lead-serious-civil-service-efficiency-review.

Gapper, J. (2017). Grenfell: An Anatomy of a Housing Disaster. *Financial Times*, 29 June.

Gershon, S. P. (2004). *Releasing Resources to the Front Line. Independent Review of Public Sector Efficiency*. London: Stationery Office.

Godden, M. (2017). KCTMO Loses Contract after Grenfell Fire. *The Times*, 28 September.

Goodin, R. (1996). *The Theory of Institutional Design*. Cambridge: Cambridge University Press.

Gormley-Heenan, C., & Aughey, A. (2015). The Coalition's Impact on Northern Ireland. In M. Beech & S. Lee (Eds.), *The Conservative-Liberal Coalition. Examining the Cameron-Clegg Government*. Houndmills: Palgrave Macmillan.

Gover, D., & Kenny, M. (2016). *Finding the Good in EVEL: An Evaluation of 'English Votes for English Laws' in the House of Commons*. Edinburgh: Centre on Constitutional Change.

Gray, A. M., & Birrell, D. (2013). The Structures of the NHS in Northern Ireland: Divergence, Policy Copying and Policy Deficiency. *Public Policy and Administration, 28*(3), 274–289.

Green, S. P. (2010). *Efficiency Review*. London: Cabinet Office.

Hartley, J., Alford, J., Hughes, O., & Yates, S. (2015). Public Value and Political Astuteness in the Work of Public Managers: The Art of the Possible. *Public Administration, 93*(1), 195–211.

HM Government. (2011). *Open Public Services*. London: Stationery Office.

HM Government. (2012). *The Civil Service Reform Plan London*. Cabinet: Office.

HM Treasury. (2017). *'Sir Michael Barber Appointed to Improve Government Efficiency' 4 March*. London: HM Treasury.

Hood, C. (1991). A Public Management for All Seasons. *Public Administration, 69*(1), 3–19.

Hood, C., & Dixon, R. (2013). A Model of Cost-Cutting in Government? The Great Management Revolution in UK Central Government Reconsidered. *Public Administration, 91*(1), 114–134.

Hood, C., & Dixon, R. (2015). *A Government That Worked Better and Cost Less? Evaluating Three Decades of Reform and Change in UK Central Government*. Oxford: Oxford University Press.

Housden, S. P. (2014). This is Us: A Perspective on Public Services in Scotland. *Public Policy and Administration, 29*(1), 64–74.

Institute for Government. (2018). *Civil Service Staff Numbers*. Retrieved from www.instituteforgovernment.org.uk/explainers/civil-service-staff-numbers.

Jeffery, C. (2016). The United Kingdom after the Scottish Referendum. In R. Heffernan, C. Hay, M. Russell, & P. Cowley (Eds.), *Developments in British Politics 10*. London: Palgrave.

Johnstone, R. (2017). Treasury Backs Plan for Disruptive Innovation in Whitehall. *Civil Service World*, 22 November. Retrieved from www.civilserviceworld.com/articles/news/treasury-backs-plan-'disruptive-innovation'-whitehall.

Kelly, R. (2017). *English Votes for English Laws*. House of Commons Library Briefing Paper Number 7339, 20 June, House of Commons. London.

Kelly, B. (2018). Northern Ireland Latest: How Did Power-Sharing Collapse at Stormont and Whybis there No Government? *Independent*, 6 September.

Kelly, G., Mulgan, G., & Muers, S. (2002). *Creating Public Value: An Analytical Framework for Public Service Reform*. London: Cabinet Office Strategy Unit.

Kensington and Chelsea Tenant Management Organisation. (2006). *Articles of Association of the Royal Borough of Kensington and Chelsea Tenant Management Organisation Ltd*. London: KCTMO.

Kickert, W. (2012). How the UK Government Responded to the Fiscal Crisis: An Outsider's View. *Public Money and Management*, 32(3), 169–176.

Knox, C., & Carmichael, P. (2005). Improving Public Services: Public Administration Reform in Northern Ireland. *Journal of Social Policy*, 35(1), 97–120.

Laws, D. (2016). *Coalition. The Inside Story of the Conservative-Liberal Democrat Coalition Government*. London: Biteback Publishing.

Manzoni, J. (2018). *Civil Service Transformation*. Speech, 24 January. Retrieved from www.gov.uk/government/speeches/civil-service-transformation-speech.

Massey, A., & Pyper, R. (2005). *Public Management and Modernisation in Britain*. Houndmills: Palgrave Macmillan.

McCann, L. (2013). Reforming Public Services after the Crash: The Roles of Framing and Hoping. *Public Administration*, 91(1), 5–16.

McDonald, H. (2015). Peter Robinson to Step Down as Northern Ireland First Minister. *The Guardian*, 19 November.

McDonald, H. (2017). Martin McGuinness Resigns as Deputy First Minister of Northern Ireland. *The Guardian*, 10 January.

McDonald, H., & Watt, N. (2015). Stormont in Crisis as Northern Ireland's First Minister Peter Robinson Resigns. *The Guardian*, 10 September.

McDowell, I. (2017). Stormont Deadlock: Need-to-Know Guide. *BBC News*. Retrieved from www.bbc.co.uk/news/uk-northern-ireland-politics-41723268.

McKay Commission. (2013). *Report of the Commission on the Consequences of Devolution for the House of Commons*. London: Cabinet Office.

McTavish, D. (2014). Debate: Scotland, the United Kingdom and Complex Government. *Public Money and Management*, 34(1), 4–8.

Menon, A., Lodge, M., & Owen, J. (2017). *The Civil Service after Article 50*. London: Institute of Government.

Moon, D. S. (2013). Rhetoric and Policy Learning: On Rhodri Morgan's "Clear Red Water" and "Made in Wales" Health Policies. *Public Policy and Administration, 28*(3), 306–323.

Moore, M. (1995). *Creating Public Value: Strategic Management in Government*. Cambridge, MA: Harvard University Press.

National Audit Office. (2018a). *Financial Sustainability of Local Authorities 2018*. HC 834, 2017–18, 8 March, NAO, London.

National Audit Office. (2018b). *Investigation into the Government's Handling of the Collapse of Carillion*. HC 1002, 2017–18, 7 June, NAO, London.

National Audit Office. (2018c). *Improving Government's Planning and Spending Framework*. HC 1679, 2017–19, 26 November, NAO, London.

Newman, J. (2005). Participative Governance and the Remaking of the Public Sphere. In J. Newman (Ed.), *Remaking Governance. Peoples, Politics and the Public Sphere*. Bristol: The Policy Press.

Newman, J. (2011). Serving the Public? Users, Consumers and the Limits of NPM. In T. Christensen & P. Laegreid (Eds.), *The Ashgate Companion to New Public Management*. Farnham: Ashgate.

Northern Ireland Executive. (2017). The Executive Office. Retrieved from www.ofmdfmni.gov.uk/civil-service-reform.

O'Brien, P., & Pike, A. (2015). City Deals, Decentralisation and the Governance of Local Infrastructure Funding and Financing in the UK. *National Institute Economic Review, 233*(1), 14–26.

O'Flynn, J. (2007). From New Public Management to Public Value: Paradigmatic Change and Managerial Implications. *The Australian Journal of Public Administration, 66*(3), 353–366.

OECD. (2016). *Northern Ireland (United Kingdom): Implementing Joined-Up Governance for a Common Purpose*. Paris: OECD Publishing.

Office of the First Minister and Deputy First Minister. (2003). *Review of Public Administration in Northern Ireland*. Belfast: OFM/DFM. Retrieved May 1, 2017, from www.rpani.gov.uk.

Osborne, S. P. (2011). Public Governance and Public Services: A "Brave New World" or New Wine in Old Bottles. In T. Christensen & P. Laegreid (Eds.), *The Ashgate Research Companion to New Public Management*. Farnham: Ashgate.

Owen, J., & Munron, R. (2016). *Whitehall' Preparation for the UK's Exit from the EU*. London: Institute of Government.

Owen, J., Lloyd, L., & Rutter, J. (2018). *Preparing Brexit. How Ready is Whitehall?* London: Institute of Government.

Painter, C. (2013). The UK Coalition Government: Contrasting Public Service Reform Narratives. *Public Policy and Administration, 28*(1), 3–20.

Parry, R. (2016). Civil Service and the Machinery of Government. In D. McTavish (Ed.), *Politics in Scotland*. London: Routledge.

Paun, A., Rutter, J., & Nicholl, A. (2016). *Devolution as a Policy Laboratory*. London: Institute for Government/Alliance for Useful Evidence.

Pollitt, C., & Bouckaert, G. (2011). *Public Management Reform. A Comparative Analysis – New Public Management, Governance and the Neo-Weberian State* (3rd ed.). Oxford: Oxford University Press.

Prime Minister. (1999). *Modernising Government*. Command Paper 4310 Session 1998–99.

Public Accounts Committee. (2015). *The Government's Funding of Kids Company*. Eighth Report 2015–16, HC504

Public Administration and Constitutional Affairs Committee. (2016a). *The Future of the Union, Part One: English Votes for English Laws*. Fifth Report 2015–16, HC523.

Public Administration and Constitutional Affairs Committee. (2016b). *The Collapse of Kids Company: Lessons for Charity Trustees, Professional Firms, the Charity Commission, and Whitehall*. Fourth Report 2015–16, HC433.

Public Administration and Constitutional Affairs Committee. (2018). *After Carillion: Public Sector Outsourcing and Contracting*. Seventh Report 2017–18, HC748.

Pyper, R. (2013). The UK Coalition and the Civil Service: A Half-Term Report. *Public Policy and Administration, 28*(4), 364–382.

Pyper, R. (2015). Public Administration, Public Management and Governance. In A. Massey & K. J. Miller (Eds.), *International Handbook of Public Administration and Governance*. Cheltenham: Edward Elgar.

Regan, E. (2017). Integrating Whitehall: The Case for a Department for Public Sector Reform. *The MJ.Co.Uk*. Retrieved from www.themj.co.uk/integrating-whitehall-the-case-for-a-department-for-public-sector-reform.

Rensch, S. (2017). CIPFA Calls for Public Service Reform in Northern Ireland. Retrieved from www.publicfinance.co.uk/news/2017/12/cipfa-calls-public-service-refrom-northern-ireland.

Rhodes, R. A. W. (1997). *Understanding Governance. Policy Networks, Governance, Reflexivity and Accountability*. Buckingham: Open University Press.

Rhodes, R. A. W., & Wanna, J. (2007). The Limits to Public Value, or Rescuing Responsible Government from the Platonic Guardians. *Australian Journal of Public Administration, 66*(4), 406–421.

Rhodes, R. A. W., Carmichael, P., McMillan, J., & Massey, A. (2003). *Decentralising the Civil Service. From Unitary State to Differentiated Polity in the United Kingdom*. Buckingham: Open University Press.

Riddell, P. (2012). *An Open Letter: Two Challenges and An Opportunity*. London: Institute for Government.

Royal Institute of British Architects. (2017). *Submission from the Royal Institute of British Architects to the Call for Evidence by the Independent Review of Building Regulations and Fire Safety*. London: RIBA.

Russell, R. (2016). *Election Report: Northern Ireland Assembly Election, 12 May 2016*. Northern Ireland Assembly Research and Information Service, Research Paper 36/16, 12 May, Northern Ireland Assembly, Belfast.

Russell, R. (2017). *Election Report: Northern Ireland Assembly Election, 2 March 2017*. Northern Ireland Assembly Research and Information Service, Research Paper 22/17, 8 March, Northern Ireland Assembly, Belfast.

Scottish Government. (2011). *Renewing Scotland's Public Services. Priorities for Reform in Response to the Christie Commission*. Scottish Government: Edinburgh.

Scottish Government. (2016). *National Performance Framework – An Outcomes-Based Approach, Measuring What Matters*. Edinburgh: Scottish Government.

Scottish Government. (2018). *Scotland's National Performance Framework*. Retrieved from http://nationalperformance.gov.scot.

Scottish Parliament. (2015). *The Smith Commission Report – Overview*. Scottish Parliament Information Centre Briefing 15/03, 8 January, Scottish Parliament, Edinburgh.

Secretary of State for the Home Department. (2011). *Independent Review of Police Officer and Staff Remuneration and Conditions Part 1 Report*, Cm 8024, March. London: The Stationery Office.

Secretary of State for the Home Department. (2012). *Independent Review of Police Officer and Staff Remuneration and Conditions Final Report*, Cm 8325-I & II, March. London: The Stationery Office.

Seldon, A., & Snowdon, P. (2015). *Cameron at 10. The Inside Story 2010–2015*. London: William Collins.

Seldon, A., & Snowdon, P. (2016). *Cameron at 10. The Verdict*. London: William Collins.

Shipman, T. (2017). *All Out War. The Full Story of How Brexit Sank Britain's Political Class*. London: William Collins.

Shipman, T. (2018). *Fall Out. A Year of Political Mayhem*. London: William Collins.

Smith Commission. (2014). *Report of the Smith Commission for Further Devolution Powers to the Scottish Parliament*. Edinburgh: The Smith Commission.

Smith, D. M., & Wistrich, E. (2016). *Devolution and Localism in England*. Oxford: Routledge.

Stoker, G. (2006). Public Value Management a New Narrative for Networked Governance? *The American Review of Public Administration, 36*(1), 41–57.

Sturgeon, N. (2016). Decisions about Scotland should be Taken by those Who Live and Work Here. *The Sunday Herald*, 18 September.

Talbot, C. (2011). Paradoxes and Prospects of "Public Value". *Public Money and Management, 31*(1), 27–34.

Talbot, C. (2012). The Civil Service Reform Plan – Mostly Old Wine in Very Old, Bit Relabelled, Bottles. *Whitehall Watch*, 21 June. Retrieved from www.whitehallwatch.org.

The Economist. (2013). One Force to Rule Them All. *The Economist*, 1 June.

Thomas, P. (2012). *Civil Service Reform: Our Verdict*. London: Institute for Government.

Thompson, J. (2016). *Transforming Health and Social Care in Northern Ireland – Services and Governance*. Northern Ireland Assembly Research and Information Service Briefing Paper 40/16, Northern Ireland Assembly, Belfast.

Thomson, B., Maudsley, G., & Payne, A. (2015). *The Thinning Blue Line*. Edinburgh: Reform Scotland.

Walker, D. (2018). 'Carillion's Collapse Shows that We Need an Urgent Review of Outsourcing. *The Guardian*, 16 January.

Walker, D., & Tizard, J. (2018). *Out of Contract: Time to Move On From the 'Love In' With Outsourcing and PFI'*. London: The Smith Institute.

Welsh Government. (2014). *Report of the Commission on Public Service Governance and Delivery*. Cardiff: Welsh Government.

Welsh Government. (2017). Improving Public Services. Retrieved from http://gov.wales/topics/improvingservices/?lang=en.

Williams, I., & Shearer, H. (2011). Appraising Public Value: Past, Present and Futures. *Public Administration, 89*(4), 1367–1384.

Woodhouse, J. (2015). *The Voluntary Sector and the Big Society*. House of Commons Library Briefing Paper Number 5883, 13 August, House of Commons, London.

Wright, B. E., & Pandey, K. (2009). Transformational Leadership in the Public Sector: Does Structure Matter? *Journal of Public Administration Research and Theory, 20*(1), 75–89.

CHAPTER 4

Modes of State Governance, Populist Pressures and Public Sector Reform

Matthew Flinders and Christopher Huggins

INTRODUCTION

The traditional account of political authority and policy-making in the United Kingdom (UK) offers a simplistic picture of governance. Under the 'Westminster model', governance capacity is seen to be centralised in a strong executive which dominates legislative and policy-making processes and exercises control through a unitary state. It is for this reason that Lijphart (2012) famously characterised the UK as an archetypal 'power-hoarding' majoritarian democracy that stood in stark contrast to more consensual 'power-sharing' democracies. This traditional approach to governing in the UK was seen to offer an appropriate balance between 'representative' and 'responsible' government (see Birch

M. Flinders (✉)
University of Sheffield, Sheffield, UK
e-mail: m.flinders@sheffield.ac.uk

C. Huggins
University of Suffolk, Suffolk, UK
e-mail: C.Huggins2@UOS.AC.UK

1964)—representative because it emphasises openness, accountability and transparency, and responsible because of its alleged decisive, clear and 'strong' decision-making capacities. These qualities relate to key public values criteria, which emphasise, *inter alia*, effective public service delivery rooted in political mandates, accountable governance informed by a public service ethos, development of public services in collaboration with relevant stakeholders and, ultimately, public satisfaction (e.g. Moore 1994; Stoker 2006). However, accounts over the last three decades have pointed to a more complex reality of governance. Indeed, it is now argued that 'Britain has moved away from a distinctive Westminster model' (Jordan and Cairney 2013, p. 234) and that governance in the UK is no longer 'representative *or* responsible' (Flinders and Judge 2017). This has raised questions about whether the so-called new modes of governance are able to deliver public value, especially in a political context characterised by public disaffection and increasing populist pressures.

It is in this context that this chapter makes a distinctive and original contribution to our understanding of modes of state governance and the nature of public sector reform. It does this by making three interrelated arguments that can be summarised as follows:

1. In recent decades, the 'Westminster model' has come under strain due to the widespread delegation of tasks, functions and responsibilities away from the direct control of national politicians.
2. The empirical analysis of two specific modes or 'types' of multilevel governance adds tone and texture to governance-theoretic arguments concerning unintended consequences, particularly around public values, by highlighting control-dilemmas, complexity questions and confusion in relation to accountability.
3. These unintended consequences have fuelled the emergence of populist pressures in ways that have not been acknowledged by existing accounts which tend to focus on economic and cultural explanations.

This chapter attempts to make a broad set of arguments about an empirical terrain in the UK. Its focus is very much on the state and the public sector (or *the state of* the public sector)—on how public services are delivered, by whom and particularly how changes in the sociopolitical context can affect reform trajectories. This speaks to broader questions about how changing modes of governance and public sector reform in the UK perform against public values criteria. We suggest that the UK provides a particularly apt context in which to explore these issues. Not only has it been a celebrated international leader for at least four decades in terms of implementing managerialist public sector reforms, but its more recent challenges vis-à-vis Brexit have put it at the forefront of debates concerning populist pressures and the changing nature of (representative) democracy.

Our core argument is that the British state is currently experiencing a period of almost fundamental structural uncertainty to the extent that it is almost impossible to assess whether what is emerging is some form of '(re)*new*(ed)' Westminster model or whether a genuinely novel mode of state governance may be emerging. At the heart of this shift in governance is a 'public values trade-off'. Here, public sector reform over the last four decades represents a 'Faustian bargain', whereby key principles underpinning the public value approach, such as effective policy delivery, accountability and ensuring public trust and satisfaction, have been traded down for the false promise of greater efficiency.

Attempting to place long-standing debates concerning the evolution of the British state *within* an account of contemporary political disaffection (essentially connecting two islands of research and theorising that might otherwise remain disconnected) nevertheless requires that we paint on a wide intellectual canvas with a fairly broad brush. We hope, however, that future studies might build upon our tentative thoughts and therefore fill-in the fine detail.

This chapter is divided into three sections which reflect the arguments set out above. The first section provides a brief account of the 'hollowing out' of the Westminster model and highlights the value of Hooghe and Marks' (2003) 'two types' approach as a valuable heuristic lens. In order to add empirical substance to these theoretical claims, the second section argues that a focus on each of these 'types' in the British context reveals a deeper set of pathologies that have implications for democratic governance. If the concept of meta-governance provides the link between the first and second sections, then the notion of a 'Faustian bargain' provides the link between the second and third due to the manner in which it exposes the existence of embedded assumptions within specific modes of governance. If these assumptions are proved to be fallacious or misleading, then counter-narratives promoting alternative modalities are likely to emerge. This is why the focus of the third section is on the emergence of democratic disaffection and populist pressures that appear to demand a very different approach to the business of governing where the role of politicians is far more direct and powers less dispersed. This is a tentative argument—but we draw upon recent survey data to underpin our position—and has implications for both the public sector and future modes of governance.

THE EROSION OF THE WESTMINSTER MODEL

In recent decades, the 'Westminster model' has come under strain due to the widespread delegation of tasks, functions and responsibilities *away* from the direct control of politicians (see Jordan and Cairney 2013; Cairney et al. 2019). Our aim is therefore to go beyond a simple restatement of this argument and instead to deepen the analytical traction and leverage of this approach through the utilisation of a specific approach that provides the framework or foundations for the next section. This, we hope, will provide a more rounded account of the erosion of the Westminster model.

The Westminster model provides both an institutional and normative map of how democratic politics should operate. Institutionally, the Westminster model revolves around a specific design or blueprint with, critically, the executive drawn from the legislature. It is therefore quite different from the presidential systems that have a far clearer division of powers. If the 'fused' nature of the executive-legislative relationship provides what Walter Bagehot (1867) described as 'the buckle' or the 'efficient secret', then the power behind the throne is a *dis*-proportional electoral system that generally ensures that political party forming a government has a majority in the legislature. It is for this reason that the UK has traditionally been interpreted as an archetypal 'power-hoarding' majoritarian democracy (Lijphart 2012). The link between this constitutional configuration and the management of the state is (theoretically at least) equally simple in the sense that since the middle of the nineteenth century, the general expectation has been that the ministerial department provides the default administrative unit. Through this constitutional innovation, a clear line of accountability and control was said to exist from public servants, through ministers, to MPs and then to the electorate. The simplicity of this chain of delegation therefore led to arguments that it was transparent and provided an acceptable balance between 'representative government' (i.e. emphasising openness, accountability and responsiveness) and 'responsible government' (i.e. emphasising stability, control and governing capacity) (Birch 1964).

In reality, the centrality of ministerial departments was something of a constitutional fiction. Non-ministerial departments continued to exist, as did a large number of agencies, boards and commissions. As political parties in parliament became more professional and better able to control their members in the House of Commons, questions also emerged concerning whether the balance between 'representative' and 'responsible' government had evolved to emphasise the latter over the former (Birch 1964). The 'parliamentary decline thesis' therefore dominated debates concerning the management of both ministers and the state throughout the twentieth century (for a review, see Flinders and Kelso 2011).

From the late 1970s and early 1980s onwards, the emergence of what was termed 'New Public Management' (NPM)—essentially an attempt to harness private sector work practices and market-type relationships in an attempt to 'make government work better and cost less' (see Hood and Dixon 2015)—exposed and further aggravated constitutional fault-lines that had in reality always existed. It did this by increasing the distance between elected politicians and those actually responsible for the day-to-day delivery of public services. One way of further understanding the link between NPM and changes in the governance of the public sector is to utilise Hooghe and Marks' (2003) distinction between 'Type I' and 'Type II' multilevel governance (see Table 4.1). The critical element being that NPM brought with it a centrifugal dynamic (i.e. it advocated the movement of functions, roles and services away from the direct control of politicians) and an emphasis on disaggregation (i.e. the breaking-up or 'agencification' of large multi-purpose bureaucracies into

Table 4.1 Types of Multilevel Governance

	Type I	Type II
Jurisdictions	General purpose	Task-specific
Memberships	Non-intersecting	Intersecting
Number of levels	Limited	No limit
Structure	System-wide architecture	Flexible design
Design	Consolidationalism	Polycenticity
Agency	Citizen	Consumer
Legitimacy	Process-based	Exit-based
Disquiet	Emphasis on voice and deliberation	Emphasis on exit
Emphasis	Democratic clarity	Economic efficiency

Adapted from Hooghe and Marks (2003)

semi-autonomous and task-specific bodies). Put simply, a large-scale transition occurred from 'Type I' to 'Type II' modes of governance in the UK, and although similar processes of 'unbundling' (Pollitt and Talbot 2003) or 'quangocratization' (Van Thiel 2001) occurred in many other advanced liberal democracies, it is possible to suggest that the extent of this process was particularly marked in the UK (for a detailed review, see Flinders 2008).

Our argument is not that Table 4.1 provides a sophisticated or perfect account of the evolution of the British state in the late twentieth century. Rather, it provides a useful heuristic or organising perspective through which to frame a discussion about key trends and their implications for democratic governance and the public sector. Five issues deserve brief comment. Firstly, our argument is not that 'the quango debate' (Ridley and Wilson 1995) first emerged in the 1980s and 1990s but that these decades did witness a major shift in the scale and complexity of delegation (see Greve et al. 1999). The paradox (secondly) being that it was the power-hoarding nature of the British constitution that allowed successive governments to engage in the wholesale delegation of state power with relatively little scrutiny. The third issue relates to layers of complexity. As already mentioned, the dominant thrust of public service reform in the 1980s and 1990s involved the dismantling of large multipurpose 'Type I' institutions into a variety of 'Type II' bodies, at the local, regional and national levels. The 'ideal type' governing model was therefore synonymous with a 'hub-and-spoke' structure where a small policy-making core (i.e. politicians and their senior staff) effectively oversaw and managed a set of contracts with delivery organisations. These delivery organisations might be 'hived-in' (i.e. still formally part of the public sector but operating with a high degree of operational autonomy) or 'hived-out' (in the sense that services were provided by private companies under contract with the state). Towards the very end of the twentieth century, this complex administrative architecture was augmented through New Labour's devolution policy that saw the creation of new 'Type I' structures in Cardiff and Edinburgh. This in itself sat alongside the increasing 'upwards' delegation of tasks and functions to the European level.

By the beginning of the twenty-first century, the institutional landscape of the public sector in the UK was labyrinthine and dense. Figure 4.1, for example, attempts to sketch out which bodies possess some responsibility for the management of transport-related carbon emissions in four UK cities, but is in itself a simplification of a far more complex empirical reality. Indeed, official committees of investigation, parliamentary inquiries and

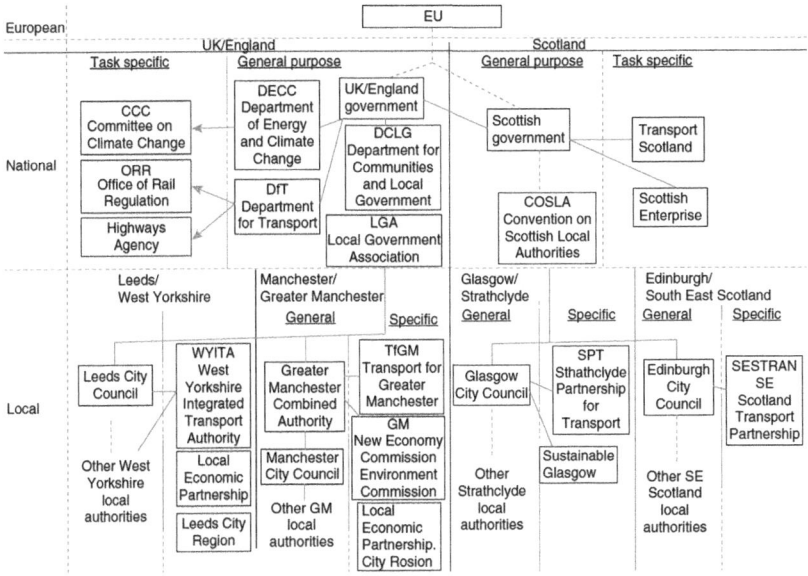

Fig. 4.1 Types of Multilevel Governance Transport-Related Carbon Emissions in Four Cities. Bache et al. (2015)

academic studies struggled to confirm exactly how many arm's-length ('Type II') bodies existed, how much public money they controlled, how many staff they employed or how they were even held to account (see, e.g. Public Administration Select Committee 2010, 2014). Put slightly differently, it seemed very hard to pull the shadow state into the sunlight of external review, but the most detailed analyses suggested somewhere around a third of all public sector spending was distributed through arm's-length bodies by the end of the twentieth century (see Flinders 2008).

The constant transfer of powers, functions and responsibilities away from the direct control of politicians is a central element of the debate concerning the perceived evisceration or erosion of the Westminster model. This has direct implications for public values. Within the context of the Westminster model, the Type I approach to multilevel governance arguably ensured key public values by providing direct lines of responsibility. However, the unitary state had been reformed into a quasi-federal structure, the logic of the market and the language of consumer-choice had infiltrated the public sector and politicians were now 'accountable' for the administration of the state but rarely 'responsible' in the sense of ever being to blame. This has had an adverse effect on public values. At the broadest level, the public sector appeared mired in 'fuzzy governance' which led to 'fuzzy accountability'. At the same time, more evidence was emerging that the economic efficiencies promised by advocates of NPM were simply not being delivered, affecting effective delivery of public services and in turn threatening public confidence and satisfaction. In order to illustrate some of these concerns in more detail, the next section provides a brief empirical account of two 'types' of MLG and their impact on the public sector.

Modes of Governing and Meta-Governance

The previous section suggested that in recent decades, the 'Westminster model' has come under strain due to the widespread delegation of tasks, functions and responsibilities away from the direct control of national politicians. This section seeks to explore the consequences and implications of this in terms of understanding the evolution of the state and the future of public sector reform. It returns to Hooghe and Marks' (2003) 'Two Types' approach in order to compare and contrast two distinctive modes of governing that have had (and continue to have) significant implications for the future of the public sector in the UK. These two brief case studies are used to illustrate how a 'muddling through' approach has tended to dominate when it comes to managing the state, in stark contrast to the UK's global reputation as a professional innovator and strategic thinker *vis-à-vis* public sector governance. The intellectual hinge that connects this section with the previous section then is the concept of 'meta-governance'. For the purposes of this chapter, meta-governance can be defined as 'the governance of governance' and essentially focuses attention on the dominant values, norms and principles that underpin modes of governing and governing approaches (see Dommett and Flinders 2015; Jessop 1997; Kooiman and Jentoft 2009). These values, norms and principles pertain both to substantive governance issues, for instance, related to the management of the health service or reducing obesity, and to governance at a more systemic level, such as the dominant paradigm shaping institutional design. Competition, for example, is a mode of meta-governance in the sense that it dictates a set of assumptions, values and principles about the appropriate relationship either between organisations or between organisations and their service users.

From this perspective, the role of politicians and senior public managers has shifted towards being 'meta-governors' rather than governing in any direct sense. This resonates with the notion of hub-and-spoke structures and speaks to a sharp division between 'policy' and delivery' which is actually highly problematic and deeply contested in reality. The research of Checkland et al. (2018) on autonomy, accountability and ambiguity in arm's-length meta-governance, for example, suggests that NHS England—itself formally an arm's-length body operating under the sponsorship of the Department for Health—is increasingly moving into a policy-making role while ministers have stepped-away from explaining the rationale for decisions to the public. In essence and against the theory, NHS England has become a meta-governor in the health sector (thereby underscoring concerns about fuzzy governance, fuzzy accountability and the evisceration of the Westminster model). The concept of meta-governance here highlights the issue of complexity. The denser and more complex the delivery or regulatory framework becomes, the more difficult it becomes for politicians to manage the business of government (Jessop 2015). In some areas, the existence of apparently intractable societal challenges may create incentives for governments to proactively create complex governance frameworks in order to facilitate 'blame games' (see Hood 2010). A more neutral interpretation, however, might simply suggest that a tipping point exists *vis-à-vis* modes of governance whereby the unintended consequences of reform agendas, such as reduced transparency and fuzzy accountability, can, in some circumstances, offset the perceived benefits. This may explain the 'pendulum swing' that has been identified in many policy sectors and several countries as periods of intense and rapid decentralisation are closely followed by equally intense periods of re-centralisation as politicians seek to reassert their control capacity and simplify structures (e.g. Axelsson 2000; De Vries 2000).

We will return to the 'pendulum swing' issue, but the main aim of this section is to briefly provide two empirical examples of the changing modes of state governance in the UK in order to corroborate a number of points and arguments that have already been made. In the previous section, we made the argument that the dominant mode of governance shifted from the 1980s onwards from a post-war emphasis on hierarchies (i.e. 'old' govern*ment*) towards an emphasis on markets and networks (i.e. the 'new' govern*ance*). This was characterised in terms of a shift from 'Type I' to 'Type II' governance (and later the creation of new levels of 'Type I' governance at the subnational level). The meta-governance of the British state therefore changed significantly, and this can be seen from the following case studies.

Type I Multilevel Governance: Decentralisation and Devolution in England

The fact that the UK is traditionally a unitary state with no constitutionally enshrined or legally protected levels of subnational government is a central element of the Westminster model. Local government has therefore always existed within a particularly precarious position, and the UK (or, more specifically, England) does not possess an established tier of regional government. The main argument of this subsection is that it is possible to identify an increasingly complex 'Type I' multilevel governance in the UK. This matters because it raises distinctive questions about the existence of concurrent modes of governance in different parts of the UK while also raising broader issues concerning meta-governance and the constitutional malleability of the Westminster model. Although the Conservative governments of the 1980s and 1990s did establish subnational bodies with responsibility for economic development in specific parts of the UK (e.g. Urban Development Corporations, Training and Enterprise Councils), their emphasis was very much on functional decentralisation through 'Type II' bodies rather than territorial decentralisation through devolution to 'Type I' structures. A critical turning point came with the New Labour government in 1997, which introduced devolution to Scotland, Northern Ireland, Wales and London in a form of 'modified majoritarianism' that attempted, as Flinders (2015) has shown, to delegate power *within* the confines of the Westminster model.

Devolution since has created a system of asymmetrical and polycentric governance, characterised by a patchwork of differing modes of governance across the UK (see Cairney et al. 2016). The most recent element of this longer devolutionary process has concerned English regional governance and a rhetorical commitment towards the notion of 'localism'. The first major step came with the *Localism Act 2011* and the creation of 'city deals' that gave specific areas additional powers and flexibilities in order to 'unlock growth and deliver jobs' (see Jones et al. 2017; O'Brien and Pike 2015). Further moves towards devolution within England were made in the form of 'devolution deals' that were more ambitious than the city deals in terms of the funding and powers and were structured around the creation of new combined authorities and, in all but one case, a directly elected mayor (a full list of 'devo deals' is available at https://local.gov.uk/topics/devolution/devolution-deals). Between November 2014 and April 2018, ten 'devo deals' were agreed, but since then, the process appears to have stalled with the Local Government Association complaining of 'devolution deadlock' and urging 'the Government to jump-start the devolution debate, providing further detail on the manifesto commitment to a 'common devolution framework' as soon as possible' (Local Government Association 2018). The government's latest annual report on devolution (March 2019—legally required under the *Cities and Local Government Devolution Act 2016*) suggests that this 'jumpstart' has not occurred with the government receiving no more formal applications between April 2017 and March 2018.

The experience of territorial devolution and English regional devolution provides insight into three issues—*clarity*, *consistency* and *complexity*—that can help us tease-out the implications for broader debates concerning democratic governance. The focus on *clarity* takes us back to the theme of meta-governance and meta-governing. These concepts, as noted above, emphasise the underlying assumptions, values and principles that dictate the introduction of reforms and the basis on which any powers are devolved to either 'Type I' or 'Type II' bodies. Put simply, the meta-governance shaping English regional devolution has been market-based. The creation of new combined authorities and the election of new mayors were designed and legitimated on the basis of their vaunted capacity to facilitate economic growth and regional productivity. The public value benefits in terms of revitalising local democracy or rebuilding civic capacity were secondary or arguably tokenistic elements of the primary agenda (see Blunkett et al. 2016; Prosser et al. 2017). As Lyall et al. (2015) put, democracy was 'the missing link' in the devolution debate. Furthermore, the manner in which these deals were brokered underlined the continuing relevance of the Westminster model in the sense that deals were brokered in private meetings between ministers, officials and local representatives. Transparency of process was not only limited but it was also clear that it was up to regions to convince the government that it could be trusted not to abuse any additional powers or resources. The notion of 'earned autonomy' captures this top-down process very well; the government set the broad aims, objectives and resource package, and it was for local authorities to decide if this was a game they wanted to play.

This flows into a focus on *consistency* and the fact that the roll-out of devolution at all levels has in recent decades taken place in an *ad hoc* and muddled manner. This lack of consistency has exacerbated not only complexity but also meant the capacity of regions to work together as sectoral powers vary significantly (see O'Brien and Pike 2015). It also raises major questions about the future of those parts of England that are not within a 'devo deal' and the extent to which they may be 'left behind'. It is for exactly this reason that the Institute for Public Policy Research (IPPR) called for an explicit 'principle-based framework' in order to 'reboot' devolution through providing a greater degree of systemic clarity and consistency (Hunter 2017). This would require the government to 'set out a statement of its vision and underlying principles, including any 'red lines' it sees on geography, powers or governance'. Despite the fact that this proposal was included within the Conservative Party's 2017 manifesto, the government has so far failed to implement the policy.

The notion of a 'deal' suggests some form of agreement that is brokered and agreed to for mutual benefit. In this way, the process is more akin to a contract-like arrangement rather than a process of democratic governance (Sandford 2017). In the case of the 'devo deals', those local authorities that signed-up were able to access relatively modest sums of money (the mayor of the Sheffield city region controls new additional funding of £30m a year over 30 years) as well as limited additional powers over issues such as local transport, strategic planning and post-16 education. With limited powers and funding on offer, it might be asked what incentives exist for local authorities to agree to 'devolution deals'. One answer to this revolves around the impact of the financial crisis on public spending and the way this has hit local government in England particularly hard (on this see Gray and Barford 2018; Sandford 2019). The National Audit Office (NAO) (2018) found that there had been a 49.1% real-terms reduction in government funding between 2010–11 and 2017–18. This resource reduction occurred at a time of increasing demand for public services, especially around adult social care. In this context, the opportunity to secure any additional finance from central government was attractive, especially when tied to broader narratives and support around regional economic development. The flip side of the deal is that accepting the deals brings with it the risk of becoming embroiled in a blame game whereby local authorities are held responsible for what were in reality centrally decided cuts. In this sense the meta-governors at the national level may have created 'devo deals' as a logical 'blame-shifting' strategy (see Bailey and Wood 2017). In this sense, they have further intensified the *complexity* of British governance in ways that speak to the notions of fuzzy governance and fuzzy accountability. The next subsection continues this focus in relation to 'Type II' multilevel governance.

Type II Multilevel Governance: Contracting-Out and Public-Private Partnerships

Although rarely framed as such, the global trend towards NPM in the 1980s can be interpreted as a shift in the meta-governance of the state. The assumptions, values and principles that had, to a greater or lesser extent, defined the evolution of the public sector during the previous century were jettisoned in favour of a far more individualised and market-based mode of governance. The notion that some public services were too important to be left to the vagaries of market forces was replaced with the introduction of profit-driven business models and private actors in areas as diverse as major utilities (water, electricity, etc.), prisons and probation and education. The aim of this section is to review the implications of this in terms of thinking about changing modes of governance and, once again, what tends to unite this subsection with the previous one is the notion of a 'deal' or 'trade-off'.

Despite the existence of numerous categories and forms, the basic 'deal' with contracting-out and public-private partnerships is very simple. A private sector organisation (which is likely to be a for-profit business but might be a not-for-profit or charity) agrees a contract with the government to deliver a specified public service, to a specified standard for a specified price. This might also include the design and build of new prisons, schools, hospitals or military camps as well as running and maintaining them over a long period of usually 25 years (Hellowell 2010). The private sector provides the initial upfront investment but then receives an annual payment. The assumption is that private sector will deliver the service at a cheaper rate than the public sector due to the pressure of competition. These efficiencies will be further enhanced as the contractor develops expertise and experience in that sector. The benefit for the government is therefore financial in what is for politicians a 'buy now pay later' scheme; the benefit for the public is that (in theory) they should receive better services at a lower cost, thereby allowing for the provision of more services or tax cuts. The benefit for the contractor is that they secure access to major public markets with the potential for significant projects but with few risks in terms of payment as the government is unlikely to go bust. The theory therefore appears to provide a win-win for all involved, and in many ways, part of the attraction of NPM for many governments, on both the right and the left, was that it appeared to be an almost apolitical and 'common sense' response to increasing fiscal pressures (Flinders 2005).

Once again, it is not possible here to provide a detailed account of Margaret Thatcher's emphasis on privatisation and the rise of 'the regulatory state', or of the use of Private Finance Agreements during the 'New Labour' years (1997–2010) (see Hellowell 2010). Nevertheless, it is sufficient to note that various forms of contracting-out and public-private partnership continue to form a central element of public governance in the UK. In other words, the specific tools of governance may have changed, but the broad (if at times reluctant) reliance on private sector finance has not diminished. Davies et al. (2018) found that the government spends £284 billion on private companies, charities and voluntary organisations which deliver goods, front-line public services and back-office support. Indeed, outsourcing is the single biggest component of government expenditure and in recent years has grown modestly. Peaking at 33.4% in 2007–08 and reaching a low of 30.3% in 2012–13, the level stood at 33.3% in 2017–18 (see Fig. 4.2).

It is critical to appreciate that Fig. 4.2 includes a range of contracting models and a vast array of suppliers from large multinational companies to small business and charities. Furthermore, securing accurate data on the nature and level of spending within this sphere is notoriously difficult (with notions of 'commercial confidentiality' grating against the demands of public accountability). Nevertheless, despite the UK pioneering the

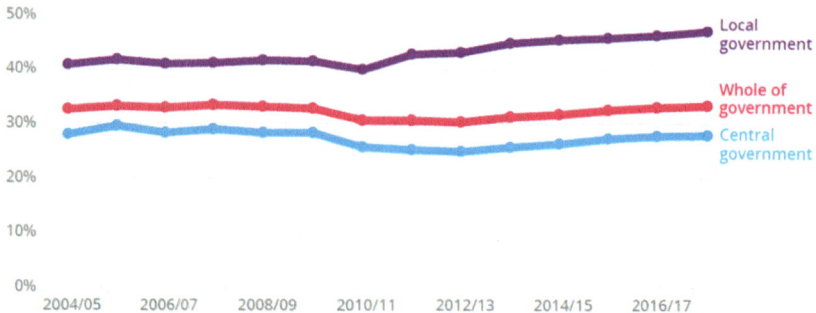

Fig. 4.2 Procurement as a percentage of government expenditure, 2004/05 to 2017/18. Davies et al. (2018, p. 6)

outsourcing of public services, recent failures in several sectors combined with profit warnings from suppliers have fuelled a wider debate about the future of contracting-out services. Three elements of this debate are particularly noteworthy given the previous issues discussed. The first takes us back to the notion of complexity and the manner in which the longer a chain of delegation through which a public service is delivered and the more potential 'veto points' that exist in this chain, then the higher the chances of 'governance failure' (see Jessop 1998; Jones 2019). A simple example brings this risk into sharp relief: Carillion, the public services company which collapsed in 2018, operated through a network of over 30,000 subcontractors. And yet the government knew very little about who they were or what they did.

The outsourcing of probation services provides a second equally stark example of governance failure. The Ministry of Justice (MoJ—the ministerial department) operating through HM Prison and Probation Service (HMPPS—an executive agency) is responsible for probation services in England and Wales. As at September 2018, 257,000 offenders were supervised by probation services, which are delivered in courts, prisons and in the community. In 2013, the MoJ embarked on major reform programme entitled 'Transforming Rehabilitation' which replaced 35 self-governing probation trusts with 21 Community Rehabilitation Companies (CRCs) to manage offenders who pose a low or medium risk of harm. It created a public sector National Probation Service (NPS) to manage offenders who pose higher risks. In February 2015, the CRCs were transferred to eight, mainly private sector, suppliers working under contracts, managed by HMPPS, which were to run to 2021–22. The Ministry considered that its reforms would deliver reductions in reoffending corresponding to £10.4 billion net economic benefits to society over the seven-year period of the contracts. In July 2018, the Justice Secretary acknowledged that the quality of probation services being delivered was falling short of expectations and announced that the MoJ would be terminating the contracts. In 2019, the National Audit Office found that the CRCs had not achieved their targets, that levels of innovation had stagnated and that significant increases in the number of people being recalled to prison had occurred (National Audit Office 2019).

The post-2013 reform of probation services provides a classic example of the imposition of market-based and NPM-inspired logic into the public sector. The reforms have been characterised as the latest example of 'hollowing out', whereby 'the state, whilst still retaining overall control, is increasingly divesting itself from probation practice in the name of marketisation, cutting costs and shrinking the state' (Deering and Feizer 2019, p. 20). At one level, this provoked a debate as to whether a marketised approach was compatible with the nature and values of probation services (Deering and Feilzer 2019); but at another more basic level, it revealed weaknesses in terms of both the ability of the state to manage private sector contracts (especially in relation to compliance and efficiency forecasts) and the ability of the private sector to understand the public sector (especially in relation to understanding the true costs of care). Despite its political salience, the reform programme, the NAO concluded, had been rushed through with insufficient testing in order to lock-in 'savings' before the 2015 General Election (and by a ministerial department that was experiencing major budget cuts and staff reductions; on this, see Dommett and Flinders 2015). Terminating the contracts cost the public purse an additional £171 million. In this sense, the probation service and other similar public sector reforms failed to deliver public value by imposing a policy model rather than developing it with relevant stakeholders and ultimately failing to deliver an effective and efficient public service.

This flows into a focus on the *capacity* of politicians and their senior officials to oversee and control an increasingly complex framework of distributed public governance. Contracting-out involves the creation of principal-agent relationships where the commissioner (i.e. the minister or 'meta-governor') is assumed to be an 'intelligent customer'. However, a series of critical reviews on the management of PFI contracts has revealed that very often, this is not the case. A lack of expertise and experience regarding the design and monitoring of major contracts often creates a situation of 'principal capture' in which the ministers and the senior civil servants who advise them become dependent on the contractor, rather than vice versa. The only way to maintain the minister as an 'intelligent customer' is to for additional resource to be invested in closely monitoring the activities of private sector contractors, but doing so may well consume any efficiency savings generated from contracting-out the service in the first place. But there is also a more political dimension to the capacity issue in the sense that market-based relationships operate on the basis of *exit* capacity (whereas democratic relationships generally emphasise *choice*). This is classic Hirschman*ian* (1990) logic, but in the case where market failure affects the delivery of a vital public service, the state cannot simply walk away in the manner expected by exit-based models. In the case of the failure of the 'Transforming Rehabilitation' reforms to probation services (discussed above), the government was obliged to make additional payments above the original terms of the contract, totalling nearly half a billion pounds in order to ensure services were actually maintained (NAO 2019)

What has been termed 'the rule of rescue' therefore demands that the vaunted risk-transfer associated with contracting-out amounts to little more than what the Office for Budget Responsibility (2017) describes as a 'fiscal illusion' because politicians cannot simply let essential public services fail. However, this can be more problematic in relation to contracting-out as the state's capacity for direct delivery may well have faded. As the Head of the NAO, Amyas Morse (2018), noted in the wake of the collapse of Carillion that 'government just doesn't have either the skill or the financial capacity to take back much delivery in-house'. This poses a distinct challenge for both the main political parties in addressing this challenge: remain committed to contracting-out but try and get better at doing it or reject market-based modes of governance and bring great swathes of activity back firmly within the public sector, in turn raising issues around capacity, efficiency and overload.

This section aimed to illustrate the existence of different modes of governance within the UK through the empirical application of Hooghe and Marks' (2003) different 'types' of multilevel governance. This underlines that it is not simply the incredibly complex bureaucratic structures that exist in the UK—a rich amalgam of layer-cakes and marble-cakes in what is in reality a relatively small territorial space—but also the tensions and trade-offs that inevitably occur in the context of making decisions about the management of the state or the future of public services. Moreover, in the context of an increasing gap between what is demanded of the state and what it can realistically deliver given the available resource package (hence the emphasis on squeezing efficiency and getting 'more bang for each buck'), the demands on the system are likely to grow. Meta-governors will have to get used to governing under pressure. As shown, this has implications for public value as successive reforms have led to policy failure and created confused accountability. This brings us to our final section and to a brief consideration of an issue that has so far escaped debate—the relationship between pre-existing modes of governance and the emergence of populist pressures.

Conclusions: Populist Pressures and Modes of Governing

This chapter has attempted to substantiate two main arguments. Firstly, that the malleability of the Westminster model has been tested and possibly even exhausted by changes in the dominant mode of governance that have delegated functions, roles and responsibilities away from the direct control of politicians. Secondly, that the analysis of different 'types' of (multilevel) governance within the UK helps reveal the empirical impact of different approaches to the meta-governance of the state in terms of contradictions, control-dilemmas and conflicts. It is, however, possible to critique the analysis that has so far been offered on at least three (inter-linked) levels. Firstly, our survey of shifting modes of governance and public sector reform restates a familiar story concerning the transition from government to governance that was first set out by Rhodes (1997) over two decades ago. Nevertheless, we have updated this basic argument concerning modes of state governance with new dimensions and more recent empirical examples. The second critique would question the intellectual breadth of this chapter and particularly its positioning very squarely at the intersection of the fields of governance, public policy and public administration. What might the complementary analysis of alternative disciplinary insights or arguments offer in terms of developing, contextualising or critiquing the arguments we have made? Following on from this, a third and final critique might look at how our argument engages with the contemporary politics of public disaffection.

These critiques are valid and lead us to locate our analysis within broader discussions around the crisis of democracy and in particular the emergence of anti-establishment populist pressures which emphasise a divide in society between 'the people' and 'the elite' and which advocate the pursuit of the popular general will. In this way, this concluding section highlights a link between the crisis of democracy and what could be termed the crisis of the state, which focuses attention very clearly on questions about modes of state governance. The 'link' between these two 'crises' is, however, complex and contestable, and our argument is therefore tentative (i.e. a proto-theory requiring further intellectual and empirical investigation). We argue that the unintended consequences of specific modes of state governance have fuelled the emergence of populist pressures in ways that have generally not been acknowledged by accounts that have tended to focus on economic and cultural explanations. This speaks to Peters and

Pierre's (2004) work on the 'Faustian bargain' that often underpins changes in modes of state governance. Simply put, their argument is that the adoption of market-based neo-liberal reforms implicitly contains a trade-off. Measures that are likely to increase the economic efficiency of an organisation, service or sector will inevitable involve some sort of trade-off in terms of public values such as transparency, accountability and democratic responsiveness. Greater efficiency comes at the cost of less democracy in a zero-sum game.

This 'Faustian bargain' is suggested in Table 4.1 and in Hooghe and Marks' work on multilevel governance, as, within the context of the Westminster model, 'Type I' governing organisations emphasise key public values such as due process, clarity and citizenship, whereas 'Type II' bodies adopt a more aggressive focus on outputs, delivery and consumer rights. In pursuing public sector reform based on Type II governing arrangements, the public values which often underpin Type I arrangement have been sacrificed. Our core argument in this chapter has been that from the 1980s onwards, consecutive governments have accepted this bargain, albeit using different tools and processes, in an attempt to make the state work better and cost less. But what if the bargain is a dud? What if the economic gains were never (or rarely) delivered and the democratic costs far higher than initially expected? What if NPM never delivered 'what it said on the tin'? What if the current crisis of democracy owes its emergence in part to the failure of this deal?

One way of engaging with these questions is to very briefly explore three broader seams of literature which, we argue, all focus attention on the link between populist pressures and previous modes of state governance in a manner that has not received attention. The first is a seam of literature on public sector accounting, audit and transparency, which seeks to assess the impact of NPM. One important reference point within this seam is made by Hood and Dixon (2015). Their conclusion is unequivocal:

> [F]ar from falling, running costs rose substantially in absolute terms over thirty years, while complaints soared. That is not exactly 'what it said on the tin' of all those grandiloquent reform makeovers aimed at containing costs and improving administration for citizens. What is notable about Hood and Dixon's (2015) findings is that what tended to drive-up running costs had little to do with the civil service or traditional public administration and more to do with the 'outsourced' elements of public services, even though

outsourcing was promoted as a cost-saving service-improving measure. Indeed, the available evidence suggests that NPM did not deliver on its side of the bargain—democratic structures and relationships were attenuated without concomitant increases in public services or efficiency levels.

This leads us to a second seam of scholarship revolving around the alleged 'crisis of democracy'. This is reflected in the titles of recent books, including: *The End of Representative Politics* (2015), *Against Elections* (2016) *The End of Democracy* (2017), *Four Crises of American Democracy* (2017), *How Democracy Ends* (2018), *The People Versus Democracy* (2018), *How Democracies Die* (2018), *Can Democracy Survive?* (2018), *Constitutional Democracy in Crisis* (2018), *Democracy and its Crisis* (2018), *Against Democracy* (2018), *Crises of Democracy* (2019), *Democracy Under Threat* (2019) and *Democracy and Crisis* (2019). The underlying message of this literature is that contemporary (liberal) democracy is in trouble. This flows into a third seam of scholarship on the emergence of 'the populist signal' (Chwalisz 2015) as the symptomatic manifestation of growing anti-political (establishment) sentiment.

This poses a question as to whether there might be some sort of link or relationship between such populist pressures and the specific debates concerning the evisceration of the Westminster model and changing modes of state governance in the UK that were discussed in the first and second sections. Put another way, is there a connection between the 'hollowing-out of the state' and broader concerns about the 'hollowing-out of public value' that may help explain the emergence of populist pressures. We suggest that there might be a connection and offer three (tentative) reasons for this that raise distinctive questions about the future of the state and modes of governance.

The first reason relates to a key criterion referenced in much of the public values literature: public trust and satisfaction (see Moore 1994; Stoke 2006). Indeed, a lack of public trust in the governance of the state by politicians is a central element of current political dissatisfaction. The Hansard Society's (2019) latest *Audit of Political Engagement* provides a number of insights—public opinion of the system of governing is at their lowest point since the audit began; the public are pessimistic about the UK's problems and their possible solution, with sizeable numbers willing to entertain political changes; feelings of powerless and disengagement are intensifying amongst specific social groups (see Box 4.1). When it comes to what the public think about the public sector more specifically, the data also raise a number of concerns. 'Nationally, more people believe public services are getting worse than they did in the late 1990s', the Deloitte (2016) *The State of the State 2016–2017* concluded, with a core finding being that the public want a more responsive and personalised public sector. More specifically, both reports found that the impact of austerity in terms of public services had hit the poorest parts of society the hardest and the majority of the public now want the government to increase public spending. The Deloitte (2017) *The State of the State 2017–2018* report found that the number of people who say they are personally willing to accept less from public services in order to restore public services has fallen to 15% (from nearly 50% in 2010). These findings suggest that the public is largely resistant to the idea of a public sector that delivers less.

> **Box 4.1 Hansard Society Audit of Political Engagement (2019)**
>
> - 72% say the system of governing needs 'quite a lot' or a 'great deal' of improvement.
> - The number suggesting it needs a 'great deal' of improvement has risen 8% in a year to 37%.
> - 75% say the main political parties are so divided within themselves that they cannot serve the best interests of the country.
> - Over half the public are downbeat about the state of Britain—56% think Britain is in decline.
> - 54% say Britain needs a strong leader who is willing to break the rules.
> - 42% think many of the country's challenges could be dealt with more effectively if the government did not have to worry so much about votes in Parliament.

The argument suggested is that the *perceived* failure of politicians to manage the state in the eyes of the public possibly provides one element of why the claims of populist politicians and parties appear to have proved effective. Moreover, the structural recalibration of the state, with its emphasis on delegation, contracting-out and an almost apolitical, depoliticised and technocratic approach to governing may have added fuel to populist pressures in the sense that it facilitated crude emotive claims about (i) disconnected, self-serving and self-interested politicians who refuse to take personal responsibility for policies, (ii) the existence of an elite that operates beyond the public's control, (iii) the rejection of experts and (iv) in the UK, context-specific claims regarding the dysfunctionality of national and European bureaucracies. The argument here is very specific. The introduction of market-based NPM-orientated reforms to the public sector is not wholly to be blamed for the emergence of populist pressures. But we are suggesting that the obvious 'governance gap' which these reforms explicitly sought to establish between elected politicians on the one hand, and those responsible for actually administering large swathes of the state on a day-to-day basis on the other, and in turn leading to failures of public sector reform to deliver public value, may well have undermined public trust and created a set of tensions and frustrations which may have had the unintended consequence of producing populist pressures.

For many frustrated with the complexities and challenges of modern governance, populism appears to offer a simplistic solution. Its focus on a strong leadership advocating the 'general will' of the people is seen to offer a more direct and legitimate democratic link than the complex institutional fragmentation of contemporary liberal democracy. Indeed, one key finding of the Hansard Society's (2019) *Audit of Public Engagement* was an indication that a majority of the public think there is a need for 'a strong leader who is willing to break the rules', and well over a third thinking that 'many of the country's challenges could be dealt with more effectively if the government didn't have to worry so much about votes in Parliament'. These findings chime with international debates concerning evidence of 'democratic deconsolidation' (Foa and Mounk 2017) in a number of advanced liberal democracies. This in itself raises distinctive questions about future modes of governance in the UK, not least because Brexit creates basic uncertainties about *where* exactly responsibility will lie or for *what*. More fundamentally, however, the results of the Hansard Society's (2019) research suggests that the basic model of *representative* democracy is currently being questioned in a way and to an extent that has simply not been seen before. Dissatisfaction with politicians, political processes and political institutions combined with a less deferential and more educated public has led 'critical citizens' to demand a greater role in the decisions that will affect their lives.

This speaks to the central theme of this chapter surrounding modes of state governance and the future of the Westminster model. Public sector reform over the last four decades has increased the complexity of governance and, through eroding public values such as clear accountability and transparency while also the failure of the private sector to deliver on its half of the 'bargain' in terms of improved public service delivery, has called into question the continued applicability of the Westminster model and its claims to offer a suitable balance between 'representative' and 'responsible' government. In this context—one defined by complexity, fragmentation and the apparent erosion of traditional public service values—highly emotive and simplistic populist messages around clarity, coherence and strong leaders can suddenly appear attractive.

The future in terms of modes of state governance therefore appears incredibly uncertain due to broader sociopolitical trends concerning the future of British democracy (and therefore of the British state). In many ways, the populist signal and events such as Brexit can be reinterpreted very much as evidence of a pendulum swing back towards a '(re)*new*(ed)' Westminster model. The aim is to reassert national control and the capacity of politicians to govern through a shorter and clearer chain of bureaucratic delegation. This may, theoretically at least, serve to restore the traditional balance between 'representative' and 'responsible' government in a manner that 'fills-in' the 'hollowing-out' effects of innumerable public sector reform initiatives over recent decades and in turn reasserts public value where it has been eroded.

However, using a populist reassertion of the Westminster model to strengthen public value presents a paradox. In the case of Brexit, for example, leaving the network of shared-risks and shared-resources provided by the European Union, British politicians may lose the control levers and resources needed to deal with most social challenges and major issues which do not respect national boundaries. The power of nostalgic promises about returning to simpler times may resonate with large sections of the public who feel trapped or 'left behind', but the reality of governing in the twenty-first century is that it is an incredibly complex endeavour. The risk in the pendulum swing, when it comes to modes of state governance and especially to capacity, is that it might leave ministers having *more control over less*. Furthermore, reasserting centralised control in such a way may not actually improve public value, especially if it leads to further policy failure. The alternative, however, takes us back into the realm of meta-governing and asking how politicians can utilise increasingly novel modes of governance, generally through networks or indirect control levers, while also promoting, maintaining and protecting a specific set of public values.

This leads us to consider whether there is a dimension to Peters and Pierre's (2004) 'Faustian bargain' that has so far escaped scholarly attention or public recognition: the public values trade-off. Put very simply, the benefit of direct control capacity through modes of state governance at the local or central level (i.e. Type I mechanisms) is that the embedded structures, socialisation processes and reward frameworks can all be geared towards promoting a very specific values or principles. In essence, the capacity to ensure a degree of consistency and uniformity is in place. Bureaucratic delegation, in general, and marketisation, in particular, disrupt this capacity and actively encourage the introduction of new value frameworks on the basis of efficiency and 'what works is what matters' (i.e. the output-driven emphasis of Type II mechanisms). Public sector values form part of a 'new public service bargain' in the sense that they have arguably been traded-down on the basis of a promise of greater efficiency—a Faustian bargain that has not paid off. The argument that public values offer a form of glue that binds not just the infrastructure of the modern state but also the essence of democratic governance is not commonly made. However, given the gap that appears to have emerged between the governors and the governed, it is possible to argue, as this chapter has, that it is an argument that needs to be made.

References

Axelsson, R. (2000). The Organizational Pendulum: Healthcare Management in Sweden 1865–1998. *Scandinavian Journal of Public Health, 28*(1), 47–53.
Bache, I., Bartle, I., Flinders, M., & Marsden, G. (2015). Blame Games and Climate Change: Accountability, Multi-level Governance and Carbon Management. *The British Journal of Politics and International Relations, 17*(1), 64–88.
Bagehot, W. (1867). *The English Constitution*. Glasgow: William Collins Sone and Co..
Bailey, D., & Wood, M. (2017). The Metagovernance of English Devolution. *Local Government Studies, 43*(6), 966–991.
Birch, A. (1964). *Representative and Responsible Government*. London: Allen and Unwin.
Blunkett, D., Flinders, M., & Prosser, B. (2016). Devolution, Evolution, Revolution … Democracy? What's Really Happening to English Local Governance? *The Political Quarterly, 87*(4), 553–564.
Cairney, P., Heikkila, T., & Wood, M. (2019). *Making Policy in a Complex World*. Cambridge: Cambridge University Press.

Cairney, P., Russell, S., & St Denny, E. (2016). The 'Scottish Approach' to Policy and Policymaking: What Issues Are Territorial and What Are Universal? *Policy and Politics, 44*(3), 333–350.

Chwalisz, C. (2015). *The Populist Signal: Why Politics and Democracy Need to Change*. London: Rowman and Littlefield.

Checkland, K., Dam, R., Hammond, J. O. N., Coleman, A., Segar, J., Mays, N., & Allen, P. (2018). Being Autonomous and Having Space in Which to Act: Commissioning in the 'New NHS' in England. *Journal of Social Policy, 47*(2), 377–395.

Davies, N., Chan, O., Cheung, A., Freeguard, G., & Norris, E. (2018). *Government Procurement: The Scale and Nature of Contracting in the UK*. Retrieved from https://www.instituteforgovernment.org.uk/sites/default/files/publications/IfG_procurement_WEB_4.pdf.

De Vries, M. S. (2000). The Rise and Fall of Decentralization: A Comparative Analysis of Arguments and Practices in European Countries. *European Journal of Political Research, 38*(2), 193–224.

Deering, J., & Feilzer, M. (2019). Hollowing Out Probation? The Roots of Transforming Rehabilitation. *Probation Journal, 66*(1), 8–24.

Deloitte. (2016). *The State of the State 2016–17*. London: Deloitte LLP.

Deloitte. (2017). *The State of the State 2017–18*. London: Deloitte LLP.

Dommett, K., & Flinders, M. (2015). The Centre Strikes Back: Meta-Governance, Delegation, and the Core Executive in the United Kingdom, 2010–14. *Public Administration, 93*(1), 1–16.

Flinders, M. (2005). The Politics of Public–Private Partnerships. *Political Studies, 7*(2), 215–239.

Flinders, M. (2008). *Walking Without Order: Delegated Governance and the British State*. Oxford: Oxford University Press.

Flinders, M. (2015). The General Rejection? Political Disengagement, Disaffected Democrats and 'Doing Politics' Differently. *Parliamentary Affairs, 68*(S1), 241–254.

Flinders, M., & Kelso, A. (2011). Mind the Gap. *British Journal of Politics and International Relations, 13*(2), 249–268.

Flinders, M., & Judge, D. (2017). Fifty Years of *Representative and Responsible Government*: Contemporary Relevance, Theoretical Revisions and Conceptual Reflection. *Representation, 53*(2), 97–116.

Foa, R., & Mounk, Y. (2017). The Signs of Deconsolidation. *Journal of Democracy, 28*(1), 5–15.

Gray, M., & Barford, A. (2018). The Depths of the Cuts: The Uneven Geography of Local Government Austerity. *Cambridge Journal of Regions, Economy and Society, 11*(3), 541–563.

Greve, C., Flinders, M., & Van Thiel, S. (1999). Quangos—What's in a Name? Defining Quangos from a Comparative Perspective. *Governance, 12*(2), 129–146.

Hansard Society. (2019). *Audit of Political Engagement 16*. Retrieved from https://www.hansardsociety.org.uk/publications/reports/audit-of-political-engagement-16

Hellowell, M. (2010). The UK's Private Finance Initiative: History, Evaluation, Prospects. In G. A. Hodge, C. Greve, & A. E. Boardman (Eds.), *International Handbook on Public-Private Partnerships* (pp. 307–332). Cheltenham: Edward Elgar.

Hirschman, A. (1990). *Exit, Voice and Loyalty*. Harvard: Harvard University Press.

Hood, C. (2010). *The Blame Game: Spin, Bureaucracy, and Self-preservation in Government*. Princeton and Oxford: Princeton University Press.

Hood, C., & Dixon, R. (2015). *A Government that Worked Better and Cost Less? Evaluating Three Decades of Reform and Change in UK Central Government*. Oxford: Oxford University Press.

Hooghe, L., & Marks, G. (2003). Unravelling the Central State, but How? *American Political Science Review, 97*(2), 233–243.

Hunter, J. (2017). *Rebooting Devolution: A Common-sense Approach to Taking Back Control*. Retrieved from https://www.ippr.org/publications/rebooting-devolution.

Jessop, B. (1997). Capitalism and Its Future: Remarks on Regulation, Government and Governance. *Review of International Political Economy, 4*(3), 561–581.

Jessop, B. (1998). The Rise of Governance and the Risks of Failure: The Case of Economic Development. *International Social Science Journal, 50*(155), 29–45.

Jessop, B. (2015). The Course, Contradictions, and Consequences of Extending Competition as a Mode of (Meta-) Governance. *Distinktion: Journal of Social Theory, 16*(2), 167–185.

Jones, M. (2019). The March of Governance and the Actualities of Failure. *International Social Science Journal, 68*(227–228), 25–41.

Jones, P., Wynn, M., Hillier, D., & Comfort, D. (2017). A Commentary on the City Deals in the UK. *Journal of Public Affairs, 17*(3), 1–6.

Jordan, G., & Cairney, P. (2013). What Is the 'Dominant Model' of British Policymaking? Comparing Majoritarian a and Policy Community Ideas. *British Politics, 8*(3), 233–259.

Kooiman, J., & Jentoft, S. (2009). Meta-governance: Values, Norms and Principles, and the Making of Hard Choices. *Public Administration, 87*(4), 818–836.

Lijphart, A. (2012). *Patterns of Democracy: Government Forms and Performance in Thirty-Six Countries* (2nd ed.). New Haven: Yale University Press.

Local Government Association. (2018). *LGA Responds to Government's Annual Devolution Report*. Retrieved from https://www.local.gov.uk/about/news/lga-responds-governments-annual-devolution-report

Lyall, S., Wood, M., & Bailey, D. (2015). *Democracy: The Missing Link in the Devolution Debate*. Retrieved from https://neweconomics.org/uploads/files/1888588d95f1712903_e3m6ii50b.pdf

Moore, M. H. (1994). Public Value as the Focus of Strategy. *Australian Journal of Public Administration, 53*(3), 296–303.

Morse A. (2018). *Risks, Resources and Government–supplier Relationships*. Retrieved from www.nao.org.uk/naoblog/risks-resources-and-government-supplierrelationships/?utm_content=andutm_medium=emailandutm_name=andutm_source=govdelivery.

National Audit Office. (2018). *Financial sustainability of local authorities 2018*. Retrieved from https://www.nao.org.uk/wp-content/uploads/2018/03/Financial-sustainabilty-of-local-authorites-2018.pdf.

National Audit Office. (2019). *Transforming Rehabilitation: Progress Review*. Retrieved from https://www.nao.org.uk/wp-content/uploads/2019/02/Transforming-Rehabilitation-Progress-review.pdf.

O'Brien, P., & Pike, A. (2015). City Deals, Decentralisation and the Governance of Local Infrastructure Funding and Financing in the UK. *National Institute Economic Review, 233*, R14–R26.

Office for Budget Responsibility. (2017). Fiscal Risks Report. Retrieved from https://cdn.obr.uk/July_2017_Fiscal_risks.pdf

Peters, B. G., & Pierre, J. (2004). Multi-Level Governance and Democracy: A Faustian Bargain? In I. Bache & M. Flinders (Eds.), *Multi-Level Governance* (pp. 75–89). Oxford: Oxford University Press.

Pollitt, C., & Talbot, C. (2003). *Unbundled Government*. London: Routledge.

Public Administration Select Committee. (2010). *Smaller Government: Shrinking the Quango State* (Fifth Report of Session 2010–2011, HC537). Retrieved from https://publications.parliament.uk/pa/cm201011/cmselect/cmpubadm/537/537.pdf.

Public Administration Select Committee. (2014). *Who's Accountable? Relationships Between Government Departments and Arm's-Length Bodies* (First report of session 2014–2015, HC110). Retrieved from https://publications.parliament.uk/pa/cm201415/cmselect/cmpubadm/110/110.pdf.

Prosser, B., Renwick, A., Giovanni, A., Sandford, M., Flinders, M., Jennings, W., Smith, G., Spada, P., Stoker, G., & Ghose, K. (2017). Citizen Participation and Changing Governance: Cases of Devolution in England. *Policy and Politics, 45*(2), 251–269.

Ridley, F., & Wilson, D. (Eds.). (1995). *The Quango Debate*. Oxford: Oxford University Press.

Rhodes, R. A. W. (1997). *Understanding Governance: Policy Networks, Governance, Reflexivity and Accountability*. Buckingham: Open University Press.

Sandford, M. (2017). Signing Up to Devolution: The Prevalence of Contract Over Governance in English Devolution Policy. *Regional and Federal Studies, 27*(1), 63–82.

Sandford, M. (2019). *Local Authority Financial Resilience* (House of Commons Library Briefing 08520). Retrieved from https://researchbriefings.parliament.uk/ResearchBriefing/Summary/CBP-8520.

Stoker, G. (2006). Public Value Management: A New Narrative for Networked Governance? *American Review of Public Administration, 36*(1), 41–57.

Van Thiel, S. (2001). *Quangos: Trends, Causes and Consequences*. Farnham: Ashgate Publishing.

CHAPTER 5

Evidence-based Policy and Public Value Management: Mutually Supporting Paradigms?

Kathryn Oliver and Alec Fraser

This chapter considers the role(s) of evidence as part of public service reform processes and what 'evidence' now represents in governance processes. Policy narratives seem to suggest that evidence-based policy (EBP) can now be taken for granted and that there has been a shift towards 'evidence-based practice'. We refute these assumptions, arguing that the rhetoric of 'evidence based policymaking' has been used to serve political agendas by legitimising various logics of public management and innovation and marginalising others over time. We explore the changes in public management cultures and discourses, and compare these with congruent changes in discourses about evidence use, including the evidence needs implied by successive paradigms of public management—namely,

---

K. Oliver (✉)
London School of Hygiene and Tropical Medicine, London, UK
e-mail: Kathryn.Oliver@lshtm.ac.uk

A. Fraser
Department of Government & Business, King's College London, London, UK
e-mail: Alec.Fraser@kcl.ac.uk

© The Author(s) 2021
J. Connolly, A. van der Zwet (eds.), *Public Value Management, Governance and Reform in Britain*, International Series on Public Policy, https://doi.org/10.1007/978-3-030-55586-3_5

traditional public administration, the new public management, and public value management as a response to networked governance (Stoker 2006). We reflect on how this has been supported by changes in the broader science policy environment, specifically the management and assessment of publicly funded research, and in funding of research to support evidence-informed policy-making.

To discuss these changes in the EBP and public management paradigms, we draw on empirical examples from the UK healthcare policy and science policy. In the UK, there has been a substantial literature on public management which we draw on to explore how fluctuating managerial emphases have evolved across different political administrations. Also in the UK, there has been a long-standing interest in the role of evidence-based medicine in the broader debates, which makes it possible to explore notions of evidence use (beyond generation) through healthcare given the particular relationships between science policy and the NHS in strategic, operational and evaluative terms, as well as highlighting relevant professional power dynamics.

To do this, we explore three themes—evidence generation, evidence use, and organisational learning—across the policy domains of higher education, healthcare policy, and broader science policy. Higher education and broader science policy create a policy and organisational environment within which significant investment in evidence generation is made. Although there exists much research and knowledge capture in civil society and within private organisations, our focus is on how predominantly publicly funded research evidence is generated, shaped, and managed. Similarly, healthcare policy has often been at the forefront of operationalising and reflecting on how administrators and managers respond to and use evidence of different kinds, and have in many cases developed techniques to enable organisations to learn about how they use data and evidence internally. Therefore, juxtaposing structural and political developments in healthcare and higher education, we discuss how these developments helped the discourse move beyond academic research evidence and consider other forms of knowledge, information, data use in situ, and the significance of these for public managers.

Evidence-Based Policy and Practice: A Historical Discourse

The role of evidence and evidence producers of different kinds has evolved over the last 50 years. Empirically, there has been a huge increase in the number of professional researchers, and governments around the world have invested more and more money in infrastructure to support evidence use (Science 2018). Alongside this expansion has been a growth in research and commentary *about* evidence production and use. Early commentators on the roles of scientists talk about the importance of 'heroic scientists' who assist governments to overcome national crises and, by harnessing the innovative capacities of technologies, bring wealth and prosperity to nations (Killian 1959; Truman 1968; Aurum 1971). In medicine too, the production of evidence was presented as the means to ensure that doctors made good, effective decisions about treatments (Cochrane 1972). Both in medicine and in public policy and management more broadly, evidence production and use was seen as a straightforward, linear process, which operated for the good of society. Uptake of new knowledge was similarly uncomplicated and seen as unequivocally beneficial. A good example of this is the formulation in the Cooksey Review, which was a review of health research funding in the UK conducted by Sir David Cooksey, commissioned by HM Treasury. His review led to a restructuring of health and medical research funding, and explicitly set out

> [T]wo key gaps in the translation of health research: translating ideas from basic and clinical research into the development of new products and approaches to treatment of disease and illness; and implementing those new products and approaches into clinical practice. (Cooksey 2006: 3)

Today, we know that knowledge production, use, and evaluation are inherently political processes, with the framing of problems, selection of methods, dissemination of results, and support and infrastructure of research understood as social processes liable to influence by a range of stakeholder and institutional processes (Jasanoff and Polsby 1991; Collins and Evans 2002; Latour and Woolgar 2013). Similarly, the processes by which evidence enters policy discourses have been interrogated, with some arguing that ideas are more likely to pervade policy environments than distinct studies (Smith 2013). Academics themselves are advised to adopt more entrepreneurial roles if they are to impact on policy and practice

(Oliver and Cairney 2019). We know that evidence is judged differently according to the contexts where it is being assessed, and that its credibility is therefore contingent on factors such as the audience, with the messenger as important as the message. We also know that the evidence base itself is a complex puzzle, with interpretations shifting as new pieces slot in or disrupt current understandings. Thus, the relationship between evidence and policy/practice is relational, contingent, complex, contested, and bounded by power disparities—much like our current understanding of the decision-making world.

In short, our understanding of how policy decisions are made has evolved over time, from linear simple models to more complex networked relationships shaped by power and context. Similarly, our understanding of the evidence-policy relationship has also shifted from a simplistic pipeline to a more contested and relational model. The discourses of evidence use and public management have mirrored one another as they changed over the last 70 years—mirrored, shaped, and, we argue, mutually supported one another.

Evidence Use and Public Management Discourses

To explore this co-evolution in discourses, we describe the changes in public management and broader governance discourses over the last 50 years, and how these correspond to shifts in the types of evidence valued by decision-makers, the discourses about evidence use, and how these have influenced both policy and research processes and environments. Political scientists have characterised the evolution of public management cultures in several ways: as 'paradigms' (Stoker 1998), 'archetypes'(Osborne 2006), or 'waves' (Dunleavy and Margetts 2010). These terms refer to relatively distinct cultures of thought within and about public administration and management which draw on different theoretical roots (Osborne 2006).

Each of these paradigms has its own internal logic and rules, which imply a distinct relationship to world of evidence. However, before exploring these relationships, we should make clear that in our view, the empirical case for distinct paradigms has not been made. Rather, we argue that elements —such as hierarchies, markets, networks—from all these paradigms coexist, albeit with differing degrees of emphasis within each paradigmatic discourse (Exworthy et al. 1999; see also Connolly and van der Zwet's chapter in this volume). Jones (2017) has written helpfully about the contemporary context of 'sedimented governance' in the UK context, drawing on the work of Bevir (2011, 2013) exploring the interactions of hierarchies, markets, and networks. Such an approach aligns with Newman's classic work on modernising governance:

> Different elements of policy and practice are overlaid on each other in complex ways. New elements of policy interact with institutionalised norms and practices established under earlier administrations, producing struggles between old and new ways of working and problems for a government determined to deliver fast and visible change to satisfy the electorate and secure re-election. All of this produces tensions in the process of institutional change and dilemmas for those working in public service organisations. (Newman 2001: 39)

This coexistence of elements has important implications for the evidence-use discourse. Users of knowledge may have competing, even contradictory, organisational aims as a direct result. For example, the imperative to foster competition implies a need to measure effectiveness; yet, this may be in direct conflict with the idea of creating services which reflect the needs of diverse stakeholders with a view to maximising public value. A good example of this can be found in relation to localised health service redesign, or regional reconfiguration in the NHS. Jones et al. (2019) highlight the critical importance of framing and the mobilising of an 'evidence' discourse to strategies of change pursued by senior clinicians and managers in order to justify decisions to centralise services in certain hospitals and consequently down-grade service provision in others. However, this 'technicist' framing in which measurement is of primordial importance neglects the countervailing importance of that which cannot be so easily measured—for instance, 'presence', 'belonging', and 'community', or a sense of what is 'ours' and 'who we are'—issues that matter to public and patients (Fraser et al. 2019). Service reconfiguration is better understood as a social phenomenon rather than merely a policy problem (Stewart 2019), and local publics have different views on what evidence is and why it might (or might not) be of importance, thereby fostering tensions between stakeholder groups. So, management and consequent evidence paradigms are in direct conflict in terms of how decisions (and problems) are framed, addressed, and evidenced. One implies a marketplace for ideas, and the other a collaborative, inclusive approach to knowledge generation. These logics also raise important questions about what types of evidence and knowledge are considered robust, credible, and legitimate within each paradigm.

Our contribution to this literature is to describe the evidence-use discourses which pervade and support each of these paradigms (see Table 5.1 for a summary). Previous attempts to map the evolution of public management have not included this aspect of governmental activity; yet, as argued above, the production and framing of knowledge is a fundamental part of public policy activity.

Therefore, we briefly describe these paradigms of management chronologically, and explore when, how, and why they overlap, and what the implications of these dynamic shifts hold for evidence generation and use. For each paradigm, we ask:

- What evidence is preferred, according to the internal logic of each paradigm of public management?
- What is this evidence used for? What purposes does it serve?
- How have organisations learned and adapted internally?

We explore these questions using examples drawn from healthcare policy, higher education, and broader science policy.

Traditional Public Administration

The post-war period in the UK involved major reconfigurations of the public sector across the UK, exemplified in the UK by the birth of the Welfare State, particularly the National Health Service (NHS). Alongside this major investment in state facilities and infrastructure following the devastation of World War II was a recognition of the importance of scientific technology and innovation (Killian 1959; Merton et al. 1968; Sapolsky 1968; Truman 1968; Wolfle 1968; Cape 1969; Aurum 1971). Governments on both side of the Atlantic invested in governmental research facilities (often repurposed from military research institutes) and created roles for 'heroic scientists' to advise government officials and politicians to help rebuild broken countries. Here, evidence is conceptualised as being essentially a means for the state to create wealth and infrastructure, in a relatively linear fashion.

Through the 1960s and 1970s, public administration scholars conceptualised the problem-solving role of government as a linear process with bureaucratic oversight and central command/control of the policy and

Table 5.1 How evidence interacts with paradigms of management

	What evidence is generated and by whom?	How is evidence used?	Organisational learning
Traditional public administration	Evidence/knowledge embodied within expert professionals Pipeline/linear models of dissemination from centre	'Evidence' is of low discursive significance in wider policy terms Professionalised knowledge is mostly static (e.g. no CPD) Weberian rule-based/task-oriented modes of organising in public sector organisations	Minimal audit/policy learning
New public management	Domination of positivist modes of thinking (power of numbers and 'facticity'; Rose 1999). Rise of technocracy Systematic review, hierarchies of evidence	'Evidence' is of high discursive significance in wider policy terms Dynamic (increased external surveillance, ongoing measurement, CPD) Disciplinary power (Bevan and Hood 2006) and economic signalling—e.g. value-for-money discourse	Single-loop learning—i.e. basic level of detection and correction of error (Argyris and Schon 1997; Davies and Nutley 2000: 339)
Public value management	Inclusivity and plurality of voices in setting the policy agenda and in interpreting the relevant evidence (Boaz et al. 2019) Varieties of knowledge, evidence matrices	'Evidence' is of medium discursive significance in wider policy terms Dynamic (increased *self*-surveillance, ongoing measurement, CPD) Deliberative, negotiated, contextualised approach to evidence	Double-loop learning—i.e. learning that leads to a redefining of the organisation's norms, goals, policies, procedures, or even structures (Argyris and Schon 1997; Davies and Nutley 2000: 340)

implementation process at a strategic level. At an operational level, public sector professional bureaucracies (hospitals, schools, universities) *tended* to be management-free zones. For instance, NHS hospitals functioned through 'consensus management' negotiations through administrator, treasurer, nurse and doctors throughout the 1970s (Harrison 1994). This approach relied on formal authority and aligns with a professional dominance narrative (Freidson 1970). Professional work was rule-bound and task-based rather than evidence-based, with high levels of professional autonomy (Timmermans and Berg 2003) and very little surveillance or audit. Throughout this period, professionals were deferentially characterised by both policy-makers and the wider public more as 'knights' than 'knaves' (Le Grand 1997), which meant that the evidence which they provided was often not questioned. Traditional public administration, therefore, paid little attention to the role and potential of evidence for policy. Evidence which was valued was that which enabled governments to build infrastructure or technologies, and expertise vested in individuals was highly weighted. Evidence producers, primarily universities, were generally provided with central funding by government and remained relatively unmonitored (Perkin 2007).

New Public Management

The rise of the New Right on both sides of the Atlantic represented by President Reagan and Prime Minister Thatcher ushered in a more aggressive environment, in which a 'value for money' discourse pervaded the relationship between government and public services throughout the 1980s and 1990s. Through this period, governments were starting to demand visible returns on investment, in terms of evidence as well as public services. Alongside greater monitoring and control of higher education and research funding, the growth of social science evidence about social interventions and policies enabled debate about *when* and *if* evidence demonstrated which policies should be supported. It is the case that from the 1970s, there was a growing recognition of the potential uses of evidence to reduce harmful practice and increase efficiency and effectiveness in healthcare (Cochrane 1972) and policy. Alongside this recognition came another development in the social sciences—that the generation and use of evaluation evidence was *de facto* a political process (Weiss 1979). This stimulated broader thinking about the nature of knowledge production and use and paved the way for a more nuanced understanding of how policy is made, the politicised nature of decision-making and evidence use, and the relational nature of both—all of which played a part in the shift towards new public management.

The role of the government was reframed so as to 'steer' rather than to 'row' (Osborne and Gaebler 1992)—in essence, the state should increasingly purchase rather than provide public services. Concurrently, the age of professional deference appeared to be over—with both practical and epistemological implications. On a practical level, in the healthcare sector, 'consensus management' as an idea was rejected by the influential Griffiths Enquiry into NHS Management in 1983 (Hood 1991; Pollit et al. 1991; Harrison and Lim 2003; Harrison 1994). In its place came the new public management (NPM) reforms in which managers 'must manage' (Hood 1991). Along with more management, more markets (notably heralded by the purchaser-provider split on 1991) and more measurement came to characterise the radical reforms to the organisation of public service delivery in the NHS and beyond (Ferlie and Pettigrew 1996). A process of disaggregation and quasi-marketisation, benchmarking, league tables and an overall 'audit explosion' (Power 1999) that characterised professionals more as knaves than knights (Le Grand 2003) represented a paradigm shift in public sector governance and management.

On an epistemological level, an internally driven reform agenda within the medical profession on both sides of the Atlantic intent on medical improvement and logics of standardisation crystallised as the evidence-based medicine (EBM) movement. This fused with both the end of the age of professional deference and a reaction to the monitoring required by NPM, supporting a predominantly positivist epistemology—valuing scientific, rational forms of understanding that consciously sought to transcend the political. This bled into the political domain with the start of the evidence-based policy (EBP) movement in the 1990s, which promised a seductive simplicity and discursive power that offered policy-makers the potential for post-ideological technocratic solutions to problems of public policy, as we see below.

The Evolution of New Public Management Towards Networked Government

Many of the rhetorical features of NPM could still be found in the New Labour administrations, in addition to an explicit focus on 'networks'. There is an enduring debate about the extent to which the New Labour reforms represented an extension or a diminution of the Conservative NPM reforms (see Chaps. 1 and 2 of this volume). There is a large political science and management literature on 'hollowing out of the state' (e.g. Newman 2001; Rhodes 2003, 2007) and growing dominance of networks as an organising force (supplanting hierarchies and markets) and competing labels or views about an appropriate management response (Dunleavy et al. 2006; Osborne 2006; Stoker 2006). It is the case that some of the unintended consequences of the NPM drive towards disaggregation were fragmented, poorly integrated services which New Labour sought to remedy through 'joined-up government' initiatives and whole-area working. However, simultaneously, other NPM aspects such as central target setting, performance management and the private finance initiative intensified (Ferlie et al. 2019). It is undeniably the case, however, that the New Labour administrations continued to exploit the evidence-based policy agenda. For instance, they invested heavily in evidence for policy and practice across all policy domains through the What Works Centres. These institutions were set up to provide evidence for policy-makers in the form of evidence briefs or even professional guidelines. The first and largest of these was the National Institute for Health and Clinical Excellence (NICE) in 1999, which has produced professional guidance on over 1400 topic, and assesses technologies, interventions, and drugs on the basis of cost-effectiveness to determine whether the NHS ought to fund their use. Since the 2000s, the What Works Centres have expanded to include education, criminal justice, and other policy domains. They now number 9 (including two affiliates) (Gough et al. 2018). These served the Labour administration by effectively depoliticising major policy decisions (Flinders and Wood 2014; Hartley et al. 2017). Being able to point to high-quality, effectiveness evidence—in other words, evidence considered most valuable under the terms of the prevailing management discourse—the government was able to disarm opposition by making dissent appear effectively irrational (Newman 2001). Alongside these, less formal policy and practice-focused research collaboratives were supported. For example, the National Institute for Health Research, the UK's primary health research funder, has put over £150 million towards the Collaboration for Applied Heath Research and Care, which are alliances between universities and NHS organisations aiming to generate actionable research evidence (NIHR 2009). As Newman (2001) has highlighted, the Blair-Brown project to modernise government was characterised by conflicting narratives that emphasised competing and sometimes contradictory models of governance through their time in power. The discursive significance of *evidence* reached its apogee under New Labour under the mantra of 'what matters is what works', which can be seen in the promotion of the systematic review (Young et al. n.d.; Boaz et al. 2002) and hierarchies of evidence which rank effectiveness evidence most highly (Petticrew and Roberts 2003).

Similarly, there was increased attention to the structural and broader environment by which evidence informs policy. The research councils, amongst other funders, supported the growth of networks such as Nesta's Alliance for Useful Evidence (https://www.alliance4usefulevidence.org), which aimed to provide a forum for evidence producers and users to develop networks. Similarly, a number of universities began to develop initiatives such as Cambridge's Centre for Science and Policy (2004), which included fellowships for policy-makers to spend time within universities. Government also responded, with the Government Office for Science setting up visiting fellowship schemes. The Parliamentary Office for Science and Technology, which operates across both the Houses of Parliament, was established in 1989, originally with charity funding, and since then has developed ways to help parliamentarians engage with scientific research. These initiatives attempted to increase the 'networks' by which evidence could infiltrate decision-making circles (Oliver and Faul 2018).

Within higher education, the assessment of how universities use public funds was strengthened through the Research Excellence Framework (REF). Universities were required to undertake regular audits of staff performance, as measured by outputs (publications) and, lately, research impact (Smith and Stewart 2017). These were undertaken roughly every four years, with increasing amounts of data collected at each round, including proportion of staff who were 'research active' (i.e. generating evidence outputs), the quality of these outputs as ranked by peers, and so forth. Most recently, in the 2014 REF, universities were asked to submit impact case studies, in which selected academics were invited to describe the societal impact of their work. This implies, once again, a linear and instrumental view of how evidence influences the world around it and how this process can be understood.

Indeed, as can be seen in contemporary critiques of the evidence-use movements, many researchers and commentators demonstrated an equally simplistic understanding of how evidence is used in policy and practice, bemoaning 'policy-based evidence' (Marmot 2004; Nutbeam 2004) and arguing strongly for a louder voice for research evidence in policy and practice decisions with an apparent linear conceptualisation of this process

(Lavis et al. 2003). Although caution was urged by others (Black and Donald 2001), the simplistic notion that more evidence would, with some effort, translate into better policy became widespread and underpinned funding mechanisms, research assessment processes, and research partnerships such as the CLAHRCs and the NIHR as a whole. More critical commentary started to appear with the recognition that traditional positivist research methods were not sufficient to guide policy and practice. This shift had already occurred within the healthcare sector, where greater attention was paid to developing research methods to allow incorporation of patient experience and organisational context to guide clinical practice (see, e.g. Greenhalgh 1999; Gabbay and le May 2004). This went alongside a health policy focus on quality improvement, patient safety, and attempts at large-scale technological innovation to gather data to guide decisions. The reflexive turn within healthcare was mirrored by policy discourses such as Patient Choice, with its 'no decision about me without me' rhetoric.

In essence, a well-cultivated evidence-based rhetoric allowed the New Labour governments to depoliticise potentially contentious issues and disarm a hostile press, enabling some (reasonably) radical reforms to be implemented, such as the minimum wage, the child poverty strategy (through Sure Start), and the abolition of smoking in public places. However, by the end of the New Labour years in office, there was general acceptance that traditional research approaches were not sufficient to inform policy and practice decisions, and it is notable that the successive Coalition and Conservative majority and minority governments appeared to feel less need to 'badge' their policies as 'evidence-based' than the previous Labour administrations. We now turn to these more recent administrations.

Networked 'Big Society'

Ferlie et al. (2019) have characterised the early coalition years (2010–12) as following a 'proto narrative' of reform guided by communitarianism (Etzioni 1995) encapsulated within the *Big Society* project. This marked a discursive shift from the neoliberal 1980s Conservatism. For instance, the 1980s for-profit mode of privatisation was replaced by much greater emphasis on the roles to be played by the third sector and the development of mutual or cooperative provider models to be spun out from traditional public sector organisations (Ferlie 2019). It also sought to mark a discursive shift from the technocratic managerialism of New Labour and its centrally driven target culture and alignment with the NPM. This new mode of thinking, re-establishing the importance of professionals and individuals (and downplaying the roles of managers) in reformed and diversified public sector service providers, builds on 'Red Tory' ideas (Blond 2010; Ferlie 2019).

This also has parallels with the narrative for networked governance found in the public value paradigm (Stoker 2006) in advocating a shift from markets towards networks and a focus on outcomes, impacts, and prevention. The logics of this paradigm would suggest that a more open, collaborative government style opens the way for a more heterogeneous evidence diet (Ferlie 2019). However, the Big Society 'proto narrative' of public management reform was subsumed under an NPM-friendly Treasury-led discourse of austerity from around 2012 (Ferlie et al. 2019), which reasserted central budgetary control and tightly mandated targets and intensified performance management across the public sector. Despite the intention to open up contracts to social enterprises, it appears that large corporate for-profit providers such as Virgin Care hoovered up the majority of contracts that shifted from NHS providers throughout the years of the coalition government (Sheaff et al. 2016; Ferlie 2019). This translates into a desire to control costs, a reassertion of the central tenets of NPM and a consequent return to the positivist evidence preferred under those rules. It is important to note here that the NPM rupture followed the economic overthrow of Keynesian orthodoxy. In many ways, the potential of PVM is constrained by ongoing neoliberal economic dominance (hence the refusal of the NPM to die).

In broad terms, we suggest the three and a half decades from 1948 were characterised by a relatively stable paradigm of Traditional Public Administration. The mid-1980s marked a decisive shift from many aspects of the Public Administration mode to the NPM. Whilst both the New Labour administration and its successor coalition government rhetorically rallied against aspects of the NPM paradigm from 1997 to 2010, respectively, and both introduced reforms that pointed towards principles of network governance and required a PVM response, empirically it appears that the NPM paradigm has not been replaced and remains embedded (Trenholm and Ferlie 2013). For this period, therefore, the prevailing discourse is of a hybrid NPM-network governance context in which evidence interacts with policy and practice.

Contemporary Paradigms of Public Management and Evidence Use

Public value management is structured around a collective and inclusive striving for 'public value' by managers and broader stakeholders as opposed to the rigid target-focused culture of the NPM. Stoker developed four propositions around the pursuit of public value in his 2006 work. These are reproduced below. In this section we explore the implications of these propositions for the generation, use, and evaluation of evidence to inform policy:

1. Public interventions are defined by the search for public value.
2. There is a need to give more recognition to the legitimacy of a wide range of stakeholders.
3. An open-minded relationship approach to the procurement of services is framed by a commitment to a public service ethos.
4. An adaptable and learning-based approach to the challenge of public service delivery is required.

These propositions set out a vision of PVM, which are both aspirational and prescriptive. A critical reading of PVM might suggest it represents a normative approach that downplays the role of ideology, power, politics, and actor interests. It might therefore be perhaps better suited to the technocratic mid-late New Labour years before the banking crisis (in which it emerged) as opposed to contemporary times subsumed by the subsequent regimes of austerity—during which ideology has very much reasserted itself. At the macro-political level, understandings around key concepts such as 'equity', 'efficiency', and 'accountability' have undergone fundamental shifts in the aftermath of the Great Recession to the point where Stoker's concluding sentence of his 2006 paper may appear somewhat naïve:

> People are, [Public Value Management] suggests, motivated by their involvement in networks and partnerships, that is, their relationships with others formed in the context of mutual respect and shared learning. (Stoker 2006: 56)

Interpretations of equity, efficiency, accountability, and, ultimately, 'public value' are fundamental to the work that public managers do.

However, judgements about what these terms mean in practice are not only subjective but also strongly directed by political ideology and trends in fiscal policy in ways more openly apparent in 2019 than in 2006. For instance, the trend towards conditionality with respect to welfare payments within the wider context of reduced public spending and the political contestation this has provoked is indicative of the difficulty in arriving at a shared conception of 'public value'. A further (and highly tragic) example might be how the actors (local residents, local council officials, the tenant management organisation, architects, and private building contractors) involved in the networks and partnerships related to the upkeep of the Grenfell House tower block in London demonstrated very different interests and understandings around 'public value' (see also Robert's Pyper's discussion of Grenfell in Chap. 2 of this volume).

The idea of what public value means then is highly ambiguous (Rhodes et al. 2008) and is open to critique from different standpoints. Furthermore, in our view, the case for public value management is yet to be empirically made. Stoker's propositions suggest that politically speaking, we all are on the same side, in the sense that there is no broad disagreement about aims, merely the specific paths we take to reach them. To us, this seems both aspirational and potentially naïve for the reasons outlined above. However, having outlined our reservations about the PVM paradigm, the propositions put forward by Stoker appear to have a degree of real-world currency and to have reified ongoing discourse in public management, and can thus be treated as social facts. Thus, cognisant of the critiques of Stoker's position, we can still use Stoker's four propositions to examine the contemporary cultures of public management and how these interact with evidence generation, use, and evaluation. Our contention is that each of Stoker's propositions implies corresponding evidence needs, which in turn require a mobilisation of research and knowledge infrastructures (see Table 5.2) and harnessing of local information and data. Whether consciously or not, public sector leaders may be seen to be aligning themselves with these precepts, and knowledge producers are responding in particular ways. Below, we set out these changes and responses, which we discuss in the context of historic evidence use discourses.

First, Stoker argues that *public interventions are defined by the search for public value*. Whilst such ideas are political and subject to contestation as already discussed, we take this to mean that public sector organisations are

Table 5.2 Four PVM propositions and their implications for evidence use:

PVM propositions (adapted from Stoker 2006: 47–49)	Implication for evidence use	Policy examples
1. Public interventions are defined by the search for public value	Impact of evidence/research/knowledge must be demonstrated Embedded assumptions of Value for money (VfM) discourse, attribution, quantitative methods	Universities—REF, counter—'biomedical bubble' (Jones and Wilsdon 2018) Health—outcomes focus
2. There is a need to give more recognition to the legitimacy of a wide range of stakeholders	Co-production/co-creation of evidence Negotiating power imbalances between different actors' epistemologies?	Discursive importance and spread of PPI, consultations, etc.
3. Collaborative commissioning for public service ethos	Role of evidence in framing questions and debates, raising issues, enabling scrutiny—but power dynamics obscured Pluralistic.	Big Society and social entrepreneurship, cooperative delivery models
4. An adaptable and learning-based approach to the challenge of public service delivery is required	Double-feedback loops (local data and reflective practice)	Health—patient-reported outcome measures to foster better local responses—in theory, better, localised actions

motivated to seek out programmes and strategies which lead to identifiable changes in population outcomes in line with strategic aims, and that there is a need to demonstrate these changes evidentially. This implies that evaluations of ongoing and new programmes and interventions are carried out in order to enable learning and to establish that desired outcomes are being met. We note the normative assumptions which underpin this use of evidence—about 'best value', such that it is clear to all what is best, that this is a shared view, and that that the desired outcomes of the interventions are equally obvious and shared. One can trace responses to this policy paradigm amongst the university infrastructures and the discourse about evidence use at a more granular level (see Box 5.1).

Taken together, this implies a valuing of research knowledge for what it can do in society. It conceptualises research as a means to an end, rather than as a useful or meaningful activity in its own right. This 'impact

Box 5.1 The search for public value: the example of higher education
Public value has been used as a justification for increased monitoring and centralised funding of research and education. In the UK university sector, this can be seen in the development of the first Research Assessment Exercise in 1986. This exercise essentially required universities to report on the extent and quality of their research through a peer-review process, with central government funding decisions (so-called quality-related funding) being based on the outcomes of these reviews. Over successive iterations (1989, 1992, 1996, 2001, and the Research Excellence Framework which followed in 2008, 2014, 2021), the amount of reporting required of universities grew. The 2014 Research Excellence Framework included for the first time a significant portion of funding awarded for research impact; that is, case studies submitted by universities in which their research was shown to have had an impact on policy and practice. In the forthcoming 2021 REF, this proportion looks likely to increase, and Universities UK have announced a new assessment framework, the Knowledge Exchange Framework, which will specifically examine how well universities translate their research into 'real-world' change: 'Impact' (Reed and Evely 2016; Holliman and Warren 2017).

In the wider higher education sector, the UK government created a number of arms-length bodies designed to monitor and guide the teaching and research activities: the Office for Students and the introduction of the Teaching Excellence Framework (TEF), and, in the near future, the Knowledge Exchange Framework (KEF). These initiatives aim to collect data about university activity and performance, although there are significant concerns about how well they are able to capture meaningful data. For example, the TEF relies heavily on student evaluations, which are known to be heavily biased against female lecturers, and does not include any assessment of teaching management (e.g. regularity of syllabus update) or administrative support. However, they are likely to continue, with the stated objective of improving the value for money offered by the higher education sector.

agenda' creates pressure on universities and research funders to show public benefits for public spend, and the increased managerialism within universities enabled leaders to institute organisational changes to how academics were performance managed against grant income and output metrics. Practices of research have themselves adapted to this public value narrative, particularly in the health sector. The rapid growth of theory and methods for improvement and implementation of science has focused the attention of researchers on demonstrating changes to outcomes and to attributing societal changes to particular interventions, usually using quantitative methods to do so. In health, as well as other sectors including probation, active labour market, and youth engagement policies, the UK government has pioneered experimentation in outcomes-based contracts including high-profile social impact bond projects (Disley et al. 2015; Fraser et al. 2019). An interest in the scaling-up of evidence-based interventions with well-funded evaluations to test attribution in the pursuit of long-term social outcomes was deemed central to such approaches (at least in the early years). However, contestation around 'public values' amongst different actors and perceptions of conflicts of interest attest to the difficulty of achieving these goals (Fraser et al. 2018, 2019). The epistemological challenges of evaluating outcomes-based payment programmes are also notable (Fox and Morris 2019).

Second, Stoker's call to *recognise the legitimacy of stakeholders* in public decision-making has an obvious corollary in the growth of interest in co-production (Durose et al. 2013). Co-production, as conceptualised by Ostrom (and discussed in Chap. 1), refers to the development of responsive, personalised public services through 'the joint working of people who are not in the same organisation to produce goods or services' (Ostrom 1996; Iedema and Carroll 2011; Durose et al. 2017).

Box 5.2 Recognising the legitimacy of stakeholders: the example of public and patient involvement

Although there has been significant interest in involving the public in research processes for some years, it is only recently that researchers have been significantly incentivised to 'engage' with different stakeholders, with some funders having this as a routine prerequisite. For most health funders, this takes the form of public and patient

(continued)

Box 5.2 (continued)

involvement (PPI), where 'lay' participants are invited to participate as advisors, or co-researchers, in research projects, with the aim of making research more useful and applicable to patient experience (Duncan and Oliver 2017). This movement aligns with similar drives to involve service users in their design and delivery (Elinor Ostrom's 'coproduction') and the recognition of 'lay' expertise in shaping public discourse (Wynne 1992).

In health, PPI has been institutionalised by funders such as the National Institute for Health Research (NIHR). For every grant application, regardless of topic, applicants must explain how patients will be involved in the research. For some, this has led to the important task of public engagement with research, and wider discussion about impact outside the academy, becoming tokenistic (Oliver et al. 2019). However, the broad consensus is that learning how to work meaningfully with potential audiences for research, and those implicated in research on interventions and policies, is the most democratic and ethical way to do research (Frickel, Albert & Prainsack 2016).

This implied a recognition of the rights to participate in decision-making, and these principles can also apply to knowledge production—indeed, joint knowledge production may be a way of achieving public participation in service design and delivery (Filipe et al. 2017). Collaborative research practices, which can include co-design, co-creation, stakeholder and public engagement, participation/involvement, and integrated knowledge translation are now widespread (Fransman 2018). The shift to co-production tallies with calls across academic disciplines to make knowledge production more accountable, transparent, and 'democratic' by including a broader range of stakeholders (Fransman 2018). Recent investigations into the value of interdisciplinary research have led to calls for joint inquiry (Prainsack 2018) and public-led innovation (Mazzucato 2011; Mazzucato and Robinson 2018) to generate public 'equity' (Ooms et al. 2014), all of which would require great attention paid to the ethics, values, and methods required to democratise knowledge for public policy. Yet, to address needs identified by a wide range of stakeholders, researchers would have to fundamentally adapt their practices; research funding streams would have to radically alter from slow, proposal-led funding towards core support for researchers enabling long-term partnership working; and performance management and career incentives for academics and universities would have to adapt (Oliver et al. 2019). This type of radical shift is, as yet, not on the foreseeable future for the higher education sector. There remain significant questions about how public universities should act (Stirling 2010; Morgan 2017; Wilkinson 2017), and how to best 'democratise' knowledge so that the possibility of publicly focused policy and practice becomes a reality (Oliver and Duncan 2018). Similarly, healthcare practitioners and other public managers would have to have capacity and capability to engage in deliberations about evidence with different partners, to be genuinely open to policy change, to be able to implement far-reaching organisational changes, and to be able to continually reflect and learn.

Third, Stoker's call for an 'open-minded, relationship approach to the procurement of services framed by a commitment to a public service ethos' (Stoker 2006: 48) implies, in our view, a practical recommendation to commission services on the basis of collaborative discussions. This proposition is rather ambiguous, but suggests moving away from strictly contract-led service provision towards a more negotiated relationship, where local stakeholders work in tandem with commissioners to determine need and make provision accordingly. Such an approach requires reconsiderations around the legal requirements and governance traditions through which local health (and other) services are put out to tender and ultimately agreed. Encouraging commissioners to be more collaborative may place stress on existing relationships and lead to dilemmas (Fraser et al. 2019).

> **Box 5.3 Collaborative commissioning**
> The Government Outcomes (GO) Lab at Oxford University was set up as a centre for both academic research and practical guidance for outcomes-based commissioning of services in 2016. The GO Lab promotes collaborative commissioning approaches whereby multiple agencies (e.g. Local Authorities, Clinical Commissioning Groups, third sector and private sector organisations) come together in order to tackle 'wicked issues' which they define as 'social problems for

(continued)

Box 5.3 (continued)

which there are no clear links between cause and effect—like homelessness, chronic unemployment or educational achievement' (Blundell et al. 2019). These approaches often draw on ideas of social entrepreneurship and sometimes cooperative models of delivery. Qualitative comparative work of collaborative commissioning across a selection of UK Local Authority areas led by the GO Lab developed a typology of collaborations:

- **Collaborative Councils**: Broad programme of change where collaboration is a mechanism for the local authority to reform their own way of working and the way other local public agencies work
- **Collaborative Markets**: Aim to transition the relationships between local social sector delivery organisations from competitive to collaborative ones in part using alternative service contracts, procurement, and contract management practices
- **Agents of Change**: External to the frontline teams and organisations whose practice they are trying to meaningfully shift, but responsibility to improve the public sector is co-owned
- **System Connectors**: Enable integration of the public and voluntary sectors to improve health and social outcomes by leveraging existing assets without fundamentally uprooting existing relationships and structures. (Blundell et al. 2019: 8)

Whilst the authors of the report identify some encouraging developments such as increasing trust amongst local actors from different organisations and evidence of a desire to more directly engage local communities in the design and delivery of services through efforts at collaborative commissioning, they also identified resistance to such new ways of working and difficulties in embedding collaborative practices within existing bureaucratic decision-making processes. Crucially too, whilst participants expressed the belief that collaborative commissioning *could* result in reduced costs and improved impact, the evidence to back this up was limited, and the authors call for further rigorous independent evaluation in this space (Blundell et al. 2019: 25).

This proposal has several implications. It suggests that stakeholder's preferences and view would frame and constitute the evidence base in order to surface the political and personal interests at play. It suggests an evidence base which draws on multiple sources and methods, including the historical and local service context and budgetary and governance constraints. All of these types of evidence would need to be valued and weighed alongside more traditional research and experimental evidence about the effectiveness of new interventions.

From a more critical perspective, we can see that evidence of different kinds here plays a role in framing questions and encouraging debate, as well as enabling scrutiny. However, with the requirement to be 'open-minded', it is likely that it becomes impossible to address the challenge of determining which types of evidence are most credible and useful for different purposes. If all problems are (said to be) solved through deliberation and discussion, the most powerful interests may dominate the understanding of these, leading to a replication of existing power dynamics (Fraser et al. 2018; Lowe-Walker 2018).

Finally, Stoker calls for 'adaptable and learning-based approach[es]' (see Box 5.4), which is echoed by the recent rise in participatory and particularly action research methods employed to evaluate public services and policies (Rycroft-Malone et al. 2015; Holmes et al. 2017). Complex systems analyses tell us that as public services adapt and evolve through double-feedback loops, research practices have also incorporated process-driven methods which enable evaluators and implementers to grapple with real-time localised actions, and to adapt and improve (Fletcher et al. 2016). The abilities of public (and increasingly third) sector providers and their commissioning partners to design systems for the collection of robust data, and capacities to use these become more important (Boaz et al. 2019).

Taken together, these propositions allow us to see the responses made by evidence providers, with a focus on evaluation, mixed methods, and inclusive and adaptive research designs. We can also trace responses at the higher education policy environment. The REF and associated polices have incentivised researchers to focus on projects with 'real-world' impact, and have emphasised a discourse of public-facing research. Stoker's propositions prescribe a set of public management values, the echoes of which can be seen in the responses made by knowledge producers. Yet, these responses are limited by current structural and governance arrangements surrounding knowledge production. PVM implies multiple processes occurring simultaneously and a shift away from simplistic ideas about markets that may distort and mitigate against collaboration towards more open systems and engagement with a more diverse approach to evidence. These cultural discourses combine to create a number of effects across the public and higher education and health sectors and create conflicting rules which determine how evidence is sought and valued. In order to produce accessible, locally relevant, adaptive, and robust evidence, there are significant changes that need to be made. Firstly, the research system, from a policy level to the micro-interactions of data interpretation, needs to radically shift to incorporate a much broader range of knowledge types. The entire venture of identifying and answering questions will need to be reconfigured if all interests and beliefs are to be represented in the generation for an evidence base. This would have enormous ramifications for how we train our scholars, how research is assessed and evaluated, and the institutional practices and environments which enable research to be done.

> **Box 5.4 Adaptable learning**
> One approach to adaptable and setting-based learning which has become popular particularly within healthcare is the use of 'embedded researchers'. There are variations, but in general an embedded researcher is one who works inside a host organisation (a hospital or primary care practice, for example), not as a member of staff, while remaining affiliated with a host research / academic institution (McGinity and Salokangas 2014). Their role goes beyond that of a traditional 'knowledge broker' who might attempt to act as a boundary spanner, bringing research and academic expertise into a new setting. Rather, these researchers act collaboratively with local partners to conduct research together 'to identify, design, and conduct research studies and share findings which respond to the need of the organisation; and accord with the organisations' unique context and culture' (Vindrola-Padros *et al.* 2017: 70).
>
> The concept of the embedded researcher therefore quite directly addresses the call for adaptable and learning-placed approaches, emphasising:
>
> - Developing trusting and meaningful relationships with local staff.
> - Becoming an 'insider' to the organisation, to meet challenges and share goals and interests.
>
> *(continued)*

> **Box 5.4 (continued)**
>
> - Generating locally relevant knowledge *with* local staff, enabling organisations to respond to highly relevant evidence to improve their own performance.
> - Facilitating greater local research capacity, and enabling critical reflection by both the embedded researcher and the local team.
>
> This last is seen as an integral part of 'embeddedness' and describes the mechanism by which locally produced learning could be shared, owned, and acted on in an adaptive manner. Indeed, the tension between becoming an insider (and losing critical perspective) and the need to maintain distance to enable this critical reflection is regarded as a key challenge for embedded research (Segalowitz and Brereton 2010; Vindrola-Padros *et al.* 2017).

Conclusions: New Evidence for Evidence-Based Policy

Evidence needs are influenced by public management and policy paradigms, and vice versa. Each paradigm implies different evidence needs, which may influence everything from research funding to the day-to-day practices of research. Epistemologically speaking, the values and assumptions underpinning these paradigms also influence what kinds of evidence are valued. Traditional public administration saw evidence as a way of producing technology and wealth for the state. Over the decades, this evolved into a desire to monitor and manage evidence production, alongside trends towards greater surveillance of public services.

New public management and evidence-based policy became mutually symbiotic. Both require investment in data collection and performance management of various kinds; both favour a positivist, data-led approach to decision-making. Political support for EBP grew throughout the late 1990s and through the New Labour administrations as a way of depoliticising potentially contentious topics. However, the approaches taken to generate evidence within this narrow framing became process-led. The 'What Works' narrative, while helpful to New Labour from a political perspective, implied a very narrow set of evidence needs—predominately gathered via quantitative and trial-based approaches. These approaches implied normative assumptions about what types of evidence are most valued, and who can and should participate in knowledge production or decision-making processes (Greenhalgh 1999). This has led to a narrowing of the debates about values in both evidence and policy production, as the EBP/PVM processes both make assumptions about which values should drive them. Austerity, managerialism, hierarchies, and networked governance bring their own values and assumptions. However, the rhetoric of EBP does not admit to these pressures and generates numerous assumptions around the research and policy processes. In both the EBP/PVM discourses, there is a naivety about the motivations of stakeholders and the feasibility and appropriateness of techniques used to further the generation and use of evidence. Interestingly, both discourses seem to have arrived at a similar place. That is, in order to *produce* the most useful evidence, stakeholders should collaborate and deliberate, and to *use* it, public managers should hold inclusive discussions and collaborate on service delivery. Yet, this solution fails to engage with the reality of public management and policy, in the sense that it is a conflicted and disputed space (Mouffe 2000). The assumption that simply bringing the relevant parties together to discuss the meaning of evidence ignores existing power dynamics, assumes that the values and meanings we attach to evidence are shared, and that all have the same political priorities. None of these assumptions are evidence-based themselves (Oliver and Boaz 2019).

Public value management, like the successor to EBP (evidence-informed policy-making), can be read as a reaction to the positivist straightjacketing of NPM and EBP. Both recognise the importance of plurality (both in epistemology and participation), and thus are moving in the right direction. However, we believe that both discourses are ultimately still hamstrung by political imperatives and power imbalances between actors. Public value management may imply a radically different attitude to evidence production and use, which would take account of many of the tensions described above. A focus on relationships within the system is helpful, but the residual rhetoric of NPM may complicate the picture, as will existing professional hierarchies and dominance. A truly responsive evidence base would certainly require radical overhaul of research institutions, training, and assessment, as well as capability and capacity within public organisations.

Commentary on EBP and research into evidence use (e.g. implementation science) has often failed to take account of this broader political agenda and to understand the policy and management processes which they are attempting to influence and the multiple and potentially conflicting regimes of governance in which these occur (Newman 2001; Jones 2017). Interventions and strategies are proposed and designed which rely on the linear model of knowledge use (Oliver et al. 2014) and often do not reflect the complexity of the policy or practice environment (Boaz et al. 2011; Head and Alford 2015). Even today, we find frequent references to the 'policy cycle' which has long been debunked by policy scholars as a useful, yet misleading, heuristic. This matters, because we know that the policy process influences which types of evidence are considered valuable and credible, and policy environments and cultures inform which types of evidence are generated and used (Nutley 2010; Nutley et al. 2013; Cairney and Oliver 2017). There are potential future opportunities for wider and deeper research and policy relationships due to the destabilising effects of the COVID-19 pandemic, but this remains to be seen (Tseng 2020).

It is clear that there are significant pressures on knowledge users and producers, which are brought to bear through the dominance of narratives like the 'evidence-based' and 'public value management' discourses. It is also clear that there are immensely complicated normative and practical issues to explore surrounding how evidence is produced, why, and what for. Yet, we still do not know what kinds of evidence are most valued or why, in different contexts, including when enough evidence is enough, and how to encourage policy makers towards change. There are also questions about the roles and responsibilities of different actors in using evidence to advocate, or advocating for the evidence, and the pros and cons of different approaches as well as how to mobilise evidence for change. We urgently need more empirical evidence about who gets to participate in knowledge production, the roles of power and different forms of knowledge, how credibility and legitimacy are framed and negotiated in different public and policy contexts, and how to best investigate these processes to deliver meaningful public value.

References

Argyris, C., & Schön, D. A. (1997). Organizational learning: A theory of action perspective. *Reis*, (77/78), 345–348.

Aurum. (1971). Letter From London : Science Policy and the Question of Relevancy. *Bulletin of the Atomic Scientists, 27*(6), 25–26. https://doi.org/1 0.1080/00963402.1971.11455376.

Bevan, G., & Hood, C. (2006). What's measured is what matters: targets and gaming in the English public health care system. *Public administration*, *84*(3), 517–538.

Bevir, M. (2011). Governance and Governmentality After Neoliberalism. *Policy & Politics*, *39*(4), 457–471. https://doi.org/10.1332/030557310X550141.

Bevir, M. (2013). *A Theory of Governance, Berkeley Planning Journal.* https://doi.org/10.5811/westjem.2011.5.6700.

Boaz, A., & Davies, H. (Eds.). (2019). *What works now?: evidence-informed policy and practice.* Policy Press.

Blundell, J., Rosenbach, F., Hameed, T., & FitzGerald, C. (2019). *Are We Rallying Together? Collaboration and Public Sector Reform*, Government Outcomes Lab, University of Oxford, Blavatnik School of Government.

Black, N., & Donald, A. (2001). Evidence Based Policy: Proceed with Care. *BMJ (Clinical research ed.).* https://doi.org/10.1136/bmj.323.7307.275.

Blond, P. (2010). *Red Tory: How the Left and Right Have Broken Britain and How We Can Fix It.* London: Faber and Faber.

Boaz, A., Ashby, D., & Young, K. (2002). *Systematic Reviews: What Have They Got to Offer Evidence Based Policy and Practice?* Retrieved February 14, 2019, from https://www.kcl.ac.uk/sspp/departments/politicaleconomy/research/cep/pubs/papers/assets/wp2.pdf.

Boaz, A., Baeza, J., & Fraser, A. (2011). Effective Implementation of Research into Practice: An Overview of Systematic Reviews of the Health Literature. *BMC Research Notes.* https://doi.org/10.1186/1756-0500-4-212.

Cairney, P., & Oliver, K. (2017). Evidence-based Policymaking Is Not Like Evidence-based Medicine, So How Far Should You Go to Bridge the Divide Between Evidence and Policy? *Health Research Policy and Systems*, *15*(1). https://doi.org/10.1186/s12961-017-0192-x.

Cape, W. H. (1969). Scientific and Technological Advice to State and Local Governments. *The American Review of Public Administration*, *3*(2), 170–171. https://doi.org/10.1177/027507406900300225.

Cochrane, A. L. (1972). Effectiveness and Efficiency: Random Reflections on Health Services. *BMJ.* https://doi.org/10.1136/bmj.328.7438.529.

Collins, H. M., & Evans, R. (2002). The Third Wave of Science Studies. *Social Studies of Science*, *32*(2), 235–296. https://doi.org/10.1177/0306312702032002003.

Cooksey, D. (2006). *A Review of UK Health Research Funding.* Retrieved January 29, 2019, from https://assets.publishing.service.gov.uk/government/uploads/system/uploads/attachment_data/file/228984/0118404881.pdf.

Davies, H. T., & Nutley, S. M. (Eds.). (2000). *What works?: Evidence-based policy and practice in public services.* Policy Press.

Disley, E., Giacomantonio, C., Kruithof, K., & Sim, M. (2015). *The Payment by Results Social Impact Bond Pilot at HMP Peterborough: Final Process Evaluation Report.* RAND.

Duncan, S., & Oliver, S. (2017). Editorial: Motivations for Engagement. *Research for All, 1*(2), 229–233. https://doi.org/10.18546/RFA.01.2.01.

Dunleavy, P. *et al.* (2006). New Public Management Is Dead—Long Live Digital-era Governance. *Journal of Public Administration Research and Theory.* https://doi.org/10.1093/jopart/mui057.

Dunleavy, P., & Margetts, H. (2010). The Second Wave of Digital Era Governance. Retrieved February 11, 2019, from https://papers.ssrn.com/sol3/papers.cfm?abstract_id=1643850.

Durose, C. *et al.* (2013). Transforming Local Public Services through Co-production. In *Arts and Humanities Research Council*, pp. 1–38. http://www.birmingham.ac.uk/Documents/college-social-sciences/government-society/inlogov/briefing-papers/transforming-local-public-services-co-production.pdf.

Durose, C. *et al.* (2017). Generating "Good Enough" Evidence for Co-production. *Evidence and Policy*, pp. 135–151. https://doi.org/10.1332/174426415X14440619792955.

Etzioni, A. (1995). *New Communitarian Thinking : Persons, Virtues, Institutions, and Communities.* Virginia: University Press of Virginia.

Exworthy, M., Powell, M., & Mohan, J. (1999). The NHS: Quasi-market, Quasi-hierarchy and Quasi-network? *Public Money and Management, 19*(4), 15–22. https://doi.org/10.1111/1467-9302.00184.

Ferlie, E. (2019). *The Politics of Management Knowledge in Times of Austerity.* Retrieved February 14, 2019, from https://books.google.co.uk/books?hl=en&lr=&id=Ok5yDwAAQBAJ&oi=fnd&pg=PP1&dq=info:XZBJCDoqIowJ:scholar.google.com&ots=Vg1eZHL9e_&sig=fS2Bf8w7VtyDKfZ3InQWq-npbuk&redir_esc=y#v=onepage&q&f=false.

Ferlie, E., & Pettigrew, A. (1996). Managing Through Networks: Some Issues and Implications for the NHS. *British Journal of Management.* https://doi.org/10.1111/j.1467-8551.1996.tb00149.x.

Filipe, A., Renedo, A., & Marston, C. (2017). The Co-production of What? Knowledge, Values, and Social Relations in Health Care. *PLoS Biology.* Edited by C. Marris. Public Library of Science, *15*(5), e2001403. https://doi.org/10.1371/journal.pbio.2001403.

Fletcher, A., et al. (2016). Realist Complex Intervention Science: Applying Realist Principles Across All Phases of the Medical Research Council Framework for Developing and Evaluating Complex Interventions. *Evaluation.* SAGE PublicationsSage UK: London, England, *22*(3), 286–303. https://doi.org/10.1177/1356389016652743.

Flinders, M., & Wood, M. (2014). Depoliticisation, Governance and the State, *Policy and Politics.* https://doi.org/10.1332/030557312X655873.

Fox, C., & Morris, S. (2019). Evaluating Outcome-based Payment Programmes: Challenges for Evidence-based Policy. *Journal of Economic Policy Reform, 2*, 1–17.

Fraser, A., Tan, S., Lagarde, M., & Mays, N. (2018). Narratives of promise, narratives of caution: A review of the literature on Social Impact Bonds. *Social policy & administration, 52*(1), 4–28.

Fraser, A. Stewart, E., & Jones, L. (2019). Editorial: The Importance of Sociological Approaches to the Study of Service Change in Healthcare. *Sociology of Health & Illness.*

Fransman, J. (2018). Charting a Course to an Emerging Field of "Research Engagement Studies" : A Conceptual Meta-synthesis. *Research for All, 2*(2), pp. 1–49. Retrieved August 6, 2018, from http://www.ingentaconnect.com/contentone/ioep/rfa/2018/00000002/00000002/art00002#.

Freidson, E. (1970). *Professional Dominance. The Social Structure of Medical Care, Profession of Medicine: A Study on the Sociology of Applied Knowledge.* https://doi.org/10.1016/S1474-7065(03)00104-9.

Frickel, S., Albert, M., & Prainsack, B. (2016). Introduction: investigating interdisciplinarities.in Investigating interdisciplinary collaboration. *Theory and Practice Across Disciplines,* 5–24.

Gabbay, J., & le May, A. (2004). Evidence Based Guidelines or Collectively Constructed "Mindlines?" Ethnographic Study of Knowledge Management in Primary Care, *BMJ.* https://doi.org/10.1136/bmj.329.7473.1013.

Gough, D., Maidment, C., & Sharples, J. (2018). *UK What Works Centres: Aims, methods and contexts.* London. Retrieved February 27, 2019, from https://eppi.ioe.ac.uk/cms/Default.aspx?tabid=3731.

Le Grand, J. (1997). Knights, Knaves or Pawns? Human Behaviour and Social Policy, *Journal of Social Policy.* https://doi.org/10.1017/S0047279 497004984.

Le Grand, J. (2003). Motivation, agency, and public policy: of knights and knaves, pawns and queens. Oxford University Press on Demand.

Lowe-Walker, R. E. (2018). *Intercultural deliberation and the politics of minority rights.* Harvard: UBC Press.

Greenhalgh, T. (1999). Narrative Based Medicine: Narrative Based Medicine in an Evidence Based World, *BMJ.* https://doi.org/10.1136/bmj.318.7179.323.

Harrison, S. (1994). Knowledge into Practice: What's the Problem? *Journal of Management in Medicine, 8*(2), 9–16. https://doi.org/10.1108/02689 239410059589.

Harrison, S., & Lim, J. N. W. (2003). The Frontier of Control: Doctors and Managers in the NHS 1966 to 1997, *Clinical Governance: An International Journal.* https://doi.org/10.1108/14777270310459922.

Hartley, S., Pearce, W., & Taylor, A. (2017). Against the Tide of Depoliticisation: The Politics of Research Governance. *Policy & Politics, 45*(3), 361–377. https://doi.org/10.1332/030557316X14681503832036.

Head, B. W., & Alford, J. (2015). Wicked Problems. *Administration & Society.* SAGE PublicationsSage CA: Los Angeles, CA, *47*(6), 711–739. https://doi.org/10.1177/0095399713481601.

Holliman, R., & Warren, C. J. (2017). Supporting Future Scholars of Engaged Research, *Research for All*. https://doi.org/10.18546/rfa.01.1.14.

Holmes, B. J., et al. (2017). Mobilising Knowledge in Complex Health Systems: A Call to Action. *Evidence & Policy: A Journal of Research, Debate and Practice*, *13*(3), 539–560. https://doi.org/10.1332/174426416X14712553750311.

Hood, C. (1991). A Public Management for All Seasons? *Public Administration*, *69*(1), 3–19. https://doi.org/10.1111/j.1467-9299.1991.tb00779.x.

Iedema, R., & Carroll, K. (2011). The "Clinalyst". *Journal of Organizational Change Management*. Edited by O. Eikeland. Emerald Group Publishing Limited, *24*(2), 175–190. https://doi.org/10.1108/09534811111119753.

Jasanoff, S., & Polsby, N. W. (1991). The Fifth Branch: Science Advisers as Policymakers. *Contemporary Sociology*, *20*(5), 727. https://doi.org/10.2307/2072218.

Jones, L. (2017). Sedimented Governance in the English National Health Service, In *Decentring Health Policy: Learning from British Experiences in Healthcare Governance*. https://doi.org/10.4324/9781315310817.

Jones, R., & Wilsdon, J. R. (2018). *The Biomedical Bubble: Why UK research and innovation needs a greater diversity of priorities, politics, places and people. Report*. Nesta, London.

Jones, L., Fraser, A., & Stewart, E. (2019). Exploring the Neglected and Hidden Dimensions of Large-scale Healthcare Change. *Sociology of Health & Illness*

Killian, J. R. (1959). Science and Public Policy: Recent Actions by the Federal Government in Helping Science and Technology Help the Nation Are Surveyed. *Science*, *129*(3342), 129–136. https://doi.org/10.1126/science.129.3342.129.

Latour, B., & Woolgar, S. (2013). *Laboratory Life: The Construction of Scientific Facts, 1986*. https://doi.org/10.1017/CBO9781107415324.004.

Lavis, J. N., et al. (2003). How Can Research Organizations More Effectively Transfer Research Knowledge to Decision Makers? *Milbank Quarterly*, *81*(2), 221–248. https://doi.org/10.1111/1468-0009.t01-1-00052.

Marmot, M. G. (2004). Evidence Based Policy or Policy Based Evidence? *BMJ*. https://doi.org/10.1136/bmj.328.7445.906.

Mazzucato, M. (2011). The Entrepreneurial State. *Soundings*. https://doi.org/10.3898/136266211798411183.

Mazzucato, M., & Robinson, D. K. R. (2018). Co-creating and Directing Innovation Ecosystems? NASA's Changing Approach to Public-private Partnerships in Low-earth Orbit. *Technological Forecasting and Social Change*. https://doi.org/10.1016/j.techfore.2017.03.034.

McGinity, R., & Salokangas, M. (2014). Introduction: "Embedded Research" as an Approach into Academia for Emerging Researchers. *Management in Education*. https://doi.org/10.1177/0892020613508863.

Merton, R. K., Cole, J. R., & Simon, G. A. (1968). The Matthew Effect in Science: The Reward and Communication Systems of Science Are Considered. *Science.* American Association for the Advancement of Science, *159*(3810), 56–63. https://doi.org/10.1126/science.159.3810.56.

Morgan, G. (2017). Science and Technology Advice to Government. In *Theory and Practice in Policy Analysis* (pp. 521–566). Cambridge: Cambridge University Press. https://doi.org/10.1017/9781316882665.020.

Mouffe, C. (2000). Deliberative Democracy or Agonistic Pluralism? *Social Research.* https://doi.org/10.2307/40971349.

Nesta. (n.d.). *The Alliance for Useful Evidence.* Retrieved February 14, 2019, from https://www.alliance4usefulevidence.org/.

Newman, J. (2001). *Modernizing Governance: New Labour, Policy and Society. Sage Publications Ltd.* https://doi.org/10.4135/9781446220511.

NIHR. (2009). NIHR Collaborations for Leadership in Applied Health research and Care (CLAHRCs): Implementation Plan 5.8. Retrieved February 14, 2019, from https://www.nihr.ac.uk/about-us/how-we-are-managed/our-structure/infrastructure/collaborations-for-leadership-in-applied-health-research-and-care.htm.

Nutbeam, D. (2004). Getting Evidence into Policy and Practice to Address Health Inequalities. *Health Promotion International.* https://doi.org/10.1093/heapro/dah201.

Nutley, S. (2010). Debate: Are We All Co-producers of Research Now? *Public Money & Management, 30*(5), 263–265. https://doi.org/10.1080/09540962.2010.509170.

Nutley, S., Powell, A., & Davies, H. (2013). What Counts as Good Evidence? *Provocation Paper for the Alliance for Useful Evidence.* https://doi.org/10.1002/trtr.1318.

Oliver, K., & Boaz, A. (2019). Transforming Evidence for Policy and Practice: Creating Space for New Conversations. *Palgrave Communications, 5*(1), 1.

Oliver, K., & Cairney, P. (2019). The Dos and Don'ts of Influencing Policy: A Systematic Review of the Advice Literature, *Palgrave Communications.*

Oliver, K., & Faul, M. V. (2018). Networks and Network Analysis in Evidence, Policy and Practice. *Evidence and Policy, 14*(3), 369–379. https://doi.org/10.1332/174426418X15314037224597.

Oliver, K., Kothari, A., & Mays, N. (2019). The Dark Side of Coproduction: Do the Costs Outweigh the Benefits for Health Research? *Health Research Policy and Systems.*

Oliver, K., Lorenc, T., & Innvær, S. (2014). New Directions in Evidence-based Policy Research: A Critical Analysis of the Literature. *Health Research Policy and Systems, 12*(1), –34. https://doi.org/10.1186/1478-4505-12-34.

Oliver, S., & Duncan, S. (2018). Editorial: The Challenges of Sharing Different Ways of Knowing. *Research for All, 2*(1), 1–5. https://doi.org/10.18546/RFA.02.1.01.

Ooms, G. *et al*. (2014). Is Universal Health Coverage the Practical Expression of the Right to Health Care?, *BMC International Health and Human Rights*. https://doi.org/10.1186/1472-698X-14-3.

Osborne, D., & Gaebler, T. (1992) *Reinventing Government: How the Entrepreneurial Spirit Is Transforming Government, Reading Mass. Adison Wesley*. https://doi.org/10.4018/978-1-4666-4852-4.ch003.

Osborne, S. P. (2006). The New Public Governance? *Public Management Review*. Routledge, *8*(3), 377–387. https://doi.org/10.1080/14719030600853022.

Ostrom, E. (1996). Crossing the Great Divide: Coproduction, Synergy, and Development. *World Development, 24*(6), 1073–1087. https://doi.org/10.1016/0305-750X(96)00023-X.

Perkin, H. (2007). History of Universities. In *International Handbook of Higher Education* (pp. 159–205). Dordrecht: Springer Netherlands. https://doi.org/10.1007/978-1-4020-4012-2_10.

Petticrew, M., & Roberts, H. (2003). Evidence, Hierarchies, and Typologies: Horses for Courses, *Journal of Epidemiology and Community Health*. https://doi.org/10.1136/jech.57.7.527.

Pollit, C., et al. (1991). General Management in the Nhs: The Initial Impact 1983–88. *Public Administration, 69*(1), 61–83. https://doi.org/10.1111/j.1467-9299.1991.tb00782.x.

Power, M. (1999). *The Audit Society: Rituals of Verification*. Oxford: Oxford University Press. https://doi.org/10.1177/135638909800400408.

Prainsack, B. (2018). The "We" in the "Me": Solidarity and Health Care in the Era of Personalized Medicine. *Science Technology and Human Values, 43*(1), 21–44. https://doi.org/10.1177/0162243917736139.

Reed, M., & Evely, A. (2016). How Can Your Research Have More Impact? Five Key Principles and Practical Tips for Effective Knowledge Exchange, *LSE Impact blog*, pp. 1–5. Retrieved July 10, 2018, from http://blogs.lse.ac.uk/impactofsocialsciences/2015/07/07/how-can-your-research-have-more-impact-5-key-principles-tips/.

Rhodes, R. A. W. (2003). *Understanding Govenance: Policy Networks, Governance, Reflexivity and Accountability*. Buckingham: Open University Press. https://doi.org/10.1111/1467-9299.00107.

Rhodes, R. A. W. (2007). Understanding Governance: Ten Years On, *Organization Studies*. https://doi.org/10.1177/0170840607076586.

Rhodes, R. A., Wanna, J., & Weller, P. (2008). Reinventing Westminster: how public executives reframe their world. *Policy & Politics, 36*(4), 461–479.

Rycroft-Malone, J., et al. (2015). Collective Action for Knowledge Mobilisation: A Realist Evaluation of the Collaborations for Leadership in Applied Health Research and Care. *Health Services Delivery Research, 3*(44), 2.

Sapolsky, H. M. (1968). Science Advice for State and Local Government. *Science, 160*(3825), 280–284. https://doi.org/10.1126/science.160.3825.280.
Science. (2018). *Congress Apporove Largest U.S. Research Spending Increase in a Decade, Science.* https://doi.org/10.1126/science.aat6620.
Segalowitz, M., & Brereton, M. (2010). An Examination of the Knowledge Barriers in Participatory Design and the Prospects for Embedded Research. https://doi.org/10.1145/1738826.1738890.
Sheaff, R., et al. (2016). A Qualitative Study of Diverse Providers' Behaviour in Response to Commissioners, Patients and Innovators in England: Research Protocol: Table 1. *BMJ Open, 6*(5), e010680. https://doi.org/10.1136/bmjopen-2015-010680.
Smith, K. (2013). *Beyond Evidence Based Policy in Public Health.*
Smith, K., & Stewart, E. (2017). We Need to Talk About Impact: Why Social Policy Academics Need to Engage with the UK's Research Impact Agenda. *Journal of Social Policy.* Cambridge University Press, pp. 109–127. https://doi.org/10.1017/S0047279416000283.
Stirling, A. (2010). Keep It Complex. *Nature.* https://doi.org/10.1038/4681029a.
Stewart, E. (2019). A Sociology of Public Responses to Hospital Change and Closure. *Sociology of Health & Illness.*
Stoker, G. (1998). Governance as Theory: Five Propositions. *International Social Science Journal.* https://doi.org/10.1111/1468-2451.00106.
Stoker, G. (2006). Public Value Management: A New Narrative for Networked Governance?, *American Review of Public Administration.* https://doi.org/10.1177/0275074005282583.
Timmermans, S., & Berg, M. (2003). The Practice of Medical Technology. *Sociology of Health & Illness.* https://doi.org/10.1111/1467-9566.00342.
Trenholm, S., & Ferlie, E. (2013). Using Complexity Theory to Analyse the Organisational Response to Resurgent Tuberculosis Across London. *Social Science & Medicine, 93*, 229–237. https://doi.org/10.1016/j.socscimed.2012.08.001.
Truman, D. B. (1968). The Social Sciences and Public Policy. *Science, 160*(3827), 508–512. https://doi.org/10.1126/science.160.3827.508.
Tseng, V. (2020). Evidence for Policy in the Wake of COVID-19: Short—Medium—Long Term Impacts, LSE Blog. https://blogs.lse.ac.uk/impactofsocialsciences/2020/05/22/evidence-for-policy-in-the-wake-of-covid-19-short-medium-long-term-impacts/.
Vindrola-Padros, C. et al. (2017). The Role of Embedded Research in Quality Improvement: A Narrative Review, *BMJ Quality and Safety.* https://doi.org/10.1136/bmjqs-2015-004877.
Weiss, C. H. (1979). The Many Meanings of Research Utilization. *Public Administration Review, 39*(5), 426. https://doi.org/10.2307/3109916.

Wilkinson, C. (2017). Evidencing Impact: A Case Study of UK Academic Perspectives on Evidencing Research Impact. *Studies in Higher Education*. https://doi.org/10.1080/03075079.2017.1339028.

Wolfle, D. (1968). Science Advice for State Governments. *Science, 160*(3828), 607–607. https://doi.org/10.1126/science.160.3828.607.

Wynne, B. (1992). Uncertainty and environmental learning: reconceiving science and policy in the preventive paradigm. *Global Environmental Change, 2*(2), 111–127.

Young, K. *et al.* (n.d.). Social Science and the Evidence-based Policy Movement, *cambridge.org*. Retrieved February 14, 2019, from https://www.cambridge.org/core/journals/social-policy-and-society/article/social-science-and-the-evidencebased-policy-movement/33D115F3218BDA8A76B7A5B510099679.

CHAPTER 6

Public Service Innovation: Challenges and Possibilities for Innovation Adoption

Adina Dudau, John Finch, James Grant Hemple, and Georgios Kominis

SETTING THE SCENE FOR PUBLIC SERVICE INNOVATION

The public sector has been subject to numerous political and structural changes worldwide. These have been informed by significant conceptual shift over what the sector is for, who it should serve, and at what cost and benefit to society. Different modes of governance, Weberian (traditional) public administration, new public management (NPM) and new public governance (NPG) had different answers to these questions (see, e.g. Dudau 2010, as well as Chapter 1 of this book). Navigating through these governance modes, the sector has now reached significant organisational complexity due to coexistence and partial overlap of diverse ownership models (e.g. arms-length agencies, state-owned enterprises, charities). Concurrently, the public sector has also seen a blurring of the 'line of visibility' (Radnor et al. 2014) where front-line professionals interact with service users (Dudau et al. 2018a, 2019), with the latter assuming various roles: of a customer, of a client or indeed a citizen who is entitled to services but may not use them.

The most paradigm-altering of these changes emerged in the context of neoliberal reforms of the end of the twentieth century—the grand global project of 'privatising the world' (Letwin 1988). Prompted by the growing divide between resource scarcity and rising demand for services, these public sector reforms aimed at 'doing more with less' (e.g. Overmans and Noordegraaf 2014; Overmans 2018). This presented an opportunity for policy-makers and organisational employees to look at processes differently, as well as to identify newer and more effective products or services. This involved using technological advances more effectively, streamlining processes and so on. This chapter focuses on the ways to enable innovation in public services by identifying conditions for innovation adoption in the UK context.

The definitional terrain for public service innovation is convoluted, but some clarity emerges around a few dominant issues. First, innovation entails a dichotomy between incremental and systemic change (Albury 2005), also referred to in the literature as the difference between 'change' and 'innovation' (Brown and Osborne 2012). Innovation scholars seems to agree on the fact that innovation goes beyond 'change', entailing discontinuity from the past and perceived novelty related to first-time usage in an organisation or a service (e.g. Bhatti et al. 2011). The concept is intuitively appealing, as novelty often is, leading some to consider innovation a goal in itself. Such a normative stance is perhaps suggestive of scholars' fascination with the concept; however, it appears to be missing out on selective or variable adoption, as well as on impact of innovation on public service outcomes, particularly where such outcomes might be negative. In their recent reviews, de Vries and Voorberg identified innovation failure as an important gap in the literature (de Vries et al. 2014, Voorberg et al. 2015). But innovation assessment, as either success or failure, can be a function of the forces driving its adoption (Dudau et al. 2018a). Dudau et al. (2018a) identified two innovation types, consumerism-driven and professionalism-driven innovation, whose evaluation criteria rest upon their drivers: consumerist criteria (such as client satisfaction) for consumerism-driven innovation, and professional criteria (such as safety, attainment, public health, depending on the professional area of expertise within the service) for professionalism-driven innovation. Another aspect influencing innovation adoption in public services is the risk associated with the new process, product, service or idea (e.g. Osborne et al. 2019). Also, institutional inertia in the public sector can be strong and requires a certain type of leaders to overcome it (e.g. Hartley 2005). Finally, generalisations about public service innovation are difficult to make because there is a great variety of services with very different characteristics, organising principles and which have been affected differently by successive modes of governance (e.g. Dudau et al. 2019).

This chapter explores a tale of innovation adoption in an innovation-intensive public service in the UK: utilities provision by a state-owned company. The analysis of this case offers an interpretation of innovation adoption as being a function of organisations' risk appetite. Our research suggests that there is a 'sweet spot' of just the right amount of risk appetite, shaped by perception of value to 'citizens' (recipients of *public value*) and to 'customers' (recipients of *private value*), which determines innovation adoption in public services like the utilities. Our tale of innovation will be interpreted through the lenses of governance modes and two important contextual developments, value creation and management (at a service level) and institutional hybridity (at an organisational level), brought about by NPM. Both these developments stem from variations in organisational configurations meant to enhance the delivery of public value in UK public services in general, and in utilities, as case in point.

UK Context: Governance Modes and Value Creation Through Institutional Hybridity

The UK is one of the first countries to implement public sector neoliberal reforms towards the end of the twentieth century (e.g. Hood 1995). The political project which accompanied these reforms became known as the new public management (NPM) and, although it is neither the first nor the last of the reform waves to affect the sector, and indeed the public services, it arguably introduced an irreversible structural and paradigmatic change (Ashworth et al. 2013). The fundamental change it brought to Weberian, traditional public administration model of governance, is that it imported private sector practices and tools into the public sector, in a drive for economy, efficiency and effectiveness (Andrews and Van de Walle 2013). The NPM reforms were supported by the rising wave of a neoliberalist paradigm which regarded the state as a realm of coercion restricting individuals' initiative and self-realisation. The intention behind adopting these reforms in Britain was to reduce the budget deficit which reached unprecedented levels at the end of 1979 (Matthews and Minford 1987). Policy-makers signed up to the idea that the way to achieving that was through measures that promoted privatisation, marketisation and decentralisation (Rhodes 1998). As public sector budgets shrunk, front-line professionals became more aware than ever of the costs involved in running a service and of the alignment between their performance and that of their service performance. Simultaneously, service users started being referred to as customers (rather than citizens or service users), the rhetoric of consumerism increasing demands and expectations from public services. The governance mode following NPM, referred to as new public governance (NPG) (Osborne 2010) or the Third Way (Giddens 2013) in the UK, cemented the NPM reforms (Newman 2001). Indeed, the 'modernisation agenda' of the New Labour in the UK (Midwinter 2001, Newman 2001) enhanced the role of the service users even further and improved transparency through which users would be able to assess quality in public services. Quality and performance management regimes became the mantra of a governance mode which aimed for 'effectiveness' in public service delivery; in other words, for services which are fit for purpose, regardless of the institutional configurations (public, private, non-profit) through which this was going to be achieved.

These developments, introduced decisively by NPM promoters and cemented by NPG, had two important consequences in the public sector: institutional hybridity (Greenwood et al. 2010) and value creation in public services (Osborne 2018). Both value creation and institutional hybridity impact on how public service innovation is adopted. This is where the chapter will now turn.

Institutional Hybridity

Institutional hybridity represents the coexistence of two or more, irreconcilably contradictory, institutional logics such as (1) that of managerialism or consumerism, brought about by NPM, essentially maximising consumers' voice, and (2) a prevailing public sector logic which pre-existed it, such as professionalism (e.g. Dudau et al. 2018a), where professional judgement is dominant and consumer judgement is minimal. Yet, as argued earlier in this section, NPM only marked the start of the hybridity

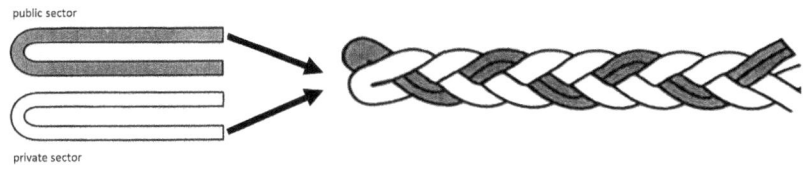

| Weberian public administration | New Public Management | New Public Governance | Post- New Public Governance |

Fig. 6.1 The process of institutional hybridity in relation to governance modes

process; then, NPG offered fertile ground for development and it allowed it to flourish into its current configuration, as Fig. 6.1 illustrates.

Previous studies concluded that organisational multiplicity, seen, for example, in public-private partnerships or privatised organisations, brought about by the NPM reforms, is associated with 'inherently incompatible' logics as organisations are confronted with 'incompatible prescriptions' (Greenwood et al. 2010). The process through which organisations combine such different institutional logics is referred to as institutional hybridity (Battilana and Dorado 2010; Van den Broek et al. 2014; Pache and Santos 2013a, 2013b; Johanson and Vakkuri 2017).

Some scholars of complexity propose that competing logics produce complexity (see Christensen and Lægreid 2011). Most authors, however, argue that multiple logics coexist or combine to formulate hybrid organisational forms or practices (Battilana and Dorado 2010; Dunn and Jones 2010; Goodrick and Reay 2011; Pache and Santos 2013a, b) and that, in doing so, they are fundamentally different from complex organisations and practices where these logics eventually converge. Therefore, hybrids do not comply blindly with institutional pressures, as those described by Dimaggio and Powell (1983), or can decouple, as Meyer and Rowan (1977) proposed, so they can blend and manoeuvre logics (Binder 2007) because they can access repertoires of institutionalised templates and combine these in unique ways.

Van den Broek et al. (2014) note possibilities for having hybrid practices within organisations, explaining that such practices combine symbols or norms from more than one institutional order—for example, a managerial practice of cost control and a professional ethos of putting client safety first at any cost. Pache and Santos (2013b) added that hybrid organisations can combine competing logics through 'selective coupling', which they explain as follows:

In contrast to decoupling, which entails the ceremonial espousal of a prescribed practice with no actual enactment, selective coupling refers to the purposeful enactment of selected practices among a pool of competing alternatives. Selective coupling allows hybrids to satisfy symbolic concerns. (Pache and Santos, 2013b, pp. 993–994)

Pache and Santos (2013b) add that selective coupling is superior to practice-level hybridising strategies such as compromising (Oliver 1991), as the latter requires negotiations to select what you will get from conflicting logics (Battilana and Dorado 2010; Pache and Santos 2013b). Consequently, selective coupling is a less costly strategy but also provides insights into using 'cultural toolkits' for agency and reflexivity to solve competing logics issues (Tracey et al., 2011). Competing logics can be unavoidable and cannot be handled easily by hybrid organisations (Pache and Santos 2013b). Public services with combined public and private sector operating logics are stages of constant selective coupling of particular practices from each *modus operandi*. When blending the two sets of practices emerging from the two competing institutional logics (see Fig. 6.1), public service providers arguably pursue one common goal: value creation to service users. It is on this basis that we identify the recent preoccupation with value creation (e.g. Osborne et al. 2015, Osborne 2018, Dudau et al. 2019) and value management (Connolly 2016) as another important development brought about by NPM, alongside institutional hybridity.

Value Creation and Management Through Public Services

With NPM, the power of consumers has grown as has their awareness of, and demand for, value. This is how value creation has become more important than (or at least as important as) the uniform delivery of public goods. Indeed, and as illustrated in Fig. 6.2, if Weberian, traditional public administration prioritised equality and neutrality in the delivery of public goods in pursuit of collective public value, NPM facilitated a move away from this norm by embracing a differential approach to value co-creation, depending on the nature of the service provided and on whether it fulfils more private or more public 'needs'. Services such as transportation, communication and utilities were among the first to acknowledge the dichotomy between, hence the need for differential offerings for, public and private value. For example, while transportation may be a basic need for

6 PUBLIC SERVICE INNOVATION: CHALLENGES AND POSSIBILITIES... 155

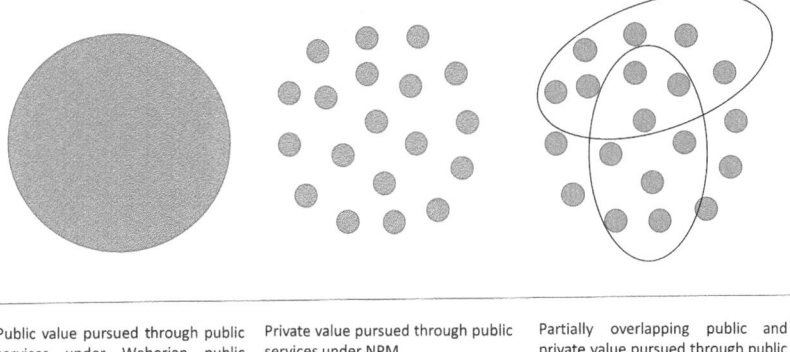

Public value pursued through public services under Weberian public administration governance mode

Private value pursued through public services under NPM

Partially overlapping public and private value pursued through public services under NPG

Fig. 6.2 Public and private value across modes of governance

some, such as to the elderly, it also provides additional, and arguably private, value through catering services, different comfort levels, convenient departure / arrival times as well as allowing for living arrangements far away from work. Public services, such as transportation, were therefore the first to introduce the need for, or awareness of, private value co-creation, alongside the more widely accepted public value creation. As such, differential pricing and consumer choice was introduced through the introduction of markets and quasi-markets in the UK (e.g. Hood 1995). Subsequent NPG reforms only cemented these developments by deepening NPM reforms in some services while, at the same time, recognising the limitations of the markets in addressing '[t]he social values inherent in public services' (Hefetz and Warner 2004: 174). In response to the latter, NPG introduced wide-ranging partnership working integrating a number of services (e.g. Osborne 2010).

Arguably, under the NPG mode of governance (Osborne 2010), public and private value creation are both pursued in public services, arguably following varying demand for each form of value, too, as suggested by different service user configurations (individuals as customers, individuals as more passive service users, communities of citizens, etc.). The kind of value extracted by clients from public services is now an integrated mix of public and private value. The mix is not uniform for all services—for example, there will be higher levels of public value managed and extracted from a service like criminal justice than for transport or utility services;

similarly, private value is disproportionately more salient to consumers and providers of water, gas and electricity, than it is, for example, to health professionals and their patients. It is also not the same for services in different countries—there are differences between Scotland and England, let alone the UK and other countries.

Public value is an elusive and multidimensional concept originating from the work of Moore (1994) and developed in earnest in the early 2000 in an attempt to break away from the neoliberal ideology and emphasise the distinctiveness of the public sector. It has been defined by O'Flynn (2007) as a reflection of collectively expressed, politically mediated preferences consumed by the citizenry—created not just through 'outcomes' but also through processes which may generate trust or fairness (O'Flynn 2007). The creation of public value is the core of public managers' work, just as that of private value is the focus of managers in the private sector (ibid.). A perspective which pushes the concept of value creation away from its original public sector focus on public value and towards a marketing-inspired conception of value realisation exclusively by service consumers (and not co-defined with service providers) is the 'public service logic' theory (Osborne 2018). It allows to move the focus away from organisations and the organisational infrastructure involved in service design and provision, and towards service outcomes, that is, service impact on—both direct and indirect—users. While public service logic (PSL) was only recently formulated (Osborne 2018), the theory is rooted in the service logic (SL) perspective developed some decades earlier (Grönroos 2006) and the 'service-dominant logic' (SDL) (Vargo and Lusch 2004, 2016). The thought revolution created by the service logic paradigm was in terms of no longer holding organisations responsible for the value they create but, rather, for the 'value promise' which then service users combine with 'value in context' and 'value in use' to create their own private value extracted individually from services. This can be problematic for public services, even after adaptation of the theory for public service use (undertaken by Osborne, see Osborne 2018).

The idea that public services are no longer seen to be implicated in the uniform pursuit of public value and, instead, are perceived to be of service to individual service users is undoubtedly linked with the evolution of institutional hybridity. Indeed, with multiplicity of needs, wants and user profiles comes multiplicity of 'logics' through which these can be addressed by service providers. The NPM mode of governance is responsible for both changes: from public to private value creation and from institutional uniformity to institutional hybridity.

Implications for Public Service Innovation

Different services experienced these ontological and organisational changes differently, depending on a number of variables. One is the degree of exposure services have to consumers, for example, there are fewer direct users of the criminal justice system than there are of public transport. Another is the need for professional input determining what service quality looks like, for example, there is less specialised advice required in determining quality public housing provision than there is in determining the right tax codes or medical treatment. A conceptual framework which allows for differentiation of public services comes from Laing (2003), who distinguishes between them on the basis of relative knowledge and power base of the professionals and of their clients in these services (see Fig. 6.3).

This spectrum differentiates professional judgement-dominant services, such as criminal justice, from consumer-dominant services, such as public transport. Professionals delivering social benefit services have far more expertise and understanding of the service than their clients do, whereas the opposite may be true for private benefits-dominant services. For example, probation officers understand the principles and practice of criminal justice far better than the people they serve; however, users of public transport have a deeper understanding of the service than those delivering it. Therefore, quality assurance mechanisms, such as user satisfaction surveys, make more sense for the latter, than for the former, category of services. As a result, professional judgement is dominant on the left side of the continuum and consumer judgement on the right side of it. Services which find themselves on the half right side of Laing's (2003) spectrum tend to

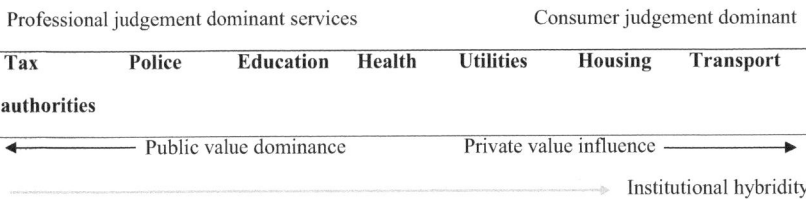

Fig. 6.3 Service continuum (adapted from Laing 2003)

be universal (i.e. everyone needs, and uses, health services, education and utilities like water, gas and electricity) and therefore public sentiment; hence consumer judgement is strong, but, equally, these services rely on specialised professional input (doctors, nurses, teachers, engineers). The two actors, professionals and consumers, are likely to be affected by conflicting institutional logics (e.g. Greenwood et al. 2010) causing organisational practices to oscillate between 'business like managerialism' driven by consumerism and 'traditional professional values' driven by professionals (Noordegraaf 2007).

The two institutional logics of 'markets' and 'professions' are evident in the ways in which service users are referred to as 'consumers', 'customers' or 'citizens'. Each of these terms comes with underlying assumptions about how public service delivery can be understood and evaluated by the public (McLaughlin 2009). Citizens have been catered for by Weberian mode of governance which prioritises equality, equity and neutrality in how services reach users who have equal right of usage as citizens. There is a certain degree of dignified passivity entailed in the concept of 'citizenship'—in that the public have rights and exercise them through political participation, but they have little power to change things individually when they experience value destruction, rather than value creation, through public services. Then, 'customers' have been the focus on NPM reforms introduced with faith in customer empowerment through choice (Jung 2010). Customers are considerably more assertive than 'citizens' are, and have more regard for private, rather than public, value through services. As such, the relationship between customers and professionals develops from a position of power, entitlement and regard for own private needs at the expense of collective needs valued by professionals (for a wider discussion, see O'Flynn 2007 and Dudau et al. 2018a). Finally, 'consumers' have been the focus of NPG, with their concern with service quality. They are reasonably empowered, but not as politically engaged as 'citizens' nor as demanding as 'customers' (e.g. Thomas 2017). Arguably, they are in the middle between the two extremes: citizens (all those entitled, whether they are direct public service users or not) and customers (direct public service users with specific demands).

With an upward trajectory for concern with customers' needs, the institutional logic of 'professionalism' suffered a decline (e.g. Denhardt and Denhardt, 2000; Mark 2013). For example, when customer satisfaction is employed as a measure of service quality, professionals may be inclined to prioritise 'pleasant' aspects of service provision over 'unpleasant' ones, even when the latter serves their clients better. In higher education, this could be seen in the increasing use of 'entertainment' in class and the decline in use of pedagogical activities founded on 'cognitive dissonance' (Festinger 1962). In utilities such as water provision, this can be seen in rankings of service quality informed by water taste—the pursuit of growth in these rankings may inform the trade-off between convenience of service (e.g. water taste) and safety.

Public service innovation is adopted and evaluated differently in every public service. Services on the right side of Laing's (2003) spectrum (Fig. 6.3) are more likely to adopt product innovation (e.g. new buses/trains, new housing and building materials transforming tenants' and passengers' lives) than services on the left side of it. Services on the left side of the spectrum (e.g. criminal justice, customs and revenue) are more likely to be conservative with respect to innovation than services with higher concerns for private benefits and private value. Arguably, in these services, innovation processes are likely to be more incremental and more measured because the stakes are higher. For example, more people get affected by innovation failure in taxation services than by innovation failure in public housing, because there are more beneficiaries of taxation than there are of public housing. Equally, innovation failure in criminal justice can mean generalised criminality putting more people at risk than, say, innovation failure in public transport which may affect the users of one vehicle or train at one moment in time. But what happens in the middle of Laing's spectrum, with universal services, such as health, education and, arguably, utilities provision? The following section illuminates the decision-making processes behind innovation adoption in services with high institutional hybridity and which sit in the middle between public value (e.g. public needs) and private value (e.g. individual 'wants') creation. This is an under-researched governance space in innovation studies (which tend to look at processes and outcomes but not at what precedes innovation adoption) and public sector management (where the interplay of risk and innovation has been investigated theoretically by Osborne and colleagues) (Osborne and Brown 2011, Brown and Osborne 2013, Flemig et al. 2016,) and only recently explored empirically (Osborne et al. 2019, Torugsa and Arundel 2016), however in services with little propensity for private value (i.e. health, environmental sustainability). In this chapter, we identify the role of risk in shaping innovation adoption in hybrid organisational settings (where public and private value pursuits are blended), increasingly an organisational form in the UK public sector (e.g. Dudau et al. 2018b), as the value of innovation is judged in relation to the risk it entails.

Zooming In: Innovation Adoption in State-Owned Enterprise

If it is for public managers to assess public value (Connolly 2016, O'Flynn 2007), private value from public services is assessed by service users (Osborne 2018). Managerial decision-making, including adopting or not adopting innovation, in hybrid organisational settings arguably takes both types of value into account. Traditionally, utilities have been provided by the public sector in most OECD countries. They are professionalised services (i.e. dominated by engineers) where professional expertise has been dominant until the recent NPM reforms brought in private sector initiatives and a consumerist mindset. While these reforms encouraged public service innovations, they also brought with them conflicting institutional logics with their own interpretation of value to the service user. The value of innovation is therefore likely to be open to constant negotiation, particularly at adoption stage, a key phase in the innovation process (Cooper 1998).

Innovation Adoption in a State-Owned Enterprise

Our interview-based qualitative study of innovation risk in a British-owned utilities company (denoted as *Public Utility Firm* for ethical reasons) revealed interesting observations about perceptions of risk in innovation in this organisational environment. The study started from an awareness of the technological innovation available to the company's engineers in line with industry standards, and investigated key respondents' perspectives of their decision-making when embarking on innovation processes. One of the authors had prolonged access to meetings and documents in *Public Utility Firm* as well as data from 60- to 90-minute interviews with seven key respondents, public managers with remit for innovation. These interviews were transcribed and analysed thematically (Gioia and Corley 2004)—see Table 6.1 for a sample of quotes clustered under the 'public value' theme and the subordinate codes of 'citizenry' and 'health and safety'.

Table 6.1 Illustration of public value pursuit in *Public Utility Firm*

Public value through citizenship	Public value through health and safety
'we're always under the scrutiny of the public... one of our regulators is the customer forum... and we will be challenged on what we're spending money on'.	'[the utility] needs to be fit for consumption... safe for human consumption'. 'we provide an essential service to the public... [we need to] make sure that our service is reliable to the public'.

RESEARCH CONTEXT

Institutional hybridity in *Public Utility Firm* is given by its state ownership, monopolistic status and strict compliance with the government's regulatory framework, therefore a concern for citizens and their safety, coupled with business demands and concern for customers. *Public Utility Firm* operates within a blended context of non-commercially focused regulated market and commercially focused non-regulated market. It is its operations on the regulated market that is of relevance to our study as this is a public utilities service, the non-regulated market being concerned with domestic and international consultancy. On the regulated market, *Public Utility Firm* serves 2.52 million households, 5 million customers and employs approximately 3500 employees. It was created in the early 2000s by an Act of Parliament that merged three independent utility authorities into one large utility firm that operates as a monopoly utility provider within its regulated geographical market. The firm's focus is on delivering its services at the lowest price possible while maintaining a high quality of service. This is exemplified by the unique regulatory framework that the public utility firm operates within to ensure that it delivers on its purpose. Figure 6.4 identifies the seven key stakeholders within its regulatory framework.

The Parliament holds *Public Utility Firm* to account and requires executives to attend parliamentary committees to offer progress updates. Government ministers act on behalf of the public by setting industry objectives and appoint the chair and non-executive members. The customer forum is situated as the most important regulator and considers what is reasonable for the customer in terms of future service levels, investment priorities and the price of service. The customer forum is populated by appointed members who have various expertise in engineering,

Fig. 6.4 *Public Utility Firm*'s regulatory framework

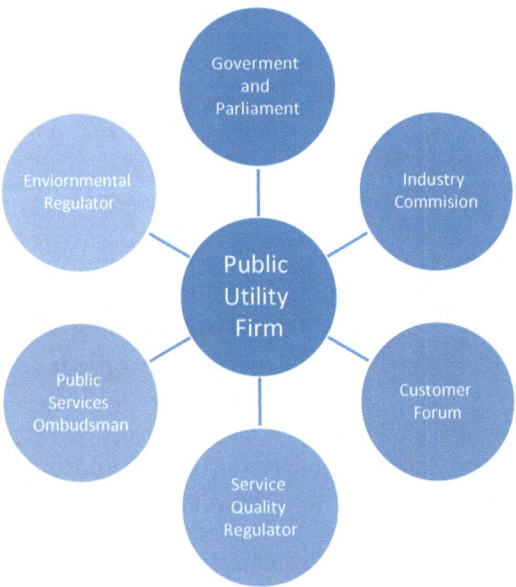

business, utilities and the public sector. The Industry Commission is a non-departmental public body with statutory responsibilities for setting the price and service quality proposed by the customer forum. The Service Quality Regulator is concerned with the safety of the services provided, monitors the quality of samples taken and inspects the assets and activities of the public utility firm against regulations. The Environmental Protection Agency is responsible for making sure that the environment and the human health are protected. Finally, the Public Services Ombudsman is responsible for investigating complaints about public services.

Figure 6.1 depicts the complex nature of the utility firm's regulatory commitments. It highlights the relationship and concern between price, service quality and risk to the public. The organisation of the *Public Utility Firm's* regulatory framework requires constant collaboration between all the stakeholders who play varying roles in acting on behalf of the public. This contextualises the unique environment of this specific case. To deliver services to the public, *Public Utility Firm* relies on the technical expertise of its employees and delivery partners. The delivery partners consist of several joint ventures between competing local and global commercially focused consultancy firms. The internal employees and members of the regulatory framework are also predominantly end users of the services that are provided by the public utility firm.

The firm's most important regulator is the 'Customer Forum', which reflects the importance conferred to customers. Yet, within *Public Utility Firm*, there is a clear and consistent distinction between customers and internal customers. Within its regulated market, customers are viewed as those who buy the utility services within the firm's geographical area of responsibility. Their internal customers, however, are employees who collaborate with each other to help fulfil job responsibilities and ultimately deliver the services to external customers (service users), as well as alliance partners and supply chain partners.

Public Managers' Perceptions of Innovation Adoption

To start with, respondents suggested that their incentive for innovation is service improvement, but this it is not an end in itself, but rather a means to another purpose—customer benefit—which could be achieved by bringing costs down (presumably transferring any savings to the consumer) or by improving the service:

> doing things differently and better for the customer's benefit … [it is] ultimately about driving down costs and driving up service.

Public Utility Firm respondents saw innovation as a process (process innovation) not related to product innovation but to providing a better service, as defined by service users—who, as noted in the quote, extract private value from this service: lowering costs and growing satisfaction with the quality of the service. They linked the idea of service (as opposed to product) dominance with being part of the public sector, yet they also refer to their consumers as 'customer', which can appear to be contradictory but may be simply a reflection of hybridity in *Public Utility Firm*. This is further illustrated by the shift in terminology used to refer to service users: on the one hand, when speaking of improved business processes, the terminology used was that of 'customer', while on the other hand, when speaking of risk of innovation, the wording changed from 'customers' (a notion which is difficult to separate from that of expectations for growing value for money) to 'the public' (entailing notions of citizenship and health and safety, hence to do with public, rather than private, value):

Service consumers represent only one side of the service's 'line of visibility'. The other side relates to service professionals, in this case engineers and operational managers (many with an engineering background), with the latter category being where we selected our interviewees. This was done for two reasons. First, we wanted to have a diversity of backgrounds rather than a strong engineering perspective on risk and innovation. Second, we wanted to centre the discussion on respondents' own involvement in decision-making around innovation adoption. *Public Utility Firm* managers revealed considerable caution around innovation adoption. The boundary of their caution domain is given by their 'risk appetite'—which one of the interviewees explained using the 'cliff edge' analogy:

> The point where you fall off a cliff ... that's the point where you are no longer at risk, you are in the danger zone and there might be a fence and there might be a sign beyond the fence and there might be a cliff. And I suppose the appetite is, do you stay at the fence or do you go to the sign and I think sometimes we could push our appetite a bit further, and have more appetite for risk.

This interviewee clearly believes that a risk appetite is an enabler, rather than an obstructer, of innovation. The interviewee continues:

> it's not about taking more risks, I think it's about having more appetite for risk. I don't see risk management about taking more or less risk, it's about what is your appetite... [it's about increasing one's] risk tolerances.

But 'risk appetite' (or lack of) can also be seen as a constraining factor for innovation, as evident here:

> the risk appetite of the organisation ... I would say would be a constraining factor. So, we have a regulatory contract that sets out over a six-year period what the priorities are from [the] Government and our quality regulators and the economic regulator then sets an amount of money to deliver all of that. The primary focus of the organisation is delivering that regulatory contract. Within that, there are a lot of milestone dates, so the fact that you have to deliver things on a set timetable is a constraining factor. If you are going to innovate, you have almost got to pause and step back ... There is an element of fear of failure within there.

As an enabler for some, and a constraint for others, risk appetite is what determines the organisation to be innovative:

> you have got innovators at the bottom end of the curve, early adopters, early majority, majority, and then fast forwarders, and people at the far end of the thing are the laggers… It depends where you are on that curve and being at the front end of the curve, [means] to be where you can get your fingers burnt. I think we are less open to that. If we are in early adopter/early majority space, we are more likely.

So, *Public Utility Firm* finds itself in the first half of that process of diffusion, but not very early on. The reference to burned fingers alludes to failure and, by association, to risk of failure. Yet the latter seems subordinate to, and indeed only one of the interpretations for, the concept of 'risk appetite' professed in the organisation. Overall, the case of *Public Utility Firm* suggests caution when adopting innovation. This could be explained, on the one hand, by the 'hybrid' assumptions of who the company serves (customers or citizens) through its universal utilities' provision, which can prompt stages for complex decision-making likely to delay the adoption of innovation, and, on the other hand, by its public ownership so an overall concern for public value in the balance of public and private value imperatives.

Discussion: Public Value Pursued Through Innovation in Hybrid Public Services

The core lesson for from *Public Utility Firm* is that hybridity matters in process innovation. Firm ownership (public, private or a configuration of both) sets organisational priorities. In the public sector, these traditionally have been to promote, manage and enhance public value in public service provision: evidence-based, safe and effective service outcomes to most, rather than few, service users, typically referred to as 'the public'. This is a very different goal than consumer satisfaction, which is more commonly pursued in the private sector, as a measure of private value attainment. In hybrid settings, the pursuit is dual. Moreover, as it appears in our case study, in hybrid organisations delivering public services (as many utilities are), this dual pursuit is subordinate to public value management.

The value of innovation in the utilities is subjected to irreconcilable duality. On the one hand, technology-heavy organisations like utility firms can hardly afford to fall considerably behind the latest innovation trends, as they can determine dramatic service improvements and cost cuts (Rennings and Rammer 2009), both of which can enhance value in private service consumption and in long-term firm sustainability. On the other hand, utilities are run by national infrastructure companies which can hardly afford to fail (Schulman et al. 2004), as failure comes with high costs to human life. As a result, they find themselves on the bleeding edge of innovation, even if, paradoxically, they stay off the cliff edge avoiding getting their fingers burned, as two of our respondents suggested.

Public service organisations such as *Public Utility Firm* exercise caution when considering the 'needs' over the 'wants' of end consumers. The former consideration employs professional judgement, while the latter, a consumerism judgement. Public service logic paradigm (Osborne 2018) suggests the latter to be paramount in the post-NPG mode of governance, therefore prompting an important schism from the more widely accepted orthodoxy in public sector management, that public value is the quintessential distinctive offering by the public sector (e.g. Moore 2000). Commentators went further, arguing that public value management can be a governance mode in its own right (e.g. Pyper 2015), with public sector professionals being managers of value (Connolly 2016). Yet public service logic (Osborne 2018) challenges this view, suggesting that value is not the sector's to manage, but the users to determine in conjunction with their personal experiences, beliefs and ability to consume the service offered (see also Dudau et al. 2019). The insights from *Public Utility Firm* show that public managers are aware of the duality between public and private values and take it into account when deciding to innovate, prioritising public value, if ever so slightly. They do so implicitly through the use of language when referring to service users and what they perceive to be their expectations of the service, and by suggesting caution due to concerns for collective service outcomes such as health, safety, reliability and value for money (as illustrated in Table 6.1). If other public service providers share *Public Utility Firm's* approach to innovation and vision of priorities, this has some interesting implications for theory, suggesting permanence in public managers' attitudes around public value imperatives, an underlay, arguably, to their commitment to private value provision, giving some weightage to Pyper's (2015) and Connolly's (2016) suggestions of public value being the core work of public managers. This is significant as the search for a post-NPG paradigm is still on and as the

Big Society did not seem to provide the right framing of public sector and public service management (e.g. Dudau et al. 2019).

CONCLUSIONS

The challenge, and at the same time, the opportunity, in public service innovation, comes from the rhetoric around innovation adoption and evaluation, emerging from either side of the hybridity mix. The level of hybridity in the service determines the direction of bias in this rhetoric – for example innovation which is deemed successful due to high customer satisfaction is likely to have been adopted for managerial purposes aiming at maximising private value for consumers; then, innovation being deemed as successful despite lower than excellent customer satisfaction scores is likely to have been designed for public, rather than private value. While deciphering evaluative messages of innovation through rhetoric analysis can be challenging, building them is an opportunity in terms of building support for innovation initiatives in public services.

REFERENCES

Albury, D. (2005). Fostering Innovation in Public Service. *Public Money & Management Journal, 25*(1), 51–56.

Andrews, R., & Van de Walle, S. (2013). New Public Management and Citizens' Perceptions of Local Service Efficiency, Responsiveness, Equity and Effectiveness. *Public Management Review, 15*(5), 762–783.

Ashworth, R., Ferlie, E., Hammerschmid, G., Moon, M. J., & Reay, T. (2013). Theorizing Contemporary Public Management: International and Comparative Perspectives. *British Journal of Management, 24*, 1–17.

Battilana, J., & Dorado, S. (2010). Building Sustainable Hybrid Organizations: The Case of Commercial Microfinance Organizations. *Academy of Management Journal, 53*(6), 1419–1440.

Bhatti, Y., Olsen, A. L., & Pedersen, L. H. (2011). Administrative Professionals and the Diffusion of Innovations: The Case of Citizen Service Centres. *Public Administration, 89*(2), 577–594.

Binder, A. (2007). For Love and Money: Organizations' Creative Responses to Multiple Environmental Logics. *Theory and Society, 36*(6), 547–571.

Brown, K., & Osborne, S. P. (2012). *Managing Change and Innovation in Public Service Organizations*. London: Routledge.

Brown, L., & Osborne, S. P. (2013). Risk and Innovation: Towards a Framework for Risk Governance in Public Services. *Public Management Review*, 15(2), 186–208.

Christensen, T., & Lægreid, P. (2011). Complexity and Hybrid Public Administration—Theoretical and Empirical Challenges. *Public Organization Review*, 11(4), 407–423.

Connolly, J. (2016). Contribution Analysis as an Approach to Enable Public Managers to Demonstrate Public Value: The Scottish Context. *International Journal of Public Sector Management*, 29(7), 690–707.

Cooper, J. R. (1998). A Multidimensional Approach to the Adoption of Innovation. *Management Decision*, 36(8), 493–502.

Denhardt, R. B., & Denhardt, J. V. (2000). The New Public Service: Serving Rather Than Steering. *Public Administration Review*, 60(6), 549–559.

De Vries, H. A., Bekkers, V. J. J. M., & Tummers, L. G. (2014). *Innovation in the Public Sector: A Systematic Review and Future Research Agenda*. Speyer: EGPA Conference.

DiMaggio, P. J., & Powell, W. W. (1983). The Iron Cage Revisited: Institutional Isomorphism and Collective Rationality in Organizational Fields. *American Sociological Review*, 48, 147–160.

Dudau, A. (2010). Managing Uncertainty: Public Administrators Dealing with 'Wicked' Issues in Public Policy. *Yearbook of Swiss Administrative Sciences*, 1(1), 1.

Dudau, A., Kominis, G., & Szocs, M. (2018a). Innovation Failure in the Eye of the Beholder: Towards a Theory of Innovation Shaped by Competing Agendas within Higher Education. *Public Management Review*, 20(2), 254–272.

Dudau, A., Favotto, A., & Kominis, G. (2018b). Boundary-Spanning Leadership in Hybrid Networks: A Case Study of English Local Safeguarding Children Boards. In A. B. Savignon, L. Gnan, A. Hinna, & F. Monteduro (Eds.), *Hybridity in the Governance and Delivery of Public Services* (pp. 243–260). Bingley: Emerald Publishing Limited.

Dudau, A., Glennon, R., & Verschuere, B. (2019). Following the Yellow Brick Road? (Dis)enchantment with Co-design, Co-production and Value Co-creation in Public Services. *Public Management Review*, 21(11), 1577–1602.

Dunn, M. B., & Jones, C. (2010). Institutional Logics and Institutional Pluralism: The Contestation of Care and Science Logics in Medical Education, 1967–2005. *Administrative Science Quarterly*, 55(1), 114–149.

Festinger, L. (1962). Cognitive Dissonance. *Scientific American*, 207(4), 93–106.

Flemig, S., Osborne, S., & Kinder, T. (2016). Risky Business—Reconceptualizing Risk and Innovation in Public Services. *Public Money & Management*, 36(6), 425–432.

Giddens, A. (2013). *The Third Way: The Renewal of Social Democracy*. London: John Wiley & Sons.

Corley, K. G., & Gioia, D. A. (2004). Identity Ambiguity and Change in the Wake of a Corporate Spin-off. *Administrative Science Quarterly, 49*(2), 173–208.

Goodrick, E., & Reay, T. (2011). Constellations of Institutional Logics: Changes in the Professional Work of Pharmacists. *Work and Occupations, 38*(3), 372–416.

Greenwood, R., Díaz, A. M., Li, S. X., & Lorente, J. C. (2010). The Multiplicity of Institutional Logics and the Heterogeneity of Organizational Responses. *Organization Science, 21*(2), 521–539.

Grönroos, C. (2006). Adopting a Service Logic for Marketing. *Marketing Theory, 6*(3), 317–333.

Hartley, J. (2005). Innovation in Governance and Public Services: Past and Present. *Public Money and Management, 25*(1), 27–34.

Hefetz, A., & Warner, M. (2004). Privatization and Its Reverse: Explaining the Dynamics of the Government Contracting Process. *Journal of Public Administration Research and Theory, 14*(2), 171–190.

Hood, C. (1995). The "New Public Management" in the 1980s: Variations on a Theme. *Accounting, Organizations and Society, 20*(2-3), 93–109.

Johanson, J. E., & Vakkuri, J. (2017). *Governing Hybrid Organisations: Exploring Diversity of Institutional Life*. London: Routledge.

Jung, T. (2010). Citizens, Co-producers, Customers, Clients, Captives? A Critical Review of Consumerism and Public Services. *Public Management Review, 12*(3), 439–446.

Laing, A. (2003). Marketing in the Public Sector: Towards a Typology of Public Services. *Marketing Theory, 3*(4), 427–445.

Letwin, O. (1988). *Privatising the World: A Study of International Privatisation in Theory and Practice*. London: Weidenfeld & Nicolson.

Mark, E. (2013). Student Satisfaction and the Customer Focus in Higher Education. *Journal of Higher Education Policy and Management, 35*(1), 2–10.

Matthews, K., & Minford, P. (1987). Mrs Thatcher's Economic Policies 1979–1987. *Economic Policy, 2*(5), 57–101.

McLaughlin, H. (2009). What's in a Name: 'Client', 'Patient', 'Customer', 'Consumer', 'Expert by Experience', 'Service User'—What's Next? *The British Journal of Social Work, 39*(6), 1101–1117.

Meyer, J. W., & Rowan, B. (1977). Institutionalized Organizations: Formal Structure as Myth and Ceremony. *American Journal of Sociology, 83*(2), 340–363.

Midwinter, A. (2001). New Labour and the Modernisation of British Local Government: A Critique. *Financial Accountability & Management, 17*(4), 311–320.

Moore, M. (1994). Public Value as the Focus of Strategy. *Australian Journal of Public Administration, 53*(3), 296–303.

Moore, M. H. (2000). Managing for Value: Organizational Strategy in for-profit, Nonprofit, and Governmental Organizations. *Nonprofit and Voluntary Sector Quarterly, 29*(1), 183–204.

Newman, J. (2001). *Modernizing Governance: New Labour, Policy and Society*. London: Sage.

Noordegraaf, M. (2007). From "Pure" to "Hhybrid" Professionalism: Present-day Professionalism in Ambiguous Public Domains. *Administration & Society*, 39(6), 761–785.

O'Flynn, J. (2007). From New Public Management to Public Value: Paradigmatic Change and Managerial Implications. *Australian Journal of Public Administration*, 66(3), 353–366.

Oliver, C. (1991). Strategic Responses to Institutional Processes. *Academy of Management Review*, 16(1), 145–179.

Osborne, S. P. (Ed.). (2010). *The New Public Governance: Emerging Perspectives on the Theory and Practice of Public Governance*. London: Routledge.

Osborne, S., & Brown, L. (2011). Innovation, Public Policy and Public Services: The Word That Would Be King? *Public Administration*, 89, 1335–1350.

Osborne, S. P., Radnor, Z., Kinder, T., & Vidal, I. (2015). The SERVICE Framework: A Public-Service-dominant Approach to Sustainable Public Services. *British Journal of Management*, 26(3), 424–438.

Osborne, S. P. (2018). From Public Service-dominant Logic to Public Service Logic: Are Public Service Organizations Capable of Co-production and Value Co-creation? *Public Management Review*, 20(2), 225–231.

Osborne, S., Brandsen, T., Mele, V., Nemec, J., van Genugten, M., & Flemig, S. (2019). Risking Innovation. Understanding Risk and Public Service Innovation—Evidence from a Four Nation Study. *Public Money & Management, Online first*, 40, 1–11.

Overmans, J. F. A., & Noordegraaf, M. (2014). Managing Austerity: Rhetorical and Real Responses to Fiscal Stress in Local Government. *Public Money and Management*, 34(2), 99–106.

Overmans, T. (2018). Innovative Austerity Management: How City Managers Create Slack for Innovation in Times of Fiscal Stress. *Journal of Public Budgeting, Accounting & Financial Management*, 30(4), 350–367.

Pache, A. C., & Santos, F. (2013a). Inside the Hybrid Organization: Selective Coupling as a Response to Competing Institutional Logics. *Academy of Management Journal*, 56(4), 972–1001.

Pache, A. C., & Santos, F. (2013b). Embedded in Hybrid Contexts: How Individuals in Organizations Respond to Competing Institutional Logics. In *Institutional Logics in Action, Part B* (pp. 3–35). Bingley: Emerald Group Publishing Limited.

Pyper, R. (2015). Public Administration, Public Management and Governance. In A. Massey & K. Johnstone (Eds.), *The International Handbook of Public Administration and Governance* (pp. 13–34). Cheltenham: Edward Elgar Publishing.

Radnor, Z., Osborne, S. P., Kinder, T., & Mutton, J. (2014). Operationalizing Co-production in Public Services Delivery: The Contribution of Service Blueprinting. *Public Management Review, 16*(3), 402–423.

Rennings, K., & Rammer, C. (2009). Increasing Energy and Resource Efficiency Through Innovation-an Explorative Analysis Using Innovation Survey Data. *ZEW-Centre for European Economic Research Discussion*, Discussion paper no. 09-056.

Rhodes, R. A. (1998). Different Roads to Unfamiliar Places: UK Experience in Comparative Perspective. *Australian Journal of Public Administration, 57*(4), 19–31.

Schulman, P., Roe, E., Eeten, M. V., & Bruijne, M. D. (2004). High Reliability and the Management of Critical Infrastructures. *Journal of Contingencies and Crisis Management, 12*(1), 14–28.

Thomas, J. C. (2017). *Citizen, Customer, Partner: Engaging the Public in Public Management: Engaging the Public in Public Management*. London: Routledge.

Torugsa, N., & Arundel, A. (2016). Complexity of Innovation in the Public Sector: A Workgroup-level Analysis of Related Factors and Outcomes. *Public Management Review, 18*(3), 392–416.

Tracey, P., Phillips, N., & Jarvis, O. (2011). Bridging Institutional Entrepreneurship and the Creation of New Organizational Forms: A Multilevel Model. *Organization Science, 22*(1), 60–80.

Van den Broek, J., Boselie, P., & Paauwe, J. (2014). Multiple Institutional Logics in Health Care: 'Productive Ward: Releasing Time to Care'. *Public Management Review, 16*(1), 1–20.

Vargo, S. L., & Lusch, R. F. (2004). Evolving to a New Dominant Logic for Marketing. *Journal of Marketing, 68*(1), 1–17.

Vargo, S. L., & Lusch, R. F. (2016). Institutions and Axioms: An Extension and Update of Service-dominant Logic. *Journal of the Academy of Marketing Science, 44*(1), 5–23.

Voorberg, W. H., Bekkers, V. J. J. M., & Tummers, L. G. (2015). A Systematic Review of Co-Creation and Co-Production: Embarking on the Social Innovation Journey. *Public Management Review, 17*(9), 1333–1357.

CHAPTER 7

Public Value Leadership in the Context of Outcomes, Impact and Reform

Janice McMillan

INTRODUCTION

Public value is not a new concept, and there have been many lenses through which it has been viewed, spanning a wide range of disciplinary areas (see, e.g. Lüdeke-Freund 2010; Mazzucatto 2018; and Lindgreen et al. 2019). There is increasing interest in the concept of leadership and what it means to lead in, and for, a public value context. This growing interest is closely related to the need for increased accountabilities stemming from the devolution of authority and responsibility in public resource use within recent public service reform agendas.

In the UK context, the importance of leadership in the creation of public value has been highlighted by Barber (2017) in his review of public value outcomes and proposal for reform set around a public value framework (also see Chaps. 2 and 3 in this volume). Leadership is increasingly being seen as the key vehicle through which public sector organisational change can be facilitated in pursuit of public value. This emphasis is

J. McMillan (✉)
Edinburgh Napier University, Edinburgh, UK
e-mail: J.McMillan@napier.ac.uk

however problematic and reflective of key questions around the concept of public value leadership—who are the leaders, what are they leading and how are they leading? Further, what are the boundaries of leadership action within the varying conceptions of public value leadership?

Within a surfeit of literature around the meaning of public value, most scholars are concerned with interpretations of 'value' and 'public' (Hartley et al. 2019). As Chap. 2 in this volume shows, discussions around both show the highly contested nature of the domain where interpretations may be used by governments, actors and commentators alike to meet or forward their own aims.

The concepts of leadership and public value can be viewed through two main lenses. The first lens considers the concept of public value from a leadership perspective and is based around exploring the approaches that are best suited to the achievement of public value. These contributions are akin to those that have pervaded the public management field since the global public reform agendas of the 1980s and 1990s, which highlighted the desirability, and relevance, of private management operating principles (see, e.g. Chiapello and Fairclough 2002). From this leadership perspective, there has been relatively little literature that discussed public value leadership from a practical point of view. This is reflective of the unsettled nature of debates around what public value is and how it may be achieved.

The second lens through which public value leadership has been considered views leadership from the public management subject base (Denis et al. 2007). Here, the literature is mostly concerned with 'how' public value outcomes may be achieved through the roles that leaders play; in other words, 'what' public leaders do within the busy, changing and conflictual domain of public service provision. How public value leadership is conceptualised underpins the practice of leadership and is important in informing the development of policy to enhance public service provision. This chapter will explore the various conceptions of leadership in relation to public value creation and maintenance and examine the practice issues that impact leaders' capacity to meet public value expectations and achieve desired outcomes.

Conceptualisations of Public Value Leadership

Whichever lens is used to consider the leadership of public value, the age-old question of leadership in the public sphere, and whether it differs (or not) from that of leadership in the private sector is an important debate within the literature. We have seen this question recast in many national and subnational governing systems, drawing on the various understandings, assumptions and terminologies of the time. The language of the debate is further influenced by the specifics of reform agendas (also see Pyper's chapter in this volume), political imperatives and ideologies.

Although there are two major approaches clearly identifiable in this debate, which have been variously termed the 'public administration approach' and the 'management approach', there are many individual interpretations that sit within and between these main approaches. Broader conceptions of political leadership propose that various accountabilities are key to understanding the role of leaders in the public domain and their resulting actions and behaviours. These may be useful in considering today's public value leadership even where discussions consider the political aspects of leadership only. Elcock (2001) argued, for example, that reform agendas of the 1980s and 1990s have driven a preoccupation with a narrow definition of performance based on outputs (also see Oliver and Fraser' chapter in this volume). This may not include wider benefits of public leadership activity. He argues that, over this period, there has been a worrying lack of debate around public value in the decisions made regarding the provision of services. In many senses, this is a compounding factor in the loss of a public administration perspective in favour of a management approach in consideration of the purpose of such provision.

The importance of leadership (rather than management) in achieving what we may consider today to be public value was highlighted by Elcock (2000, 2001), and was the focus of later work (see, e.g. Elcock and Fenwick 2012). Through his work, Elcock emphasised the need for leadership at all levels and in all types of governance; this leadership, based on creativity and collective learning which he viewed as key to public service provision, is most likely to meet the needs of the various stakeholders in the public domain. Elcock viewed leadership as a transcender of political concerns that could ameliorate the worst excesses of political expediency. Elcock's argument is compelling; however, any consideration of leadership in the public domain is complicated by the fuzzy boundaries between politicians as leaders and public servants as leaders.

Moore's (1995) original exposition of the public value framework, and specifically the 'strategic triangle', does not directly address leaders or leadership but rather talks of managers in the public sector. While this may be reflective of the time when there was generally less concern with differentiating leadership from management (and the terms were commonly used synonymously as can be seen in the description of the Kennedy Project in Moore 1995), questions about whether public value creation is, and should be, a concern of public managers and/or leaders remain important for the public administration of today. In other words, should public value creation be the main concern of their practice, and what are their respective roles in creating public value?

The development of the public value approach (PVA) poses fundamental questions for leaders regarding their practice and has implications for the broader concept of leadership. In particular, it raises questions around the legitimacy of public leaders in determining public value outcomes, given that public servants are not directly accountable to the public in electoral terms (also see Massey's chapter in this volume). From the public administration perspective, the theoretical development of PVA and its espoused meaning has been set against the failings of the new public management (NPM) reform agendas in Western democracies and globally in Westminster-style governance systems. These failings are well documented and can be argued to span continents (see, e.g. Fenwick and McMillan 2010). The works of Dunleavy (1995) on policy disasters and of Rhodes (1996) on network governance are early contributions to the debates surrounding key issues in the unintended consequences of such reform programmes. The search for a post-NPM organising paradigm has been a major concern for public administration scholars ever since. The failure to agree to such is reflective of the complexity of public service provision and of the concerns of actors involved.

Fenwick and McMillan (2010, p. 4) argue that 'the search for a unifying prescription for public service reform is fraught with theoretical and practical pitfalls and is likely to be futile… actors make sense of the public sector environment through complex and/or anti-foundational responses. There is no simple or single answer in considering the future of public policy and management: the future derives from (and will be interpreted by others through) the lived experience of the actors involved and the meaning assigned to what they do'. They further propose 'the inevitability of anti-foundationalism in a post-modern world…this [is] the only possible response in an environment where all previous positions, not least those associated with neo-liberalism, have failed' (2010, pp. 4–5).

Key theoretical contributions that have impacted this search for an organising paradigm have included that of Moore (1995) through the development of the concept of public value and subsequent interpretations of such by Stoker (2006), Rhodes and Wanna (2007), Benington

(2009) and Talbot (2009), for example. The development of public value is presented as a desirable and pervasive force in public service provision and may be considered to be an all-encompassing concept, as many alternative propositions in service delivery can be considered integral elements of the public value concept as defined by Moore (see, e.g. Rhodes' network governance).

Public value suggests that those charged with the provision of public services work within a strategic triangle; a system of accountabilities and strategy domains. In Moore's original conception, any preferred public service strategy should be capable of constituting public value through the production of outcomes that are deemed valuable by actors. Outcomes should be achievable within the finite resources available and be supported by all stakeholders. Public value is essentially an organising paradigm that demands an anti-foundational approach, where strategy is developed 'bottom-up' from interpretations of those that are closest to the situations and resultant needs of public service users, not from those far removed from the realities of the society they seek to serve.

Public managers, according to Moore's approach, have a key role in creating value through their balancing of various concerns in the strategic triangle. The triangle represents three areas of activity in service provision that must be aligned to promote public value creation and outcomes. Moore (1995) argues that public managers should identify a public value proposition that defines desired outcomes, work actively within the authorising environment to establish support for the proposition and enable the organisational capacities to achieve public value. In Moore's conception, managers must work both within organisational boundaries and beyond to achieve such. Here, they must lead provision through their melding of the concerns of actors within the domains. Importantly for Moore, the main leadership task is to interpret the value placed on outcomes (and not just outputs) by the actors involved and to mediate between them to maximise the meaning and resultant perceived benefit for individuals, publics and civil society. This involves a key leadership task of gauging the significance of certain outcomes for individuals and groups within the citizenry. In this way, public service leaders have to manage a moral obligation to society that distinguishes them from private sector leaders who, it may be argued, are concerned solely with the meeting of an individual's expectations within individualised contract arrangements.

Critiques of Moore's conception of public value (see, e.g. Bryson et al. 2017) highlight a main area of contention as involving the definition and evaluation of the base concept itself. Does public value differ from, for example, public good, and further how are the public (recipients of services) to be defined? It is argued by some that public value has the benefit of building on two previous paradigms—public administration and NPM—and drawing out elements of both to create a 'double strength' paradigm (Stoker 2006; Talbot 2009). However, the practice of public value creation will be greatly influenced by how the citizenry chooses to define themselves.

Within public value, the construction of the meaning of value is one that has implications for leaders and for the place of democracy and politics in public service provision. Benington (2009) offers a redefinition of value that goes beyond Moore's original conception and provides an alternative to the narrow performance focus therein. Benington's definition encompasses 'all that adds value to the public sphere' (p. 237) and includes aspects of political, social, economic, cultural, ecological and economic values. He further posits that public value is not a concern of the public sector acting in isolation but that necessarily outcomes are created by actors operating in the private and voluntary domains through their interactions with the public sector (and each other). For leaders, then, one of the challenges of the PVA involves influencing beyond the boundaries of public organisations through outward-facing, rather than inward-facing, leadership practice solely focussed on the sourcing of goods and services from other sectors. Leadership in the public sector is now broader in its concern than has previously been seen. Ayres (2019) argues that public leadership is now best represented as meta-governance and suggests that service delivery is best served through enactment of public leadership actions and behaviours that highlight process management, enabling of participation and the setting of clear service goals and boundaries. She further contends that 'many policy interventions rely on a distributed operational capacity so metagovernors also need to "manage out" to consider and align the broader value chain of which their organizations will form only part' (p. 284).

Various conceptions of what constitutes public value have also impacted the evaluation of such and how this may in turn influence future public reform agendas (see Pyper's chapter in this volume). Evaluation methodologies are underpinned by a set of philosophical assumptions about how the public domain should be viewed and developed. As with other concepts in governance (e.g. public worth and public good), public value evaluation is largely based on qualitative indicators as reform trajectories globally try to reposition the citizen at the heart of public service provision. Such repositioning has driven a concern with the views of citizens that are more fully expressed through qualitative means. However, public value and its evaluation suffer from the same issues of strategic positioning as, say, human resource development (HRD) where a vicious circle may develop between the consideration of impact and value in its totality versus that which can be easily measured (also see Oliver and Fraser's chapter in this volume). The difficulty for public sector leaders is simply that the more they are asked to justify resource use within governing systems that require 'evidence' and 'proof' of value, the more they are required to use quantitative indicators that do not represent the ethos behind public value nor easily capture the 'meaning' of public value for those that are the recipients of public services, and the ultimate arbiters of the value of public outcomes.

Jordan (2019) alludes to this issue in her review of value creation in the Wigan Deal, a social deal established in 2010 between Wigan Council and its publics (citizens, communities and business interests) to create better outcomes in the face of central government austerity measures and substantial funding cuts. She argues that the informal deal has worked on many levels in creating shared understandings of what value can be achieved but that the Council has yet to establish measures that consider how the Deal is working in relation to its specific objectives. Measures exist around integral elements of the Deal, but there is no mechanism for overarching evaluation or for gauging the public value created. This is reflective of the difficulties in measuring a totality where many value judgements are displayed and where, as a result, proxy measures become the most appealing (and manageable) default.

Drawing from Benington's (2009) definitional concepts above, for the practice of public value leadership, there is also the issue of the way in which public value may be successfully achieved. Working through considerations of Moore's strategic triangle, questions abound as to how leaders lead *in* a public value setting to ensure that outcomes are achieved and to develop feelings of trust and legitimacy in what they do. How does leading in a public value setting then differ from leading/managing in other domains?

Whilst the similarities and differences in leading and managing are well articulated in the leadership literature, the terms have been used synonymously in studies of public value and within the public administration literature more widely. Writing from a leadership perspective, Northouse

(2013) provides a meta-description of the key similarities and differences in leadership and management, stating that 'although there are clear differences between management and leadership, the two constructs overlap. When managers are involved in influencing a group to meet its goals, they are involved in leadership. When leaders are involved in planning, organizing, staffing, and controlling, they are involved in management. Both processes involve influencing a group of individuals toward goal attainment' (p. 14).

Building on Northouse's definition, it may be argued then that it is the way that leaders perform their tasks that differentiates them from managers, rather than a differing set of skills being employed. The foregrounding of direction setting, aligning people and maintaining motivation defines leadership beyond the planning, organising and controlling activities of managers. Hartley et al. (2019) provide a useful classification of recent conceptions of leadership in public value creation from a public administration perspective, highlighting three strands of influence. The first, they argue, moves towards systems-centric understandings through consideration of leadership as a collaborative activity, both within public organisations and across organisational networks. The second strand involves consideration of this systems-centred view of public value but highlights the different domains in which leadership takes place—between organisations in the public, private and voluntary sectors reflecting the definition of public value leadership offered by Benington (2009) above. The third strand involves leadership with political astuteness following Hartley et al. (2015), who argue that leadership happens within public value creation but that this is not unidirectional with clearly defined, shared understandings of purpose. Thus, leadership processes involve service provision articulated through careful manoeuvring of, and through, the constellation of provider organisations to reach best-fit solutions that are those deemed most acceptable to the greatest number of stakeholders. Importantly, they further identify the use of formal and informal political processes as one means through which public leaders can achieve public value outcomes.

Leading *in* a public value setting then is not the same as leading *in* the private domain or any other. While public value may still be developing as the dominant organising perspective for public service provision, the basic long-held differences between leadership and management in public and private organisations still provide a useful benchmark. This leads us to a question of *what* then is being led. Here, Rhodes' contention that there is something special about leadership in the public domain resonates in his argument that leadership in the public sector has 'a dual task of collective choice and encouraging the politics of participation' (1991, p. 549). Public value concerns can only strengthen this focus.

LEADERS AND LEADERSHIP PRACTICE

The leadership of public value creation involves promoting the co-production of services. For leaders, the 'what' of leading within a public value context necessarily involves engaging in co-production not only of service provision but also of public value. As with the public value concept itself, co-production is an area that has multiple theoretical bases, approaches and understandings. The practice of co-production is then not a free-standing activity but is set within varying organisational, professional and societal conventional wisdoms that each contains expectations in the form of desired outcomes and underlying assumptions which steer, and may sometimes undermine, the achievement of these desired outcomes. Filipe et al. (2017) talk to this very issue in their investigation of co-production of healthcare in London, stating that:

> As a policy term, co-production benefits from retaining a degree of ambiguity. Although the lack of a strict definition can complicate efforts to get collaborations off the ground, it also allows more flexibility by expanding rather than constraining what they might entail. This challenge is not simply a problem of translational "gaps" between policy and practice: it is a matter of organisational dispositions and positions, of personal attributions, and of conflicting assumptions about what co-production is and does in the context of health care. (p. 3)

Osborne et al. (2016) outline the various theoretical approaches to co-production and highlight the tensions within this aspect of public value. Drawing on both public administration and management perspectives, they define co-production as 'the voluntary or involuntary involvement of public service users in any of the design, management, delivery and/or evaluation of public services' (p. 640) and argue that recent reform agendas mean that 'co-production is intrinsic to the process of public service delivery and is linked directly to the co-creation of value both for service users and for society' (p. 644). In recognising one design outcome of recent reforms as the re-centring of the service recipient within co-production processes, they determine that a key public leadership challenge concerns the creation of channels through which recipients can engage in co-production processes and activities.

Within co-production processes and activities, what is it that public leaders can do to enable achievement of such? It is argued here that one critical leadership role involves environmental scanning to consider the power relationships between stakeholders so that imbalances may be ameliorated within the processes of co-production. Most reform agendas assume that public sector organisational and system change will benefit all equally and at the specific time points when certain public value outcomes are desired and/or required. Practice suggests that there are major difficulties in achieving this (Filipe et al. 2017), and again then we return to the issue of who constitutes 'the public' in public value.

Benington (2009) argues that the PVA requires a rethinking of the relationship between the individual and state in service provision. He considers that using civil society as an organising base is useful in allowing public leaders to engage in different communities and also to consider how best public value may be measured. Suggesting a definition of civil society by Cohen and Arato (1992) as compromising spheres of interactions between the economy and the state (however broadly that may be cast), he contends that 'more active engagement with civil society, in which much public service is "co-produced" with a range of formal and informal partners rather than by the state alone, implies a need for governments to discover new ways of indirect influence on the thinking and activity of other organisations and actors' (p. 241).

Questions of, and issues around, the relationship between civil society and state are no more keenly seen than in examples of co-production in the integration of health and social care services. Involving health services and local government agencies, reorganisation projects aim to create integrated joint boards across jurisdictions with the responsibility for the local health and care needs of patients. An extensive policy reform throughout the world of health and social care integration is dependent on leaders from the various sectors involved (and this will vary across governing systems) working together to produce outcomes that have value for, and are valued by, the recipients of services.

Leadership of co-production is however fraught with difficulties and requires new mind-sets, and ways of doing, for the leaders involved. There are, of course, as in any change process, procedural requirements, but how these are enacted is where leaders can directly influence and reset the ways in which services are valued by recipients. This may not in itself represent a return to top-down thinking, but certainly in the case of the UK, and Scotland in particular, it may be seen as representing a degree of relational turn in public value thinking and practice. Generally, unified leadership is seen as key to the success of integration projects (Carnochan and Austin 2002), but the degree of unification and indeed direction of travel of any new leadership constellation is really at the core of success no matter whether viewed from a top-down or bottom-up perspective. Within health and social care integration in the Scottish context, unified leadership is considered central in achieving the policy aims of the Scottish Government through the National Health and Wellbeing Outcomes where 'embedding outcomes requires support to frontline practice and strong leadership' (Scottish Government 2015, p. 21). The Scottish Government's Health and Social Care Delivery Plan (2016) further identifies leadership as critical and highlights the need for leadership development to 'ensure that current leaders are equipped to drive the changes required in health and social care …[and] also ensure sustainability of approach by identifying the next cohort of future leaders' (Scottish Government 2016, p. 20).

Integration may be seen as having two key purposes clearly identified by Capitman (2003) as efficacy and efficiency. When relating these purposes to a PVA, then efficacy may be seen as representing public value for the recipients and efficiency as representing public value for the broader civil society. The challenge for public leaders is to bring these sometimes competing concepts together in a context where resources are always at a premium. Yet how far can public leaders really counter political masters whose purpose, it may be argued, is self-satisfying and often disguised as attempting to achieve public value? This question is one that underlies many studies of public value creation. The power of politicians is an ever present for public leaders. Blaug et al. (2006) argue that

> Public value stands astride the fault that runs between politicians and public managers. It offers a new perspective on the trade-off between democracy and bureaucracy. Yet the importance it attaches to authorisation, democracy and dialogue cannot negotiate away this trade-off by simply dismissing efficiency. The public value approach must somehow locate and express public notions of value, and be viable and effective. An orientation to public value recognises both the need for efficiency and for democracy. (p. 16)

Studies of health and social care integration in the UK have shown the pervading influence of politicians and of politics. In a review of the success of the Greater Manchester experiment in health and social care devolution (colloquially known as the Devo Manc Project), Walshe et al. (2018) highlight the problems around facilitating meaningful devolution for integration, concluding that

> Most of the policy agenda that is being pursued in Greater Manchester reflects closely the national priorities of the government and the Department of Health and Social Care, and the NHS mandate and priorities and planning guidance of NHS England. In that sense, devolution has not been an exercise in allowing local autonomy or control over policy, but over its implementation. (p. 6)

> A National Audit Office report considering health and social care integration in England also highlighted the impact of political concerns on integration success arguing that 'shifts in policy emphasis and reorganisations… have complicated the path to integration'. (Comptroller and Auditor General 2017, p. 7)

Research investigating the leadership of early health and social care integration projects identified that outcomes were often overlooked in favour of achieving the organisational change itself. For leaders, the success of 'joining–up' was the main means by which they were held accountable (Sandfort 1999). Leadership actions were then focussed on creation of integrated structures rather than on what those structures could enable. But such an approach represents bounded, or low-level, integration of ideas and of service delivery structures rather than a higher level systems integration. Systems integration (e.g. of information technology or human resources) requires leaders to let go and work in new ways. It requires organisations to break their cultures, to abandon conventional wisdoms and to undertake holistic organisational change. As Sandfort (1999) argues, however, such integration must be unidirectional and conducted in a timeous way as there will be no individualised organisational systems to return to.

In achieving systems integration, organisational cultures provide the greatest challenge for public leaders. Unidirectional change towards new integrated boards may be hindered by the existence of strong organisational subcultures often based around professional identities, for example, of clinicians and allied health practitioners. Integration requires a weaving together of subcultures which must often be achieved within a situation of power differentials between various organisational actors. Thus, jolting and incremental change towards an integrated culture forms the new operating environment for most leaders within health and social care integration (Lyngso et al. 2014).

Managing power relationships between organisations and the possible resultant cultural discord within organisations is one of the major challenges for leaders trying to ensure public value outcomes (as highlighted earlier in this chapter). The complex nature of organisational cultures means that cultural integration is often approached in a prescriptive manner outlining what needs to happen to facilitate change rather than considering how this may be achieved. As culture is integrally linked to organisational context, this is not an unsurprising approach; however, relative power bases are also at play in efforts to create integrated cultures. In health and social care integration, professional tensions are common, and these can translate into value judgements being made about the importance of the knowledge and practice of others (Peck et al. 2001; Scragg 2006).

Changes in the relative power balance between integration actors are a cause of relational turn as witnessed in in examples of health and social care integration in the UK. Relational turn makes it more difficult for leaders to achieve planned change and militates against the creation of meaningful public value for all. Drawing on Moore's original conception of the public value landscape, there are three major players within today's integration domain: politicians (at national and local levels), provider organisations (public, private and voluntary) and the publics (individual recipients and the wider civil society). Relational turn, it may be argued, has now been through two phases: the first represented by the rising power of the publics in determining what services *should* be provided and how these should be manifest (examples of early stage and low level integration) and the second (examples of later stage and systems integration) by the rising power of leaders (both organisational and political) in determining what *can* be provided within the resources available. The publics are no longer in the ascendency in the power dynamics of the integration domain in the UK.

The policy objectives of health and social care integration in the UK are aimed at the creation of patient-centric care which, as Hutchison (2015) notes, 'correlate[d] to improved individual outcomes as well as single points of patient contact and consistent streamlined service' (p.133). Early-stage integration has been evidenced through local strategies focussing on the management of long-term conditions and on the reduction in the reliance on institutionalised care in favour of community-based interventions. Public health service delivery has also been refocussed, with the main responsibility for provision being transferred to local authorities (Edwards 2013; Hutchison 2015). These developments, within an overall drive to empower service recipients, allowed user voice in service decisions through, for example, the establishment of service user forums in provider organisations. It is also argued that moves towards strengthening regulation dissipated existing health and social care organisation's power bases (Edwards 2013).

The salience of systems integration cannot be overstated. In particular, information technology integration allows information to be shared in meaningful ways and for leaders to plan provision more effectively. Although such later-stage integration is still developing, Atherton et al. (2015) show the importance of transparency and trust in information sharing in their study of the linking and use of health and social care data in Scotland. Resultant robust management of the expectations of users has allowed leaders to strengthen their relative power bases in determining what provision possibilities exist at specific points within service provision processes. Certainly, there is scope for further integration as projects explore the mining of big data to enhance the effectiveness of planning processes (Buchanan et al. 2017).

Yet public leaders, and especially political leaders, are open to the influences of the pendulum of popularity and must recognise that relational turn may have an ongoing impact on *what* they are leading. Leaders may well be hindered in public value creation by their own, and their organisations', capacities and capabilities. These capacities and capabilities have been identified as primarily concerning the processes required for integrated practice. So, issues around overall aim of the integration, the respective roles and responsibilities of the actors, management of provider organisations' differing visions, willingness to share information, differing professional ideologies, building and maintenance of provision relationships and financial uncertainty, for example, are most commonly cited as influences (Cameron et al. 2013).

Integration processes also impact *how* public leaders lead; increasingly, traditional top-down models of leadership and followership are cast aside in favour of practices around co-leadership and followership (West et al. 2014; Klinga et al. 2016). The principles of co-leadership are variously termed in the literature, but as Williams (2012) notes, co-leadership assumes the central positioning of tasks in defining service provision practices rather than, for example, individual organisational leadership roles. Co-leadership is structured through leaders in each principal provider organisation (usually two), leading in pairings around specific service tasks. Co-leadership also positions followers in a co-followership relationship. The advantages of such arrangements for service provision and public value creation are clear—allowing a direct link to the services provided. But equally, questions of rhetoric and reality are levelled at the leadership of integration projects with what is espoused as co-leadership being far from the realities of organisational (and professional) silo leadership (Ling et al. 2012).

Recent studies of co-leadership as a vehicle for public value creation in health and social care integration highlight the barriers to co-leadership and the leadership shortcomings that lead to difficulties in achieving the ultimate goal of value for all. Stewart (2017), in his consideration of the integration project in Scotland, highlights the scepticism of leaders in co-leading and proposes that trust is a key bulwark against co-leadership. It may be that leaders are not openly, or even knowingly, hostile to such co-leadership; however, difficulties in co-production and service co-ordination across organisational boundaries are premised on the strength of individual organisational cultures (Fenwick and McMillan 2013). Where cultures resist, trust is lessened. The irony of the impact of organisational culture on co-leading for public value is that, as identified by Schneider and Barbera (2014), leadership is central to the creation and maintenance of cultures. For public leaders, there is a choice that must be made as to how far they open up to 'real' co-leadership rather than either acting as one at the margins or partially committing to joint decision-making for the services they seek to provide.

Klinga et al. (2016) argue that there are certain preconditions that are required to facilitate co-leadership, arguing that co-leadership support and practice at the top of the integrating organisations is essential along with the co-location of leadership activity. They also identify personal and interpersonal preconditions as important in impacting facilitation. Klinga et al. highlight openness of leaders and an acceptance of the equal value of the two leadership parties as critical. Further, in the practice of co-leadership, they argue a series of factors are important in maintaining such an approach. They highlight leader flexibility in resource allocation. Leaders are required to think beyond the boundaries of the individual organisation and to consider task (or individual user) paramount so that resources become centred rather than split according to whether the task is rooted in the health or social care domain.

Yet, for many leaders, the practice of co-leadership is fraught with difficulties, and co-leadership rhetoric is not being replicated in their lived experiences. For example, Beswick (2014), in a study of leadership challenges in the integration of health and social care in the Scottish Highlands, suggests that practice issues revolve around the lack of trust between leaders, thus impeding how they engage with integration reform processes. In particular, lack of trust between leaders in co-leadership practices impacts negatively how leaders view the motives of their 'partner' leaders.

Brown and Head (2019) also argue that there are tensions in leadership co-production of public value outcomes through the enduring influence of traditional models of public administration. In their study of public value leadership in the integration of services for indigenous communities in Australia, they conclude that success for leaders is based on the balancing of the elements in Moore's strategic triangle and that 'public leaders need to strategically balance authorization, capability and public value creation throughout a reform process…policy failure is not necessarily a result of either policy or implementation or capacity deficiencies, but may arise as a complex interplay between all three factors' (p. 261).

Within the British context, leadership has also been highlighted as central to the achievement of public value outcomes (however these may be evaluated). Hutchison (2015) begins to identify the 'what' of leadership in terms of specific leadership competencies required rather than considering 'what' public leaders are leading in terms of the process architecture of public value creation. This view is interesting as it addresses not what leaders need to do, and the perceived difficulties, but identifies where there are gaps in individual leadership skills and practice and thereby offers a new lens on issues in public value creation. Hutchison (2015) argues that 'the success or failure of a local change effort may not rest with the indicated structures, either national or local, but the ability of the key leaders to exhibit assured traits throughout implementation' (p. 137). Through enhancing the competences of leaders, Hutchison (2015) contends that integration projects may be more likely to be successful and that integration may require leaders to lead differently through either engaging with new skills or enhancing skills that are less obvious, and critical, in traditional public administration approaches to service provision. Indeed, he goes further to suggest that 'each local area should therefore investigate fully the leadership characteristics of the key personnel involved in the change process and question their ability to deliver organisational transformation' (p.137).

What, then, may these new, or recast, competencies be? What is it that leaders need to do differently in enabling public value creation? Research around this question foregrounds the importance of entrepreneurialism. Morse (2010) usefully draws on the notion of public value leaders as 'boundary spanners' looking beyond individual organisations and formal partnerships to the wider public service domain and contends that 'integrative leaders are entrepreneurs who create public value' (p. 243). In unpacking what this means for leaders, then risk-taking, innovativeness and pro-activity appear central to success in public value creation. Risk-taking, it is argued, is certainly not a trait encouraged in traditional conceptions of the leadership of public services (Currie et al. 2008).

Even where leaders may have personal traits akin to those of risk-taking and innovativeness, there remain issues around how these may be evaluated within a public value climate where organisational cultures are still underpinned by fear, blame and trust issues (Hutchison 2015). Certainly, a light touch from national and local policy-makers (politicians) may ameliorate some of the manifestations of fear, blame and trust, but this may not be readily experienced by public leaders due to the extended accountabilities that the public value approach encourages. Interpretations of public value outcomes developed through formal and informal evaluation mechanisms act as a key influence on the ways in which public leaders choose to lead (Vedung 2017). Leadership in public value creation is therefore a complex phenomenon and one critical to the sustainability of the public value approach.

Public Value Leadership: Challenges and Prospects

Leaders within the public value domain have to think beyond simply *what* they are leading to consider their leadership *for* public value. Sustainability of public value leadership is now a key concern both in terms of personal sustainability and the resultant outcomes leaders may achieve for their publics.

The need for sustainable leadership may be aligned with concerns highlighted by Hartley et al. (2019) in their call for studies of loss and displacement of public value so that a comprehensive view and understanding of public value may be achieved. Sustainability of public value outcomes is critical in guarding against loss and displacement through ensuring the efficient use of limited resources and reducing the need for multiple, differing and simultaneous delivery strands to reinforce value outcomes for particular publics.

Hartley et al. (2019) argue that public value is not always a 'win-win-win' situation for the politicians, organisations and publics involved and that displacement may be a more common outcome than much of the research implies. Displacement occurs where certain publics, or communities within specific publics, lose or have declining value from public services in order to provide increases in service value for publics elsewhere. Public value then is neither complete nor static—it is a moving feast of gains and losses that leaders have to manage themselves, their organisations and their publics through. Indeed, leaders may themselves have to create loss and displacement realities in order to achieve higher level public value and/or value for certain publics and communities in the longer term. This is reflective of the second wave of relational turn in public value creation through integration. However, success in value creation may also be an outcome of the sustainability of public leaders themselves rather than of organisational systems impacting in isolation.

Sustainable leadership is one paradigm response to the global financial crises of 2008, and the years that followed, where organisations suffered a series of shock events that tested conventional understandings of the primacy of the shareholder-first model of leadership generally espoused in the private sector. Stakeholder-first approaches to leadership were required in order to broaden the operating environments of many organisations in the private sector where their traditional markets were no longer assured. Sustainable leadership was also borne of the growing concern around the moral obligations of organisations where leaders were viewed as responsible for ensuring ethical, ecological and, to a certain extent, the emancipatory operation of business so that all stakeholders are considered and societal value created (Porter and Kramer 2011).

The study of sustainable leadership is a developing field where the main focus moves between the organisational and individual levels of analysis. Grounded in conceptions of environmental sustainability, sustainable leadership has been discussed by major proponents. Avery and Bergsteiner (2011) as primarily comprising a long-term vision achieved through the interplay of higher level leadership practices including trust, knowledge sharing, devolved decision-making, team orientation, self-management and creating an enabling culture. Considering the multiple definitions and frameworks of sustainable leadership, it is argued that there is no one best way of ensuring its achievement as 'sustainable leadership emerges from the interplay of many factors ... there is no one "right" way within the overall sustainable leadership paradigm' (2011, p. 5).

Gerard et al. (2017) provide a meta-conception of, and framework for, sustainable leadership for organisations. They argue that sustainable leadership is an outcome of the relationships and exchanges between three dimensions: stakeholder considerations, organisational processes and the external environment. They further contend that

> 'the successful implementation of sustainable leadership arguably depends on an effective sustainable culture within the organisation and how this is affected by the external environment... the leadership of an organisation can hugely impact its culture. A pivotal argument here is the role and development of employees and leaders which must be central to an organisation's sustainable success. If there is not a culture of development and conservation within an organisation then the underpinnings of sustainable leadership are crucially missing' (p.133).

Given the importance of relationship building in creating public value outcomes, it is important that maintenance of such is supported at the individual level through developing the sustainability of leaders. Non-deliberate public value displacement is reduced when a long-term view is taken by public service providers. Casserley and Critchley (2010) have identified that sustainability of leadership and of organisations is predicated on three core individualised processes: reflection on action; psychological intelligence and psychological well-being. Psychological intelligence, they argue, is defined as 'having a clear sense of personal purpose and an awareness of personal assumptions and motivations' (p. 290) and is reflective of the self-awareness domain in Goleman's (1998) *Emotional Intelligence* model of competencies and skills that drive leadership performance.

For Casserley and Critchley (2010), sustainable leadership is a move away from the top-down control-based view of organisational leadership where 'unilateral decision making, or decision making by a small inner circle, is the norm even on business activities involving significant business risk... Moreover, it is all too easy for leaders to extend this illusion of control to believing they can predict and control the consequences of their decision making for society as a whole' (p.288). In public value creation, this may help allay the concerns of many public administration scholars around placing the public servant in prime position in determining public service delivery and defining value.

In developing a sustainable leadership approach, there is a need for a new way of thinking and doing in developing organisational leaders' competency and capacity (Casserley and Critchley 2010). The traditional paradigms of leadership development advance a concern with performance, development of individual competencies, modification of behaviours, off-the-job training and prescriptive solutions to perceived leadership failings. In contrast, sustainable leadership requires development through reflection on action, emphasis on sustainability as precondition to performance and enhancing the integration of leaders' core processes with the culture of the organisation (p. 292).

However, the underlying requirements for sustainable leadership development for public value creation are extremely difficult to enact in current service systems. Reflecting on action in dealing with real-life adversity, for example, is predicated on the assumption that leaders have safe space in which to reflect. Where public value is determined by all service stakeholders, this makes for a crowded and often conflictual leadership space where the outcomes of reflection may not always be positively received. Again a hands-off approach by politicians is necessary so that blame does not partner reflexive leadership practices. In similar vein, service performance is a pervasive influence on how public value is evaluated. Creating desirable outcomes remains the main aim of leadership action rather than a concern with how these are produced, further blurring the focus on the quality of relationship between the individual leader's core processes and organisational culture.

Given the issues raised in this chapter, there is a need to make sense of leadership for public value and to consider the ways in which leaders can lead for sustainable public value. Hartley et al. (2019) have provided an argument that leading for public value requires a set of competencies to be developed and enacted that may, when taken together, represent the overarching organising concept of political astuteness. Such a position clearly differentiates public value leadership from traditional shareholder models and draws on the assertion that context is critical.

Political astuteness or variations thereof have long been considered an important influence on the leadership of public services. Hartley et al. (2019) argue that 'political astuteness enhances value creation through improving the capability of actors to understand, manage, and coordinate various of the interests at stake…[t]here is, therefore, an argument to be made that political astuteness is an important missing ingredient linking leadership and public value in many contexts' (p. 244). It can also be argued that political astuteness is important in enhancing the sustainability of public leaders through enabling them to be more proactive and orchestrate public value creation more fully. Through removing stresses that may be an outcome of reactive leadership practices, burnout may be avoided and psychological and physiological well-being improved. In this respect, burnout is a key challenge in improving the sustainability of leaders (Casserley and Critchley 2010).

Investigations of political astuteness in creating public value for groups, publics and civil society suggest that there is impact on how leaders lead for public value (Hartley et al. 2017; Ayres 2019). Competencies range from the more deliberative network negotiation to less deliberative or 'soft' type competencies, reflecting attributes related to emotional intelligence such as the ability to 'read' others. However, recognition of the link between leadership and political astuteness in creating public value has potential pitfalls for the practice of public value creation and sustainability of value outcomes.

Further questions are raised around the place of public servants vis-a-vis political leaders in influencing public value. The democratic position of public servants has traditionally been that of advisor to those who are democratically accountable to wider publics through the electoral process. Rhodes and Wanna (2007) question the desirability of a deliberate breaching of the boundary between decision-maker and producer for democratic accountability and future governance (also see Massey's chapter in this volume). A bigger question that challenges fundamental values in governance is raised by the possibilities of public organisation leaders playing a higher level role of arbiter in who should gain and in what ways from publicly funded service provision.

Second, in successful public value creation, the relationships between public leaders and leaders in provider organisations outwith the public sphere require to be based on principles of co-leadership. Questions arise around the levels of political astuteness of the partner leaders and what levels are required. Further, is political astuteness used by public leaders to strengthen bonds between leaders or weaken the influence of external leaders in the relationship? Recent research by Ayres (2019) suggests that political astuteness should be available across sectors through the metagovernance of provision networks. She argues that 'soft metagovernance involves utilizing social contacts and relationships to pursue network objectives and can be particularly important to metagovernors who may not be resource-rich or do not command formal authority' (p. 280), even where leaders 'employ soft metagovernance intuitively as a consequence of "happenstance" as opposed to a decisive and coordinated organizational strategy' (p. 292). However, there is still relatively little research around the possibilities of achieving meta-governance and importantly the possible unintended consequences that may ensue. Where nongovernmental leaders are engaging in meta-governance, then the issues around the de-democratisation of public value creation are writ large.

Third, it raises issues around training and development for political astuteness and meta-governance. Calls for programmes to equip leaders in required skills and competences usually stop at the 'need for' stage and do not consider how these may be facilitated or indeed what the focus should be. We must also remember that for those nongovernmental leaders, it is likely that facets of political astuteness may run counter to the skills and competences desired in their wider organisational and/or business settings. All leaders engaging in creation of public value outcomes must be aware of the ways in which outcomes may be valued by groups within, and levels of, society. However, such evaluation is a complex phenomenon impacted by issues such as rationality, recency and reflection. Vedung (2017) hints at the complicated nature of evaluation through reference to definitional issues, describing evaluation as a semantic magnet, and through breadth of public service provision, where areas of activity are often interlinked and interdependent in creating public value outcomes.

For leaders, evaluation of public value is a key concern as a judgement of their leadership performance. It is argued here, however, that leaders are not wholly divorced from how that evaluation is constructed and how value is ultimately forged in the minds of the publics concerned. Leaders are not passive recipients but are key agents influencing the evaluation process. The way that leaders influence evaluation is an output of the purpose of evaluation. Certainly in public value creation and maintenance, evaluation may lead to service improvement, termination or public policy debate, or sometimes mixtures of the three, but evaluation for accountability still has a purpose and is a strong driver in evaluation processes. This is not surprising given that evaluation is usually retrospective and publics will refer to a narrow set of meanings in evaluation which have accountability at their root. As Vedung (2017) contends, 'exercising evaluation for accountability reasons, that is, principals undertaking evaluation with the aim of holding their executives responsible for what they have done, is a perfectly valid purpose for evaluation' (p. 13).

Leaders impact public value evaluation through direct actions and indirectly through the shortcomings shown by various publics in the co-production and co-evaluation of services. A central influence is the advantage leaders have through professional knowledge of, and experience in, service production. Professional knowledge is something that most publics will not possess in great enough quantity to be able to map the possibilities for service provision. Obviously, public leaders are part of the broader civil society, but evaluation at this level is less likely to impact directly on specific and/or localised service provision but rather impacts higher level policy directions. More directly, leaders legitimise evaluation methodologies and through this define the boundaries for evaluation. For publics wishing to impact public value outcomes, there is a premium to expressing evaluations within accepted methodologies as bounded public value is preferable to loss or displacement as a result of difficulties in articulating value judgements clearly to providers. This is especially important in evaluations of public value for ongoing activities where improvement may be more timeously and directly impacted. Again, however, we return to a core concern within democratic systems of the degree to which leaders should be concerned with the evaluation of public value outcomes. Is there a moral obligation to provide quality services that meet the needs of users, however these may be valued?

Conclusions

Public leadership is a complex concept in terms of both theory and practice. Many of the problems in understanding, changing and ultimately improving leadership in and for public value settings are an outcome of competing views of the role and scope of leadership, and the influence of multiple stakeholders' control over leadership actions. The capacity of public leaders, both collectively and individually, to align concerns across leadership dimensions, where each may be considered a distinct microsystem, is critical for successful and sustainable public value leadership practice. Yet, there are distinct opportunities for public leaders to positively impact outcomes for the citizenry they serve. Leaders can, and do, influence outcomes in the face of the contextual challenges they face through collaborative action in particular. Joined-up leadership is possibly the greatest test, and yet greatest success for leaders in service provision. This can be seen within health and social care integration where public value leaders have come together across sectors, professions and disciplines to form leadership constellations. If we consider this as positive in impacting individual outcomes and value, then the possibilities for purposeful public value leadership may be less limited than we imagine.

It is argued here then that hallmarks of public value leadership should include considerations that will strengthen leadership constellations: through personal mastery (e.g. sustainability and innovativeness), considerations of skills (e.g. negotiation and risk management) and considerations of competencies (e.g. emotional intelligence and relationship building). Through development of hallmarks (at organisational and individual levels), the practice of public value leadership may be understood more fully and improvements defined and ultimately evaluated within the contexts in which it operates. In order to fully appreciate the affective capacity of public value leadership, despite the need for evidence-based evaluation in certain instances, those with political authority should resist the quantification of public value leadership evaluation through the development of a hands-off approach that allows those closest to the needs of civil society to provide value outcomes for that civil society.

References

Atherton, I. M., Lynch, E., Williams, A. J., & Witham, M. D. (2015). Barriers and Solutions to Linking and Using Health and Social Care Data in Scotland. *British Journal of Social Work, 45,* 1614–1622.

Avery, G. C., & Bergsteiner, H. (2011). Sustainable Leadership Practices for Enhancing Business Resilience and Performance. *Strategy & Leadership, 39*(3), 5–15.

Ayres, S. (2019). How Can Network Leaders Promote Public Value through Soft Metagovernance? *Public Administration, 97,* 279–295.

Barber, M. (2017). *Delivering Better Outcomes for Citizens: Practical Steps for Unlocking Public Value.* London: HM Treasury.

Benington, B. (2009). Creating the Public in Order to Create Public Value? *International Journal of Public Administration, 32*(3–4), 232–249.

Beswick, E. (2014). What are the Leadership Lessons from the Integration of Health and Social Care in the Scottish Highlands? *International Journal of Integrated Care, 14*(6). https://doi.org/10.5334/ijic.1624.

Blaug, R., Horner, L., & Lekhi, R. (2006). *Public Value, Politics and Public Management: A Literature Review.* London: The Work Foundation.

Brown, P. R., & Head, B. W. (2019). Navigating Tensions in Co-Production: A Missing Link in Leadership for Public Value. *Public Administration, 97*, 250–263.

Bryson, J., Sancino, A., Benington, J., & Sørensen, E. (2017). Towards a Multi-Actor Theory of Public Value Co-Creation. *Public Management Review, 19*(5), 640–654.

Buchanan, W., Thuemmler, C., Spyra, G., Smales, A., & Prajapati, B. (2017). *Towards Trust and Governance in Integrated Health and Social Care Platforms.* In C. Thuemmler & C. Bai (Eds.), *Health 4.0: How Virtualization and Big Data are Revolutionizing Healthcare* (pp. 219–231). Switzerland: Springer International Publishing.

Cameron, A., Lart, R., Bostock, L., & Coomber, C. (2013). Factors that Promote and Hinder Joint and Integrated Working between Health and Social Care Services: A Review of Research Literature. *Health & Social Care in the Community, 22*(3), 287–295.

Capitman, J. (2003). Effective Coordination of Medical and Supportive Services. *Journal of Aging and Health, 15*(1), 124–164.

Carnochan, S. & Austin. M. J. (2002). Implementing Welfare Reform and Guiding Organizational Change. *Administration in Social Work, 26*(1), 61–77.

Casserley, T., & Critchley, B. (2010). A New Paradigm of Leadership Development. *Industrial and Commercial Training, 42*(6), 116–126.

Chiapello, E., & Fairclough, N. (2002). Understanding the New Management Ideology: A Transdisciplinary Contribution from Critical Discourse Analysis and New Sociology of Capitalism. *Discourse & Society, 13*(2), 185–208.

Cohen, J., & Arato, A. (1992). *Civil Society and Political Theory.* Cambridge, MA: MIT Press.

Comptroller and Auditor General. (2017). *Health and Social Care Integration.* Session 2016–17, HC1001, National Audit Office.

Currie, G., Humphreys, M., Ucbasarfan, D., & McManus, S. (2008). Entrepreneurial Leadership in the English Public Sector: Paradox or Possibility? *Public Administration, 86*, 987–1008.

Denis, J.-L., Langley, A., & Rouleau, L. (2007). *Rethinking Leadership in Public Organizations.* In E. Ferlie, L. E. Lynn Jr., & C. Pollitt (Eds.), *The Oxford Handbook of Public Management* (pp. 446–467). New York: Oxford University Press.

Dunleavy, P. (1995). Policy Disasters: Explaining the UK's Record. *Public Policy and Administration, 10*(2), 52–70.

Edwards, N. (2013). Implementation of the Health and Social Care Act. *British Medical Journal, 346*, 2090.

Elcock, H. (2000). Management is Not Enough: We Need Leadership! *Public Policy and Administration, 15*(1), 15–28.

Elcock, H. (2001). *Political Leadership*. Cheltenham: Edward Elgar.
Elcock, H., & Fenwick, J. (2012). The Political Leadership Matrix: A Tool for Analysis. *Public Money & Management, 32*(2), 87–94.
Fenwick, J., & McMillan, J. (2010). Public Management in the Postmodern Era: An Introduction. In J. Fenwick & J. McMillan (Eds.), *Public Management in the Postmodern Era: Challenges and Prospects* (pp. 3–11). Cheltenham: Edward Elgar.
Fenwick, J., & McMillan, J. (2013). Management Development and Co-Production: Myths and Realities. *Journal of Management Development, 32*(9), 971–983.
Filipe, A., Renedo, A., & Marston, C. (2017). The Co-Production of What? Knowledge, Values, and Social Relations in Health Care. *PLoS Biology, 15*(5), e2001403.
Gerard, L., McMillan, J., & D'Annunzio-Green, N. (2017). Conceptualising Sustainable Leadership. *Industrial and Commercial Training, 49*(3), 116–126.
Goleman, D. (1998). *Working with Emotional Intelligence*. New York: Bantam.
Hartley, J., Alford, J., Hughes, O., & Yates, S. (2015). Public Value and Political Astuteness in the Work of Public Managers: The Art of the Possible. *Public Administration, 93*, 195–211.
Hartley, J., Alford, J., Knies, E., & Douglas, S. (2017). Towards an Empirical Research Agenda for Public Value Theory. *Public Management Review, 19*, 670–685.
Hartley, J., Parker, S., & Beashel, J. (2019). Leading and Recognizing Public Value. *Public Administration, 97*, 264–278.
Hutchison, K. F. (2015). An Exploration of the Integration of Health and Social Care within Scotland Senior Stakeholders' Views of the Key Enablers and Barriers. *Journal of Integrated Care, 23*(3), 129–142.
Jordan, E. (2019). *The Wigan Deal*. The Future of Government Series, Centre for Public Impact.
Klinga, C., Hansson, J., Hasson, H., & Sachs, M. (2016). Co-Leadership—A Management Solution for Integrated Health and Social Care. *International Journal of Integrated Care, 16*(2), 1–9.
Lindgreen, A., Koenig-Lewis, N., Kitchener, M., Brewer, J. D., Moore, M. H., & Meynhardt, T. (Eds.). (2019). *Public Value*. London: Routledge.
Ling, T., Brereton, L., Conklin, A., Newbould, J., & Roland, M. (2012). Barriers and Facilitators to Integrating Care: Experiences from the English Integrated Care Pilots. *International Journal of Integrated Care, 12*(3), 1–12.
Lüdeke-Freund, F. (2010). Towards a Conceptual Framework of 'Business Models for Sustainability'. In J. Wever, A. Quist, J. Tukker, F. Woudstra, N. Boons, & N. Beute (Eds.), *Knowledge, Collaboration and Learning for Sustainable Innovation*. Delft.

Lyngso, A. M., Skavlan, N., Host, D., & Frolich, A. (2014). Instruments to Assess Integrated Care: A Systematic Review. *International Journal of Integrated Care, 14*(9), e027.

Mazzucatto, M. (2018). *The Value of Everything*. London: Penguin.

Moore, M. H. (1995). *Creating Public Value*. Cambridge, MA: Harvard University Press.

Morse, R. (2010). Integrative Public Leadership: Catalyzing Collaboration to Create Public Value. *The Leadership Quarterly, 21*, 231–245.

Northouse, P. (2013). *Leadership: Theory and Practice* (6th ed.). Thousand Oaks: Sage.

Osborne, S. P., Radnor, Z., & Strokosch, K. (2016). Co-Production and the Co-Creation of Value in Public Services: A Suitable Case for Treatment? *Public Management Review, 18*(5), 639–653.

Peck, E., Towell, D., & Gulliver, P. (2001). The Meanings of Culture in Health and Social Care: A Case Study of the Combined Trust in Somerset. *Journal of Interprofessional Care, 15*(4), 319–327.

Porter, M. E., & Kramer, M. R. (2011). Creating Shared Value. *Harvard Business Review, 1*, 62–77.

Rhodes, R. A. W. (1991). Theory and Methods in British Public Administration: The View from Political Science. *Political Studies, 39*(3), 533–554.

Rhodes, R. A. W. (1996). The New Governance: Governing without Government. *Political Studies, 44*(4), 652–667.

Rhodes, R. A. W., & Wanna, J. (2007). The Limits to Public Value, or Rescuing Responsible Government from the Platonic Guardians. *Australian Journal of Public Administration, 66*, 406–421.

Sandfort, J. (1999). The Structural Impediments to Human Service Collaboration: Examining Welfare Reform at the Front Lines. *Social Service Review, 73*(3), 314–339.

Schneider, B., & Barbera, K. M. (Eds.). (2014). *Oxford Handbook of Organizational Climate and Culture*. New York: Oxford University Press.

Scottish Government. (2015). *National Health and Wellbeing Outcomes: A Framework for Improving the Planning and Delivery of Integrated Health and Social Care Services*. Edinburgh: Scottish Government.

Scottish Government. (2016). *Health and Social Care Delivery Plan*. Edinburgh: Scottish Government.

Scragg, T. (2006). An Evaluation of Integrated Team Management. *Journal of Integrated Care, 14*(3), 39–48.

Stewart, A. (2017). *Understanding Key Challenges in Health and Social Care Integration in Scotland: Principal Stakeholders' Perspectives*. Edinburgh Napier University.

Stoker, G. (2006). Public Value Management: A New Narrative for Networked Governance. *The American Review of Public Administration, 36*, 41–57.

Talbot, C. (2009). Public Value—The Next "Big Thing" in Public Management? *International Journal of Public Administration, 32*(3–4), 167–170.

Vedung, E. (2017). *Public Policy and Program Evaluation*. Oxford: Routledge.

Walshe, K., Lorne, C., Coleman, A., McDonald, R., & Turner, A. (2018). *Devolving Health and Social Care: Learning from Greater Manchester*. Manchester: The University of Manchester.

West, M., Eckert, R., Steward, K., & Pasmore, B. (2014). *Developing Collective Leadership for Healthcare*. London: The King's Fund.

Williams, P. (2012). The Role of Leadership in Learning and Knowledge for Integration. *Journal of Integrated Care, 20*(3), 164–174.

CHAPTER 8

Accountability and Networks: Mind the Gap

Andrew Massey

This chapter focuses on the properties and contours of accountability within the context of the contemporary UK reform agendas. Furthermore, it sets this alongside the public value debate and discusses the potential ways in which the increased complexity of new kinds of accountability, that is, ways in which accountability is differently emphasised and targeted, can adversely affect the pursuit of public value. The chapter also considers issues such as blame-gaming, culpability avoidance and how network-based approaches to reform pose difficulties for transparent lines of accountability. We need to remember that states, and their public administration systems, are comprised of individuals who are also members of institutions. Institutions cannot possess a human personality, but consist of people all with a persona. Institutions are designed to control people and to serve them simultaneously. John (2018, p. 1) neatly encapsulates this:

> We live in an age of large public policy problems that governments find hard to solve. These include obesity, climate change, terrorism, race discrimination,

A. Massey (✉)
International School for Government, Kings College London, London, UK
e-mail: andrew.1.massey@kcl.ac.uk

© The Author(s) 2021
J. Connolly, A. van der Zwet (eds.), *Public Value Management, Governance and Reform in Britain*, International Series on Public Policy, https://doi.org/10.1007/978-3-030-55586-3_8

corruption and youth unemployment ... these problems share their origin in human behavioural traits that persist over time. Behaviours create and sustain poor outcomes, both for individual citizens and communities .... Effective policy outcomes usually depend on some degree of citizen action and responsiveness.

Individual behaviour and response to policy initiatives, however, are often transmitted through peer groups and 'close social networks' (John 2018, p. 1). As governments have restructured, reformed and re-engineered the state and its institutions, the interactions and citizen responses to global issues with a local impact, such as recycling, immunisation or cultural integration, have become integral to governance. The issue of accountability, therefore, often lies at the heart of institutional responses. Individuals, however, are members of a range of formal and informal institutions, such as families, cultural groups, civil society groups, employing organisations, religious groups, social media sites and occasionally even political parties. These all contribute to a society's governance structures and are integral to overlapping networks of individuals and institutions, some of which are engaged in the policy process and, in the case of many parts of civil society, are also part of a governance network that clouds lines of political and social accountability (Bevir 1995, p. 171).

In this chapter, literature on policy networks and accountability is examined in order to bring such challenges to the fore in the context of public value debates in Britain. There are clear and intentional links and intersections with earlier chapters on governance and new public management (NPM) reform. Although this volume is concerned with governance and reform in Britain and by implication focussed on 'good governance', it is important to remember that the context of UK public reform is both local and global, and many of the lessons learned in the UK are watched and pondered from afar. Likewise, the UK would do well to reflect on lessons from other jurisdictions. Mungiu-Pippidi and Johnston (2017) note that in this broader development context, even affluent and stable countries may discover that their

> (S)ound institutions can weaken or become out of touch; anti-system parties and would-be strongmen can capitalise on economic and cultural stresses and on global and regional population movements, to undermine consensus, legitimacy, tolerance and democratic values. (p. 262)

The chapter begins by defining the concept (or rather different concepts) of accountability and continues with an exploration of the different types and levels of accountability. It then sets this into the public administration and public management context. Short discussions to illustrate the concepts and problems of blame-gaming and culpability avoidance are in the section that follows in order to illustrate the lessons for accountability flowing from reform. The use of policy network theory to explain these issues, alongside policy transmission (through coercive and mimetic structural and policy isomorphism), policy learning and policy transfer, is discussed, with public value management being a constituent of this.

Accountability

Accountability is a slippery concept; it exists in many forms, and as complex government and governance become ever more multifaceted, then so does understanding accountability. We must ask the Socratic questions:

1. Accountability to whom? Stakeholders? Politicians? Citizens?
2. Accountability for what purpose?
3. What type of accountability?

Accountability is often used differently in Anglo-American contexts to that which applies in the EU and the wider global context, and this also causes confusion to those exposed to this diversity of perceptions. Accountability matters because it forms the basis of responsible governance, but increased complexity does not always mean increased accountability and indeed may conspire to make some intended aspects of accountability somewhat elusive. It may be argued, therefore, that although the concept of accountability lies at the heart of good government and governance, it is not always straightforward and reforms intended to make public institutions more accountable (to elected politicians or to stakeholders) may have unintended consequences at odds with the original purpose (also see Pyper's chapter in this volume).

It may also be argued that the issues addressed and debated in terms of 'public value' are further complicated by the increasing complexities of accountability. For example, from the outset of Moore's original proposition—that it is the task of public managers to create public value (1994) while navigating a strategic triangle including producing valued outcomes, while operating within the constraints of resources and capability and within a legal framework and jurisdiction (Katsonis 2019)—it is apparent that there is the possibility of intended outcomes coming into some conflict with public sector managers' personal and professional ethics and judgements. This could be in terms of their understanding of social standards, principles and ideals (Katsonis 2019). These are informed by their perceptions of what it means to be accountable and their understanding of what it is they are expected to do in terms of delivery and performance. An extensive review of the public value literature found there are eleven public value dimensions in which public value can be measured. These are:

1. public satisfaction
2. economic value—generating economic activity/employment
3. social and cultural value—social capital/cohesion
4. political value—democratic dialogue, public participation
5. ecological value—sustainable development, reducing pollution, waste, global warming
6. service delivery—take-up, satisfaction, choice, fairness, cost
7. financial performance—revenues, expenditure value for money, efficiency
8. non-financial performance—efficiency, customer satisfaction, service quality
9. social value from the user perspective, tangible economic value from the administration perspective, intangible economic value from the administration perspective
10. trust and legitimacy
11. protecting citizens' rights (Faulkner and Kaufman 2017, in Katsonis 2019).

These can be grouped together to suggest that public value can be measured across four main areas: outcome and achievement, including social, economic, environmental and cultural outcomes; trust and legitimacy, that is the extent to which public organisations are trusted and deemed legitimate by the public; service delivery quality; and efficiency (Katsonis 2019). If 'good governance' also includes elements of public value, then the enmeshing of these notions with increased levels and types of accountability across these eleven dimensions can lead to confusion which in turn may cause shortcomings in terms of governance and service delivery. This is described later with some examples.

On the surface, accountability is deceptively simple; for example, McGarvey (2001) notes the traditional model of public accountability is represented by a:

> coherent chain of accountability—from official to official in the bureaucracy, from official to minister, from minister to Parliament, from Parliament to the people. Each official is technically accountable, through the hierarchical structure of the bureaucracy, to elected politicians and to the citizenry at large. This is underpinned by Weberian conceptions of bureaucracy. Honesty, integrity, impartiality and objectivity inform the behaviour of officers as they administer rules decided by politicians. (p. 18)

These traits, plus openness, transparency and effectively functioning systems of accountability, are positive attributes of a dynamic political system (Massey and Pyper 2005, p. 151). As previous chapters have discussed, however, the traditional perspective on accountability has been challenged and subjected to the same stresses as the public administration to which it refers throughout a generation of public sector reform in Britain. The conception and development of the civil service (and alongside that the broader public administrative apparatus) of the UK can be mapped by a series of reports that gave meaning to the structures that evolved, with the modern reform process being initiated by the 1982 Financial Management Initiative. But, it began with the nineteenth-century Northcote–Trevelyan report, heavily influenced by Trevelyan's brother-in law, Thomas Babington Macaulay:

- 1853 Northcote Trevelyan (published 1854)
- 1854 Macaulay Report on the Indian Civil Service
- 1918 Haldane
- 1955 Priestley
- 1961 Plowden
- 1968 Fulton
- 1982 Financial Management Initiative
- 1987 Ibbs (Next Steps) Report (published 1988)
- 1993 Oughton
- 1994 Continuity and Change
- 1999 Modernising Government
- 2004 Civil Service Reform: Delivery and Values
- 2004 Gershon

- 2009 Putting the Frontline First
- 2012 Civil Service Reform Plan. (List adapted from Stanley 2019)

Alongside these central reports were a constant stream of reports, statutes and reforms for education (schools and university expansion), health, social care, and from the early 1980s, a new and often heuristic approach to regulation. We can see that the eleven dimensions of public value outlined above map easily onto the focus of these reports, even though (of course) the concept had not been developed while much of this change was being formulated and implemented.

All of this led to a development of different perspectives of accountability. McGarvey (2001, pp. 18–25) notes:

1. *The Traditional Perspective* (already discussed and largely Weberian, though based on Haldane in the UK);
2. *The Democratic Perspective*; based on the view that elected bodies scrutinise as well as influence policy and government activity and expenditure. It tends to view the public as being passive consumers of public services.
3. *The Professional Perspective*; in the period 1945–1980, professional power was often viewed as being apolitical, and professional/technocratic solutions to issues and problems were sought out (Massey 1988). By 1980, this had been challenged by the political left and right. The professionals were seen as adopting professional modes of accountability that emphasised professional power and autonomy and drove resources towards solutions and activities defined by those same professional groups, often defining themselves as the guardians of standards and of the public interest.
4. *The Managerialist Perspective*; the advance of NPM deliberately sought to demote traditional and professional accountability. It took the perspective of a reform agenda that championed managerial ability and strengths as drawn from the private sector; indeed, the nomenclature of the public sector was gradually adapted over some years to mimic that of business with, for example, senior civil servants transforming from being deputy permanent secretaries into grade two and now director generals, and undersecretaries of state becoming grade three and now deputy director general. It was a form of both mimetic and coercive isomorphism in that policymakers insisted on the reforms, but often left the individuals leading

them to select best practice from private sector management. These reforms are well-documented (Stanley 2019) and shifted the emphasis onto a major decentralisation and reduction in civil service numbers, but throughout the public sector to an emphasis on the benefits of competition, choice and service outputs and outcomes. The governance of central departments has been remodelled to include (in most cases) a Departmental Board which has, amongst its members, people from business as non-executive directors. The permeation of business, industry and public service executives has led to a revolving door of personnel between the public and private sectors in a deliberate policy of culture change (Wilks et al. 2002; Wilks 2013).

5. *The Governance Perspective*; which represents a move beyond government to recognising that policy formation and service delivery are now conducted using a range of public, private and third-sector institutions within a legal framework of regulation. There is an emphasis on partnerships and co-governance employing a range of managerialist innovations such as private-public partnerships and regulatory and fiscal support for social innovation (Massey and Johnston 2016).

6. *The Regulatory Perspective*; a consequence of the rise of the managerialist form of accountability is an increase in the audit, surveillance and regulation. Much of the privatised and semi-privatised delivery of services is conducted within a complex regulatory framework of law and institutions.

7. *The Rational Choice Perspective*; the new forms of accountability take place 'in forums consisting of individual political actors. A rational choice perspective on accountability emphasises that only by focusing on individual political strategies of these actors could a true picture of accountability emerge' (McGarvey 2001, p. 24). This often provides an explanation as to how autonomy-motivated officials still seek to evade ministerial control, even after all the managerialist and regulatory reforms.

Connected to these different perspectives, there are also different modes of accountability:

1. Answerability or explanatory accountability;
2. Amendatory accountability—change bad things;
3. Redress of grievance—put right wrongs;

4. Sanctions—punish poor behaviour and/or poor performance. (Massey and Pyper 2005, p. 153)

People may be accountable for a range of responsibilities, and they may be answerable for things but not liable for them. True accountability, however, implies more than simply a commitment to answering questions. Full accountability implies a willingness to deliver a redress of grievance. Based on the ancient English notion of 'redress of grievance before the granting of supply', it is the basis of parliamentary democracy, with some writers tracing it back to Saxon times (Hennessey 1989; Stanley 2019; Parliament 2019). In legal, constitutional and political terms, therefore, accountability must come before any pursuit of public value.

The haze of layers of modes, traits and perspectives of accountability can be further explored when we try to answer the foregoing questions as to whom, what, how and why organisations are accountable. The stewardship model is one that has been intrinsic to much of the pre-NPM focus on accountability; one party trusts another party with resources and/or responsibilities (Massey and Pyper 2005, p. 154). They must then present an account of and answer for the use of those resources and execution of those responsibilities. These resources and responsibilities may be defined very broadly to encompass 'the public interest' or more specifically the duties and standards expected from public office holders (Gray and Jenkins 1985, p. 138, cited in Massey and Pyper 2005, p. 154). It may be observed that this formulation draws on traditional Weberian and similar explanations and may be seen in the nineteenth-century Northcote-Trevelyan reforms of the UK (Hennessey 1989). Hughes (2018) appreciates, however, that accountability in the public sector is different to that of the private sector; it has a much wider role in terms of social justice, control of corruption and symbolic virtue. As such, attempts by NPM adherents and modernisers to depict reform as an endeavour to enhance general notions of accountability stray from relevance if they fail to accept that accountability (as a noun) is always political. Johnston reinforces this point with her observation that whatever form public administration and public policy take, it is the study of politics and the nature of accountability within the public sector that are always going to be concerned with political issues and political realities (Johnston 2012, p. 2; Massey 2019a, p. 4).

Different reform agendas, with different perspectives on modes of accountability, have occurred as distinct phases over the last forty years in the UK:

1. The Thatcher period (1979–1990), where a highly ideological neoliberal central government began to deliberately, but at first hesitantly, attempt to dismantle facets of the post-war welfare state and social contract through retreating from strategic industrial and energy policies and engaging in large-scale privatisation (Adonis 1994; Ascher 1987; Dunleavy 1986).
2. The Major period (1991–1997), which saw the consolidation of the neoliberal agenda and further privatisation, but with a deepening and broadening of notions of accountability to the 'citizen', notably through Citizen's Charters and viewing citizens as consumers and stakeholders. It was in this period that the term public value came into being, though it was under New Labour that it became a more common currency (Seldon 1997; Moore 1994).
3. The New Labour (Blair/Brown) period (1997–2010), where a wholly reformed Labour Party embarked upon an attempt at political and social transformation (modernisation) of the UK, part of which involved accepting the market capitalist basis of economic development in order to deliver high employment and redistribute the proceeds from a growing economy, but to do so through new approaches to social innovation and co-delivery of services. It also continued a policy of deregulation, especially of the finance industry (in conjunction with similar deregulation in the USA), which led directly to the financial crisis of 2008 (Seldon 2007; Moore 1994; Massey 2019b).
4. Coalition—May period (2010–2019), a period dominated by fiscal austerity, and there were social and public innovation experiments combined with continued varieties of privatisation (Stanley 2019; Brandsen et al. 2018).

The scale of the privatisation process, which began in the early 1980s, can be appreciated when the list below is explored. As noted above, however, this is part of a global pattern, and the pathway to privatisation and revenues raised have fluctuated in different countries, with the OECD (2018) noting the scale varies since 2008. In Britain, the rate has slowed down because so much has already been ejected from the public domain, the full income from which is difficult to calculate due to the different types of sale occurring over different times and using a range of procedures. In the UK, the privatisation of important utilities integral to modern life also gave rise to the new regulation structures. The privatisation list is as follows: AEA Technology Plc and UKAEA Limited

- Amersham International
- Associated British Ports (ABP) and trust ports
- British Aerospace
- British Airports Authority
- British Airways
- British Coal
- British Energy
- British Gas
- British Leyland
- British Nuclear Fuels Limited (BNFL)
- British Petroleum
- British Rail
- British Shipbuilders and Harland and Wolff
- British Steel Corporation
- British Sugar Corporation
- British Technology Group
- British Waterways
- Britoil
- British Telecom
- Buses
- Cable & Wireless
- Electricity Supply Industry
- Enterprise Oil
- Export Credit Guarantee Department
- Girobank
- London Underground
- National Air Traffic Services (NATS)
- QinetiQ
- Rolls Royce
- Royal Dockyards
- Royal Mail
- Royal Ordnance Factories
- Short Brothers
- Horserace Totalisator Board
- Thomas Cook
- Water Industry (Source: adapted from Rhodes et al. 2014, p. 1).

Yet, different though they are, it may be argued, all these reform agendas really take place within the egregore of liberal authoritarianism, driving change through a series of ideologically liberal dynamics (Massey 2019b). Although constructed via this egregore, the emphasis varies over time and place as the increasing complexity of public sector reform has evolved. Some have led to approaches that place less emphasis on the matters *for which* officers and officials are said to be accountable and stress instead the persons and institutions *to whom* they are accountable and the processes and mechanisms *through which* accountability can be achieved. Often, and confusingly, these models are employed at the same time. For example, ministers in central government are:

1. Accountable for a series of both 'role' and 'personal' responsibilities.
2. Accountable to Parliament, their ministerial colleagues collectively and the prime minister individually.
3. Accountable through a wide variety of mechanisms such as parliamentary questions, auditors, debates, select committees, standing committees, ombudsmen, the courts, official enquiries into their political party.

Similar sequences may be used to chart the accountability of officers and officials in the UK and elsewhere generally (Massey and Pyper 2005). In addition (and to partly recapitulate), these somewhat descriptive accounts of traits and perspectives are designed by public sector reforms to impose both external and internal forms of accountability. They are:

1. External, when officials have to account to individuals beyond their own organisation, for example, to Parliament, the audit bodies, regulators and the courts. As with many of the new accountabilities, these often overlap.
2. Internal, when individuals or groups account to line managers, civil servants, minister's etcetera, using appraisal, rules and regulations, budgeting and internal financial accountability, codes of conduct, professional ethics (Massey and Pyper 2005; Hughes 2018).
3. The newly privatised bodies have to account variously to global shareholders operating in a range of jurisdictions, regulators and market forces.

Accountability, therefore, can move upwards to senior politicians, outwards to colleagues and downwards to citizens/consumers. Or it may be categorised by type: managerial, market-led, political, legal, consumer and professional (McGarvey 2001; Hughes 2018).

From the early 1980s, the reform emphasis emphatically moved towards a more managerial, regulatory and consumer-based approach with the introduction of explicit contracts and service-level agreements, improved and more visible budgetary arrangements within and between departments and agencies and a concerted effort to enforce stakeholder power, however that was defined. New and improved regulatory regimes led increasingly to accountability through accountancy as well as audit and inspection (Power 1999). It is important to note, however, that these increased modes of accountability, although partially designed to drive efficiency, were not in and of themselves without considerable financial cost in terms of compliance and costs in terms of human resources. With the increased complexity of accountability, it was often easy to lose sight of the direction and focus of accountability; the increased use of appointed rather than elected bodies diminished direct accountability through the ballot box. As a footnote to the debate on managerialism from the focus of accountability, it is an interesting debate as to whether the reduction of professional power and consequent de-professionalisation of public sector occupations aided or hindered accountability. It may be seen that the producer power exercised by public sector professionals kept citizens at arm's length from decisions affecting their own welfare and that of their children. But it is moot as to whether the barrage of new regulatory institutions and layers of management have actually improved the delivery of services in education, health and local government, or simply shifted the producer dominance to a different kind of institution, for example, the NHS failings identified in the study in later sections of this chapter (Rhodes and Wanna 2009). An interesting observation connected to this managerialisation and marketisation of public sector professions is that made by Rhodes and Wanna regarding public value management in Westminster-style democracies. In their view, much of public value management has to be seen in the context of US-style new public management (though they do not use that term in their paper critical of Moore (1994)). They point out that '[p]ublic value pretends public managers can supplant politics and play at being the new Platonic guardians of society. In Westminster systems the idea is fraught with enormous political risk' (Rhodes and Wanna 2009, p. 418). They argue that the way Moore lumps elected and appointed officials together with others delivering public services fails to account for the difference between different kinds of public administration; one size does not fit all. While professionals lost a degree of autonomy and power over their field of expertise, the new managerialism set within the framework of networks did have to account for various policy problems and recurring failures in health, education and social welfare; it accelerated the gradual evolution of a blame culture and the avoidance of culpability, and it is to this we now turn.

ACCOUNTABILITY IN THE AGE OF NETWORKS

In this section, we will explore the notion of networks as part of governance and as a result of public sector reform, before considering the issues of blame and culpability avoidance. Rhodes' (1997) analysis of policy networks and administrative reform (including wider developments such as the core executive, hollowing out of the state, multi-level governance) is the perspective most closely adopted for this section of the chapter. This is because it is based on an informed analysis of the British political system and relevant literature. It also theoretically analyses the reform process from its location as part of the political process (political science), rather than from a business school perspective which adopts a more fundamentally managerialist criteria and context for public sector management. This latter standpoint is the main critique of Moore's public value model by the later works of Rhodes and Wanna (2009), but also (to a lesser extent) by Bozeman's (2007) societal perception of public value being concerned with the rights, benefits and prerogatives to which the public are entitled and Meynhardt et al.'s (2017) assessment that public value has a relational perspective—the relationship between subject and object—adapting a psychological perception, but from a predominantly US outlook. In the context of this volume, viewing networks and public value from a British *political* perspective, therefore, allows a broader discussion of the dynamics for change.

Rhodes defines a policy network as a 'cluster or complex of organizations connected to one another by resource dependencies' (1997, p. 37). Although refined both by Rhodes and his critics over subsequent years, this definition remains a suitable starting point for understanding network theory. Building on the work of the US and European authors (and concepts such as 'iron triangles', professionalism, pluralism and elitism), he identifies five types of networks:

1. Policy communities.
2. Professional networks.
3. Intergovernmental networks.
4. Producer networks.
5. Issue networks.

Rhodes develops an explanation around each of these types, but there is not sufficient room here to reiterate the entire analysis. It is suffice to note the obvious links into professional power and the growth of managerialism explored in the forgoing sections. His seminal policy network theory building (Rhodes 1997, pp. 29–45) aimed to offer a meso-level concept that provides:

> A link between the micro-level of analysis dealing with the role of interests and government in particular policy decisions and the macro-level of analysis, which focuses on broader questions about the distribution of power within modern society.... The existence of a policy network both influences, although clearly it does not determine, policy outcomes *and* reflects the relative status, or even power, of the particular interests in a broad policy area. (p. 29)

Expanding on the US and European literature, Rhodes (1997, p. 37) argues that:

1. Any organisation is dependent upon other organisations for resources.
2. In order to achieve their goals, the organisations have to exchange resources.
3. Although decision-making within the organisation is constrained by other organisations, the dominant coalition retains some discretion. The appreciative system of the dominant coalition influences which relationships are seen as a problem and which resources will be sought.
4. The dominant coalition employs strategies within known rules of the game to regulate the process of exchange.
5. Variations in the degree of discretion are a product of the goals and the relative power potential of interacting organisations. This relative power potential is a product of the resources of each organisation,

or the rules of the game and the process of exchange between organisations.

In further developing the theory, Rhodes argued that the macro-level of the theory analyses intergovernmental relations and this can involve multilevel governance looking up to global and EU levels as well as down to meso-levels. The meso-level of analysis focusses on the 'variety of linkages between the centre and the range of sub-central political and governmental organizations' (1997, p. 37), while the micro-level analysis explores the behaviour of individual actors, both individuals and organisations. In other words, and linking back in this chapter to the section on accountability, we can argue that the permanent reform process of the public sector in the UK has moved from traditional Weberian bureaucratic structures to a complex web of interactions and government conducted through governance (see Flinders and Huggins' chapter in this volume). It is the complexity of networks in both the formulation of policy and the delivery of services that makes this possible. As the state apparatus shrinks, it has led to what Rhodes (1997) has labelled 'governing without governance', though this is a contested perspective by those who argue the powers of the state have simply been redistributed rather than removed or hollowed out (Smith 1999; Fenwick et al. 2012).

At the same time, as networks have become part of the academic currency, Hughes (2018, pp. 143–148) demonstrates that many observers question how novel they are or how pervasive. He notes that while Klijn (2012) supports much of the Rhodes' analysis, agreeing that networks are more or less stable patterns of social relationships, a form of governance, others make the point that network theory simply 'reminds us of the (longstanding) importance of informal relationships between organisations and groups' (Pollitt 2003, p. 67). In other words, it is a different way of understanding interest groups and their role in the state. We must remember that prior to the development of the modern state in the UK, governments relied on merchants, parishes, private companies and individuals to deliver services, and in the case of parts of the former Empire, to actually govern in the name of the Crown (Robins 2012). Network theory assists us to understand the modern evolution of government and governance and the contemporary challenges to transparency and accountability. In this sense, there are concerns as to how networks interact with traditional systems of accountability (Hughes 2018, p. 144). Hughes cites Peters (1996) to explain that, 'the creation of a more participatory style of governing does not mean that government is in reality less powerful. It does mean, however, that state and society are bonded together in the process of creating governance' (Hughes 2018, p. 145). It may be argued that this may actually strengthen the state and its ruling agents through this kind of interaction in society with its hegemonic control over certain resources such as power, wealth and regulation (Davies 2011, pp. 47–62). As noted at the outset of this chapter, accountability is a slippery concept. Networks suggest three dynamics for accountability:

- bureaucratic rules-based public administration;
- the market and the law of contract;
- network intermediation based on consultation, coordination and the powers of diplomacy.

It may also be argued, however, that in mature states with a settled mode of government, there is only one hegemony: the state. It is the government that sets the rules and makes the laws under which contracts are policed and networks function. But the way in which this occurs and operates is dependent upon the context, the context that is geographical, temporal, political, economic, cultural and based on control over resources including people. We may also ask, who controls the state? Whatever the answer, it will be a deeply political, and not a managerialist, response. The fluidity of networks and accountability may be found within this miasma.

Context and Culpability

This section will begin with a short discussion of challenges facing parts of the NHS and the conflict between accountability and public value in different ways to different stakeholders. The Labour politician credited with the formation of the NHS, Aneurin Bevan, was born in South Wales. The area where he grew up is now medically served by Swansea Bay Health Board, the successor to Abertawe Bro Morgannwg (ABM) University Health Board following a recent restructuring of healthcare in Wales. Given the mapping of public sector reforms discussed in this volume, and the changing nature of accountability and growing policy networks as outlined in this chapter, it is likely that Bevan would not recognise the public sector he did so much to construct with the creation of the post-war welfare state. It is doubtful he could have guessed at the way the NHS would have grown and developed. Few, if any, commentators prior to 1980 could have confidently predicted the way in which public administration has developed as a result of public sector reform and the technological revolution in IT, telemetry, material science and robotics. Many of the issues confronting public sector professionals and managers are encapsulated in recognition by the former CEO of the Abertawe Bro Morgannwg Board that medicine has become so complex, the management structures so complicated and lines of accountability so blurred that individuals can often feel lost and over-managed but under-used, leading to mistakes and disaffection. In a short message to the staff, he quoted Bevan's renowned phrase, based on the traditional Weberian view of accountability, to illustrate how in the region of his birth, there has been astonishing change leading to the need to constantly reform management structures and lines of accountability. He drolly noted that in:

> Aneurin Bevan's famous words that "if a hospital bedpan is dropped in a hospital corridor in Tredegar, the reverberations should echo around Whitehall" has been interpreted a number of ways by those working in and leading the NHS. Does it mean that we should have a target for reducing dropped bedpans? Or that the Westminster Government should take direct responsibility for and control over every tiny detail of care provided in the NHS? Or was he saying something more general about accountability for services in the NHS? (Williams 2015, p. 1)

Before proceeding to list some of the challenges of change facing his team:

> In 1948 the UK NHS had a budget of £437 million which is roughly £9 billion in today's money, the Welsh share of which would have been around £17.5 million (about £360m in today's money); ABMU Health Board alone has a budget of £1.2 billion in 2015. In 1948 the NHS employed 144,000 people today this has risen to around 1.7 million staff making it the fifth largest employer in the world! … So the NHS has become much larger, more complicated, more accountable and therefore sadly sometimes more bureaucratic. We are technologically capable of doing more for patients but seemingly expected to do more than we have the capacity and resources to do as we age and our needs become more complex. The NHS continues to be very political,

Before concluding:

> If a bedpan is dropped in one of our hospital corridors it may not reverberate in Whitehall, Cardiff Bay or even my office—but I expect locally based management teams to know what is going on in their hospital or services and for staff to be able to answer the question—who is in charge here? (Williams 2015, p. 2)

The answer to that question is more difficult than it at first appears to be. The complexity of management and accountability structures means that even the most junior hospital doctor, or ward nurse, porter or radiologist has a complex list of accountabilities. Certainly, they have a line manager, but given the sheer size of the average General Hospital, it is doubtful they will ever meet their own director of medicine or director of nursing, let alone the CEO of the board of NHS Trust. These senior managers and professionals may be in charge, but it is difficult to see how they can be made answerable or accountable in a meaningful sense for the actions of junior staff and in turn junior staff are often resentful of having to be personally accountable for mistakes that occur in what they often perceive to be an under-resourced, over-managed system where they have little control over their work and are forced to deliver services structured by key performance indicators over which they have no control. There is evidence to suggest that they often feel bullied and join in the blame-gaming and avoidance of culpability (Kline and Lewis 2019, pp. 166–174; Blackwood et al. 2017, pp. 349–356). Even where they have line managers, there is often a complex matrix management system that further complicates accountability. Then there is the added issue of successive contracting out and marketisation of cleaning and ancillary services, such as catering and routine maintenance to private sector firms. Sir Paul Williams may well have expected an answer to his question, but it is probable that in the NHS (and indeed in much of the public sector), front-line staff do not know who is in charge beyond their immediate line manager who may or may not be an NHS-employed professional or civil servant, but may well be a private contractor seeking to operate at a profit. The point made about how in the UK public administration is always about politics, and that in the reform period since the 1980s, politics and new forms of accountability 'outrank' notions of public value, is important here.

A series of reports and investigations have highlighted how in the NHS there have been serious flaws and errors resulting in harm coming to patients, yet it is often those who speak out, the whistle-blowers, who suffer from victimisation at the hands of managers who seek to avoid blame. One of the most comprehensive, because he used and referred to a range of similar reports regarding recent public service failures, was that of Robert Francis into the appalling failures of the Mid Staffordshire NHS Foundation Trust (HC 2013). He listed the failures as:

- A culture focused on doing the system's business—not that of the patients;
- An institutional culture which ascribed more weight to positive information about the service than to information capable of implying cause for concern;
- Standards and methods of measuring compliance which did not focus on the effect of a service on patients;
- Too great a degree of tolerance of poor standards and of risk to patients;
- A failure of communication between the many agencies to share their knowledge of concerns;
- Assumptions that monitoring, performance management or intervention was the responsibility of someone else;
- A failure to tackle challenges to the building up of a positive culture, in nursing in particular but also within the medical profession;
- A failure to appreciate until recently the risk of disruptive loss of corporate memory and focus resulting from repeated, multilevel reorganisation (2013, p. 4).

This led to cases where:

- Patients were left in excrement in soiled bedclothes for lengthy periods;
- Assistance was not provided with feeding for patients who could not eat without help;
- Water was left out of reach;
- In spite of persistent requests for help, patients were not assisted in their toileting;
- Wards and toilet facilities were left in a filthy condition;
- Privacy and dignity, even in death, were denied;
- Triage in A&E was undertaken by untrained staff;
- Staff treated patients and those close to them with what appeared to be callous indifference.

Successive Secretaries of State for Health apologised for the poor care received by patients, but none resigned, and it was many years before Francis Report was able to apportion blame and then to make over 200 separate recommendations to improve care standards and seek to ensure there would be no repetition. Francis also dealt with the blame culture head-on, arguing:

> There is a tendency when a disaster strikes to try to seek out someone who can be blamed for what occurred, and a public expectation that those held responsible will be held to account. All too frequently there are insufficient mechanisms for this to be done effectively. A public inquiry is not a vehicle which is capable of fulfilling this purpose except in the limited sense of being able to require individuals and organisations to give an explanation for their actions or inaction. (HC 2013, p. 35)

After noting that the UK public sector in general, and the NHS in particular in this case, had failed to learn the lesson of Sir Liam Donaldson's report into the Bristol hospital failings and move away from the blame culture, Francis argued that in this case:

> On the whole, the purpose of identifying where individuals have fallen below relevant standards should be to show examples of conduct or judgements to be avoided in future. In a system failure as widespread as that identified in this Inquiry, it becomes a futile exercise to undertake; so many are in one sense accountable, it is far more effective to learn rather than to punish. To place too much emphasis on individual blame is to risk perpetuating the illusion that removal of particular individuals is all that is necessary. That is certainly not the case here. To focus, therefore, on blame will perpetuate the cycle of defensiveness, concealment, lessons not being identified and further harm. (HC 2013, p. 35)

The recommendations for improvement proceed to 'emphasise what is important':

- Emphasis on and commitment to common values throughout the system by all within it;
- Readily accessible fundamental standards and means of compliance;
- No tolerance of non-compliance and the rigorous policing of fundamental standards;
- Openness, transparency and candour in all the system's business;

- Strong leadership in nursing and other professional values;
- Strong support for leadership roles;
- A level playing field for accountability;
- Information accessible and useable by all allowing effective comparison of performance by individuals, services and organisation.

The emphasis on these standards, with implicit and explicit recommendations for better communication, better training, more open and transparent management systems and a recognition of the need to embrace criticism and learn from it, not to punish those who engage in honest debate, echoed much that was in the earlier Bichard Report (2004). Bichard Report was forensic, skilled, analytical and used his three decades of experience at a senior level in public service to criticise the response of two police forces, social services and others involved in the tragedy. He, like Francis, noted the lack of proper training in current techniques in different public institutions, poor use of resources, poor communication, lack of transparency, lack of clear guidance and overall clarity of accountability and procedures and a general failure initially to take responsibility. His recommendations were clearly set out to remedy this.

Conclusion

In conclusion, Rhodes and Wanna (2009, p. 173) remind us of the importance of politics and politicians in forcing through the changes that have taken place in the public sector and the various dynamics for those changes. But the overriding lesson is that politics is the driving force, not managerial concerns; rather, managerialism is a tool of control. In the cases outlined above, no politicians resigned or took responsibility for the problems that occurred as a direct result of managerialist reforms. Reports across time and subject area have made similar recommendations to those above, and in social services, education, healthcare and transport, the core issues of clear lines of amendatory accountability have not been brought back into the public sector. Rhodes and Wanna took case studies from across sectors and made the following observations:

> Here, we are not exploring the virtues or sins of political leaders. We focus on the dangers for public officials of challenging, supplanting and undermining those leaders. With this aim in mind, our cases illustrate the following propositions.

1. Governments are not inherently benign—political leaders will often seek to protect themselves at the expense of their officials (the Dr David Kelly case from the UK).
2. Spearheading decisions and 'doing the politics' for a minister is dangerous territory—'excessive responsiveness' leads to public servants being criticized for unethical or unduly partisan behaviour (the 'children overboard' case from Australia).
3. Authorizing environments can be wicked and mendacious—they display the pervasive characteristics and deleterious effects of partisan self-interest—and the political courtiers not the officials remain king (the BSE 'mad cow disease' case from the UK).
4. The public sector is fundamentally different—there are real dilemmas in copying private sector behaviours (the 'Yorkshire tea-parties' case from the UK).
5. Taking the entrepreneurial initiative can lead to both unintended consequences and the problem of 'many hands'—the tragic consequences of public value explorers behaving without clear lines of accountability (the Cave Creek case from New Zealand). (Rhodes and Wanna 2009, p. 173)

In other words, the real lessons learned regarding accountability and policy networks and blame-gaming are certainly those we find in reports such as those of Francis and Bichard, but the wider lesson is that the recommendations and actions for greater clarity, transparency and amendatory accountability can only be effectively made with a political commitment that is carried through and regularly audited. It may be argued that redemption for the failures in public service that have occurred could be found in a less complex web of accountabilities, in the adoption or readoption of a simple, transparent clarity of responsibility and accountability. After all, if the Saxons could (mythically) achieve this through the redress of grievance before the granting of supply, then so should we.

References

Adonis, A. (1994). The Transformation of the Conservative Party in the 1980s. In A. Adonis & T. Hames (Eds.), *A Conservative Revolution? The Thatcher-Reagan Decade in Perspective*. Manchester: Manchester University Press.

Ascher, K. (1987). *The Politics of Privatisation: Contracting Out Public Services*. Basingstoke: Macmillan.

Bevir, M. (1995). *A Theory Of Governance*. University of California Press.

Blackwood, K., Bentley, T., Catley, B., & Edwards, M. (2017). Managing Workplace Bullying Experiences in Nursing: The Impact of the Work Environment. *Public Money & Management, 37*(5), 349–356.

Bozeman, B. (2007). *Public Values and Public Interest: Counterbalancing Economic Individualism.* Washington, DC: Georgetown University Press.

Brandsen, T., Steen, T., & Verschuere, B. (Eds.). (2018). *Coproduction and Co-creation: Engaging Citizens in Public Service Delivery.* Milton Park: Routledge.

Davies, J. (2011). The Limits of Post-Traditional Public Administration: Towards a Gramscian Perspective. *Critical Policy Studies, 5*(1), 47–62.

Dunleavy, P. (1986). Explaining the Privatisation Boom: Public Choice Versus Radical Approaches. *Public Administration, 64*(2), 13–34.

Faulkner, N., & Kaufman, S. (2017). Avoiding Theoretical Stagnation: A Systematic Review and Framework for Measuring Public Value. *Australian Journal of Public Administration, 77*(1), 69–86.

Fenwick, J., Johnston, K., & McTavish, D. (2012). Co-Governance or Meta-Bureaucracy? Perspectives of Local Governance 'Partnership' in England and Scotland. *Policy and Politics, 40*(3), 405–422.

Gray, A., & Jenkins, W. (1985). *Administrative Politics in British Government.* Brighton: Wheatsheaf.

HC 635. (2004). *The Bichard Inquiry Report: A Public Inquiry Report on Child Protection Procedures in Humberside Police and Cambridgeshire Constabulary, Particularly the Effectiveness of Relevant Intelligence-Based Record Keeping, Vetting Practices Since 1995 and Information Sharing with Other Agencies. This Report Makes Recommendations on Matters of Local and National Relevance.* London: The Stationary Office Limited.

HC 974. (2013). *Report of the Mid Staffordshire NHS Foundation Trust Public Inquiry.* Chaired by Robert Francis. London: The Stationary Office Limited.

Hennessey, P. (1989). *Whitehall.* London: Pimlico.

Hughes, O. (2018). *Public Management and Administration: An Introduction* (5th ed.). Basingstoke: Palgrave.

John, P. (2018). *How Far to Nudge? Assessing Behavioural Public Policy.* Cheltenham: Edward Elgar Publishing.

Johnston, K. (2012). The Future of the Discipline: Trends in Public Sector Management. In J. Diamond & J. Liddle (Eds.), *Emerging and Potential Trends in Public Management: An Age of Austerity* (pp. 1–24). Bingley, UK: Emerald Publishing.

Katsonis, M. (2019, March 3). How Do We Measure Public Value? *The Mandarin.* Retrieved July 2, 2019, from https://www.themandarin.com.au/104843-measuring-public-value/.

Klijn, E.-H. (2012). New Public Management and Governance: A Comparison. In D. Levi-Faur (Ed.), *Oxford Handbook of Governance*. Oxford: Oxford University Press.

Kline, R., & Lewis, D. (2019). The Price of Fear: Estimating the Financial Cost of Bullying and Harassment to the NHS in England. *Public Money & Management*, 39(3), 166–174.

Massey, A. (1988). *Technocrats and Nuclear Politics*. Aldershot: Avebury/Gower.

Massey, A. (Ed.). (2019a). *A Research Agenda for Public Administration*. Cheltenham: Edward Elgar Publishing.

Massey, A. (2019b). Persistent Public Management Reform: An Egregore of Liberal Authoritarianism? *Public Money & Management*, 39(1), 9–17.

Massey, A., & Johnston, K. (2016). Governance: Public Governance to Social Innovation. *Policy and Politics*, 44(4), 663–675.

Massey, A., & Pyper, R. (2005). *Public Management and Modernisation in Britain*. Basingstoke: Palgrave.

McGarvey, G. (2001). Accountability in Public Administration: A Multi-Perspective Framework of Analysis. *Public Policy and Administration*, 16(2), 17–28.

Meynhardt, T., Brieger, S., Strathoff, P., Anerer, S., Baro, A., Hermann, C., et al. (2017). Public Value Performance: What Does It Mean to Create Value in the Public Sector? In R. Andebner, D. Greiling, & R. Vogel (Eds.), *Public Sector Management in a Globalised World* (pp. 135–160). Wiesbaden: Springer.

Moore, M. (1994). Public Value as the Focus of Strategy. *Australian Journal of Public Administration*, 53(3), 296–303.

Mungiu-Pippidi, A., & Johnston, M. (Eds.). (2017). *Transitions to Good Governance: Creating Virtuous Circles of Anti-Corruption*. Cheltenham: Edward Elgar Publishing.

OECD. (2018). *Privatisation and the Broadening of Ownership of State-Owned Enterprises*. Paris: OECD.

Parliament. (2019). Retrieved January 3, 2019, from https://www.parliament.uk/about/living-heritage/evolutionofparliament/originsofparliament/birthofparliament/overview/origins/.

Peters, B. G. (1996). *The Future of Governing: Four Emerging Models*. Lawrence: University of Kansas Press.

Pollitt, C. (2003). *The Essential Public Manager*. Maidenhead: Open University Press.

Power, M. (1999). *The Audit Society: Rituals of Verification*. Oxford: Oxford University Press.

Rhodes, R. A. W. (1997). *Understanding Governance: Policy Networks, Governance, Reflexivity and Accountability*. Buckingham: Open University Press.

Rhodes, R. A. W., & Wanna, J. (2009). Bringing the Politics Back in: Public Value in Westminster Parliamentary Government. *Public Administration, 87*(2), 161–183.

Rhodes, C., Hough, D., & Butcher, L. (2014). *Privatisation: Research Paper 14/16.* London: House of Commons Library.

Robins, N. (2012). *The Corporation that Changed the World: How the East India Company Shaped the Modern Multinational.* London: Pluto Press.

Seldon, A. (1997). *Major: A Political Life.* London: Weidenfeld and Nicholson.

Seldon, A. (2007). *Blair's Britain, 1997–2007.* Cambridge: Cambridge University Press.

Smith, M. (1999). *The Core Executive in Britain.* Basingstoke: Macmillan.

Stanley, M. (2019). Retrieved January–February 28, 2019, from https://www.civilservant.org.uk/library.html.

Wilks, S. R. M. (2013). *The Political Power of the Business Corporation.* Cheltenham: Edward Elgar.

Wilks, S. R. M., Ahn, B., & Halligan, J. (2002). *Reforming Public and Corporate Governance: Management and the Market in Australia, Britain and Korea.* Cheltenham: Edward Elgar.

Williams, P. (2015, June 29). *Chief Executive's Message.* Retrieved February 18, 2019, from http://www.wales.nhs.uk/sitesplus/documents/863/Chief%20Executive%20Message%2029th%20June%202015%20version2.pdf.

CHAPTER 9

Public Value Management in Brexit Britain

Janice Morphet

INTRODUCTION

The fact that Brexit entered mainstream public discourse from 2016 onwards has led to subsequent recognition and debate about the contribution that European Union (EU) membership has made to the UK since its entry in 1972 (Bulmer and Quaglia 2018). Much of this consideration has related to a range of specific and tangible benefits associated with the wider understanding of 'what the EU does for us', rather than the overarching ideology of the role of achieving public value through joint state action that is implicit within EU membership. While the tangible benefits of European Health Insurance Cards (EHIC) and mobile phone roaming charges, together with student exchanges through ERASMUS and funding for research and development such as Horizon programmes, are understood, the wider public purposes are not (Dellmuth and Stoffel 2012; Sigalas 2010; Busse et al. 2011; Veugelers et al. 2015). The role of the structural funds and their support for economically lagging regions has been recognised where it has been overt, but, like much of the EU's policy, legislation and funding in the UK, this has frequently been coated

---

J. Morphet (✉)
University College London, London, UK
e-mail: j.morphet@ucl.ac.uk

© The Author(s) 2021
J. Connolly, A. van der Zwet (eds.), *Public Value Management, Governance and Reform in Britain*, International Series on Public Policy, https://doi.org/10.1007/978-3-030-55586-3_9

with domestic policy (Morphet 2013). Nor has there been much discussion in the UK about why such interventions are made within this EU context or their public objectives. There has been little recognition of the role that the UK has played in shaping both EU agenda priorities and the mechanisms through which they have been delivered. These examples include the creation of the single market (Cockfield 1994), the Trans-European Networks (Morphet 2016) and the creation of the administrative space within which much of the business is conducted (Olsen 2003; Trondal and Peters 2013). While there has been a consensus within EU member states for the prioritisation of public over private values within the state, there has been less focus on foregrounding these underlying principles. However, the forces of Thatcherism and then of austerity since 2010, particularly the dismantling of the welfare state in England, have separated UK state values and principles from the EU mainstream. This shift away from the role of the state in pursuing public value for its people has arguably reinforced and confirmed the UK state's isolationism that is now expressed through Brexit.

Since the UK's membership of the EU in 1972, much of the support generated for specific places and sectors has been provided by the principles, legislation and funding that have not been acknowledged or understood by the media in the UK (Morphet 2013). To do so is often perceived as a reduction of the UK's standing as a leading economy, acting as a recipient rather than as a donor. This recognition of the need for economic support from the EU appears to have been equally welcomed and reviled for the same reasons. Hence, it is no surprise that this uneasy donor/dependency relationship was reflected in Brexit referendum voting patterns within those areas most in receipt of funding in England and Wales (Becker et al. 2017; Goodwin and Heath 2016; Rodríguez-Pose 2018).

On the other hand, the EU, particularly the European Commission (EC), has been circumspect in identifying the scale of the impact that membership has brought to the internal and substate institutional structures of the member states. This was confirmed by the *Balance of Competences Reviews* undertaken by the UK Civil Service in 2014 before the referendum was called (Foreign and Commonwealth Office 2014). Instead, the EC has preferred these to be regarded as domestic responses to the implementation of decisions made by the member states. Pollack (2003) argues that this is achieved through a combination of agenda setting, agency and delegation. Further, where there are policy, legislative and programme evaluations, these have tended to be undertaken within the frameworks provided by the EC's own vertical institutional structures.

The European Parliament has provided a wider overview of the impacts through its multiple studies on the impact of Brexit, for example,[1] although none of the EU institutions have publicly assessed the cumulative impacts of membership of any member state. This diffidence about identifying the scale and impact of the application of such joint decision-making is now being addressed in the forthcoming programme period 2021–2027, where the territorial impacts of EU policy, legislation and programmes will be a key focus of EC, and its internal organisation may change to reflect this territorial shift (CEC 2018). However, this lack of exposition of the effects of EU membership, to reduce any member state concerns about power relations, has also created an opportunity for fear about this power to grow and fed into the rise in populism (Hobolt 2016; also see Flinders and Huggins' chapter in this volume). Within the UK Brexit referendum campaign, it made it difficult for those in favour of remaining in the EU to demonstrate the positive outcomes of membership and made it easy for those in favour of Brexit to make generalised claims and use the Vote Leave organization's campaign slogan of 'taking back control'.

The creation of public value through other aspects of membership of the EU is seldom recognised within these debates, including the wider context in creating systems of regulatory alignment for its member state economies, including for the UK. There is little understanding of the EU policy framing provided to the UK through its pooling of a range of key policy areas within the EU, including transport, energy, environment, macroprudential policy, public health, employment rights, rural policy, local economic policy and citizens' rights. There are also other contexts where the effects of EU membership on public policy have not been recognised at all. In 2010, the joint poll for assessing effective policy-making in the UK since 1979, conducted between the Political Studies Association and the Institute for Government (Rutter et al. 2012), selected the ten most effective policies. Although not recognised in this poll, all ten policies selected had all been implemented through EU agreements and in ways determined by legislation agreed within the EU (Morphet 2013). Given this, the position of the EU in support of public value is hard to decipher in the guiding principles of EU policies, programmes and practices and how these have been conveyed into UK public policy during the UK's membership of the EU.

---

[1] http://www.europarl.europa.eu/unitedkingdom/en/brexitpublic/brexitstudies.html accessed 19th June 2019.

In this chapter, the role of the EU in promoting public value is discussed, and there will be some consideration of the effects of the potential loss of this framing context for British public policy in the implementation of any Brexit model, from 'no deal' to soft alignment. The EU's approach to public value, that is embodied in the Treaties that create its operational code, has had both defining and constraining effects on the role and operation of all EU public bodies including those within the UK. This is through their public and democratic accountability, operational and delivery mechanisms and practices of public administration. We can see this in a range of policy fields, which have been defining for UK public practice in the period of the UK's membership of the EU. These are discussed in more detail below and include differential spatial and territorial policies introduced when the UK joined the EU that have subsequently been supported by the EU principle of subsidiarity. The creation of the single market has also embodied public value within the operational principles adopted by the EU which are have been additional to those in the UK (Meunier and Nicolaïdis 2006). The EU as a trade power is included within the trade agreements with the World Trade Organization which are entered into by each member state through the Government Procurement Agreement (GPA). The public value principles within the GPA were developed by the EU in the single market implementation, although they were initially denied and then suppressed by the UK Conservative Government up to 1997. These principles were applied across the other member states who utilised the quality and public value components of public procurement to balance market interests. To the EU, the principle of public value is central to all its activities and is one of its core objectives, and it is used as a paradigm for its role (O'Flynn 2007). While the UK was predominantly operating on the welfare state model, its notion of public value was like that in the EU. Since the marked changes in the objectives of UK public policy from 1979 and accelerated since 2010 (Mooney and Neal 2010; Grimshaw and Rubery 2012), the underpinning principles of EU public value have been growing in importance in UK public policy.

The Role of Public Value in UK Public Policy

Public value, according to Moore (1995), can be defined as achieving mandated objectives efficiently and effectively with politically neutral competence. However, here Moore does not question the basis of the public ethos, how democratically elected politicians communicate that ethos to their administrations and how they set the priorities for their executive to implement their policies including using their budgets, setting minimum standards of operation and service delivery. Benington and Moore (2011) state that the role of government is in adding benefit to society but suggest that it is challenged by the neoliberal ethos that has been pervasive since the introduction of competition in the public sector through the WTO GPA. They partly relate this to a more consumerist approach to public services at the level of the individual, exemplified by using the term *customer* rather than the democratically accountable term of *citizens*. However, they also suggest that in order to achieve public value, there should be horizontal and vertical integration between those engaged in wider governance rather than discussing solely the responsibilities of government (see the chapter by Huggins and Flinders in this volume). This extension of the use of governance, though, can also be undermining of democratic accountability and is itself suggestive of neoliberal practices of government where directly elected politicians are influenced and their decisions can be diluted by external public and private partner interests (Peters and Pierre 1998). These approaches have been developed further into notions of social capital which are regarded as the beneficial outcome of governance models if they are achieved successfully in practice (Schuller et al. 2000). In the concept of social capital, social value is achieved through outcomes supported by networks of organisations in common approaches such as those achieved through horizontal and vertical integration. However, these may reflect governance rather than government structures, and these relationships may not be susceptible to the mechanisms of democratic accountability, unless there are contractual relationships between them.

The welfare state was the embodiment of public value in the UK, with the state undertaking its activities for the benefit of the people and where interventions were primarily based on eliminating harm as issues emerged to promote more equal changes for people in the light of evidence as set out in the Fabián approach to welfarist public policy (Timmins 2001). With the introduction of competition within public services in the EU, including the UK, the identification and externalisation of public values through codes of governance have been developed as changes in the forms of public delivery that have emerged (Woolcock 2016; Dür and Elsig 2011). The externalisation of the client contractor relationships in public services has changed the fundamental principles and practices of the welfare state (Hills 2011). The application and implementation of the WTO

GPA (1979), which opened public services to competition from other providers in the private sector, was agreed by the UK government in 1976. If public services were to be provided by contractors, then the values imbued in public bodies had to be made explicit and, to some extent, monetised. If private suppliers had to comply with the same public value requirements as existing public providers, then this had to be specified in contracts and managed through compliance processes (Warner 2013). This would not necessarily mean that services would be cheaper for the public sector, although much of the narrative around the GPA suggested this (Jensen and Stonecash 2005). However, this externalisation of public value could mean that it might be able to be more systematically delivered than when internalised within public organisations relying on their ethos, culture, custom and practice and was an argument for the introduction of new public management (NPM) (Dunleavy and Hood 1994).

The second driver for the external representation of public value in the UK was to make services more customer- rather than producer-focused. This derived from Osborne and Gaeblar's *Reinventing Government* (1993), Rhodes (1996) and the work of Krugman (1991) where the role of the central state was seen to be working against national prosperity if it was overly dominant and centralising. This was also reinforced through the move towards sustainability in the Rio Earth Summit in 1992, which promoted the benefits of more local approaches to longer term environmental benefits. However, in establishing a more systemic approach to assessing public value in practice, there remain concerns about conflicting elements of the 'modes' and the 'role' of cost benefit analysis, or measurement systems. An example of this in the construction of public service competition is the use of balanced score cards as a means of demonstrating how decisions have been made. Even where there are absolute objectives, such as improving reading ages or increasing household income, there will be different ways of measuring these targets and gaming their achievement (Guthrie and Russo 2014). The externalisation and transparency of public values within administrative frameworks can allow some comparison between organisations and countries but also provides mechanisms through which administrators can make specific decisions (Boyne 2002; De Graaf et al. 2016). It has also allowed a more technical approach to evaluation, which can again be a focus on inputs rather than policy outputs or as the Blair government proposed on outcomes (Alford and O'Flynn 2009). For much public policy, the public values are enshrined as a basis of administrative functioning and political decision-making. Nevertheless, the decision-making, which is at the heart of politics at all levels, is set within these frameworks and presented to decision-makers in common ways—based on choice or evaluation systems, options appraisal or cost-benefit analysis. It is less clear to what extent these technocratic methods are informed more by political or local values in determining the precise decisions about a contract, a decision about a major planning application or organisational restructuring (Schott et al. 2015).

It is possible to see the debates on the role of public value in UK public policy that emerged in 2002 were temporally aligned with the administrative reforms that were being introduced within the EU through the creation of the administrative space and the open methods of coordination (OMC). In their Cabinet Office paper *Creating Public Value An Analytical Framework for Public Services Reform*, Kelly et al. (2002) externalise the principle of public value as a restatement of the core role of the state in a neoliberal context. It marks a shift in thinking away from NPM and a reconnection to trust, local priorities and, like the EU reforms, the quality of public decision-making. This debate continued by defining the practices that can support the delivery of public value—through leadership, re-engineering of organisations and networks—but without discussing the objectives of public value (Jørgensen and Bozeman 2007).

This is an issue in England, where public value creation has been most challenged by the application of austerity and 'rolling back the state' ideologies since 2010. In Scotland, Wales and Northern Ireland, and in the EU, the prevailing ideology of welfarism remains and is the guiding principle for providing public value within the state; it remains an unreconstructed view that the state intervenes for the public good and this in turn creates public value that is closest to the welfare state (Mooney and Williams 2006; MacKinnon 2015). This view links to a second approach which identifies the role of the creation of public value through public actions which benefit the whole of society including the private sector. Mazzucato (2018) argues that public interventions, particularly by the UK central state, have been undervalued and have undermined one of the main purposes of the state in support of its people.

In the UK, it can be argued that the role of public value in holding the state to account has been lost, particularly through its replacement by responsibilisation as an overriding principle for maintaining a functioning society including the provision of health care, education and other public services (Chandler 2017). Since 2010, these public services have been marginalised by successive governments and seen as a cost rather than as a benefit to society. Taking such an approach is inherently contradictory to achieving the full expression of public value as it has reduced the level of public trust in government (Pollitt and Bouckaert 2004) and excludes the potential of user or citizen engagement in decision-making (James and Jervier 2017), which are key tenets of public value. Thus, the welfare state at national and local levels has been destabilised (Powell and Miller 2013; Cochrane 2004) and does not provide the protective insurance against unexpected changes in personal circumstances in health, housing or employment that has been available since its inception.

This 'small state' approach has created a gap between the UK and the EU that characterises public value as continuous improvement and state intervention in addressing the quality of services offered to citizens to support their welfare including access to jobs, culture, energy provision and transport. Further, the EU's treaties require it to intervene to achieve social and economic cohesion—taking interventionist action where economies are lagging or EU citizens are less advantaged in comparison with the average. On a continuum, the EU's role in promoting public value through its treaties and programmes has advanced as the UK government's interest in public intervention has reduced (Painter 2012). The ideology of the EU in favour of public value is so ingrained in the public life of the other member states that it has been adopted without further questioning. Hartley et al. (2017) set out three dimensions of public value, and it is the second of these, 'the notion of public value as the addition of value through actions in an organizational or partnership setting' (Hartley et al. 2017, p. 671), that characterises the motivation and underlying ethos of EU institutional values. This is in comparison with the first dimension of public value they cite—'the notion of public value as a contribution to the public sphere' (Hartley et al. 2017, p. 617) which is more applicable within a post-2010 setting in England. For the UK government, particularly in its management of England, public value is an 'add on', whereas in the EU, it is a core principle and objective.

Much of the debate about public policy in the UK and the EU in the period since 1990 has been on the role of new public management (NPM) and its perceived antithetical position in relation to public value (Ferlie et al. 1996; Hoggett 1996). There are underlying assumptions that NPM has replaced the practices of public policy and administration that embodied public value in the UK before its introduction. Some of the concern about NPM has been expressed by those who consider that they are losing their control over the definition of public value operated through professional codes and administrative practices (Woodman 1999). While NPM might be part of a community-based approach to governance that challenged professional control over decision-making, it could also be a return to a more Fabian-like approach to the use of evidence; for example, are the policies working as intended and are they offered in the same ways to all (Beresford 2002)? NPM represented a move away from the control held by those producing public services in a 'we know best what is good for you' way and 'we will determine how it will be delivered', to a position where consumer/user choice and voice was given a greater role in determining policy priorities and delivery standards across a range of public services (Simmons et al. 2012; Shand 2018). It also included co-production and 'choice and voice' within private or mixed production approaches (Bovaird and Loeffler 2012; Mintrom 2003).

Performance management, as part of NPM, has been a tool of this process of moving from a range of service delivery outputs to ones that are expected to be more consistent, although this is characterised as a 'tick box' approach by its detractors (Van Dooren et al. 2015; Arnaboldi et al. 2015). In its application, the role of the NPM became associated with input rather than outcome measures, which have been particularly critical in Australia and New Zealand (Di Francesco 2001; Adcroft and Willis 2005). In England, it can be argued that the post-2010 age of austerity has crowded out government interest in public value in policy-making, with the focus being more on whether its political agenda has been met (Hupe and Hill 2016; Taylor-Gooby 2016). Examples of this approach include universal credit and house building. In terms of housing, however, the UK government policy-making in England has been overtaken by a political agenda with policy driven by public opinion polling for party approval such as that on landlord policies and home ownership driven by survey responses made by 'generation rent', rather than attention to its responsibilities to the people as a whole (Lund 2013; Lowndes and Gardner 2016).

So, what difference does any policy make in achieving public value? This focus on outcomes was less popular in the central British state where careers are made in innovation and input rather than on assessment of the effectiveness of the policy in the longer term (Pollitt and Bouckaert 2004). Here, there is a variation in values and objectives between cosmopolitans and locals in public services (Gouldner 1957, 1958). Cosmopolitans seek wider public recognition for initiatives from either the domestic or international policy community. In comparison, locals spend a longer time in localities or as specialists and are judged on the effectiveness of policies in meeting the objectives as set out at the point of their adoption. In this view, it is the 'locals' that are frequently associated with understanding and maintaining public value located in more traditional practices, whereas the cosmopolitans are seen to be in favour of change using external reference points. Locals expect to influence and for others to follow them based on their knowledge and competence. Within the UK/EU debate, it is the UK that self-identifies as the 'local', that is, knowing what is best for the country or communities without any wider reference to outcomes. This is in comparison with the EU, which is regarded by the central government public policy community as cosmopolitan and other, despite the role that the UK has played in influencing these policies and programmes. The default position of Whitehall in the implementation of EU pooled and agreed policies within the UK has been to domesticise them into 'local' policies and submerge those elements that are associated with public value provided through their EU provenance. The list of 'successful' policies generated by the Political Studies Association and Institute for Government Poll provides some examples that include devolution, smoking ban, independence of the Bank of England and the minimum wage (Morphet 2013).

Role of Public Value Within the EU

The role of public value in the EU has developed over time, and this can be considered in three main ways. Firstly, the role of *governance* as a tool of public value is expressed at the point of accession of any member state. This includes the embodiment of the EU's ethos and the role of decision-making, particularly in relation to funding, including evidence of anti-corruption measures (Van Der Wal et al. 2008). The accession process includes not only the requirement to align with the *acquis* at the point of joining the EU but also a range of democratically accountable institutions and processes that are in support of decision-making and public accountability (Moravcsik and Vachudova 2003; Schimmelfennig and Sedelmeier 2004). This development of democratic accountability has changed with time, and should the UK wish to rejoin the EU after leaving, this may require some significant domestic constitutional changes. Other subnational structures included within the treaty principles of subsidiarity and decision-making are set out in the 2009 Lisbon Treaty.

While the EU, particularly under Delors, European Commission President 1985–1995, took a more top-down approach to the consumer interest in public value practices, the widening of EU membership to the accession of new states in 2004 suggested that a more open and transparent approach to determining public policy and delivery. This recognised that funding would be required to achieve some convergence in the practices of government (Cappelen et al. 2003). Delors also understood that in a widening membership, it was important to find ways of demonstrating a positive and democratically accountable relationship with the EU at all scales of government (Grant 1994). The member states could not be relied upon to communicate this within their tiers of government, and the European Parliament would need more powers to lay claim to being more than a talking shop (Kohler 2014). The creation of the Committee of the Regions was another way of reinforcing the role and legitimacy of multilevel governance (MLG), not least at the level which was most in contact with the EU's citizens (Tömmel 1998). If the EU was to expand its territory and its role, it needed the legitimacy that could be demonstrated to its citizens, and applying public value tests could be one way of achieving this recognition of the EU's role (Jenson 2007).

While the British prime minister led in the establishment of the subsidiarity principle, in the Treaty for the EU ('Maastricht Treaty') 1992, Whitehall managed a devolution process that would move ahead in Scotland, Wales, Northern Ireland and London, but it had little or no intention of implementing devolved decision-making within England. Instead, it introduced a set of substate structures which were centrally controlled such as government offices for the regions, regional assemblies and regional development agencies that managed EU programmes and funding (Pemberton and Morphet 2014). These quasi-devolved bodies continued until 2010, when they were abolished by the New Labour government. They were replaced by local enterprise partnerships (LEPs) by the incoming Conservative and Liberal Democrats Coalition Government in 2010 until such time, and after further application of territorial subsidiarity in the Lisbon Treaty (2009), the EU called a halt in 2014. The UK government subsequently commenced a devolved programme of government for England through the establishment of combined authorities with directly elected mayors (Sandford 2016).

Within the EU, the practices of NPM as a tool of achieving public value were identified as being important in the process of convergence if the adoption of the *acquis* was to be meaningful in practice. This would also become more important when increased the application of subsidiarity was introduced after 2009. It has been one of the means of changing administrative systems from being primarily clientelist to meeting public value objectives as broadly understood (Moore 1995). Within the EU, the techniques of NPM became a means of demonstrating the process of this cultural and practical convergence within accession states and was also spread to examine the effectiveness of EU policies, governments and expenditure in meeting wider social, economic and environmental objectives (Pollitt and Bouckaert 2004; Chandler 2017). It was also a means of demonstrating compliance with policies and implementation agreed by member states within the EU. In this case, it became both an input and an output technique for establishing what was defined as practices of public value within the EU (Haughton 2007; Vachudova 2008). These may come to be represented as codes in public life (Francesco 2012) that provide practical approaches to ensuring public value with sanctions if public organisations, politicians and officials are not in compliance with them. These were the objectives set for the process of accession by the Blair government and Presidency in 1998. These objectives were used to guide the processes of accession. They were also then included within the *Agenda 2000 for a stronger and wider union* that established the objectives, policies and processes for the whole EU, as it expanded to include the accession states into membership (Henderson 1998; CEC 2000). *Agenda 2000* incorporated the notion of public value in the principles of these arrangements for accession, particularly through the first which was concerned with government and decision-making.

Secondly, public value approaches within the EU are *dynamic* rather than static. For example, they reflect a growing relationship between the EU and the OECD about the role of international standards within the EU as it becomes more outward-facing. This means that long-standing member states have also been involved in reforms of their own practices in part introduced into the EU by Tony Blair (Bulmer 2008; Morphet 2013; Daddow 2016). Within the EU, this was resolved as the creation of an administrative space where officials could discuss alternatives and make agreements outside the formal structures that had previously been the only mechanisms available within member states (Radaelli 2003; Tholoniat 2010; Trondal and Peters 2013). This involved the use of codes and written statements of public value and could be seen not only as being a frame for NPM but also as a safeguard to the increasing requirements to open public services to competition and to public providers in other member states. As the extensive literature on public sector outsourcing demonstrates, there is both a fear about the loss of a public value ethos in this process and the potential reduction in values that bind the state together as a socially cohesive whole (Jensen and Stonecash 2005; Grimshaw et al. 2002). The rise in populism could be related to reducing role of the state and responsibilisation of individuals that has left a sense of insecurity and a search for an alternative provider as a form of security (Lowe and Meers 2015). While the populist parties cannot offer material support, they can offer political reassurance though recognition of this fear of loss of protection, not least in an uncertain economic future (Ketola and Nordensvard 2018).

The third contribution that the EU makes to the *institutionalisation* of public value practices has been through its assumptions that state provision and intervention through regulation has positive benefits for society. The adoption of positive legal practices towards the management and delivery of public goods and services includes the citizens' rights in relation to them (Petersmann 2017)—such as for free movement and the access to the benefits of citizenship across all member states. The same approach applies to companies and their operations. EU intervention and regulation also supported access to services across all member states, for example, for mobile phone charging and the standards within which companies work such as the General Data Protection Regulation (GDPR) (2016). These public values are also imbued at different levels of government and in cross-border areas where there is no current EU-wide legal framework in place. Within the EU, decisions must be taken as close as possible to the citizen and in a transparent way. As Petersmann (2017) shows, the EU legal framework for decision-making must also apply in external agreements which third countries such as the trade agreement with Canada.

The Relationship Between EU Public Value Norms and Practices and the UK

Since the UK has been a member of the EU, there have been changes in policy practices and influences over outcomes, both of which relate to public value. While influences have been two-way between the EU and the UK, the spheres of influence have varied. A key influence of the UK's membership of the EU on its forms of governance has been the application of vertical and horizontal integration in government. The UK's membership of the EU in 1972 was accompanied by the introduction of spatial economic policies, which included structural funding programmes and were meant to replicate the approaches that had been operational in the UK for assisted areas before then (Mitchie and Fitzgerald 1997; Marshall and Glasson 2007). While the policy operated as a centralist redistribution policy in the UK, membership of the EU started to have some influence on the nature of the UK's centralism, which shifted to a more regularised rather than random approach, in particular, through the introduction of the Barnett formula in 1978 (Bell and Christie 2001). This was also a response to a growing interest in devolution within the UK in the context of the Scottish referendum in 1979. However, the EU started to extend this approach to develop and incorporate subsidiarity—at first at the member state level as part of the Treaty for the EU (1992) and then extended to substate government in the Lisbon Treaty (2009). This initial influence of the UK on the EU to extend its role in public value had turned in a way that the UK government did not expect nor generally welcomed, particularly in relation to England (Morphet 2017b). What had been a specific and focused UK regional policy had been extended to a universal and wide-ranging approach to devolved decision-making that increasingly became expressed as multilevel governance (MLG).

The form of vertical integration through MLG approaches is most frequently discussed as it represents the ways in which subsidiarity is most recognised in action. What is the purpose of MLG within the EU principles and objectives, and how has it influenced the delivery of public value within the UK? It is possible to contextualise the EU's position within its policy of MLG (Morphet 2013) as part of institutionalised relationships between the EU and its localities. The EU has also reinforced the linkages between MLG and economic growth through a set of economic policies as it has aligned with the OECD in pursuit of fiscal federalism and increase in GDP (OECD 2018). A third area of EU priority has located the development of MLG through the UN's Sustainable Development Goals (SDGs) (UN 2016) and particularly the New Urban Agenda (NUA) (UN 2017). This focuses on the development of joint work across functional economic areas to align administrative boundaries to these, even where they may cross state borders. The EU has incorporated this through the adoption of its own Urban Agenda. This approach has had implications for public value not least because of the ways in which the EU, OECD and UN are establishing comparable evaluative data for the performance of these subregions (Brezzi and Veneri 2015). Where it might be argued that NPM focused more on service delivery, the comparative evaluation of subregions within this MLG context allows for some consideration of the state's role in supporting these outcomes. Where they are not constrained by the central state, the role of the subregions, together with their increasingly directly elected political leadership, is developing their own initiatives and optimising them for their areas. In this way, public value could be enhanced and derived locally to meet specific priorities, but the methods are not prescribed by inputs and the integrated and cumulative impact of these initiatives. Moreover, policies and programmes may also be considered for their effectiveness.

While there has been some devolution in the UK following the development and deepening of the subsidiarity principle in the Treaty for the EU (1992) and later the Lisbon Treaty (2009), leading to evolving processes of devolution in Scotland, Wales, Northern Ireland and London, the form of devolution within England has remained curtailed by Whitehall. Subsequently, as pressure from the EU increased towards more devolution and decentralisation in England, there was some acknowledgement of this through the potential for administrative reform through the creation of regional assemblies in 2004 (ODPM 2002). However, the regional scale appeared to be too large to fit within the emerging new economic geography (Fujita and Krugman 2004) and at the same time not acceptable to the electorate when the 2014 referendum in the northeast region for a regional assembly was lost. In line with the growing subregional agenda, the number of local authorities in the northeast has now been reduced, with two-tier local government abolished in two areas and new strategic combined authorities emerging for functional economic areas within the region for areas including Teesside and around the Tyne.

This change in direction away from regionalism towards smaller substate areas was discussed in a series of significant papers by the Treasury on devolved decision-making between 2004 and 2006 under the chancellorship of Gordon Brown (HMT 2004; Morphet 2008). This was followed by the review of subregional areas in England (HMT 2007). Together with Brown becoming prime minister in June 2007, these might have suggested a more radical approach to meeting the increasing pressure for devolution from the EU, as set out in the Lisbon Treaty, particularly for England. However, despite all these portents and preparations, the UK was the last of all member states to sign the Lisbon Treaty, thus delaying its implementation from the 2007–2013 to 2014–2020 EU cohesion programme period. Some scalar government reforms in England were made through the Local Democracy, Economic Development and Construction

Act 2009, but these reforms were ponderous in their application and appeared to be working on 'variable geometry' (Jones and Macleod 2004), with no common approach across the whole of England or the wider UK territory. The government did not introduce devolved decision-making to local areas and as local authorities expected these reforms to be selective initiatives for favoured local authorities rather than universal in application, they did not press for change (Blunkett et al. 2016). The government regional structures were dismantled by April 2010, leaving the policy agenda clear for local devolved decision-making.

While the creation of new local enterprise partnerships (LEPs) in 2010 promised no devolution to local authorities, in one move they created new subregional alliances of greater and lesser economic effectiveness (Jones 2010). It also launched yet another round of quasi-devolution to these new LEPs which were wholly owned by the continuing clientelist arrangements between them and their sponsoring government departments (Pemberton and Morphet 2014). However, unsurprisingly, these LEPs remained top-down in their character and were able to directly appoint their own boards and had no requirements or practices for public engagement (Pike et al. 2015; Johnston and Blenkinsopp 2017). There was also little consideration of the role of LEPs in generating public value. Instead, they were used by government to direct central policies to substate locations, using the competitive mechanisms and language of 'deals' for EU programmes which were intended to be universal rather than selective.

It was also becoming clear that the new EU 2013 Cohesion Regulation (1303/2013) would extend the notion of universal approaches to substate policy-making through two specific formats—Integrated Territorial Investment (ITI) (van der Zwet et al. 2014; Miller and van der Zwet 2018) and Community-Led Local Development (CLLD) (Piattoni and Polverari 2016) that were introduced to develop common approaches across the whole of the EU territory. In the EU, defining the substate scales for implementation of the 2014–2020 programme brought together substate funding together including that for rural areas, transport, energy, structural funds, research and development, environment and sustainability. The EU also developed territorial pacts between the state and the localities as contracts between partners as part of *Europe 2020*, the post-economic 2008 crisis programme (Antonescu 2015). At the macro-regional scale, vertical and horizontal integration programmes were developed at substate level that included member states as partners for the Baltic, the Adriatic, the Danube and the Alps (Neuman and Zonneveld 2018).

The UK's initial approach to implementing the 2013 Cohesion Regulation was centralised and appeared to be more about retaining centralised control than generating the public value that was intended through the devolved programme. This UK approach was not accepted by the European Commission. Rather than risk failure of its submission for the way it would deliver the Cohesion Regulation, the UK government shifted its position, and the Chancellor of the Exchequer, George Osborne, confirmed that the UK would devolve power and funding decisions to substate levels in England (Sandford 2016). However, this was to occur over the programme period to 2020, during which time some Combined Authorities have been created. Notwithstanding this, the centralised approach to managing funding and decision-making in England continued through a range of centralised programmes such as growth deals operated through non-democratically accountable LEPs (Harrison 2014; Johnston 2015). When the UK was challenged to achieve these reforms by the end of the EU programme period in 2020, instead of instituting a universal implementation of combined authorities, as might have been expected, the government acted to formalise the role of LEPs as agencies of the government. This confirmed their centralising role over local decision-making. Further, elsewhere in the UK, through City Deals, the government moved to recentralise the EU programmes that had previously been devolved (Morphet 2017b).

As a continuing member of the EU, the UK would be facing the next programme period for substate policy implementation (2021–2027), which includes further advances in the application of subsidiarity. Without this, there are more forces for government recentralisation in the UK than any continuation of decentralisation. It has been argued that Brexit has pushed devolution off the government's agenda given there is insufficient 'bandwidth' within the civil service (Wright 2017; Wincott 2018). However, an alternative reading could be that the government is hedging its position. If the UK leaves the EU, then there will be no need to continue with this wider devolved approach as the supra-legal agreements for subsidiarity in the EU treaties will be lost. Central government can reduce devolution and could promote the policies for austerity and centralisation, already in place in England, to the rest of the UK. Here there is no sense of government adding public value but rather abandoning this role. On the other hand, with any future relationship between the UK and the EU remaining uncertain, there may be some risk mitigation being applied just in case the devolution approaches have to continue in some way. It is also the case that the OECD, which could emerge as a more important influence on UK economic policy-making post-Brexit, is firmly of the view that pubic value should be created by government and that governments best do this by devolving power (O'Flynn 2007; OECD 2019).

The EU's approach to public value has had a second influence on UK public policy, and this has been through its dynamic aspect. This influence can be seen on British legislation and public policy that are episodic in their character. That is, they are bounded by the terms of five-year parliamentary terms. In the UK, there is a role for case law which can be used in interpretation of legislation and can create a more dynamic pathway for decision-making but only if the legislation is not changed by the Parliament when new sets of case law must be established. The only consistency will be how case law is determined and how it is applied in practice. The processes of legislation are dynamic, but the content of the legislation could be static unless changed by subsequent legislation. In contrast, the EU's approach to legislation and policy-making is cumulative, and this has made it more dynamic. In this way, as most frequently represented by the 'whereas' clauses at the beginning all EU regulations and directives, there is an assumption that EU policy and legislation is committed to continuous improvement and incorporation of change (Porte et al. 2001). The role of the European Court of Justice (ECJ) and the role of EU citizens are seen to be more important than the member state governments and other private sector organisations that operate within this legislation. Under EU law, it is possible for any citizen to bring a case against its own government or a corporation if it considers that they were not operating within the legislation that is in effect at the time. The ECJ is incorporating the role of public value through its decision-making. It has therefore been possible for UK citizens, for example, to take public value cases against the UK government to the ECJ for failure to meet air or water quality standards. In these cases, once proven against the government, the ECJ has powers to fine the government and to make it demonstrate how it will act in future. The ECJ can then pass over the delivery of these judgements to domestic courts. In the case of data privacy, the ECJ can rule in the practices of companies in their use of data and fine them if the EU rules are breached. Court cases again can be brought by individuals. In the UK, it is not possible for individuals to bring general cases against the government in this way, and then, where cases are found against corporations, it is not possible for the courts to require remedial action by the government apart from the payment of damages. This is a static and not a dynamic approach to legislation and public value, and the UK's approach remains residual unless it has been required to act based on EU decisions or legislation.

Thirdly, turning to consider the effects on the UK of EU membership on its institutionalised policy practices, there have been some direct and indirect influences in the approach to public value. In terms of a direct influence, the UK civil service has lost some of its skill and experience in policy-making (Hallsworth 2011; Rhodes 2016). While the focus of domestic policy-making has been split between the negotiation of specific policy issues within the EU, conducted between a range of UK Government Departments and channelled through the Cabinet Office and the UK's Representative in the EU (UKREP), much of the domestic role of the civil service has been finding ways of implementing this agreed policy and legislation into practice (Bulmer and Burch 2013; Morphet 2013). As Rutter et al. (2012) demonstrated, there is a concern in the civil service to understand how policies are made and what contributes to their effectiveness. This effectiveness may increasingly be regarded as internally referential within the UK civil service rather than considering its public value, which was more typical of governments before 2010. However, the conclusions of Rutter et al.'s work overlooked the overriding contextual factor that the policies that have been deemed to be successfully implemented in the UK were agreed within the EU first. The basis of these 'successful' policies was not subject to political disputation within the UK. Instead, only the methods of implementation, which could be aligned to prevailing political ideologies of governments and preferences of ministers by civil servants, were regarded as being successfully delivered (Morphet 2013). At the same time, there has been a distancing between the UK civil service and policy-making which has been through the operation and application of the GPA and the EU's role in delivery through aspects of the single market and procurement legislation. This has meant that services that could be amenable to outsourcing in their delivery have been distanced from Whitehall where before they would have been part of the government departments' work and contributed to a wider understanding of the delivery of the departments' responsibilities (Froud et al. 2017). At the same time, the centre of the civil service has protected its position from the potential for outsourcing, and it has introduced agencies into its own structures to distance policy from operational responsibilities (Pollitt 2013). In the GPA, government policy is not expected to be open to competition. Hence, for civil servants, there has been a shift away from any association with the practices of government at the interface with citizens and users, and this distancing has been a factor in the government's departmental hierarchy (Dommett et al. 2016). Hence, those departments with the greatest amount of public interface such as DWP and MHCLG have a lower influence in determining policy and outcomes than the Treasury and the Cabinet Office. In responding to the EU's programming cycles, the UK has adopted the comprehensive spending review (CSR) to ensure that policy shifts agreed as part of EU decisions can be implemented using this as a mechanism for domesticating EU policy and programme implementation. This has led to implementation using an episodic approach of policy projects within the CSR (in managing them as start and finish policy delivery rather than taking the cumulative approach and binding them into policy which is the practice in the EU and other member states). There has been a failure to use the CSR to incorporate the public value elements of EU policy within the UK government system as a whole.

What Are the Potential Effects of Brexit on Achieving Public Value in the UK?

The effects of the UK leaving the EU can only be determined when the mode of departure is finalised and the nature of the future arrangements between the UK and the EU is agreed. There are some aspects of public value that can be maintained in the UK (Morphet 2017a). These relate to the provision of public value through competition and environmental obligations that will continue to be required based on UN and WTO treaties. The public value elements of the SDGs, the GPA and the WTO trade and environment treaty will remain, although the opportunity to call the government to account for breaches in their observation by UK citizens will be limited by the prevailing model of UK law. Even if UK law for environment and employment policy shadows that of the EU's law following Brexit, it will not be effective in the same way because it will be subject to UK interpretation in the courts and there will be no access to the ECJ and its remedies. This is a potential loss in the practice and delivery of public value even while the principles remain in trade policy. Former Prime Minister Theresa May made some promises to maintain alignment between EU and UK environmental and employment legislation. While such approaches adopted by subsequent prime ministers might give some benefits to UK citizens, in the dynamic and continuing improvement of EU standards, it will be less effective if the legal mechanisms for requiring compliance are not as strong as those currently within the EU (Reid 2016). There may also be external pressures such as those exercised by companies that will not trade with the UK unless there is clear and active compliance with the EU's standards. At the same time, those companies from the USA that do not have a similar recognition of public value are campaigning for lower standards and may make this a requirement of their trading relationships with the UK (Balls et al. 2018). This is particularly the case as the USA has withdrawn from the UN climate change agreement and may wish to pressurise its trading partners into taking the same path.

The second area where Brexit may influence the delivery of public value will be on devolution and governance within the principles of subsidiarity. Here, the EU treaties have provided longer term certainty for the Scottish, Northern Ireland and Welsh governance arrangement that are protected within this higher-level legislation, while the UK has made no changes in the constitution to incorporate their role in government and decision-making. Without this, while these governance arrangements can be included within UK's post-Brexit domestic settlement, they cannot, by UK law, be guaranteed by more than one parliamentary term. The same will apply to other structural features of substate governance such as combined authorities in England. There are no guarantees that these would continue or that additional combined authorities could be established. While there would be no formal requirements to apply subsidiarity in the UK, the OECD and UN may provide some pressure on the UK government. The OECD has considerable influence over the UK economic and social policy and has close links with the EU and the IMF. The UK government could be strongly encouraged to support the policies of fiscal federalism that are being pursued by the OECD but cannot be required to do so. The UN might take a different view. In signing up to the SDGs in 2016, SDG 11 for the New Urban Agenda may be represented as requiring the UK to continue with subsidiarity and devolving powers to substate government (UN 2016). This is a treaty obligation and therefore stronger than OECD membership. It is also the case that the UN will be monitoring all signatories to assess their compliance or movement towards achievement of SDG standards (Office for National Statistics 2019). SDG 11 includes an assessment of devolved governance, and while this might be helpful, the UK might consider this to be advisory rather than a commitment. Compliance with the EU subsidiarity principle has only had a residual effect in the devolution of decision-making in the UK state, and it could be that the UN approach will be equally dismissed or ignored and public value principle could be undermined.

Finally, Brexit removes the EU's commitment to continuous improvement and welfarist intervention through legislation, policies and programmes that were applied to the UK during its membership. Since the 2016 referendum, there has been no public discourse about the loss of public value principles following Brexit, and it appears to have been overlooked (Gingrich and King 2018). Within England, there is an absence of an overarching welfarist ideology in public policy, no incorporation of public value outcomes for government actions and the default position could result in more neoliberal policies. None of the political parties have focused on the EU's role in framing all public policy within public value principles as a post-Brexit issue, as the debates about the various options for departure have concentrated on very few specific topics such as employment and environment law and have been further obscured by the COVID-19 pandemic. In a post-Brexit UK, there is likely to be a public value lacuna in the guiding principles of government that remains unrecognised and will further distance England from the rest of the UK and the EU.

Conclusion

The potential effects on achieving public value through government policies and interventions are uncertain in a post-Brexit world. However, there are questions and challenges that will face the delivery of public value in the future. As shown in this chapter, some of these values are imbued in international treaties with the UN and WTO to which the UK will still be committed to and which will require UK compliance. However, there are other factors at work that suggest that if public value is to be an agreed objective through the delivery of public policy and services in the UK, it will need to be specifically addressed in the parliamentary processes and through government practices. Without this, it is likely that it will be overlooked and eroded. Instead, there may be a drift to other operational principles in government policy without any specific objectives to do so but as an unintended consequence.

These outcomes may cover a range of practices, some of which have already emerged through preparations for Brexit since the 2016 referendum. These include a strong focus on recentralisation of public policy administration through the undermining and removal of devolved powers in Scotland, Wales and Northern Ireland. The European Union (Withdrawal) Act 2018 recentralises the powers for transport, agriculture and the environment, initially for a fixed period but one that can be extended. It is also possible to see the recentralisation of substate governance decision-making through the use of City Deals in Scotland, Wales and Northern Ireland that, in practice, are bypassing the devolved governments to make new direct relationships between functional economic areas and Whitehall (Ward 2018).

Secondly, with its episodic approach to government, the UK will see a shift back to short-termism, rather than through a cumulative approach to achieving public value outcomes. This will have both general and specific consequences such as undermining commitments to longer term infrastructure projects. Where EU membership has provided policy and programme commitments for 20–30 years, the UK Parliamentary system does not allow this. There may be difficulties in sustaining commitments to nationally significant infrastructure projects over the shorter term political and parliamentary cycles (Davies et al. 2018). These will not be able to be secured even through the establishment of specific UK institutions such as the National Infrastructure Commission. Furthermore, this lack of a longer term view and a focus on short-termism will lead to greater priority for polling-led public policy with electoral horizons dominating government actions. The implementation of longer-term EU programme cycles in the UK led to the establishment of the CSR, but this process could be lost as a mechanism to refocus government activities and expenditure within agreed timescales. As Brexit's legacy, this will leave government agendas being defined by the absence of proactive action guided by public value principles.

REFERENCES

Adcroft, A., & Willis, R. (2005). The (Un) Intended Outcome of Public Sector Performance Measurement. *International Journal of Public Sector Management, 18*(5), 386–400.

Alford, J., & O'Flynn, J. (2009). Making Sense of Public Value: Concepts, Critiques and Emergent Meanings. *International Journal of Public Administration, 32*(3–4), 171–191.

Antonescu, D. (2015). Territorial Pact in Context of Europe 2020. *Procedia-Social and Behavioral Sciences, 188*, 282–289.

Arnaboldi, M., Lapsley, I., & Steccolini, I. (2015). Performance Management in the Public Sector: The Ultimate Challenge. *Financial Accountability & Management, 31*(1), 1–22.

Balls, E., Sands, P., Sethi, M., Hallam, E., Leape, S., & Weinberg, N. (2018). On the Rebound: Prospects for a US-UK Free Trade Agreement.

Becker, S. O., Fetzer, T., & Novy, D. (2017). Who Voted for Brexit? A Comprehensive District-Level Analysis. *Economic Policy, 32*(92), 601–650.

Bell, D., & Christie, A. (2001). Finance–The Barnett Formula: Nobody's Child? In A. Trench (Ed.), *The State of the Nations, 2001* (pp. 135–151). Exeter: Imprint Academic.

Benington, J., & Moore, M. (2011). Public Value in Complex and Changing Times. In J. Benington & M. Moore (Eds.), *Public Value Theory and Practice* (pp. 1–30). London: Palgrave Macmillan.

Beresford, P. (2002). Participation and Social Policy: Transformation, Liberation or Regulation? *Social Policy Review – Harlow*, 265–290.

Blunkett, D., Flinders, M., & Prosser, B. (2016). Devolution, Evolution, Revolution… Democracy? What's Really Happening to English Local Governance? *The Political Quarterly, 87*(4), 553–564.

Bovaird, T., & Loeffler, E. (2012). From Engagement to Co-Production: The Contribution of Users and Communities to Outcomes and Public Value. *Voluntas: International Journal of Voluntary and Nonprofit Organizations, 23*(4), 1119–1138.

Boyne, G. A. (2002). Public and Private Management: What's the Difference? *Journal of Management Studies, 39*(1), 97–122.

Brezzi, M., & Veneri, P. (2015). Assessing Polycentric Urban Systems in the OECD: Country, Regional and Metropolitan Perspectives. *European Planning Studies, 23*(6), 1128–1145.

Bulmer, S. (2008). New Labour, New European Policy? Blair, Brown and Utilitarian Supranationalism. *Parliamentary Affairs, 61*(4), 597–620.

Bulmer, S., & Burch, M. (2013). *The Europeanisation of Whitehall: UK Central Government and the European Union.* Manchester: Manchester University Press.

Bulmer, S., & Quaglia, L. (2018). The Politics and Economics of Brexit. *Journal of European Public Policy, 25*(8), 1089–1098.

Busse, R., van Ginneken, E., & Wörz, M. (2011). Access to Health Care Services Within and Between Countries of the European Union. In *Crossborder Health Care in the European Union–Mapping and Analyzing Practices and Policies* (pp. 47–90).

Cappelen, A., Castellacci, F., Fagerberg, J., & Verspagen, B. (2003). The Impact of EU Regional Support on Growth and Convergence in the European Union. *JCMS: Journal of Common Market Studies, 41*(4), 621–644.

CEC. (2018). *EU Budget.* Brussels: CEC.

CEC. (2000). *Agenda 2000: For a Stronger and Wider Union.* Brussels: CEC.

Chandler, J. (2017). *Questioning the New Public Management*. London: Routledge.
Cochrane, A. (2004). Modernisation, Managerialism and the Culture Wars: Reshaping the Local Welfare State in England. *Local Government Studies, 30*(4), 481–496.
Cockfield, A. (1994). *The European Union: Creating the Single Market*. London: Wiley Chancery Law.
Daddow, O. (2016). *New Labour and the European Union: Blair and Brown's Logic of History*.
Davies, N., Atkins, G., & Slade, D. (2018). *How to Transform Infrastructure Decision Making in the UK*. London: Institute for Government.
De Graaf, G., Huberts, L., & Smulders, R. (2016). Coping with Public Value Conflicts. *Administration & Society, 48*(9), 1101–1127.
Dellmuth, L. M., & Stoffel, M. F. (2012). Distributive Politics and Intergovernmental Transfers: The Local Allocation of European Union Structural Funds. *European Union Politics, 13*(3), 413–433.
Di Francesco, M. (2001). Process not Outcomes in New Public Management? 'Policy Coherenin Australian Government. *The Drawing Board: An Australian Review of Public Affairs, 1*(3), 103–116.
Dommett, K., MacCarthaigh, M., & Hardiman, N. (2016). Reforming the Westminster Model of Agency Governance: Britain and Ireland After the Crisis. *Governance, 29*(4), 535–552.
Dunleavy, P., & Hood, C. (1994). From Old Public Administration to New Public Management. *Public Money & Management, 14*(3), 9–16.
Dür, A., & Elsig, M. (2011). Principals, Agents, and the European Union's Foreign Economic Policies. *Journal of European Public Policy, 18*(3), 323–338.
Ferlie, E., Fitzgerald, L., & Pettigrew, A. (1996). *The New Public Management in Action*. USA: Oxford University Press.
Foreign and Commonwealth Office. (2014). *EU Balance of Competences Review*. London: FCO.
Francesco, F. D. (2012). Diffusion of Regulatory Impact Analysis Among OECD and EU Member States. *Comparative Political Studies, 45*(10), 1277–1305.
Froud, J., Johal, S., Moran, M., & Williams, K. (2017). Outsourcing the State: New Sources of Elite Power. *Theory, Culture & Society, 34*(5–6), 77–101.
Fujita, M., & Krugman, P. (2004). The New Economic Geography: Past, Present and the Future. *Papers in Regional Science, 83*(1), 139–164.
Gingrich, J., & King, D. (2018). Americanising Brexit Britain's Welfare State? *Political Quartery, 90*(1), 89–98.
Goodwin, M. J., & Heath, O. (2016). The 2016 Referendum, Brexit and the Left Behind: An Aggregate-Level Analysis of the Result. *The Political Quarterly, 87*(3), 323–332.
Gouldner, A. W. (1957). Cosmopolitans and Locals: Toward an Analysis of Latent Social Roles. I. *Administrative Science Quarterly*, 281–306.

Gouldner, A. W. (1958). Cosmopolitans and Locals: Toward an Analysis of Latent Social Roles. II. *Administrative Science Quarterly*, 444–480.

Grant, C. (1994). *Delors: Inside the House That Jack: Inside the House That Jacques Built*. London: Nicholas Brealey Publishing.

Grimshaw, D., & Rubery, J. (2012). The End of the UK's Liberal Collectivist Social Model? The Implications of the Coalition Government's Policy During the Austerity Crisis. *Cambridge Journal of Economics, 36*(1), 105–126.

Grimshaw, D., Vincent, S., & Willmott, H. (2002). Going Privately: Partnership and Outsourcing in UK Public Services. *Public Administration, 80*(3), 475–502.

Guthrie, J., & Russo, S. (2014). Public Value Management: Challenge of Defining, Measuring and Reporting for Public Services. In *Public Value Management, Measurement and Reporting, Emerald, Bingley* (pp. 3–17).

Hallsworth, M. (2011). Policy-Making in the Real World. *Political Insight, 2*(1), 10–12.

Harrison, J. (2014). The Rise of the Non-State 'Place-Based' Economic Development Strategy. *Local Economy, 29*(4–5), 453–468.

Hartley, J., Alford, J., Knies, E., & Douglas, S. (2017). Towards an Empirical Research Agenda for Public Value Theory. *Public Management Review, 19*(5), 670–685.

Haughton, T. (2007). When Does the EU Make a Difference? Conditionality and the Accession Process in Central and Eastern Europe. *Political Studies Review, 5*(2), 233–246.

Henderson, D. (1998). The UK Presidency: An Insider's View. *Journal of Common Market Studies, 36*(4), 563–572.

Hills, J. (2011). The Changing Architecture of the UK Welfare State. *Oxford Review of Economic Policy, 27*(4), 589–607.

HMT. (2004). *Devolving Decision Making: 1-Delivering Better Public Services: Refining Targets and Performance Management*. London: HMT and Cabinet Office.

HMT. (2007). *Review of Sub-National Economic Development and Regeneration*. London: HMT.

Hobolt, S. B. (2016). The Brexit Vote: A Divided Nation, a Divided Continent. *Journal of European Public Policy, 23*(9), 1259–1277.

Hoggett, P. (1996). New Modes of Control in the Public Service. *Public Administration, 74*(1), 9–32.

Hupe, P. L., & Hill, M. J. (2016). 'And the Rest Is Implementation.' Comparing Approaches to What Happens in Policy Processes Beyond Great Expectations. *Public Policy and Administration, 31*(2), 103–121.

James, T. S., & Jervier, T. (2017). The Cost of Elections: The Effects of Public Sector Austerity on Electoral Integrity and Voter Engagement. *Public Money & Management, 37*(7), 461–468.

Jensen, P. H., & Stonecash, R. E. (2005). The Efficiency of Public Sector Outsourcing Contracts: A Literature Review. *Journal of Economic Surveys, 19*, 5.

Jenson, J. (2007). The European Union's Citizenship Regime. Creating Norms and Building Practices. *Comparative European Politics, 5*(1), 53–69.

Johnston, K. (2015). Public Governance: The Government of Non-State Actors in 'Partnerships'. *Public Money & Management, 35*(1), 15–22.

Johnston, L., & Blenkinsopp, J. (2017). Challenges for Civil Society Involvement in Civic Entrepreneurship: A Case Study of Local Enterprise Partnerships. *Public Money & Management, 37*(2), 89–96.

Jones, A. (2010). Here We Go Again: The Pathology of Compulsive Re-Organisation. *Local Economy, 25*(5-6), 373–378.

Jones, M., & MacLeod, G. (2004). Regional Spaces, Spaces of Regionalism: Territory, Insurgent Politics and the English Question. *Transactions of the Institute of British Geographers, 29*(4), 433–452.

Jørgensen, T. B., & Bozeman, B. (2007). Public Values: An Inventory. *Administration & Society, 39*(3), 354–381.

Kelly, G., Mulgan, G., & Muers, S. (2002). *Creating Public Value: An Analytical Framework for Public Service Reform.* London: Cabinet Office.

Ketola, M., & Nordensvard, J. (2018). Social Policy and Populism: Welfare Nationalism as the New Narrative of Social Citizenship. *Social Policy Review 30: Analysis and Debate in Social Policy, 2018*, 161.

Kohler, M. (2014). European Governance and the European Parliament: From Talking Shop to Legislative Powerhouse. *JCMS: Journal of Common Market Studies, 52*(3), 600–615.

Krugman, P. (1991). Increasing Returns and Economic Geography. *Journal of Political Economy, 99*(3), 483–499.

Lowe, S., & Meers, J. (2015). Responsibilisation of Everyday Life: Housing and Welfare State Change. *Social Policy Review, 27*, 55–72.

Lowndes, V., & Gardner, A. (2016). Local Governance Under the Conservatives: Super-Austerity, Devolution and the 'Smarter State'. *Local Government Studies, 42*(3), 357–375.

Lund, B. (2013). A 'Property-Owning Democracy' or 'Generation Rent'? *The Political Quarterly, 84*(1), 53–60.

MacKinnon, D. (2015). Devolution, State Restructuring and Policy Divergence in the UK. *The Geographical Journal, 181*(1), 47–56.

Marshall, T., & Glasson, J. (2007). *Regional Planning.* Abingdon: Routledge.

Mazzucato, M. (2018). *The Value of Everything Making and Taking in the Global Economy.* London: Allen Lane.

Meunier, S., & Nicolaïdis, K. (2006). The European Union as a Conflicted Trade Power. *Journal of European Public Policy, 13*(6), 906–925.

Miller, S., & van der Zwet, A. (2018). Integrated Territorial Investment in the UK: A Tale of Two Regions. *European Structural & Investment Funds Journal, 6*(1).

Mintrom, M. (2003). Market Organizations and Deliberative Democracy: Choice and Voice in Public Service Delivery. *Administration & Society, 35*(1), 52–81.

Mitchie, R., & Fitzgerald, R. (1997). The Evolution of the Structural Funds. In I. Turok & J. Bachtler (Eds.), *The Coherence of EU Regional Policy Contrasting Perspectives on the Structural Funds* (pp. 14–28).

Mooney, G., & Neal, S. (2010). 'Welfare Worries': Mapping the Directions of Welfare Futures in the Contemporary UK. *Research, Policy and Planning, 27*(3), 141–150.

Mooney, G., & Williams, C. (2006). Forging New 'Ways of Life'? Social Policy and Nation Building in Devolved Scotland and Wales. *Critical Social Policy, 26*(3), 608–629.

Moore, M. H. (1995). *Creating Public Value: Strategic Management in Government*. Harvard University Press.

Moravcsik, A., & Vachudova, M. A. (2003). National Interests, State Power, and EU Enlargement. *East European Politics and Societies, 17*(1), 42–57.

Morphet, J. (2008). *Modern Local Government*. London: Sage.

Morphet, J. (2013). *How Europe Shapes British Public Policy*. Bristol: Policy Press.

Morphet, J. (2016). *Infrastructure Delivery Planning: An Effective Practice Approach*. Bristol: Policy Press.

Morphet, J. (2017a). *Beyond Brexit*. Bristol: Policy Press.

Morphet, J. (2017b). Sub-Regional Strategic Spatial Planning: The Use of Statecraft and Scalecraft in Delivering the English Model. *Town Planning Review, 88*(6), 665–682.

Neuman, M., & Zonneveld, W. (2018). The Resurgence of Regional Design. *European Planning Studies, 26*(7), 1297–1311.

O'Flynn, J. (2007). From New Public Management to Public Value: Paradigmatic Change and Managerial Implications. *Australian Journal of Public Administration, 66*(3), 353–366.

ODPM. (2002). *Your Region, Your Choice—Revitalising the English Regions Cm 5511*. London: ODPM.

OECD. (2018). *Rethinking Regional Development Policy-Making*. Paris: OECD Multi-level Governance Studies, OECD Publishing.

OECD. (2019). OECD Recommendation on Public Service Leadership and Capability. Retrieved April 28, 2019, from http://www.oecd.org/employment/pem/recommendation-on-public-service-leadership-and-capability.htm.

Office for National Statistics. (2019). UK Reporting Platform: UK Data for Sustainable Development Goal Indicators. Retrieved May 1, 2019, from https://sustainabledevelopment-uk.github.io/.

Olsen, J. (2003). Towards a European Administrative Space? *Journal of European Public Policy, 10*(4), 506–531.

Osborne, D., & Gaebler, T. (1993). *Reinventing Government: The Five Strategies for Reinventing Government.*

Painter, C. (2012). The UK Coalition Government: Constructing Public Service Reform Narratives. *Public Policy and Administration, 28*(10), 20.

Pemberton, S., & Morphet, J. (2014). The Rescaling of Economic Governance: Insights into the Transitional Territories of England. *Urban Studies, 51*(11), 2354–2370.

Peters, B. G., & Pierre, J. (1998). Governance Without Government? Rethinking Public Administration. *Journal of Public Administration Research and Theory, 8*(2), 223–243.

Petersmann, E.-U. (2017). EU Citizenship as a Constitutional Restraint on the EU's Multilevel Governance of Public Goods. Retrieved February 2, 2019, from http://cadmus.eui.eu/bitstream/handle/1814/47505/LAW_2017_12.pdf?sequence=1&isAllowed=y.

Piattoni, S., & Polverari, L. (Eds.). (2016). *Handbook on Cohesion Policy in the EU.* Edward Elgar Publishing.

Pike, A., Marlow, D., McCarthy, A., O'Brien, P., & Tomaney, J. (2015). Local Institutions and Local Economic Development: The Local Enterprise Partnerships in England, 2010. *Cambridge Journal of Regions, Economy and Society, 8*(2), 185–204.

Pollack, M. A. (2003). *The Engines of European Integration: Delegation, Agency, and Agenda Setting in the EU.* Oxford: OUP.

Pollitt, C. (2013). The Evolving Narratives of Public Management Reform: 40 Years of Reform White Papers in the UK. *Public Management Review, 15*(6), 899–922.

Pollitt, C., & Bouckaert, G. (2004). *Public Management Reform: A Comparative Analysis.* USA: Oxford University Press.

Porte, C. D. L., Pochet, P., & Room, B. G. (2001). Social Benchmarking, Policy Making and New Governance in the EU. *Journal of European Social Policy, 11*(4), 291–307.

Powell, M., & Miller, R. (2013). Privatizing the English National Health Service: An Irregular Verb? *Journal of Health Politics, Policy and Law, 38*(5), 1051–1059.

Radaelli, C. M. (2003). *The Open Method of Coordination: A New Governance Architecture for the European Union?* Swedish Institute for European Policy Studies.

Reid, C. T. (2016). Brexit and the Future of UK Environmental Law. *Journal of Energy & Natural Resources Law, 34*(4), 407–415.

Rhodes, R. A. W. (1996). The New Governance: Governing Without Government. *Political Studies, 44*(4), 652–667.

Rhodes, R. A. (2016). Recovering the Craft of Public Administration. *Public Administration Review, 76*(4), 638–647.

Rodríguez-Pose, A. (2018). The Revenge of the Places that Don't Matter (and What to Do About It). *Cambridge Journal of Regions, Economy and Society, 11*(1), 189–209.

Rutter, J., Marshall, E., & Sims, S. (2012). *The "S" FACTORS Lessons from IFG's Policy Success Reunions.* London: Institute for Government.

Sandford, M. (2016). Devolution to Local Government in England. In *House of Commons Library Briefing Paper, 7029.* London: House of Commons.

Schimmelfennig, F., & Sedelmeier, U. (2004). Governance by Conditionality: EU Rule Transfer to the Candidate Countries of Central and Eastern Europe. *Journal of European Public Policy, 11*(4), 661–679.

Schott, C., van Kleef, D. D., & Steen, T. (2015). What Does It Mean and Imply to Be Public Service Motivated? *The American Review of Public Administration, 45*(6), 689–707.

Schuller, T., Baron, S., & Field, J. (2000). Social Capital: A Review and Critique. In *Social Capital Critical Perspectives* (pp. 1–38). Oxford: Oxford University Press.

Shand, R. (2018). The Role of Ethics and Targets in Environmental Governance and the Enduring Importance of New Public Management. *Political Studies Quarterly, 16*(3), 230–239.

Sigalas, E. (2010). The Role of Personal Benefits in Public Support for the EU: Learning from the Erasmus Students. *West European Politics, 33*(6), 1341–1361.

Simmons, R., Birchall, J., & Prout, A. (2012). User Involvement in Public Services: 'Choice About Voice'. *Public Policy and Administration, 27*(1), 3–29.

Taylor-Gooby, P. (2016). The Divisive Welfare State. *Social Policy & Administration, 50*(6), 712–733.

Tholoniat, L. (2010). The Career of the Open Method of Coordination: Lessons from a 'Soft' EU Instrument. *West European Politics, 33*(1), 93–117.

Timmins, N. (2001). *The Five Giants: A Biography of the Welfare State.* London: Harper Collins.

Tömmel, I. (1998). Transformation of Governance: The European Commission's Strategy for Creating a 'Europe of the Regions'. *Regional & Federal Studies, 8*(2), 52–80.

Trondal, J., & Peters, B. G. (2013). The Rise of European Administrative Space: Lessons Learned. *Journal of European Public Policy, 20*(2), 295–307.

UN. (2016). *New Urban Agenda.* New York: UN.

UN. (2017). *New Urban Agenda.* Habitat lll Quito, New York: UN.

Vachudova, M. A. (2008). Tempered by the EU? Political Parties and Party Systems Before and After Accession. *Journal of European Public Policy, 15*(6), 861–879.

Van Der Wal, Z., Pevkur, A., & Vrangbaek, K. (2008). Public Sector Value Congruence Among Old and New EU Member-States? Empirical Evidence from the Netherlands, Denmark, and Estonia. *Public Integrity, 10*(4), 317–334.

Van Der Zwet, A., Miller, S., & Gross, F. (2014). *A First Stock Take: Integrated Territorial Approaches in Cohesion Policy 2014–20.*

Van Dooren, W., Bouckaert, G., & Halligan, J. (2015). *Performance Management in the Public Sector.* Routledge.

Veugelers, R., Cincera, M., Frietsch, R., Rammer, C., Schubert, T., Pelle, A., et al. (2015). The Impact of Horizon 2020 on Innovation in Europe. *Intereconomics, 50*(1), 4–30.

Ward, M. (2018). *City Deals. House of Commons Library Briefing Papers SN07158.* London: House of Commons.

Warner, M. E. (2013). Private Finance for Public Goods: Social Impact Bonds. *Journal of Economic Policy Reform, 16*(4), 303–319.

Wincott, D. (2018). Brexit and the State of the United Kingdom. In *Routledge Handbook of the Politics of Brexit* (pp. 31–42). Routledge.

Woodman, C. L. (1999). The Evolving Role of Professions in Local Government. *Local Governance, 25*(4), 211–220.

Woolcock, S. (2016). *European Union Economic Diplomacy: The Role of the EU in External Economic Relations.* Routledge.

Wright, N. (2017). Squeezed Mandarins: The Four Big Challenges Facing the Civil Service. *LSE Brexit.*

Public Value Management: A Paradigm Shift?

Arno van der Zwet and John Connolly

> *A new scientific truth does not triumph by convincing its opponents and making them see the light, but rather because its opponents eventually die, and a new generation grows up that is familiar with it.*
> —(Max Planck 1949)

Introduction

A paradigm shift is commonly understood as a fundamental shift in the understanding and underlying assumptions which changes the prism through which we look, interpret and understand the world around us. Such a shift does not need to occur suddenly, and it rarely does. Indeed, as the above quote by Planck[1] suggests, in many cases, paradigms evolve, they slowly emerge and they can even die out. This chapter takes an evaluative stance by reflecting on the previous chapters to make an assessment of what the evidence from the British context tells us about the debate

---

[1] Max Planck was an eminent German theoretical physics who was awarded the Nobel Prize in Physics for his discovery of energy quanta.

A. van der Zwet (✉) • J. Connolly
University of the West of Scotland, Paisley, Scotland
e-mail: arno.van-der-Zwet@uws.ac.uk; john.connolly@uws.ac.uk

regarding whether we are living in a time of post-new public management, whether public value management (PVM) fills a conceptual vacuum or whether this represents the 'emperors new clothes'. Ever since the 'discovery' of new public management (NPM), scholars have been predicting its demise. The original works that identified NPM by Hood (1991) and Pollitt (1990) voiced strong criticism against the approach and they cannot be considered advocates of NPM in a purist sense (Alford and Hughes 2008). Talbot (2009: 130) argued that PVM may well be 'the next big thing' in public management. Similarly, O'Flynn (2011: 2) tentatively concluded that there is 'some potential for paradigmatic change and setting out what might be some of the practical implications for public sector management and managers'. PVM therefore can be argued to provide a new interpretation that is more flexible and avoids a more narrow-minded 'one best way' approach of previous paradigms (Alford and Hughes 2008).

However, critics argued that the approach was of limited value in terms of understanding public service reform (Rhodes and Wanna 2009, also see Pyper's Chapter in this volume). The particularities of British public administration are such that PVM has been argued to be unsuitable to accommodate the dynamics of the Westminster system (Rhodes and Wanna 2009), which thrives on competition between different value systems (i.e. political ideologies), rather than a more consensus-based approach (Moore 1995).

Against this background, and taking into account the analysis of the preceding chapters in this volume, this chapter considers the levels of congruity between PVM and new public management. It concludes that there has not been a paradigmatic shift away from new public management ideas but that there has been an incremental shift in terms of how public value outcomes are being considered by policy-makers. What has been missing is a comprehensive reform agenda that allows public value management to be a consistent and integral part of UK governance. However, the twin crisis of Brexit and the COVID-19 pandemic may offer a springboard for reform in the medium- to long-term.

The chapter will briefly reflect on some of the conceptual discussions (especially linked to Chap. 1 in this volume) to consider to what extent there is sufficient conceptual clarity to identify a shift towards PVM and to assess to what extent the core conceptual characteristics of PVM are unique to the concept or whether they are shared with pre-existing approaches to public management. It will be argued that PVM has merit in terms of understanding public reform and management. In contrast to the outcome-based orientation of new public management, public 'value' management offers a more relational and network-based perspective of public service delivery. It offers the potential to understand outcomes and the results of public interventions as a consequence of stakeholder engagement within complex governance environments.

The chapter also considers the more practical use of public value management as a narrative for policy-makers. The key evaluative question here is as follows: to what extent does public value management offer an appropriate discursive framework to communicate policy innovation? Scholars such as Smith (2004) have argued that public value offers a powerful narrative for the public sector as well as a defence against the dominance of NPM narratives. This question can be directed to experts and the general public. The new public management paradigm found it useful to establish a managerial narrative for both expert policy communities to stress, in particular, effectiveness elements (i.e. result orientation). However, a public narrative around the efficient delivery of public services has also been highly favoured in order to demonstrate value for money. In order to structure the analysis in the chapter, we will evaluate PVM framework across three dimensions: as a process of policy design, as a programme of policy implementation and as a type of politics.

Defining Public Value Management for Practical Purposes

NPM takes its cue from a private sector approach to government policy-making whereas PVM challenges this rationale and proposed a clear distinction between private managers who create private (economic) value and public managers who should create public (social) value (Moore 1995). In this sense, PVM returns to more traditional understandings of public policy management by identifying clear differences between the ways in which the private sector and the public sector operate (Stoker 2005). Kelly et al. (2002) further clarify this relationship by arguing that private sector value, unlike public value, can be measured in terms of corollary returns to shareholders. Instead, public value includes other values such as fairness, equal access and justice. This does not mean that public value cannot be delivered through private sector means, but the results are measured against public value outcomes. Or, as Alford and Hughes (2008: 131) state, 'it is not who produces it that makes value public. Rather, it is a matter of who consumes it'. The 'collective consumptions' by citizens, rather than the individual consumption by clients, is what sets public value apart from private value (Moore 1995).

From this perspective, PVM also affords more room for politics in policy-making approaches when compared to NPM, by increasing the relative weightage of democratic participation as a feature in the policy-making process (also see Pyper's chapter in this volume). However, the importance of politics cannot be interpreted from a narrow electoral perspective. Instead, PVM affords attention to a wider range of deliberative and participatory mechanisms that allow value-based decision-making. Yet, as Pierre and Peters (2000: 49) argue, 'the creation of a more participatory style of governing does not mean that government is in reality less powerful'. It does mean, however, that 'state and society are bonded together in the process of creating governance'.

In order to understand the origins of PVM as a concept, it is useful to consider how it differs from its predecessor in terms of its rationale. Comparing PVM to traditional public administration's rationale, we note that public administration employs a hierarchical worldview of how society and politics should be organised (Hood 2000; Stoker 2004). The main idea is that humans require rules to maintain order but also to take decisions for the common good. Without such rules and hierarchy, modern societies would not be able to function. Public input in these processes is quite limited, and instead policy-making is dominated by politicians and experts in relatively closed communities (Stoker 2003). In contrast, NPM emphasises the individualistic and entrepreneurial nature of individuals (Stoker 2005) and originates from a rational model which regards individuals as 'utility maximisers'. This worldview leaves society at risk of a 'tragedy of the commons' as rational decisions within the context of one particular policy or institutional setting may maximise its utility but have negative spill-over effects for others and society as a whole. NPM does not fully let go of the idea of a hierarchical structure to support common decisions, but the emphasis is placed on incentives to act towards the common good. Rather than rules and restrictions that are employed under traditional public administration models, NPM affords weightage to targets and personal accountability for not meeting such targets. The individual preferences are aggregated and captured by politicians or policy managers. These preferences are formulated in a framework of 'customer choices' (Stoker 2003; also see Dudau et al. in this volume) which allow, in theory, for a maximum number of options to be available to satisfy diverse interests.

PVM provides an approach to policy-making which, to an extent, goes back to ideas of public administration in terms of its emphasis on societal rather than individual inputs. PVM is more closely linked to communitarian ideologies in which the individual has responsibilities towards the common good (Stoker 2005). From this perspective, bonds and relationships are important to shape consensus-based decision-making. Stoker (2005) argues that the key difference between public administration and NPM on the one hand, and PVM on the other, is that for the latter, preferences are not formed in isolation. The PVM paradigm assumes that public opinion is more subtle and that people are capable of changing their opinions through meaningful deliberations and achieving consensus positions. It also reassesses the role of public managers in terms of achieving legitimacy for policies and organisations in the eyes of the public. As Blaug et al. (2017: 7) note:

> Far from advocating a return to inefficient public services, public value embraces notions of valued public services and efficiency. It calls for more rounded accountability whereby organisations face their citizens as well as their political masters, rather than static, top-down models that focus public managers on meeting centrally driven targets.

This short discussion dovetails previous more detailed analysis in this volume (particularly in Chap. 2). However, for the purpose of this chapter, we can say that conceptually, on the one hand, PVM does represent a new set of ideas on public policy and public administration but that, on the other hand, it also remains firmly rooted in NPM (and even looks back to more traditional ideas of public administration). These linkages are likely to make it difficult to distinguish any shifts in public administration approaches that can be described as 'paradigmatic'.

A New Process of Policy-Making?

In order to evaluate an apparent shift in UK policy-making to PVM and to provide some clarity of its conceptual underpinnings, this chapter identifies three interrelated dimensions of the PVM framework. First, PVM can be linked to the *processes that shape decision-making*. Although PVM takes a value-based perspective which can be interpreted as an outcome of the policy process, the process by which this outcome is achieved forms an integral part of the public value framework (Alford and Hughes 2008). It is the greater involvement of citizens who ultimately provide legitimacy for policy decisions that distinguishes PVM from other policy frameworks (Talbot 2008). Historically, social democratic systems have had a weak link between civil society and the state with citizens only having real influence on politics and policy-making through the election of political actors that best represent their views, confining political and policy processes to formal institutions of the state (Schumpeter 1995). One of the consequences is that citizens do not feel connected to the management of public services, which in turn creates an environment in which the management and resource requirements of public services are often misunderstood (Corrigan and Joyce 1997). Such a lack of understanding leaves citizens susceptible to political narratives about the inefficiencies and ineffectiveness of public service delivery (Blaug et al. 2017). Kelly et al. (2002: 4) point to 'an implicit—and sometimes explicit—contract, whereby, the legitimacy of government…depends on how well it creates [public] value'. However, leaders do not simply follow established preferences; they also assert and must 'shape as well as accommodate public preferences' (Kelly et al. 2002: 7). This tension problematises the role of citizens in the processes of decision-making and leaves us to question the extent to which public value is driven by inputs from society or shaped by elites. Although it goes beyond the focus of this chapter to assess this question in full, PVM clearly advocates a greater contribution of citizens' views in policy-making processes. However, the mechanics by which these inputs are delivered are often less apparent.

Nevertheless, a process through which the aggregation of values takes place is a fundamental feature of Western liberal democracies. At a political level, parties fulfil this function and provide representation of a wide spectrum of values. Yet, the apparent crisis of political parties, evidenced by lower turnouts in elections and falling memberships (see Dalton 1995) and the distrust of elites, evidenced by the rise of populist parties, raises further doubts about whether electoral processes on their own are sufficient in terms of establishing trust and legitimacy in policy-making processes. Long-mooted ideas of public engagement in policy-making processes, such as participatory governance and co-creation, have suggested a more iterative approach to aggregation of values in policy-making. These processes also attempt to accommodate what can be described as a fickle public in the sense that people do not have stable preferences and are prone to changing their minds (Marshall 2007). The contradictory nature of motivations and actions of individuals and institutions has developed into an important strand of research (Talbot 2008) and provides grounds for an iterative process which continuously re-evaluates, redefines and recreates public policy to ensure the closest possible alignment to public value (Moore 1995). As discussed below, the idea of iterative implementation processes is closely linked to the issue of trust in public policy.

Scholars such as Hudson et al. (2019) and Head and Alford (2015) propose a more pluralistic approach to policy-making which includes policy target groups in terms of identifying policy problems and solutions. Hudson et al. (2019) argue that the 'top to bottom' approach that continues to be a major feature of many policy frameworks is one of the main reasons for continued policy failure in the public sector. One of the main challenges is that top-down policy implementation seems to be more susceptible to path dependencies as they provide limited room for new inputs and shifting values within society. Furthermore, a shift to a more 'bottom to top' approach in policy approaches not only has the potential to create legitimacy and trust but can also help to tackle wicked policy problems in a more holistic manner (Head and Alford 2015). Understanding multidimensional policy challenges requires input from the many groups that are affected. The perspectives of these groups will provide valuable input in the policy process based on the lived experiences of groups and individuals. However, from a PVM perspective, what is perhaps even more important is that it allows groups with different positions to engage with each other and create an understanding of different values in a discursive manner. Ultimately, this could facilitate shifts towards consensus positions, a theme that we will return to later. As PVM recognises the fluidity and complexity of public value, it emphasises the need for continuous engagement to align and realign policy inputs to these shifts in expected outcomes whilst balancing the often contradictory nature of the public's policy positions.

The idea of a more bottom-up approach to policy-making does not mean that the role of experts and public managers would become less important, neither does it mean that public managers are considered all-knowing neutral protectors of the public good (Talbot 2009). PVM emphasises a more active role of public managers, but this falls well short of making them the decision-makers, which is a role that is reserved for politicians (Moore 1995). Instead, the public manager's role is threefold. First, they facilitate the articulation of value positions by different groups. Second, they identify and vocalise contradictions in different value positions (either within groups or between groups). Third, they actively look for, and establish, consensus positions. Such an approach is closely linked to ideas of networked governance (Stoker 2005), whereby different actors work closely within a policy system to establish policy frameworks that are based on a common understanding of the issues and the outcomes that are desirable. In order to find the appropriate policy solutions that balance values and that reflect public views and needs, public managers and policy stakeholders are required to operate in a collaborative manner. In this context, the idea of partnership working and the creation of agile agencies that are able to adapt to shifting value patterns in the public domain and collaborate across a range of public policy areas, has become an important feature (Demos 2007).

Assessing the extent to which policy processes in the UK have shifted towards more collaborative and bottom-up approaches is clearly challenging given the fuzziness of the concept and the overlap with other styles of policy-making. It is difficult to argue that participatory governance, co-creation, network management and partnership working are all exclusive features of a PVM paradigm. Yet, a more explicit recognition of the strength of these mechanisms in the policy process could well be perceived as indication of a shift towards a different policy paradigm. It is also important to note that there is spatial dimension to the extent to which certain processes that allow us to capture public values are appropriate and feasible. In other words, the way in which public value is aggregated in the public domain varies according to the level at which aggregation takes place (local, regional, national or supranational).

Over the past two decades, bottom-up processes interpretations of policy-making, which take into account values, have gained prominence. A plethora of new mechanisms and approaches have been introduced to provide more inputs in policy-making decisions. These mechanisms vary substantially in terms of their reach and influence, but what they have in common is that they are designed to give the public (whether they are conceived as citizens, service users, customers) more input in the policy design, implementation and evaluation processes. At one end of the spectrum, we see the use of referenda and petitions. Referenda combine traditional electoral processes with direct policy inputs. Before 1997, the UK had three regional referenda[2] and one UK-wide referenda.[3] In terms of representing a PVM process, they do not adhere to principles of iterative decision-making and are, at least when it comes to controversial issues,

---

[2] 1973 Northern Ireland Border Poll and 1979 Scottish and Welsh Devolution referenda.
[3] 1975 EC Membership referendum

poor mechanisms to establish consensus and can be considered rather blunt tools that do not allow for nuanced positions to be formulated in relation to wicked policy challenges. Indeed, as demonstrated by the Brexit referendum, and the Scottish Independence referendum, they can deepen divisions within society. On the other hand, referenda can have legitimising effects, particularly when they have a decisive outcome. Since 1997, the UK has held seven regional referenda[4] and two UK referenda.[5] These numbers indicate a more frequent use of referenda to take constitutional policy decisions.

Public petitions systems have also been introduced at the national, regional and local levels in order to increase the inputs from the public in policy decisions. The UK government launched its public petition system in 2006, and relaunched it in 2011. Also, regional governments have their own public petition systems. Petitions are well-suited to inform policy during the agenda-setting stage, although they can also target policy formulation processes. From a public value perspective, these systems can have an important role in terms of underpinning the legitimacy of representative institutions and policy decisions (Bochel 2013), and they also have a significant effect on participation in political processes (Carman 2012). On the other hand, they form barriers for certain groups; in particular, certain social classes and age groups have less access to these mediums (Carman 2012). Similar to referenda, petitions can be divisive in that they simplify complex policy issues in a binary format. On the other hand, they are consultative and have the potential to form the basis of more nuanced debates which take into account views from different petitions in order to achieve consensus positions.

Public consultation has become a commonly used mechanism for policy inputs at all levels of government and in many policy domains (planning, environmental, etc.). It is often regarded as a way to deal with heightened democratic discontent and a way for governments to increase inputs in policy-making processes from citizens (Culver and Howe 2004). Consultation can take many forms ranging from approaches that provide a degree of citizen power to noting more than tokenism (Arnstein 1969). Thomas (1990) identifies five categories of decision-making process:

---

[4] 1997 Scottish and Welsh Devolution, 1998 Greater London Authority, 1998 Northern Ireland Good Friday Agreement, 2004 North East England Devolution Referendum, 2011 Welsh Devolution referendum, 2014 Scottish Independence referendum.

[5] 2011 Additional Vote referendum and 2016 EU membership referendum.

- autonomous managerial decision: The manager solves the problem or makes the decision alone without public involvement;
- modified autonomous managerial decision: The manager seeks information from segments of the public, but decides alone in a manner which may or may not reflect group influence;
- segmented public consultation: The manager shares the problem separately with segments of the public, getting ideas and suggestions, then makes a decision which reflects group influence;
- unitary public consultation: the manager shares the problem with the public as a single assembled group, getting ideas and suggestions, then makes a decision which reflects the groups interests; or
- public decision: The manager shares the problem with the assembled public, and together the manager and the public attempt to reach agreement on a solution.

The public value paradigm champions the latter two approaches, and in particular the latter in terms of facilitating a process in which consensus positions can be achieved but are dependent on public managers providing leadership (see also McMillan's chapter in this volume).

In 2018, the UK government published new consultation guidance which highlights that consultations should only be conducted in cases where decisions have not been taken and should be part of a process of engagement. Public managers are asked to consider whether informal iterative consultation is appropriate, using new digital tools and open, collaborative approaches (UK Government 2018). Yet there remain strong doubts about whether such processes have a desired effect in terms of encouraging engagement through which a range of values can be captured, create better decision-making processes, and ultimately increase trust in policy-making processes. Studies show that there is a lack of incentives for citizens to participate; there are insufficient resources to accommodate consultations; there often is a closed design process which invites 'usual suspect responses'; and the process can raise expectations of citizens only for them to experience regulatory capture (Bloomfield et al. 2001; Maciejewski-Scheer and Hoppner 2010). Under such circumstances consultation can do more harm than good.

Moreover, co-production can be considered an extended consultation mechanism which invites 'professionals and citizens [to make] better use of each other's assets, resources and contributions to achieve better outcomes or improve efficiency' (Governance International cited in Bovaird et al. 2015). Co-production emphasises an iterative process by which values and resources are carefully balanced. The above definition suggests that consultation processes only qualify as co-production if there is a significant contribution by citizens. Bovaird et al. (2015) note that most co-production in the UK can be characterised as an individual endeavour where the contributions made, and the benefits received, by citizens are at an individual level. Evidence of collective co-production, where the benefits are collective but the inputs by citizens may be provided individually or together, is rarer. Nonetheless, collective co-production has the ability to establish consensus policies around a wider range of values but it is more difficult to achieve. Political self-efficacy and pre-existing satisfaction with public services are key drivers in co-production. The latter suggest a "catch 22" dilemma—satisfaction is achieved through consultation processes but is also a prerequisite to participation. Yet, as mentioned in Chap. 2 of this book, co-production as well as participatory governance has been given more emphasis in the design of many public policy programmes. One of the key benefits is thought to be that by bringing the end-user into the design process, the risk of policy and programmatic failures are reduced (Bovaird 2007; McConnell 2015).

Further mechanisms of participatory action are citizens' juries (CJ) and citizens' assemblies. These mechanisms combine elements of representative democracy and direct democracy by randomly selecting a group of citizens that is representative of the population as a whole. As a mechanism for gathering citizens' views, they are not new, but they are well suited to determine public value in the broadest sense and as part of a deliberative process through which the participants are able to cross-examine experts and debates are supported by an advisory panel. As such, citizens' juries and assemblies aim to address the concerns of the 'growing difference and distance between the subjectivity, motives and intentions of citizens and the political decisions made in their name' (Smith and Wales 2018). They provide space for continuous reflection on public value concerns between election cycles and also can afford 'voice' to those that are more marginalised. However, juries and assemblies are costly and questions can be raised about their representativeness. They remain open to top-down framing and issue selection. Although these approaches have become reasonably common place as part of social research strategies (for example, a 2014 study that identifies 66 citizens' juries in research projects (Street et al. 2014)) their results are often not considered by decision-makers, which limits the influence of the outcomes of such juries on policy-making (similar to the debates regarding the relationship between evidence and policy more generally—see Chap. 4 in this volume). That being said, citizens' assemblies have been organised on a number of high-profile topics including devolution and Brexit.[6] Others have been proposed recommendations on issues such as climate change but these were rejected by the UK government (Electoral Reform Society 2019). The Scottish Government has recently expressed a strong interest in adopting more permanent assembly following the Irish example whereby, in the latter context, juries had considered issues such as abortion, climate change and the challenges of an ageing population (Herald 2019). In conclusion, these type of mechanisms have the potential to strengthen public value in the policy-making process but are currently too 'fringe' and sporadic in their use in Britain to be considered a galvanising force for governance reform.

PROGRAMMING FOR PUBLIC VALUE

Public value principles can also be applied to the *way in which policy programmes are implemented and measured.* In particular, when compared to NPM, a public value paradigm moves beyond the values of efficiency and effectiveness of NPM and considers a wider range of values linked to community benefit, common good and democratic processes as being central to policy-making. Ultimately, this means that a public value perspective puts emphasis on the outcomes of policies (Kelly et al. 2002) and links these to what the public considers valuable. Yet establishing what policies and services are valued by the public is challenging for a number of reasons. First, perceptions of value evolve over time and can change rapidly; therefore, continuous inputs are required to inform policy programmes. The previous section of this chapter discussed different mechanisms by which public value could inform policy, but changing perceptions also influences what should be measured as part of monitoring and evaluation processes. Second, societies consist of many divisions and PVM avoids a majoritarian view of policy implementation. As an approach, it is geared towards providing a voice for a more diverse range of policy actors in policy implementation. In order to avoid the 'tyranny of the majority', a more consensual approach to the development of policy programmes has to be adopted. In this respect, targets and outcomes have to reflect societal divisions in order to ensure that public value is considered from the broadest possible base and takes

---

[6] For more information, see: https://citizensassembly.co.uk/

into account consensus positions. Third, public value-based policy programmes require careful implementation and, therefore, this necessitates bottom-up inputs from the most appropriate spatial scale. In many ways, public value-based policy programmes can therefore be regarded as 'place-based' rather than what sometimes is called 'people based' (Barca et al. 2012). This is not to say that place-based policies do not target people; it is simply a recognition that people in different places may have different understandings of public value and therefore require policy programmes that are more tailored to their local needs. For example, economic development policy is organised around the principle that different places require context-specific interventions in order to stimulate endogenous growth.

Public value conceives its goals beyond simply meeting targets and protecting or expanding the existing organisational structures (Blaug et al. 2017; Kelly et al. 2002). Instead, the legitimacy of policy-making and governance structures are key features. Talbot (2008) adopts the competing values framework (CVF) which emerged in the 1980s (Quinn 1988; Cameron et al. 2006; Newman 2001) to fit public value goals. This framework recognises four quadrants (collectivity, autonomy, security and personal utility) but places trust and legitimacy at the heart of the framework as a dimension that relates to all other aspects. A fundamental feature of CVF is that the quadrants should not be understood as an 'either/or' choice. Linked to this, PVM has more of an eye for certain types of outcomes which consider the impact of policy decisions from a more holistic perspective. This takes into account spill-over effects from an early stage in the policy-making process.

What is evident, then, is that what constitutes public value in policy terms is, at least in part, a subjective assessment of results/outcomes. From a policy analysis perspective, it involves measuring the value of policy interventions against other options as opposed to some universal standard (Alford and Hughes 2008). The process of matching policy programmes to values is not an exact one, and, as Kelly et al. (2002) note, public value provides a rough yardstick measure for assessing the performance of the public sector. Such an approach to measuring public value requires a framework to enable evidence gathering and reporting, which goes beyond measuring hard results. It also needs to take into account softer aspects combining public attitudes with expert views of public managers that are closely involved in the implementation of programmes. These approaches need to take into account unpredictability, non-linearity, complexity and adaptability of policy implementation (Hudson et al. 2019). They also point towards potential contradictions with an NPM-based framework for gathering evidence which focuses on market competition and effectiveness rather than on services that require collaboration between a wide range of stakeholders. This is not to say that 'effectiveness' (made up of several indicators) does not remain a core aspect of a monitoring and evaluation framework, but that the contradictory nature of different measurement approaches is recognised. In this sense, monitoring systems need to take into account a broader range of measurements that can provide more nuanced information in terms of policy success and failure (McConnell 2015).

The NPM paradigm emphasises formal performance measurement systems, which have become a prominent feature throughout most of the public sector. These systems attempt to capture information in a quantitative framework in order to assess and communicate policy results. The measures are concerned with policy efficiency and effectiveness but make little attempt to capture evidence in relation to wider notions of public value. The supposed evidence-based approach to policy programming that occurred as part of the NPM depoliticised policy decisions by quantifying evidence (see the discussion by Oliver and Fraser in this volume). Yet public perceptions of policy decisions are important within this approach, and technocratic statistical performance indicators are complemented with indicators that aim to quantify subjective opinions in order to ascertain public opinion. These types of indicators go some way to capture public value in the sense that they provide an additional perspective on whether a policy is perceived as successful. However, their perceived neutrality and objectivity obscure the 'untidiness of reality and the choices that underlie their collection and interpretation' (Reddan 2019). Furthermore, not all policy areas have consistently captured public perceptions. For example, Jefferson et al. (2015) noted the need for more positive connections between society and the marine environment and that surveys play an important role in capturing public attitudes towards marine policies. Their one-off study reported that 'results show that perceptions are far from uniform across the population, and such diversity of perceptions is likely impact upon methods to catalyse societal engagement with marine conservation' (Jefferson et al. 2015: 327). More regular monitoring of public perceptions towards marine policy would provide more opportunities to adjust the policy to public values. However, these measures remain static in the sense that they do not engage with public perceptions in a more deliberative and contextual way and allow more consensus positions.

A further issue in terms of technocratic managerial approaches in relation to public value is that the type of indicators used might not represent minority positions sufficiently. This means that the ability to achieve consensus positions between majority and minority views is limited. Moreover, the Thatcherite agenda of advancing majoritarian middle-class policies (Evans 2018), and the subsequent move of New Labour towards the centre (Newman 2001), can be conceived as a type of politics that informs policies that afford limited attention to those that do not fall within the dominant positions of the ideological spectrum.

Although more recent policy frameworks have emphasised collaborative partnership-based approaches, in general, the positivist paradigm continues to be the starting point (and in many cases, the end point) of monitoring and evaluation frameworks. Despite calls for post-positivist approaches towards measuring policy outcomes that emphasise discursive governance (Korkut et al. 2015), quantification remains prominent. On the other hand, more recent concepts, such as sustainability, have increased the awareness of a need for a wider range and better integrated indicator framework within a multilevel policy environment (Turcu 2013). Scotland is a case in point. For example, as part of the adoption of a social dimension to sustainable growth (i.e. inclusive growth), the Scottish Government has demonstrated a strong commitment to the idea of inclusive growth agenda which 'creates opportunities for all and distributes the benefits of increased prosperity fairly' (Scottish Government 2018). These types of policy commitments require more detailed monitoring frameworks in order to capture public value across the different target groups. However, in Scotland, for example, there is evidence to suggest that such macro-policy commitments have not been met with meaningful strategic public value leadership to provide the capacities and support needed in order for outcomes to be demonstrated locally due to an 'empowerment-heavy' approach to public sector governance (Connolly and Pyper 2020). This points to the need to ensure that public value is not simply a task for local actors, but it is for national policy-makers to unlock potential, build capacities and to address fragmentary systems in order for the embedding of outcomes-focused evaluation practices to not fall short, which, unfortunately, has been the case in Scotland (this has also been exacerbated by the policy distractions of the Scottish Government towards constitutional questions).

Furthermore, and as discussed in Chap. 2 of this book, there has been an increased awareness of the power of storytelling as part of evaluation in relaying complex policy issues through the creation of policy narratives. Bevir (2011) has formulated one of the strongest defences of storytelling in public administration. Aligning public values to policy decisions and programmes is inevitably a complex undertaking. Empiricism provides a meagre basis for demonstrating values, and interpretation through storytelling establishes policy narratives, which give meaning to decisions and programmes (Jones et al. 2014).

The Politics of Trust

A third dimension of public value relates to the *type of politics* that underpins policy decisions. If public value management approach challenges the unclear accountability structures that were established as part of the NPM doctrine (Stoker 2003), then it would suggest that the democratic reform of politics to counteract this imbalance would be at its heart. At the end of the noughties, the global financial crisis was thought to have discredited an NPM approach underpinned by a private sector logic. Consequently, some have argued that a different type of politics is being pursued and that the experiences in the first decade of the new millennium have led to a reappraisal of the role of the public sector and public management more specifically. This new logic gives rise to renewed attention public value ideas (Talbot 2009). This politics is characterised by attempts to establish trust with the electorate in relation to reform programmes and policy decisions. As Kelly et al. (2002) note, the notion of trust is closely linked to legitimacy of policies and accountability (also see Massey's chapter in this volume).

Within this context, it is important to note that the role of public managers, in terms of achieving public value, has a political dimension. This is not to suggest that public managers are political in the sense that they are partisan. Yet, they do require to be actively engaged with politics. At a minimum, this would involve listening to how political masters interpret public value and provide advice with regards to how this can be translated into policy programmes. However, this role ranges from passively responding to political inputs to more proactively alerting elected officials to emerging challenges and framing these in the context of public value.

Alford and Hughes (2008: 134) summarise the political dimension of the role of public managers as follows:

> public managers can play an entrepreneurial role in discerning or imagining solutions to problems in our natural or social environment that are politically acceptable as well as administratively feasible. In this context, the manager's role is not so much to define public value on behalf of society as to put forward value propositions for consideration by the citizenry and their various political representatives.

A dynamic role in the political process is not without its challenges. The role of public manager is of particular importance when considering the gap that exists between policy implementation and politics. A well-recognised challenge in modern policy-making is the overly optimistic expectations of in particular large policy initiatives (Hudson et al. 2019). Some time ago Hogwood and Gunn (1984) emphasised the need to examine implementation gaps and noted the challenges of translating policy initiatives into actual results. The distance between initiatives and results is, at least in part, created by the over-selling of what policies will achieve by elected representatives and civil society actors who support policy programmes. Within a competitive system, policy actors have a strong incentive to emphasise positive outcomes and downplay the negative outcomes of policy initiatives, such as potential spill-over effects and opportunity costs, in order to gain public approval. The de-politicisation of many policy decisions as part of the NPM approaches (also see Oliver and Fraser's chapter in this volume) further distanced policy-making from politics and the public and created fuzzy boundaries between politicians and public servants (see McMillan's chapter in this volume). One of the consequences of overselling policy outcomes and depoliticising policy decision-making is that it can create skewed perceptions and understandings of the potential results of policy programmes. It can also raise expectations of the public which, in the long run, negatively impacts trust when those expectations are almost inevitably not being met. Furthermore, the depoliticisation of decision-making produces unclear and blurred lines of accountability, and therefore, public accountability becomes a tricky terrain to navigate.

Although this counts for public policy-making approaches across the board, it is particularly relevant from a public value perspective, as the results of more public value-orientated policy initiatives tend to be softer and less tangible, and they are perhaps particularly susceptible to overly optimistic public expectations. The public manager plays an active role in terms of providing evidence that allows for a deliberative process in which more nuanced positions can be communicated and, ultimately, more realistic expectations of policy initiatives in terms of their contribution to public value inform public debate. The simplification of wicked problems in public debate is inevitable but requires sensitive communication and leadership (see McMillan's chapter in this volume). Boiling complex policy decisions down to simple 'yes' or 'no' questions without deliberation provides a hot bed for divisions and lack of legitimacy, which ultimately lead to distrust and populism.

From a comparative research perspective, the Britain usually performs well in relation to good governance. Yet, many reports identify, at least on occasions, weak accountability structures: 'a lack of clarity about who was responsible; a lack of consequences for poor performance; a lack of transparency and information' (Guerin et al. 2018: 4). Furthermore, trust in government institutions has remained very low over the last decade, with data suggesting that distrust in government is now the default position for most citizens (Edelman 2018). This has not been helped by the British government's lacklustre response to the COVID-19 pandemic and political decisions taken during the lockdown (including the Prime Minister Boris Johnson's support of his aide, Dominic Cummings, when he contravened the government's own lockdown restrictions) (Fancourt et al. 2020). More broadly, people can feel unrepresented within the narrow confines of the majoritarian system. The competitive and adversarial political culture fostered by majoritarian politics leads to blame-gaming and political posturing (Guerin et al. 2018). Yet, studies by Ombudsmen have shown that future prevention and lesson learning, rather than retribution for failures, is the public's major concern when things go wrong (Mellor et al. 2014). Assigning blame in relation to policy failure is symptomatic of a political culture that oversimplifies decision-making. Another example of this same trend is the idea that public interest can only be raised through 'big' policy announcements. Moreover, research has shown that the public are more interested in how policy will be implemented (Institute of Government 2016). This, at least, suggests that there is an appetite for a type of politics that allows for increased deliberation and avoids 'dumbing down' policy decisions. Filling the communicative gap between politicians, policy-makers and the public is an important aspect of this process.

The levels of distrust in government and institutions, as in many other parts of the Western world, have reached levels where populism, in the form of anti-establishment movements, has gained support. The rise of populism in the Western world is a complex phenomenon. As noted by Flinders and Huggins in this volume, public sector reform is 'defined by complexity, fragmentation and the apparent erosion of traditional public service values', which provides a breeding ground for populism. In this sense, populism only increases the communicative gap by increasing blame-gaming as part of an anti-establishment rhetoric. On the other hand, a politics-based perspective of public value would aim to provide leadership that allows for public debate and understanding of policy complexities (also see McMillan's chapter in this volume).

Paradigm Shift?

This chapter, and in fact the book, has evaluated the extent to which, in recent years, there has been a shift towards public value in policy-making approaches. It has examined 'new' processes of policy-making in relation to programming and monitoring policy outcomes and how the politics of communicating these outcomes can be viewed through the prism of public value. In this conclusion, we will place these issues in the context of the analysis and discussion of the key themes associated with public value, governance and reform discussed in this book. The book has made a contribution to understanding key debates around whether we have seen the advancement towards a post-NPM agenda, which is more focused on 'public value' linked to debates on co-production, leadership, outcomes and deliberative forms of governance. What all of the chapters point to, in different ways via varied academic lenses, is about how politics has continued to shape the nature and architecture of public administration in Britain. Clearly, politics will (and should) always shape public administration, although it can sometimes distract from important governance questions and issues that concern matters of effectiveness and capacities within and across bureaucracies.

Since 2010 (the dominant focus of this book in terms of time period), austerity, Brexit politics and the COVID-19 pandemic have been major distractions away from a public service reform agenda. The post-1997 New Labour years were marked by more of a focus on how government works and what the role of the civil service should be (as illustrated by Tony Blair's quote at the start of Chap. 1). Indeed, several chapters of this book have commented on how the 2017 Barber Review has challenged the government to place more emphasis back onto value-seeking behaviour within the public sector. This is to ensure that the modern civil service and civil servants have the capacities and skills required to be innovate, to lead through complexities, and to embed evaluation at the heart of government business.

That being said, this book has shown how the public sector, despite the challenges of governance distractions (such as austerity, Brexit and COVID-19), has had to continually adapt and respond to demands for increased focus on public value in policy-making. This has not been to the extent to which it can be convincingly claimed that 'New Public Management is dead' or that it has been replaced by a new paradigm; rather, it is the case that there has been a degree of path dependence created by the New Labour agenda. Nonetheless, there has been a crowding out of the creative policy space for modernisation and reform to be nurtured, maintained and developed. The focus on efficiency savings and cuts to public expenditure following the financial crisis (linked to the austerity agenda) has undermined the attention that should have been paid to public sector leadership and management. It may, therefore, be the case that several NPM battles have been fought, but the war has not yet been won, a victorious successor has not yet emerged and academics should avoiding the temptation of pretending that this has happened. The concluding argument for this book is one which calls for the British government to raise the profile of the importance of governance and to formulate a comprehensive public sector reform agenda. Public value should be the dominant governing framework for undertaking such an endeavour.

In our assessment, the Brexit developments and the COVID-19 pandemic clearly demonstrate the *need* for a public value-based approach. Indeed, this approach may offer a window of opportunity for a more comprehensive governance reform agenda informed by PVM ideas that is better able to 'mount a charge' against the wicked problem of persisting spatial and socio-economic inequalities across the UK. The result of the Brexit referendum crystallised a socio-demographic chasm between those who have benefitted from European integration, immigration and globalisation and those that feel threatened by these processes (Ford and Goodwin 2017). Education, income and housing were all key predictors in terms of the Brexit vote (Swales 2016: 4). Those that have felt threatened have long felt marginalised within Britain's current governance system. The UK government under Prime Minister Boris Johnson has promised to tackle the deep-rooted spatial and socio-economic divisions by introducing a 'levelling up' agenda. For example, in the 2019 Queen's Speech, the British government stated that 'The integrity and prosperity of the United Kingdom is of the utmost importance' and promised 'measures to ensure that every part of the United Kingdom can prosper' (UK Government 2019). Many of the places that are considered 'left behind' and require levelling up, for the first time in generations, returned Conservative MPs in the December 2019 election. Although the Conservative vote was heavily influenced by the Brexit debate, the UK government was keen to demonstrate that it can represent these traditional working class areas. However, so far, the policy proposals have been rather limited. There have been a number of infrastructure project announcements, but a comprehensive policy programme that supports the levelling-up agenda has not yet been developed. More fundamentally, and more relevant to the themes of this book, there has been no real debate about governance reform and, in particular, how the values that underpin the attitudes and policy positions in these marginalised communities can be better represented in what could be perceived as an elite-driven policy process. This leads to further questions about having a public service architecture, and the quality of public leadership spanning it, to respond to such deep-rooted challenges in the post-Brexit and post-COVID-19 pandemic context. Public sector leaders also need to ensure that public trust is maintained in the democratic credentials of the state, which, in an era of post-truth politics (coupled with the reactionary and haphazard policy style of the post-2019 Conservative administration), will be an enduring governance challenge (Skleparis 2020).

The COVID-19 pandemic has also unearthed health inequalities in terms of social, age and race context. In economic terms, it has exposed the vulnerability of people in casual work and some of the flexible self-employment regulations. The measures to control the spread of the virus have a greater impact on more vulnerable groups, both socially and economically, and the economic recession will also most disproportionally affect vulnerable groups (Bibby et al. 2020). The fundamental values of healthcare access, protection of those working in vulnerable professions, health and social care have all challenged the integrity of extant governance arrangements. The pandemic crisis has also been cause to reflect on the extent to which governance processes are geared towards those at the sharp end of policy implementation at the 'street-level' (Lipsky 2010). Part of the answer lies in developing a more inclusive and diverse civil service (Smith 2020). More broadly, PVM can offer a more inclusive model for governance that provides room for a fuller appreciation of public values. Structural inequalities in British society are obviously deep-rooted and long-standing, but the twin acute uncertainties posed by Brexit and COVID-19 have served to crystallise the gaps more clearly. The quality of government depends on the quality of future public sector leadership at multiple levels of governance. Related to this point is the fact that intra-governmental development programmes for public servants has, unfortunately, fallen off of the UK government's radar over the past decade (Connolly and Pyper 2020).

The chapters of this book have also documented, using specific themes and analytical lenses, the importance of how outcomes-based approaches underpin public value. Evidencing the impact of public sector initiatives and programmes facilitates more of an innovative mindset when it comes to public value governance. Embedding the user of services, through co-productive practice, in the design and evaluation of services helps public managers to be more deliberative in their approach. This, however, is not to shy away from the acute challenges of being co-productive—for example, it is not always clear to public servants about *who* should be the co-producers (or how to reach them). It might be the case that users do not want to co-produce. The process itself can be resource-intensive. Moreover, a shift to outcomes, in a co-produced way, risks becoming a tokenistic exercise if there is a lack of leadership orientated towards building organisational cultures which are geared towards value-seeking behaviours. There is no doubt that any reform paradigms, be it NPM or public value, will always be a hostage to social, economic, political and institutional challenges. However, institutions, and how they are led, *matter* for shaping the cultural conditions for unlocking public value and, despite the challenges, we should all persevere towards enabling public value within modern governance processes.

Final Thoughts

This book provides an overview of governance reform through multiple lenses of public value management. It aims to provide a nuanced account recognising that approaches to public value cannot be 'blue printed' within different governance settings but there is merit in considering public value as an analytical lens for governance reform. It has hopefully provided key insights into the fragilities surrounding moving from the principles of public value to its implementation and sustainability based on the British context. For modern public servants, it should not be a case of viewing public value as a desirable or 'nice to do' endeavour, but perhaps it should be seen as a *moral responsibility* to make the best effort possible to govern and evaluate programmes based on public value principles. These principles are *effectiveness* (focusing on how well the outputs of a service achieve the stated objectives of that service); *efficiency* (how well services use their resources to produce outputs and achieve outcomes); *outputs* (accounting for what activities have been produced in line with objectives); *outcomes and quality* (evaluating the impact and quality of a service on the status of an individual or a group, and on the success of the service area in achieving its objectives), and *access and equity* (ensuring that services are physically accessible, affordable to access, and that inequalities of access are addresses through careful policy planning and delivery) (see Blaug et al. 2006: 52).

The next decade will continue to present major challenges and distractions away from a focus on public administration (i.e. the governance and political consequences of Brexit, post-COVID 19 recovery as well as other constitutional questions, such as Scottish independence). The organisation of the state and its public services require public servants to have the skills and qualities to navigate through the complexities and multi-stakeholder contexts that such changes will bring. The advantage of public value ideas is that they enable public servants to evaluate how, and by which means, governance should be led and managed in such an environment. A focus on measurement, evidence and evaluation for improvement and innovation is what will help multi-level actors to understand what works, when and how. This will require institutional mechanisms to foster learning across governance systems in order to avoid the pitfalls of *not* embedding meaningful evaluation. The result of not paying attention to these aspects of public leadership and management will lead to weak institutional memory retention within the system, which undermines public value and its sustainability. Overall, and looking to future (post-Brexit or otherwise), we are calling for greater macro-level political attention to be given to public value in the future. A value-based approach to 'reinventing government' needs to be prioritised and sustained within the multiple levels of modern British governance.

REFERENCES

Arnstein, S. (1969). A Ladder of Citizen Participation. *Journal of the American Institute of Planners, 35*(4), 216–224.

Alford, J., & Hughes, O. (2008). Public Value Pragmatism as the Next Phase of Public Management. *The American Review of Public Administration, 38*(2), 130–148.

Barca, F., McCann, P., & Rodrıguez-Pose, A. (2012). The Case for Regional Development Intervention: Place-based vs Place Neutral Approaches. *Journal of Regional Science, 52*(1), 134–152.

Bevir, M. (2011). Public Administration as Storytelling. *Public Administration, 89*(1), 183–195.

Bibby, J., Everest, G., & Abbs, I. (2020). Will COVID-19 Be a Watershed Moment for Health Inequalities? The Health Foundation, available on: https://www.health.org.uk/publications/long-reads/will-covid-19-be-a-watershed-moment-for-health-inequalities.

Blaug, R., Horner, L. & Lekhi, R. (2006). *Public Value, Politics and Public Management—A Literature Review*. London: The Good Work Foundation.

Blaug, R., Horner, L., & Lekhi, R. (2017). *Public Value, Politics and Public Management—A Literature Review*. London: The Good Work Foundation.

Bloomfield, D., Collins, K., Fry, C., & Munton, R. (2001). Deliberation and Inclusion: Vehicles for Increasing Trust in UK Public Governance. *Environment and Planning C: Politics and Space, 19*(4), 501–513.

Bochel, C. (2013). Petitions Systems: Contributing to Representative Democracy? *Parliamentary Affairs, 66*(4), 798–815.

Bovaird, T. (2007). Beyond Engagement and Participation: User and Community Coproduction of Public Services. *Public Administration Review, 67*(5), 846–860.

Bovaird, T., Stoker, G., Jones, T., Loeffler, E., & Pinalla-Roncancio, M. (2015). Activating Collective Co-production of Public Services: Influencing Citizens to Participate in Complex Governance Mechanisms in the UK. *International review of Administrative Science, 82*(1), 47–68.

Cameron, K., Quinn, R. E., Degraff, J., & Thakor, A. (2006). *Competing Values Leadership*. Cheltenham: Edward Elgar.

Carman, C. (2012). Barriers Are Barriers: Asymmetric Participation in the Scottish Public Petition Systems. *Parliamentary Affairs, 67*(1), 151–171.

Connolly, J., & Pyper, R. (2020). Developing Capacity within the British Civil Service: The Case of the Stabilisation Unit. *Public Money & Management*, 1-10.

Corrigan, P., & Joyce, P. (1997). Reconstructing Public Management: A New Responsibility for the Public and a Case Study of Local Government. *International Journal of Public Sector Management, 10*(6), 417–432.

Culver, K., & Howe, P. (2004). Calling All Citizens: The Challenges of Public Consultation. *Canadian Public Administration/Administration publique du Canada, 47*(1), 52–75.

Dalton, R. (1995). Political Parties and Political Representation: Party Supporters and Party Elites in Nine Nations. *Comparative Political Studies, 18*(3), 267–299.
Demos. (2007). *Agile Government: A Provocation Paper*, available on: https://lx.iriss.org.uk/sites/default/files/resources/Agile.pdf.
Electoral Reform Society. (2019). *Local Citizens' Assemblies Could Break Our Political Deadlock—But the Government Have Vetoed Them*, available on: https://www.electoral-reform.org.uk/local-citizens-assemblies-could-break-our-political-deadlock-but-the-government-have-vetoed-them/.
Edelman. (2018). *Edelman Trust Barometer*, available on: https://www.slideshare.net/Edelman_UK/edelman-trust-barometer-2018-uk-results/1.
Evans, E. (2018). *Thatcher and Thatcherism*. London: Routledge.
Fancourt, D., Steptoe, A., & Wright, L. (2020). The Cummings Effect: Politics, Trust, and Behaviours during the COVID-19 Pandemic. *The Lancet, 396*(10249), 464–465.
Ford, R., & Goodwin, M. (2017). Britain After Brexit: A Nation Divided. Journal of Democracy, 28(1), available on: https://muse.jhu.edu/article/645534.
Guerin, B., McCrae, J., & Shepheard, M. (2018). *Accountability in Modern Government: What Are the Issues? A Discussion Paper*, Institute for Government, available on: https://www.instituteforgovernment.org.uk/sites/default/files/publications/IfG%20accountability%20discussion%20paper%20april%202018.pdf.
Head, B. W., & Alford, J. (2015). Wicked Problems: Implications for Public Policy and Management. *Administration & Society, 47*(6), 711–739.
Herald. (2019, April 24). Nicola Sturgeon Wants to Set Up a Citizens' Assembly. But What Is That? Retrieved May 29, 2019, from https://www.heraldscotland.com/news/17595139.nicola-sturgeon-wants-to-set-up-a-citizens-assembly-but-what-is-that/.
Hogwood, B. W., & Gunn, L. A. (1984). *Policy Analysis for the Real World*. Oxford: Oxford University Press.
Hudson, B., Hunter, D., & Peckham, S. (2019). Policy Failure and the Policy-Implementation Gap: Can Policy Support Programs Help? *Policy Design and Practice, 2*(1), 1–14. https://doi.org/10.1080/25741292.2018.1540378.
Hood, C. (1991). A Public Management for All Seasons. *Public Administration, 69*(1), 3–19.
Hood, C. (2000). *The Art of the State*. Oxford, UK: Oxford University Press.
Institute of Government. (2016). *Trust in Government Is Growing—But It Needs to Deliver*, available on@ https://www.instituteforgovernment.org.uk/sites/default/files/publications/IfG_polling_note_WEB3.pdf.
Jefferson, R., McKinley, E., Capstick, S., Fletcher, S., Griffin, H., & Milanese, M. (2015). Understanding Audiences: Making Public Perceptions Research Matter to Marine Conservation. *Ocean & Coastal Management, 115*, 61–70.

Jones, M. D., McBeth, M. K., & Shanahan, E. A. (2014). *The Science of Stories*. New York: Palgrave Macmillan.

Kelly, G., Muers, S., & Mulgan, G. (2002). *Creating Public Value: An Analytical Framework for Public Service Reform*. London: Prime Minister's Strategy Unit, Cabinet Office.

Korkut, U., Mahendran, K., Bucken-Knapp, G., & Cox, R. (Eds.). (2015). *Discursive Governance in Politics, Policy and the Public Sphere*. New York: Palgrave Macmillan.

Lipsky, M. (2010). *Street-level Bureaucracy: Dilemmas of the Individual in Public Service*. New York: Russell Sage Foundation.

Maciejewski-Scheer, A., & Hoppner, C. (2010). The Public Consultation to the UK Climate Change Act 2008: A Critical Analysis. *Climate Policy, 10*(3), 261–276.

Marshall, B., Duffy, B., Thompson, J., Castell, S., & Hall, S. (2007). *Blair's Britain: The Social and Cultural Legacy*. London: Ipsos-MORI Social Research Institute.

McConnell, A. (2015). What Is Policy Failure? A Primer to Help Navigate the Maze. *Public Policy and Administration, 30*(3–4), 221–242.

Mellor, J., Martin, J., & Bradley, A. (2014). My *Expectations for Raising Concerns and Complaints*, www.ombudsman.org.uk/sites/default/files/Report_My_expectations_for_raising_concerns_and_complaints.pdf.

Moore, M. (1995). *Creating Public Value: Strategic Management in Government*

Newman, J. (2001). *Modernising Governance—New Labour, Policy and Society*. London: Sage.

O'Flynn, J. (2011). All Praise Public Value? The Ideas, The Debate, and Some Applications, *Australian Journal of Public Administration*.

Piere, J., & Peters, G. (2000). *Governance, Politics and the State*. New York: St. Martin's Press.

Pollitt, C. (1990). *Managerialism and the Public Services: The Anglo-American Experience*. Oxford, UK: Basil Blackwell.

Quinn, R. E. (1988). *Beyond Rational Management*. San Francisco: Jossey-Bass.

Reddan, G. (2019). *Questioning Performance Measurement: Metrics, Organizations and Power*. London: Sage Publications.

Rhodes, R. A. W., & Wanna, J. (2009). Bringing the Politics Back In: Public Value in Westminster Parliamentary Government. *Public Administration, 87*(2), 161–183.

Schumpeter, J. (1995). *Capitalism, Socialism and Democracy*. Moscow: Eksmo.

Scottish Government. (2018). *Scotland's Economic Strategy*. Retrieved May 29, 2019, from https://www.gov.scot/policies/economic-growth/inclusive-growth/.

Skleparis, D. (2020). 'All Animals Are Equal': The Relationship Between the Cummings Row and Public Trust in Democracy, *LSE Blog*, https://blogs.lse.ac.uk/politicsandpolicy/trust-in-democracy-lockdown/.

Smith, R. F. I. (2004). Focusing on Public Value: Something New and Something Old. *Australian Journal of Public Administration, 63*(4), 68–79.

Smith, B. (2020). 'We Still Fall Short': Sedwill Pledges More Action on Inequality in the Civil Service, Civil Service World, available on: https://www.civilserviceworld.com/articles/news/we-still-fall-short-sedwill-pledges-more-action-inequality-civil-service.

Smith, G., & Wales, C. (2018). 'Citizens' Juries and Deliberative Democracy. In d'Entreves (Ed.), *Democracy as Public Deliberation*. New York: Routledge.

Stoker, G. (2004). *Transforming Local Governance*. Basingstoke, UK: Macmillan Palgrave.

Stoker, G. (2005). Public Value Management—A New Narrative for Networked Governance? *American Review of Public Administration, 36*(1), 41–57.

Stoker, G. (2003). Public Value Management (PVM): A New Resolution of the Democracy/efficiency Tradeoff, unpublished paper, Institute for Political and Economic Governance (IPEG), University of Manchester.

Street, J., Duszynski, K., Krawczyk, S., & Braunack-Mayer, A. (2014). The Use of Citizens' Juries in Health Policy Decision-making: A Systematic Review. *Soc Sci Med, 109*(1-9), 1.

Swales, K. (2016). Understanding the Leave Vote, NatCen, available on: http://natcen.ac.uk/media/1319222/natcen_brexplanations-report-final-web2.pdf.

Talbot, C. (2008). *Measuring Public Value*. London: The Work Foundation.

Talbot, C. (2009). Public Value–The Next 'Big Thing' in Public Management? *International Journal of Public Administration, 32*(3–4), 167–170.

Thomas, J. C. (1990). Public Involvement in Public Management: Adapting and Testing a Borrowed Theory. *Public Administration Review, 50*(4), 444–469.

Turcu, C. (2013). Re-thinking Sustainability Indicators: Local Perspectives of Urban Sustainability. *Journal of Environmental Planning and Management, 56*(5), 695–719.

UK Government. (2018). Consultation Principles 2018, available on: https://www.gov.uk/government/publications/consultation-principles-guidance.

UK Government. (2019). Queen's Speech December 2019, available on: https://www.gov.uk/government/speeches/queens-speech-december-2019.

Index[1]

A
Accountability, viii, ix, 3, 7–9, 16, 18–20, 22, 26, 28–30, 46, 48, 62, 64, 66, 67, 71, 76, 88–90, 95, 99, 100, 103, 105, 109, 128, 173, 175, 177, 189, 193, 194, 201–222, 230, 231, 236, 262, 263, 274–276
Advocacy, 25, 36
Agriculture, 17, 249
Asylum, 2
Austerity, ix, x, xvi, 7, 19, 21, 32, 47, 51, 54–55, 61–63, 65, 73, 107, 127, 128, 139, 179, 209, 228, 233, 235, 243, 277, 278

B
Barber, Michael (Sir), 22–24, 50–53, 61, 173
Barber review, 22, 24, 53, 278
Benchmarking, x, 123
Big Society, 61–64, 126–127, 167

Blair, Tony, 1, 2, 31, 32, 48, 50, 60, 61, 209, 232, 238, 277
Blame games, 28, 95, 98
Brexit, xvi, 2, 9, 10, 17, 18, 21, 32, 56, 58–60, 62, 71–73, 89, 108, 109, 227–249, 260, 267, 270, 277–281
Britain/British, ix, x, xii, xv, xvi, 1–9, 15–36, 45, 47, 59, 68, 73, 88, 89, 92, 95, 98, 107, 109, 152, 188, 202, 205, 209, 213, 227–249, 259, 260, 270, 277, 278, 281
Brown, Gordon, ix, 241
Business, Innovation & Skills Committee, 34

C
Cabinet Office, 3, 31, 50, 51, 60, 64, 67, 74, 233, 245, 246
Cameron, David, 58, 61, 62

---
[1] Note: Page numbers followed by 'n' refer to notes.

Capacity, 4, 6, 16, 26–32, 35, 87, 88, 90, 95, 97, 98, 102, 103, 109, 110, 117, 134, 136, 138, 139, 174, 177, 178, 186, 188, 192, 195, 196, 217, 273, 278
Chancellor of the Exchequer, 64, 243
Christie Commission, 69
Citizens, ix, xi, xii, 4, 18, 20, 27–30, 33, 48–50, 61, 63, 69, 71, 105, 150–152, 155, 158, 161, 165, 179, 202–204, 209, 212, 229, 231, 234, 237, 239, 244, 246, 261, 263, 264, 266–270, 276
Citizenship, 17, 105, 158, 164, 239
City Deals, 64, 68, 96, 243, 249
Civil servants, 31, 34, 102, 206, 211, 218, 245, 278
Civil service, 2, 16, 31, 51, 59–62, 68, 72–74, 105, 205, 207, 243, 245, 277, 278, 280
Civil society, 35, 47, 116, 177, 182, 183, 185, 193, 195, 196, 202, 264, 275
Climate change, viii, 20, 201, 247, 270
Coalition, xv, 7, 17, 47, 48, 54–57, 61, 63, 74, 126, 127, 209, 214
Co-creation, 28, 48, 63, 68, 133, 154, 155, 181, 264, 266
Co-delivery, 209
Co-design, 133
Co-leadership, 186–188, 193
Collaboration, xi, 16, 22, 25n1, 26, 29, 36, 48, 63, 66, 68, 69, 71, 88, 135, 137, 162, 181, 272
Commissioning, x, 51, 134–136
Committee of the Regions, 237
Committee on Standards in Public Life, 21
Community Planning, 69
Complexity, xv, 5, 7, 8, 16, 18–19, 21, 29, 34, 36, 53, 57, 66, 70, 71, 75, 88, 92, 95, 97, 98, 101, 108, 109, 140, 149, 153, 176, 201, 203, 211, 212, 215, 218, 265, 271, 277, 278, 281
Conservative Party/Conservative, xv, 2, 7, 36, 47, 54–56, 58–62, 96, 98, 124, 126, 159, 237, 279
Constitutional Affairs Committee, 57, 63, 64, 68
Consumerism, 3, 152, 158, 166
Contractualisation, 46, 60, 65–68
Contribution analysis, 24
Cooksey Review, 117
Co-production/co-producing, 6, 16, 18, 26–30, 48, 68, 132, 133, 181, 182, 187, 188, 195, 235, 268, 269, 277
Covid-19, xvi, 2, 5, 10, 140, 248, 260, 277–280
Criminal justice, 124, 155, 157, 159
Crisis, ix, 2, 7, 20, 21, 32, 53–55, 65, 98, 104–106, 128, 209, 242, 260, 264, 274, 278, 279
Customers, 150–152, 155, 158, 161, 163, 165, 167, 204, 231, 266

D
Debt, ix, x, 55
Decentralisation, 64, 77, 95–99, 152, 207, 241, 243
Decision-making, 4, 27, 34, 64, 72, 88, 118, 123, 125, 132, 133, 135, 138, 139, 159, 164, 165, 187, 190, 191, 214, 229, 232–244, 247–249, 262–264, 266–268, 275, 276
Defence, 68, 261, 274
Delivery Unit, 50, 51
Democracy, 27, 87, 89, 90, 92, 97, 104–106, 108, 109, 176, 178, 183, 208, 212, 264, 269

Democratic, 4, 19, 26, 35, 48, 49, 89, 90, 92, 97, 98, 102, 105, 106, 108, 110, 133, 193, 195, 202, 204, 230, 231, 236, 262, 264, 267, 270, 274, 279
Democratic Unionist Party (DUP), 54, 57, 58
Department for Exiting the European Union, 60
Devolution, 3, 17, 48, 54–56, 61, 63, 65, 68, 72–78, 92, 96–99, 173, 184, 236, 237, 240–243, 247, 248, 270

E

Economy, vii, 17, 18, 151, 182, 209, 228, 229, 234
Education, vii, viii, x, 2, 28, 33, 48, 51, 53, 55, 69, 72, 98, 99, 116, 120, 122, 124, 125, 131, 134–137, 158, 159, 206, 212, 213, 221, 233, 278
Effectiveness, 18, 21, 25, 30, 32, 48, 50, 76, 119, 122, 124, 125, 136, 151, 152, 186, 235, 236, 238, 241, 242, 245, 261, 270, 272, 277, 281
Efficiency, 3, 18, 19, 27, 32, 35, 46–48, 50–53, 61, 69, 76, 89, 94, 99, 102, 103, 105, 106, 110, 122, 128, 151, 183, 204, 212, 263, 268, 270, 272, 278, 281
Empowerment, 6, 7, 49, 158
England/English, 56, 57, 64, 65, 70, 75–77, 95–99, 101, 156, 184, 208, 228, 233–237, 240–243, 247, 248
Equity, 33, 128, 133, 158, 281
Ethics, ix, 133, 204, 211

European Court of Justice (ECJ), 244, 246
Europeanisation, 7, 17
European Parliament, 229, 237
European Union (EU), 3, 17, 58, 109, 203, 227, 267n5
Evaluation, 9, 16, 18–19, 21, 22, 24, 25, 25n2, 30, 32, 35, 36, 117, 122, 128–132, 135, 136, 150, 167, 178, 179, 181, 189, 194–196, 228, 232, 233, 240, 266, 270, 272–274, 278, 280, 281
Evidence-based medicine (EBM), 116, 123
Evidence-based policy (EBP), 115–140
Evidence-based practice, 115
Expenditure, ix, xi, 7, 52, 55, 65, 100, 204, 206, 238, 249, 278

F

Financial crisis, ix, 7, 21, 32, 53–55, 65, 98, 209, 274, 278
First Minister, 57, 72
Fisheries, 17
Foreign and Commonwealth Office, 60, 228
Foster, Arlene, 57
Fulton Report, 61

G

General Election, 18, 58, 102
Globalisation, 3, 20, 21, 47, 278
Governance, xv, 2–8, 15–18, 46, 55–58, 87, 96–103, 115, 149, 151–152, 175, 202, 231
Government Office for Science, 125
Grenfell, 66, 67, 129

H
Health, vii, 2, 32, 46, 94, 117, 150, 181, 206, 229, 279
Health and safety, 160, 164
Higher education, 116, 120, 122, 125, 131, 134, 136, 137, 159
House of Commons, 57, 64, 91
Housing, 66, 157, 159, 234, 235, 278

I
Ideology, 3, 16, 128, 129, 156, 175, 186, 227, 233, 234, 245, 248, 260, 263
Immigration, 2, 17, 278
Independence, 17, 18, 34, 53, 55–59, 68, 236, 281
Inequalities, 19, 20, 27, 32, 278–281
Innovation, xi, 7, 9, 21, 26, 29, 32, 36, 46, 48, 71, 73, 90, 101, 115, 120, 126, 133, 149–167, 207, 209, 235, 261, 281
Input, x, 30, 157, 158, 232, 235, 238, 241, 262–267, 269–271, 274
Institutional hybridity, 151–154, 156, 157, 159, 161
Integration, 3, 17, 21, 47, 69, 70, 72, 74, 75, 78, 135, 182–188, 190, 192, 196, 202, 231, 239, 240, 242, 278

J
Johnson, Boris, 59, 278
Joined-up government, 26, 31

K
Keynesian, 127
Kids Company, 63, 64
Kilmister, Lemmy, 34
Knowledge broker, 137

L
Labour Party/Labour, 2, 17, 26, 54, 55, 74, 124, 126, 132, 209, 216
Leadership, xv, 3, 6, 7, 9, 15, 18–22, 25–27, 30, 36, 49, 50, 52, 58, 59, 62, 70, 71, 74, 78, 108, 173–196, 221, 233, 241, 268, 273, 276, 277, 279, 280
Learning, xi, 6, 22, 25, 27, 32, 34, 36, 50, 75, 78, 116, 128, 130, 133, 137–138, 175, 203, 276, 281
Legitimacy, xi, 29, 31, 48, 128, 132–133, 140, 176, 179, 202, 204, 237, 263–265, 267, 271, 274, 276
Liberal Democrats, xv, 2, 7, 17, 54, 63
Lisbon Treaty, 236, 237, 240, 241
Local Enterprise Partnerships (LEPs), 64, 237, 242, 243
Local government, 22, 63, 65, 69, 72, 96, 98, 182, 212, 241
Localism, 63–65, 76, 96

M
Maastricht Treaty, 237
Managerialism, 5, 49, 127, 132, 139, 152, 158, 212–214, 221
Markets, viii, 3, 16, 47, 54, 93, 95, 97, 99, 102, 103, 105, 108, 118, 119, 123, 124, 127, 132, 135, 137, 155, 158, 161, 163, 190, 209, 211, 216, 228, 230, 245, 272
May, Theresa, 58, 59, 62, 246
McGuinness, Martin, 57
Member states (of the EU), 59, 228–230, 234, 236–242, 244, 246
Migration, 20

INDEX   291

Modernisation, 3, 7, 26, 46, 47, 49–51, 53, 54, 61, 63, 65, 77, 209, 278
Monetarism, 3, 16
Monitoring, 10, 25, 30, 32, 102, 122, 123, 131, 219, 247, 270, 272, 273, 277
Morgan, Rhodri, 75
MPs, 34, 56, 63, 90, 279
Multi-level governance, 7, 17, 213

N
National Audit Office (NAO), xii, 53, 65, 67, 98, 101–103, 184
National Health Service (NHS), 75, 77, 95, 116, 119, 120, 122–124, 127, 184, 212, 216–218, 220
National Infrastructure Commission, 249
National Institute for Health and Clinical Excellence (NICE), 124
National Performance Framework (NPF), 69, 70
Neo-liberal, 105, 126, 127, 150, 151, 156, 209, 231, 233, 248
Network governance, 6, 70, 127, 176, 177
New Labour, 31, 47, 54, 62, 92, 96, 100, 123–128, 138, 152, 209, 237, 273, 277, 278
New public governance (NPG), 4, 46, 49, 149, 152, 153, 155, 158
New public management (NPM), xv, 2–5, 7–9, 15, 16, 18, 19, 24, 30, 35, 36, 46–49, 53, 65, 77, 91, 94, 99, 100, 105, 106, 116, 122–128, 138, 139, 149, 151–156, 158, 160, 176, 178, 202, 206, 208, 212, 232–235, 237, 238, 240, 260–263, 270, 272, 274, 275, 278, 280

New Public Service (NPS), 4, 110
New Right, 3, 16, 122
No deal, 230
Northcote-Trevelyan, 62, 205, 208
Northern Ireland, 3, 17, 53–59, 68, 72, 74, 75, 77, 96, 233, 237, 241, 247, 249
Northern Ireland Assembly, 57

O
OECD, 72, 160, 209, 238, 240, 244, 247
Office for National Statistics, ix, 19, 247
Osbourne, George, 64, 243
Outcome evaluation, 16, 32, 132
Outcomes, vii–xii, 7, 9, 10, 16, 19, 21–26, 31, 32, 48, 52, 58, 69, 70, 73, 77, 78, 127, 130–132, 134, 135, 150, 156, 159, 165, 166, 173–196, 202–204, 207, 214, 229, 231, 232, 235, 236, 239, 241, 246, 248, 249, 260, 261, 263, 265–271, 273, 275, 277, 280, 281
Outputs, vii, x, 3, 19, 24, 30, 32, 105, 125, 132, 175, 177, 194, 207, 232, 235, 238, 281

P
Paradigm, xv, xvi, 2–5, 36, 46, 50, 94, 115–140, 151, 156, 166, 176–178, 190–192, 230, 259–281
Participatory approaches/governance, 18, 25, 264, 266, 269
Partnerships, 7, 21, 24, 25, 25n1, 25n2, 29, 48, 61, 63, 66, 68–70, 74, 78, 126, 128, 129, 134, 155, 189, 207, 234, 266, 273

Path dependency, 54, 60, 265
Permanent secretary, xi, 51, 64, 206
Police, vii, viii, 64, 70, 75–77, 136, 221
Policy failure, 7, 29, 103, 109, 188, 265, 272, 276
Policy instruments, 70
Policy networks, 202, 203, 213, 214, 216, 222
Policy success, 6, 7, 19, 29
Populist/populism, 9, 87–110, 229, 239, 264, 276, 277
Poverty, viii, 20, 126
Prime Minister, 1, 22, 48, 50, 58, 59, 122, 237, 241, 246, 278
Private sector, vii, viii, 16, 18, 49, 91, 99–102, 109, 134, 151, 154, 156, 160, 165, 174, 177, 190, 206–208, 218, 222, 232, 233, 244, 261, 274
Programme for Government, 71, 72
Public Accounts Committee (PAC), 23, 24, 30, 32, 64
Public administration, 3, 4, 6, 15, 16, 19, 26, 29, 31, 33, 35, 36, 46, 48, 49, 104, 105, 116, 118, 120–122, 127, 138, 149, 151, 154, 175, 176, 178–181, 188, 192, 201, 203, 205, 208, 213, 216–218, 230, 249, 260, 262, 263, 274, 277, 281
Public choice, 47
Public engagement, 72, 133, 242, 264
Public good, 154, 178, 233, 239, 265
Public manager, 4, 16, 19–22, 24, 25, 25n2, 30, 32, 33, 49, 50, 95, 116, 128, 134, 139, 156, 160, 163–166, 176, 177, 183, 203, 212, 261, 263, 265, 266, 268, 271, 274–276, 280
Public policy, vii, 20, 21, 27, 29, 35, 59, 104, 117, 120, 123, 133, 176, 194, 201, 208, 229–237, 244, 248, 249, 261, 263, 265, 266, 269
Public-private partnerhsips (PPP), 66, 99–103
Public servants, ix, 90, 175, 176, 192, 193, 222, 275, 280, 281
Public service logic (PSL), 156, 166
Public services, ix, xi, 5, 7, 9, 16, 18, 19, 24, 27, 29, 31, 35, 46–49, 51, 53–55, 60–64, 67–73, 76, 77, 88, 91, 92, 94, 98–103, 105–107, 109, 119, 122, 123, 128, 132, 134, 136, 138, 149–167, 173–182, 189–192, 194, 204, 206, 207, 213, 219, 221, 222, 231–233, 235, 238, 260, 261, 263, 264, 269, 277, 279, 281
Public sphere, 49, 174, 178, 193, 234
Public value management (PVM), xv, 2, 4, 6–8, 10, 15, 45, 46, 48–50, 53, 61, 63, 65, 66, 68, 70, 73, 74, 78, 115–140, 165, 166, 203, 212, 227–249, 259–281

R
Reagan, Ronald, 122
Referendum, 17, 18, 54, 56, 58–60, 68, 228, 229, 240, 241, 248, 267, 278
Reform, 2–5, 7, 9, 10, 15, 16, 18, 21, 25, 26, 32, 36, 45–78, 87–110, 115, 123, 124, 126, 127, 135, 150–153, 155, 158, 160, 173–196, 201–203, 205–208, 211–213, 215–218, 221, 233, 238, 241–243, 260, 270, 274, 277–281

Regulation, ix, 3, 64, 162, 186, 206, 207, 210, 211, 216, 239, 244, 279
Regulatory, 95, 161–164, 207, 212, 229, 268
Reinventing government, 32, 281
Research Excellence Framework (REF), 125, 131, 136
Results-based management, 24
Review, 23
Robinson, Peter, 57

S

Scotland/Scottish, 3, 17, 18, 53–59, 68–70, 74–77, 96, 156, 183, 186, 187, 233, 237, 240, 241, 247, 249, 273, 281
Scottish government, 17, 56, 69, 74, 75, 183, 270, 273
Scottish National Party (SNP), 17, 18, 55, 56, 59
Select committees, 34, 35, 64, 211
Service delivery, 32, 33, 46, 53, 61, 64, 67–71, 88, 109, 123, 128, 139, 152, 158, 177, 178, 181, 184, 186, 192, 204, 207, 231, 235, 240, 261, 264
Single market, 228, 230, 245
Sinn Fein, 54, 57
Social capital, 27, 204, 231
Stakeholders, 16, 21, 22, 25n2, 29, 30, 88, 102, 117, 119, 128, 132–134, 136, 139, 161, 162, 175, 177, 180, 182, 190–192, 195, 203, 209, 212, 216, 261, 266, 272
Sturgeon, Nicola, 56
Sustainability, viii, 25, 69, 159, 166, 183, 189–193, 196, 232, 242, 273, 281
Sustainable Development Goals (SDGs), 240, 246, 247
Sustainable leadership, 189–192

T

Thatcher, Margaret, 18, 100, 122, 209
Thatcherism, 3, 228
Third sector, 3, 60, 63, 69–71, 126, 134, 136, 207
Third Way, 62, 152
Transparency, 9, 29, 60, 88, 95, 97, 105, 109, 152, 186, 205, 215, 220–222, 232, 276
Transport, viii, 67, 92, 93, 98, 155, 157, 159, 221, 229, 234, 242, 249
Treasury, x–xii, 22, 23, 30, 31, 50–53, 68, 241, 246
Trust, 16, 22, 26–29, 31, 48, 75, 89, 101, 106, 108, 135, 156, 179, 186–190, 204, 208, 210, 233, 234, 264, 265, 268, 271, 274–277, 279

U

United Kingdom (UK), 17, 45–78, 87, 116, 150, 173, 201, 227, 260
United Nations (UN), 240, 246–248
Utility services, 155, 163

V

Value creation, 151–152, 154–158, 174, 176–181, 183, 186–194, 233
Value for money (VFM), 25, 28, 72, 122, 131, 163, 166, 204, 261
Values, vii, 2, 15–36, 88, 119, 151, 173–196, 201, 227, 260
Voluntary organisations, 63, 100, 185

W

Wales, 3, 17, 54, 55, 57, 68, 70–71, 74–77, 96, 101, 216, 228, 233, 237, 241, 249
Weberian, 16, 19, 149, 151, 154, 158, 205, 206, 208, 215, 217
Welfare reform, 32
Welsh Assembly, 34
Welsh Government, 70, 71, 75
Westminster, 56, 212, 260
Westminster model, 17, 18, 87–97, 104–106, 108, 109
What Works Centres, 124
Whitehall, 30, 50–53, 58–63, 65, 74, 76, 217, 218, 236, 237, 241, 245, 249
Wicked problems, 20, 276, 278
Work and Pensions Committee, 34, 67
World Trade Organization (WTO), 230, 246, 248